Complete Fertility

Solutions for **Natural Fertility** and Improving **IVF Success** Everyone Should Know

Dr. Kiera Lane

N.M.D., MSAc., L.Ac., Dipl.Ac., FABORM

Copyright 2020 by Kiera Lane, NMD, PLLC
Naturopathic Medical Doctor, Acupuncturist, and Fertility Expert

All rights reserved.

No part of this document may be reproduced or transmitted in any form or by any means, electronic, mechanical, photocopying, recording, or otherwise, without prior written permission of Dr. Kiera Lane.

Requests for permission to make copies of any part of the work should be submitted to Dr. Kiera Lane at info@drlanecompletefertility.com.

Book cover and interior designed by Danielle Radden.
Edited by Rachel Pass.

Published February 2020.
Printed in the United States of America.
ISBN: 978-1-952313-00-4

Winner of 23 Best New Fertility Books To Read In 2020
--Book Authority

DISCLAIMER

This book is designed to provide information and motivation to our readers. The recommendations, views, strategies and opinions offered by the author are general in nature and should not be interpreted to be tailored to your unique situation; nor does it establish a physician patient relationship with Dr. Kiera Lane.

The information contained in this book may not be current or comprehensive. The author makes no representation of the accuracy provided since advances in medical research, procedures, treatments and opinions can change in the medical community over time.

This book is sold with the understanding that the author is not engaged to render any type of psychological, medical or other kind of professional advice. The content of this book is the expression and opinion of its author only and may not represent the opinions of other medical professionals.

This book is not intended as a substitute for the medical advice of your physician, counselor, therapist, psychologist or other health care provider. Nothing in this book is intended to provide specific medical advice to you individually. Nothing in this book will prevent, treat or diagnose any disease or illness (mental or physical).

Nothing in this book is intended to exclude and/or take the place of proper medical diagnosis and treatment by a medical professional. Never disregard professional medical advice or delay seeking medical treatment because of something you have read in this book. You should seek independent medical advice regarding the proper diagnosis and treatment of your individual health condition or concern including infertility. Always seek the advice of your own medical provider and/or mental health provider before implementing any recommendations contained in this book. Additionally, consult your physician regularly to address new or on-going symptoms or medical treatment you may need. And if new symptoms or condition arises consult a physician for immediate medical diagnosis and interventions.

DEDICATION

This book is dedicated to my daughter who inspires me every day to reach beyond what I believe is possible and shows me that love can conquer all. A special thanks to my mother for her unwavering support toward my journey to motherhood. I am grateful for the mentors and teachers in my life that bestowed upon me their great wisdom and knowledge while still allowing me to grow in my own right as a physician and be my own unique person, encouraging me to pursue my passion for knowledge and my calling to serve others. To the women, men, and families yearning to have a baby, I hope the perseverance, love, and commitment that propels you forward allows you to realize your baby dreams.

C

TABLE OF CONTENTS

Foreward — i
Introduction — iv

1. Understanding The Menstrual Cycle: Creating Knowledge Through Success
1

2. Interpreting Fertility Lab Reports: What Do They Really Mean?
7

3. Clearing Emotional Blocks
23

4. Advanced Maternal Age: Can I Really Reverse the Hands of Time?
39

5. How to Naturally Restore Ovarian Function: Learning About the Missing Link to Improving FSH and LH Levels
51

6. Optimizing Egg Quality: It Only Takes One Good Egg
73

7. Correcting Luteal Phase Defects
85

8. Estrogen Dominance and Liver Function: How This May Be Impeding Your Fertility Success & Your 7-Step Detox Toolkit to Correct It
93

9. PCOS Impacts Fertility: How to Identify If You Have It and How to Improve Your Fertility Success

10. Optimizing Thyroid Function to Improve Fertility
123

11. Immunology and Unexplained Infertility: What No One Talks About
133

12. MTHFR and Infertility: A Possible Cause of Infertility and Pregnancy Loss
153

13. Male Factor: Maybe It's Not Just You
163

14. Traditional Chinese Medicine (TCM) & Acupuncture: How It Can Improve Your Fertility
177

15. Eating for Fertility Success: How Diet Plays an Important Role in Conception
193

16. The Top Four Reasons IVF May Not Work and What To Do Differently to Increase Your Success
209

17. Advocating for Yourself & Challenging Your Doctor
217

18. Fulfilling Your Baby Dreams: Your Complete Fertility Checklist
223

Notes and References — 230
About the Author — 284
Programs and More Information — 285

FOREWARD

Reproductive choices for women have changed radically in the past fifty to sixty years. We have gone from fear of pregnancy and lack of knowledge about the female sexual response to women's control of our bodies through effective contraceptive options. Free from the pressure to marry and have families in our prime reproductive years, we can have satisfying careers and financial independence. We can even have both careers and families. Or can we?

Infertility has become a growing problem for women who desire to become mothers, as many are waiting longer to have families. Could a rise in infertility be due to environmental pollutants and lifestyle factors? Reproductive endocrinology and fertility treatments are becoming increasingly common. In our current medical model, we turn ourselves over to the specialist to rescue us from childlessness. Sometimes these expensive treatments work, sometimes they don't. Is there another way? Can we influence specific factors to increase the success of these procedures?

Dr. Kiera Lane, N.M.D., MSAc., L.Ac., Dipl. Ac., FABORM has written one of the most comprehensive books available with ways to influence fertility factors to increase the success of assisted reproductive technology (ART) and natural fertility. While some books focus on specific aspects of infertility, *Complete Fertility: Solutions for Natural Fertility & Improving IVF Success*

Everyone Should Know has a breadth and depth of information that surpasses many of the books written on the subject. Rather than just focusing on one course of standard treatment, *Complete Fertility* provides readers with the understanding needed to regain control of their own reproductive function and enhance their natural ability to conceive.

As a board-certified Naturopathic Physician, the first obstetric resident at the first accredited Naturopathic medicine school in the United States (Bastyr University), a Certified Professional Midwife (CPM), a Facility Professor of Obstetrics/Midwifery at the Southwest College of Naturopathic Medicine for the past twenty-five years, and a practicing physician and midwife for over thirty-eight years, I am well versed in the challenges women can face when it comes to reproductive options to start and expand their families. I have known Dr. Lane for over twenty years and have served as one of her professional mentors. I have watched her professional life evolve and have seen her dedication and passion for her work, especially assisting women with infertility struggles to conceive. In fact, I have even delivered some of her successes.

What Dr. Lane offers in this book goes far beyond the current medical approach of intervening with drugs and surgery. There is a time and place for such treatments, but infertility is more highly complex. As a Naturopathic physician, Dr. Lane has been trained in a professional doctoral program with focuses on biomedical sciences and clinical training, similar to conventional medical training in addition to integrative modalities. In keeping with the principles of Naturopathic Medicine which asks practitioners to focus on the healing power of Nature, to identify and treat the cause, to treat the whole person, to focus on prevention, to see a doctor as a teacher, and to do no harm, Dr. Lane, in her role as teacher, has written a book that fills a void and need for information that is usually not provided to someone struggling with infertility.
Having knowledge is very empowering and enables the infertile couple to be partners in their treatment, actively participating in their quest for a family.

In Dr. Lane's twenty years of clinical practice, she has attained a unique level of expertise in fertility. Her repertoire of modalities includes nutrition, botanical medicines, prescription medications, homeopathy, counseling, as well as an expertise in the area of Acupuncture and Traditional Chinese Medicine. As a Fellow of the American Board of Oriental Reproductive Medicine, she has expert training in the area of integrative evidence-based interventions to address infertility problems. This comprehensive book includes all of the above, and is so well researched that it can be a manual for other practitioners to follow.

In addition, having used ART combined with integrative natural interventions to have her own beautiful daughter, Dr. Lane understands what it is like to experience the "road less traveled." She is passionate and inspired to help others have positive and successful experiences on this path.

As a physician and midwife, I have delivered thousands of babies, supporting women through this pivotal transition in their lives. Some have said in my many years of practice that "The Birth Angel" hovers around me and my patients, opening the door to would-be parents realizing their baby dreams. Having worked with so many women and families who have been able to conceive, I like to think The Birth Angel is with me, helping those I serve. I have seen the successful outcomes of Dr. Lane's work in helping women conceive in spite of the serious infertility hurdles they have struggled with. It appears to me that The Birth Angel also guides Dr. Lane in her fertility work. So, if you are having problems conceiving, please read this book. The information contained here creates new options and possibilities in your quest to build a family. May The Birth Angel be with you.

--Farrah Swan, ND, CPM

INTRODUCTION

Complete Fertility: Solutions for Natural Fertility & Improving IVF Success That Everyone Should Know contains vital tools that may be the key to transforming your fertility struggles into success. Do you feel like you should have already been successful in conceiving? Are you frustrated and needing help to conceive? Do you want to get pregnant quickly? If you are reading this book, your fertility has likely been anything but quick, and you may be at a loss for just how to transform your story into a success story. Don't despair. It is possible that not having had the right obstacles removed before trying to conceive has made your attempts unsuccessful. This book was created to empower women by giving them knowledge and tools to restore natural function in their bodies and, in turn, help them get pregnant as quickly as possible. If you have been trying to conceive naturally, or with assisted reproductive technology (ART) such as in vitro fertilization (IVF) or intrauterine insemination (IUI) without success, you might not be addressing the root cause or roadblock that is preventing you from getting pregnant.

"Unexplained infertility" is just that—unexplained; it has no definitive cause. What does that really mean? There may be causes affecting your ability to conceive that you have not considered. You must first identify a myriad of possible causes in order to address them. You might not have identified these causes because you have not been asking the right questions. Those questions and the answers to them could be contained in the pages of this book.

Could your adrenal function, which modulates stress, be preventing you from getting pregnant? Are your emotions blocking your ability to move forward? Is your liver creating hormone imbalances that are affecting your fertility? Do you have inflammation that is holding you back from conceiving? Is your partner's sperm fragmented, making it almost impossible to have a baby? These may not be the first questions that pop into your head when you are wondering why you are not getting pregnant, but they should be questions you ask. The answers may hold the key to your success.

My name is Dr. Kiera Lane. I am a Board Certified Licensed Naturopathic Medical Doctor, a Board Certified Licensed Acupuncturist, and a Fellow of the American Board of Oriental Reproductive Medicine (FABORM). ABORM is an international organization first established in 2008 as a benchmark for pioneering best practices in acupuncture and oriental reproductive medicine. Fellows of ABORM are considered experts in the area of reproductive health and fertility. They are skilled Chinese medicine clinicians and educated researchers who contribute to the current body of knowledge with cutting-edge innovations and integrative evidence-based care in the area of reproductive health and fertility (1). Fellows have expert knowledge in Western procedures, laboratory testing, and Western medications used in IUI and IVF. They are also adept in all fertility interventions, both Western and Eastern, including Chinese medical diagnosis and patterns, acupuncture, Chinese herbs and herbal formulations, supplements, and lifestyle factors related to fertility and reproductive health.

Fellows of ABORM pass rigorous coursework and examinations that reflect an essential understanding of the integration of all Western and Eastern integrative modalities used to achieve success in the area of fertility. Many practitioners like myself already had years of clinical experience in the area of reproductive health before ABORM was established. In the state where I practice, I am one of only a handful of practitioners who are Fellows of ABORM. In addition, I am a Licensed physician with over twenty-five years of experience in the health care field, including a Bachelor's degree with a focus on dietetics (clinical nutrition).

Naturopathic physicians go through rigorous medical training by accredited schools that focus on biomedical sciences and clinical training that is similar to conventional medical training. Additionally, they are trained in integrative therapeutic modalities as well as pharmacology, and are experts in disease prevention, addressing the whole person, providing individualized patient-centered treatment, and focusing on maximizing the body's function. My extensive medical background helps me to integrate the best of Western, Chinese, and Natural medicine to better serve my patients. I have been successfully assisting women with their reproductive health care needs for over eighteen years. I am passionate about supporting and assisting women to conceive naturally, as well as in cooperation with assisted reproductive technology (ART) and in vitro fertilization (IVF).

I have helped women and couples conceive naturally, with IVF, with IUI, with a sperm donor, and with donor eggs. My patients have had different fertility challenges including a history of recurrent pregnancy loss, polycystic ovarian syndrome (PCOS) and everything in between.

Throughout almost two decades, I have worked with countless women and couples. Although each patient, each story, and each journey is unique, I have identified common patterns that create roadblocks to fertility success.

Most women I see are in a big hurry to get pregnant. It can be an emotional and arduous journey to conceive when you are dealing with unknown infertility. I totally understand that. There can be a deep gravitational pull so strong to have a baby and start or expand your family that it starts to take over your daily thoughts and your life. You have the desire to have a baby. You have the longing and the love to have a baby. You have the vision and the hope to have a baby. That is great. But is your body on the same page with you? Is your body ready to have a baby? And jump in head first? Unfortunately, the body and mind might be on totally different pages of your story. That is where I come in. I want to provide you with tools to help your body become ready and stay on the same page as your desire and longing.

The body, like anything else, needs preparation and assistance to prepare for pregnancy. Maybe twenty or thirty years ago in our parent's generation it was easier, but in today's world with high stress, high pressure, poor diet, and pollutants in the environment, it takes work to get pregnant. I see fertility issues in women in their thirties and forties. Many women are having babies later in life, which can lead to greater challenges. If you are having a baby when you are thirty-five years old or older, you are considered to be at "advanced maternal age." I know you don't feel old or think of yourself as old, but the body may not be functioning like it used to. Don't get discouraged. I'm right there with you, having had a baby at forty-three years old. Talk about pressure! Whatever age you are when you start or expand your family, you need to devote energy and attention to preparing your body for natural conception or for a successful IUI or IVF cycle. I understand that you are excited to move forward and create a new life, but I recommend preparation and a calculated approach to getting pregnant quickly.

I have many patients who live in areas without access to integrative medicine. They, too, need tools. Many of my patients ask, "Why is my doctor not looking at restoring function in my body if that could help me get pregnant?" Many doctors have not had training outside of traditional Western approaches to fertility treatment. *Complete Fertility* is about addressing the root cause of your roadblock with natural and integrative interventions in order to prepare your body quickly to increase your chances of conceiving naturally, or with IVF and IUI. You can't expect your body to perform as it did when you were twenty years old. You must help and support the physiology of your reproductive system so that it can perform at its top level. *Complete Fertility* is about having a plan of action to help restore normal physiological function, create a homeostasis in the body, remove blockages, and support reproductive health. Like they say, it's not enough to survive, you want to thrive. When it comes to fertility, it's not enough just to conceive, it's important to enhance egg quality and fetal development. Healthy pregnancy and healthy babies are equally important. *Complete Fertility* is about empowering you, removing roadblocks, and creating the right opportunities for success. My hope in writing this book is that you may find the tools you need to expedite your successful conception.

Nothing in this book is intended to provide specific medical advice to you individually. Please seek independent medical advice regarding your fertility before pursuing any recommendations in this book.

It is my intention that the information contained in these pages will empower you to ask the right questions of your health care provider, help you determine the roadblocks that are preventing you from reaching full success, and create the support you need to thrive in your fertility journey and find the happy ending to your personal story.

MY GOAL IS TO HELP YOU GET PREGNANT.

UNDERSTANDING THE MENSTRUAL CYCLE:

CREATING SUCCESS THROUGH KNOWLEDGE

My goal is to help you get pregnant. What is the best way to approach getting pregnant quickly? It starts with the basics of understanding the menstrual cycle. Knowledge is empowerment. It is important to understand what is normal. How many days should your period last? What color should your menstrual flow be? Are you ovulating? Is your luteal phase, the second half of your cycle, long enough? When is your fertility window the best for conception? Do you know the answers to these questions?

Many women I talk to don't know if they are even ovulating. They don't know what a normal menstrual cycle looks like. Many of my patients tell me that after they visit their gynecologist (GYN) for a checkup, they are told variations of "Your cycle is 'normal.'" "Oh, you have heavy bleeding and dark clots? Well, that's normal." Actually, that is **not** normal. Heavy bleeding is a sign of dysregulation and reflects imbalances in hormonal regulation. In Chinese medicine, dark clots represent stagnation and/or a deficiency pattern, which is abnormal. Your period is the single most tangible tool that you have to understand what is happening with your reproductive health. The body can talk to you, if you truly listen. Although it may speak another language at times, I can help you interpret what your body is telling you. If you are having heavy periods, painful cramps, a menstrual cycle longer or shorter than twenty-eight days, or no indication of ovulation, your body is saying that something is imbalanced.

Maybe no one ever told you what a period should really look like. Maybe you thought it was normal to experience a painful period every three weeks. Many women do. In order to know what is abnormal, you need to know what is normal. Is there such a thing as a perfect period? Actually, there is; it's not an urban myth. Let's discuss what a perfect period would look like.

A PERFECT PERIOD

A perfect period lasts about four to seven days and has mild to moderate blood flow that is bright red without clots, which indicates fresh, vibrant blood. It does not cause cramps. The flow of blood would not start and stop, but would be consistent throughout the day and night. It would be a little lighter in the beginning, with moderate flow in the middle, and lighter again at the end of the period. If you were to graph the blood flow, it would look much like a bell-shaped curve. You would not see or feel any symptoms prior to the period, such as low back pain, breast tenderness, mood changes, sweet cravings, or irritability. There would be no excruciating cramps, no clots or tissue with the flow of your menses. There would be no sharp excruciating pain during ovulation. Instead, there would be ease during the flow, and your period would not feel like an event, rather a normal part of daily living. During the period, your energy level would feel stable, and you would not experience additional symptoms like headache, fatigue, nausea, or cramps. The quantity of blood flow would be moderate, not too heavy and not too light. The perfect period would occur every twenty-eight days with regularity and consistency. You would see a spike in body temperature midcycle, with healthy discharge, and all discharge would be clear and sticky, denoting a fertile window.

The perfect period is not elusive—it actually does exist. But most women are told that their periods are normal when, in fact, they are quite abnormal. A perfect period indicates hormonal balance, increased fertility potential for conception, and healthy ovulation. The perfect period is what we strive for. In order to create the perfect period, we must first understand the menstrual cycle.

UNLOCKING THE MYSTERY OF YOUR MENSTRUAL CYCLE

There are many barriers that make it difficult to understand what your menstrual cycle is telling you. Like many women, you may have grown up not talking about your period to your mother, your sisters, or even your doctor. Even if you understand and have a dialogue with your body, there might be a disconnect between that understanding and interpreting what your body is saying to you. Even if you understand what your body is telling you about imbalances that affect your fertility, you may not have been given the tools to correct these imbalances before trying to get pregnant. If you, like many women, have been on birth control pills for many years, you will not have a true picture of your natural cycle. Once you remove barriers like these, the true picture of your cycle will be revealed. You must figure out what your body is saying to you. I know that you're capable of understanding your body's unique signs and symptoms so that you can get support and assist your body to improve your fertility.

To understand the menstrual cycle, let's look at the following diagram, which depicts the changes in hormones and egg development that occur throughout the menstrual cycle.

The Follicular Phase
(Day 1—Day 14)

Day one of the period is the first day of regular, red blood flow. If you spot a few days prior to the flow of red blood that is not considered day one. Let's look at the diagrams, and I will talk you through changes that occur throughout the cycle.

The first half the cycle is called the follicular phase because it is all about the follicles. Your eggs were created while you were developing in your mother's womb. You have all the eggs you are ever going to have from the very beginning of life, and they stay resting until puberty. These immature eggs rest in small envelopes called follicles, which are stored in your ovaries.

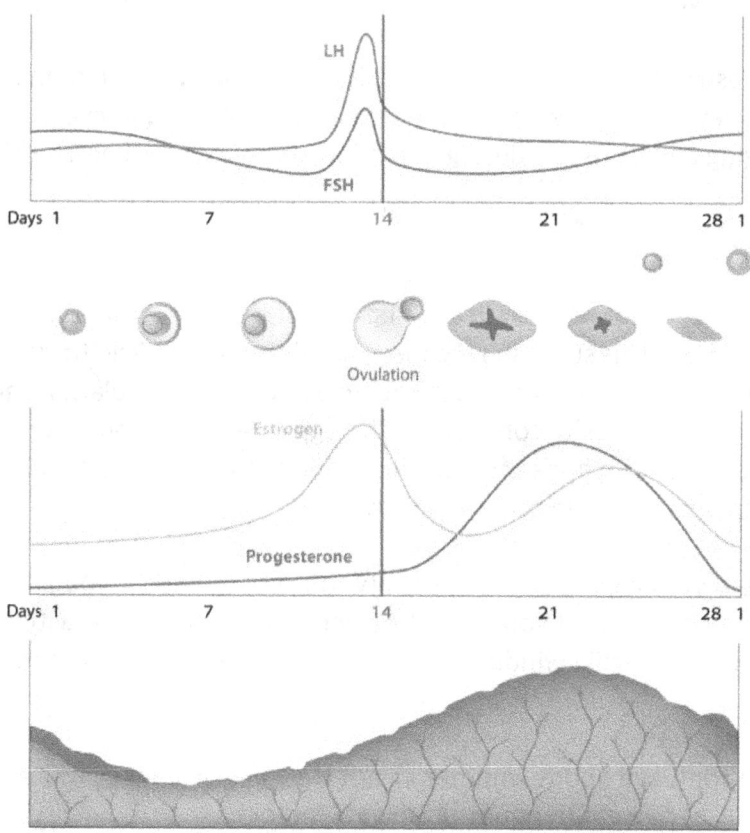

When puberty hits, follicle stimulating hormone (FSH) is produced by the pituitary gland. FSH wakes up a few follicles, known as antral follicles, each month. One of these follicles becomes dominant with each menstrual cycle. Direct stimulation from estrogen and FSH helps one lucky egg in that follicle grow and become dominant. During this process, the egg grows and becomes mature so that it can be fertilized. The follicular phase is vital to maturing an egg so it can be fertilized. An unmatured egg may be released during ovulation, but is unlikely to be fertilized. The hormonal influence of FSH and estrogen in the follicular phase is important to fully mature the egg, which is a key step to conception.

FSH also stimulates a number of follicles in the ovary that are responsible for producing the hormone estrogen. Your level of estrogen is at its lowest on the first day of your period. From then on, it increases as the follicles grow.

So at the same time that the egg is maturing, there is an increase in the amount of estrogen in your body, which ensures that the lining of your uterus thickens with nutrients and blood. A thick and vascular uterine lining ensures that a fertilized egg will have all the nutrients and support it needs to grow. High estrogen levels are also associated with the sperm-friendly cervical mucus that is secreted vaginally during ovulation. Cervical mucus looks much like the white of an egg before it is cooked. It is thin and mostly clear--though sometimes slightly opaque in color, odorless, and slightly stretchy. These characteristics create an easy environment for sperm to swim and survive for several days.

Because FSH and estrogen are essential to growing and maturing one dominant egg, they need to be at optimal levels over the first fourteen days of the follicular cycle. This gives you the best chance of releasing a mature egg during ovulation, in hopes of it being fertilized.

Ovulation (Day 14)

Rising estrogen levels along with FSH in the first half of the menstrual cycle cause a rapid rise in luteinizing hormone (LH). This surge in LH causes the dominant follicle to rupture and a release the mature egg from the ovary. This process is known as ovulation. Ovulation can vary from cycle to cycle. Generally, during successful conception, the egg is released and travels through the fallopian tubes where the sperm finds the egg and fertilizes the egg. The fertilized egg then forms an embryo, which implants in the endometrial lining.

You are most fertile during ovulation and twenty-four hours after. If you are not ovulating, then pregnancy is not possible. So if you are not having timed intercourse with your partner or spouse during the proper fertile window, you are missing the mark and conception will not happen.

Many women are confused about whether or not they are ovulating. Your fertility window can be a bit ambiguous because it depends on several factors.

Factors That Affect Your Ovulation

1) Irregular menstrual cycles
2) The levels and strength of your Luteinizing Hormone (LH)
3) Fluctuating stress levels altering hormone levels
4) When you have intercourse

5) High levels of androgens, like testosterone in women with polycystic ovarian syndrome (PCOS), may inhibit ovulation

6) Other factors, such as, thyroid function that influence ovulation

Healthy sperm can survive up to seven days, but they live three to five days on average. This means that timed intercourse before ovulation still leaves time for the egg to be released, and for the sperm to find the egg and fertilize it. Other factors that affect whether or not sperm find the mature egg include the health of the sperm, the health of the cervical mucus, and the regularity of the menstrual cycle. Generally, a woman's fertile window is the day of ovulation (usually twelve to sixteen days before the menstrual period begins) and the five days preceding it. For the average woman, that occurs somewhere between days ten and seventeen. We'll talk about ways to help monitor ovulation later in the book to help you better track your fertile window.

The Luteal Phase (Day 14—Day 28)

The luteal phase is the second half of the menstrual cycle. It usually lasts fourteen days, spanning from ovulation to Day 28. It is all about rising levels of the hormone progesterone, which help to further vascularize the lining of the uterus. If you remember, the first half the cycle starts to increase estrogen levels, which start to increase blood flow and nutrients to the lining of the uterus. Progesterone is essential in furthering this vascularizing blood flow to the lining of the uterus in order to thicken it and create a hospitable environment for an embryo to implant and grow. Many women today lead stressful, busy lives. Stress hormones influence progesterone levels and can deplete them sooner than they should. Luteal phase defects are very common and can present a roadblock to getting pregnant. It's important to know if your progesterone levels are adequate to support the development and growth of a fertilized egg. If fertilization does not occur, the drop from high progesterone levels to low levels triggers the uterine lining to shed and the period to start.

This cycle repeats each month until you get pregnant. During pregnancy, maintaining high levels of progesterone can prevent miscarriages.

IS YOUR PERIOD NORMAL?

I think we all know the answer to this. Probably not. Not everybody ovulates on Day 14 or has a period every twenty-eight days. The more irregularities in your cycle, the higher the likelihood that it's hard to conceive. Irregularities can lead you to miss the window for your fertile time, or cause you not to have enough lining to feed the embryo. Irregular hormone levels may not allow your follicle to become mature enough to be fertilized. The list goes on.

So first and foremost, pay attention and track your menstrual cycle. Then reflect on what you see. Is your luteal phase too short? Do you seem to have menstrual difficulties during the first two weeks of your period? Maybe you don't have a clue if you are ovulating. First start with tracking your cycle. There are many wonderful apps to assist you in tracking your period. Tracking your period for at least three months will allow you to see a pattern that could tell you what your body is doing. Remember that times of high stress or trauma can affect the period drastically and may not give you a normal picture of what's happening. Using over-the-counter ovulation tests, starting on Day 8 until you get a positive ovulation indicator, can show that you are or are not in ovulation. Basal body temperature can also show if your temperature is rising to indicate if you are ovulating.

Don't let problems in your cycle get you down. Understanding where you are starting from is the empowering part. You can't fix what you don't know is broken. I mean that loosely; your body is not broken, and it has the most amazing ability to heal itself. Trust in yourself and your body. Understanding what your menstrual cycle is doing will also help you to have informed conversations with your doctor to create the best strategy to increase your fertility. It also helps you to actively advocate for yourself. You deserve the opportunity to improve your fertility. Your failed attempts to conceive are not due to a defect in the body, but to a lack of knowledge that would help you identify a way to optimize your ability to conceive. Knowledge allows you the ability to make the right changes to create success.

INTERPRETING FERTILITY LAB REPORTS:

WHAT DO THEY REALLY MEAN?

Lab reports can be daunting and overwhelming, and many times they are not explained in a manner that you can understand. My patients come to me saying, "I was told my FSH is too high and I will never have a baby of my own." First of all, can a doctor really say that you will never have a baby because of your lab results? To an extent, yes. Labs are a reflection of body function; however, if your body function can be improved and you only need one good egg to have a healthy baby then your ability to conceive naturally may not just be a reflection of your labs alone. Many of my patients in their late thirties and early forties get a similar prognosis. They are told that they will never have a baby of their own naturally, based only on their age. I don't just look at the numbers. I assess the person and their body function and figure out where the roadblock is, so that we can restore balance and make opportunities for conception possible.

Whatever your situation is in your unique fertility journey, it is important to empower yourself by understanding the basics of the lab reports on which your doctor bases their decisions for your fertility. You are in control of your choices. Knowledge is power and equates to better decision-making for you and your family. In addition, there may be labs that should be done that your doctor has not ordered. Making sure that you have an in-depth view of the body before making a decision about your fertility choices is essential. You don't want to miss a roadblock that can be easily rectified.

It is hard to understand what your lab results mean when you're not a doctor and you have not gone to medical school. Even if you have, the area of fertility and reproductive health is complex and if it's not your specialty, it can be confusing. I have patients who are doctors and nurses and even they are confused about their labs. The reality in healthcare is that you have to be your own advocate. That doesn't mean you have to understand everything the doctor knows. No one is asking you to understand what comes with years of schooling and practice. However, since fertility doctors base many of the choices given to you on your FSH, LH, and AMH levels as well as other results, you should have a basic understanding of these labs and what they represent.

It can be completely disheartening when your doctor tells you that, based on your labs, you have to use donor eggs. Since the consequences of the interpretation of your labs have such an impact on the recommendations your doctor makes, you need to know the basics. This way, you can better understand where your doctor is coming from and have more insight into their recommendations. It also gives you the knowledge you need to ask better questions and to make informed decisions about your healthcare options. I believe that most doctors want you to understand their recommendations and the lab results they are based on, but they may not have the time or ability to explain or articulate things in a way that you can understand. Regardless, it is important that you have enough knowledge to ask educated questions and be involved in your own health care, especially for decisions that relate to having a baby.

You may have to be your own advocate and ask your doctor to conduct other labs that are pertinent to uncovering and understanding the roadblocks in your fertility journey. You may need to ask many questions that challenge your doctor. This is not about being adversarial with your doctor; it's about working in collaboration with your doctor so that you can make good decisions with your physician. It is about understanding your doctor's recommendations and your choices to pursue additional testing, or to make decisions about which avenue to follow next in your fertility journey.

If your doctor is not receptive to answering your questions, then you need to evaluate if you want to work with that doctor. It's important to have a good doctor-patient relationship in which you feel comfortable and can address your fears and concerns. Your doctor should be part of your supportive team.

Fertility laboratory basics are tests that are most frequently ordered in assessing fertility options. Below, you will find information on these tests that will help you understand what they are and what your results can reveal. Having a reference point to understand what each lab is and how to interpret them is vital to helping make informed decisions.

WHAT LABS YOUR DOCTOR WILL MOST LIKELY DO TO ASSESS YOUR FERTILITY

If you go to your OB, GYN, or reproductive endocrinologist (RE), they will conduct a few basic tests. One of these tests is Day 3 blood work. Labs tested on Day 3 generally include blood work on Day 3 of your menses (Day 1 is the first day of bleeding), which includes follicle stimulating hormone (FSH), luteinizing hormone (LH), and estradiol (E2, the main type of estrogen). Your levels of FSH, LH, and E2 reflect the stimulation of egg maturation and ovulation, along with ovarian reserve. Your doctor will likely conduct additional tests that do not need to be completed on Day 3. These include thyroid stimulating hormone (TSH) and anti-Müllerian hormone (AMH). These tests do not have to be conducted on Day 3. AMH is commonly tested as a marker of ovarian reserve, which is basically an assessment of how many eggs you have left. Your doctor will also conduct a pelvic ultrasound to look at the antral follicle count, which shows how many follicles are starting to wake up and grow during your menstrual cycle. These are your core fertility labs, however, there are many other labs that are done routinely and we will discuss them as well.

PAP

Having a routine Pap and pelvic exam is important to rule out high risk HPV strains 16 and 18, which are associated with increased risk of cervical cancer. A PAP gives your OB GYN, PCP, or RE the opportunity for a physical exam, the collection of cultures to rule out other infections such as yeast and bacteria, and the chance to look for tissue changes that reflect hormone imbalances that need to be addressed prior to becoming pregnant.

TESTS TO RULE OUT INFECTIONS

It is important to rule out sexually transmitted diseases (STDs) and vaginal infections that may alter your ability to conceive. In addition to STDs you can have other types of infections in the vaginal area that impede your fertility. This seems pretty common sense, but if your PAP is normal, many physicians will not do additional testing. This is unfortunate because you may be harboring bacteria, mycoplasma and ureaplasma, or other infections in the vaginal area that are changing the pH of the cervical mucus and creating a hostile environment for sperm. Rather than testing for a PAP, bacterial vaginosis, and yeast, which are all separate tests commonly used by your OBGYN, there are now labs that can test for up to fifteen or more infections from one simple vaginal sample, just like the one your doctor takes when you get a PAP. Ruling out infections and imbalances that are often missed can help to identify any roadblocks that may affect your vaginal pH and the ability of sperm to survive in their journey to reach the egg. Keeping an immunological healthy vagina environment is always important, and becomes crucial in natural conception.

These tests will help you take the steps you need to keep an immunologically healthy vaginal environment.

ADDITIONAL TESTS THAT YOUR OBGYN OR RE MIGHT CONDUCT

Many doctors will test just the basics discussed above, including FSH, LH, estradiol, AMH and antral follicle count. These labs are helpful, but may be missing valuable information that can affect your fertility. Other tests that are common, but not always conducted are TSH (thyroid stimulating hormone), A1C (blood sugar), Prolactin, testosterone, and sperm analysis. Whether or not these tests are done depends on your doctor.

Some REs conduct a much more in-depth set of lab tests, which may include: ruling out clotting disorders if you have experienced pregnancy loss, genetic testing, immunological markers, progesterone levels, and more.

Below, we will discuss the details of these standard and additional tests.

Follicular Phase Lab Work for Day 3: Follicle Stimulating Hormone (FSH), Luteinizing Hormone (LH), and Estradiol (E2)

Typically, your doctor will draw your blood on Day 3 of your menstrual cycle to assess follicle stimulating hormone (FSH), luteinizing hormone (LH) and estradiol (E2). You count the first day of your period when you have the first day of red blood flow. This does not include spotting. Your blood is tested on Day 3 of your cycle counting from Day 1. Whether you bleed during your menstrual cycle for one, two, or seven days, you must get your blood drawn on Day 3 to accurately evaluate these markers. If your OB is checking your FSH and LH levels on any other day of the cycle, the results will not accurately reflect follicular function. It is imperative to test these labs on Day 3 to get an accurate reflection of your own follicular function. If you're not having regular periods and it is too difficult to predict your cycle, you can either wait for your next cycle or you can test your levels to get a baseline of where things are at. In addition, your doctor can help you to get your period to start, usually with progesterone, and then test your labs on Day 3 after it begins.

FSH

Follicle stimulating hormone, or FSH, is tested on day three of the menstrual cycle. FSH levels reflect the amount of stimulation on the ovaries to mature an egg. As the ability of the ovaries to produce good eggs decreases, the level of FSH rises. On Day 3, the levels of FSH along with estradiol and LH are markers for ovarian function and reserve. FSH is also used by fertility experts to determine if you might be a good candidate for IVF. The chart below breaks down FSH levels to give you better understanding. My interpretation of FSH levels is based on the traditional medical standard in addition to an integrative and traditional Chinese medical interpretation of FSH blood tests. We will discuss how to optimize FSH levels to improve fertility in future chapters.

Key to Understanding Your Day 3 Labs: FSH

TEST	VALUE	MEANING
FSH	2–4	TCM View – Qi Depleted
FSH	5–6	Optimal/Excellent
FSH	6–9	Good – Fair
FSH	10–12	Diminished Reserve
FSH	12–15	Low Egg Reserve - IVF Often Recommended
FSH	>15	Poor Reserve & Qi - Donor Eggs Often Recommended

*Traditional Chinese Medicine (TCM)

LH

Luteinizing hormone (LH) levels in the blood, tested on Day 3 of your menstrual cycle, are used to monitor for an LH surge prior to ovulation. In addition, this test provides another marker for egg quality and quantity. As the LH level rises, there is a decline in ovulatory function. An LH of 10 is worse than an LH of 5 for example. In addition, from a Western standpoint, an LH of 4 might be considered normal, but from a Chinese Medicine perspective, an LH under the optimal levels shows depletion of Qi and represents a lack of ovulatory action as well. Standard evaluation of LH levels in the blood also looks at FSH to LH ratios. A very high LH relative to FSH may represent PCOS or other hormonal abnormalities. It is optimal to have LH and FSH in a 1:1 ratio. For example, an LH of 5 and an FSH of 5 would represent optimal ovulatory function. If your LH levels are not optimal, you can take steps to improve them, and in turn, improve your ability to stimulate ovulation. We will discuss how to do this in future chapters.

Key to Understanding Your Day 3 Labs: LH

TEST	VALUE	MEANING
LH	1–4	Deficiency Pattern/ Poor Ovulation
LH	5–6	Optimal Levels
LH	7–9	Normal but not Optimal TCM View—Qi Depleted
LH	≥10	Reduced ovulation

Estradiol

There are three types of estrogen in your body that can be tested in your blood. Estradiol is the primary type of estrogen in the body. In fact, this is the form contained in oral birth control pills and hormone replacement therapy (HRT). It reflects the body's ability to stimulate follicular development and egg maturation, and to start to vascularize the endometrial lining. High levels of estradiol suggest poor egg quantity and quality.

I give my patients the following reference points for estradiol levels:
- A woman who is going through menopause or who is post-menopausal with an estradiol level of 20 will report having low energy and problems with poor memory. For example, she might walk into a room and forget why she went there and what she was looking for.
- A woman going through menopause or who is post-menopausal might have an estradiol level of 50 while on bioidentical hormone replacement and have improved energy and mood.
- When you are trying to conceive, a good goal for your estradiol levels is 80–100, with 100 being optimal.
- Having an estradiol level of 150 would be an abundant supply, like icing on the cake for your fertility.
- However, having an excess of estradiol in estrogen dominant conditions like endometriosis works against your fertility.

In Chinese medicine, declining levels of estrogen indicate a deficiency pattern. Low estrogen equates to blood deficiency of the liver, and deficient kidney Yin and Jing. These low levels can be improved with acupuncture and Chinese and Western herbs. Elevated estrogen levels found in women with conditions such as PCOS, endometriosis, and fibroids indicate a stagnation of Qi and an accumulation of damp. This requires clearing the damp and moving the Qi with acupuncture and Chinese herbs, along with lifestyle and diet changes to improve estrogen levels.

Anti-Müllerian Hormone (AMH)

Anti-Müllerian hormone or AMH reflects ovarian reserve. Ovarian reserve is the follicle pool of primordial or resting follicles that you have from birth. These follicles house eggs that will mature in the future and that can result in creating new life. AMH is the gold standard used to assess the store of eggs you have left to try to conceive. Keep in mind that AMH reflects the quantity, but not the quality of the eggs you have. There are several variables that may influence AMH levels. AMH along with FSH, LH and estradiol are used to determine whether you potentially can conceive naturally, or if you are a candidate for IVF, donor eggs, or donor embryo adoption. AMH is thought to be the best measure that we have currently to measure ovarian reserve, but there is some debate about whether it is one-hundred percent accurate.

In Chinese medicine, AMH levels reflect what is called the Jing. The Jing is the energy or essence of the kidney Qi. The Jing is important because it must be built up so that it can be given to the baby. In Chinese medicine, AMH levels can be improved with the nourishing of the essence or the essential Qi through acupuncture and Chinese herbs.

Antral Follicle Count

Antral follicles, also known as resting follicles, are generally in the range of two to ten millimeters in diameter. These small follicles show up on an ultrasound, so your doctor will determine your antral follicle count and examine the size of these follicles using pelvic and intravaginal ultrasound. This lab is another tool for estimating ovarian reserve, which is an indicator of both potential egg quality and quantity. REs use this measure in conjunction with FSH, LH and Estradiol to determine ovarian function and if you are a candidate for IUI, IVF, or natural conception.

Semen Analysis

Semen analysis is used to examine the count, motility and morphology of the sperm. The normal range for sperm count is between 40- and 300-million sperm per milliliters of ejaculate. A low sperm count is fewer than 20 million. Sperm motility refers to the ability of the sperm to move in a forward direction. Low sperm motility may reduce the chances of conception, especially when paired with low sperm count. Morphology refers to the shape of the sperm. Abnormal shaped sperm are often unable to swim effectively or penetrate an egg. (Please see Chapter 13 for a detailed explanation of semen analysis.)

Depending on the results of the semen analysis, your doctor may do more in-depth testing related to your partner's sperm. For example, if the semen analysis shows clumping or signs of infection, a semen culture, prostate fluid culture, and analysis may be ordered. If the doctor is concerned about an antibody reaction to sperm, an antisperm antibody test may also be indicated. In addition, a fructose test can be used to evaluate structural problems or a blockage of the seminal vesicles in the testicles. Another test known as the Sperm Chromatin Structural Assay (SCSA®) measures the level of DNA fragmentation in the sperm which may reduce fertility potential.

Antisperm Antibodies

In some cases, an antisperm antibody test will be recommended by your doctor. The presence of antisperm antibodies or proteins found in semen is one cause of immunoinfertility (1). Antibodies in semen cause an immune response in the woman's vaginal secretions. In addition, antisperm antibodies can cause abnormal sperm production, impair transport of sperm, and impair infertility.

Sperm Chromatic Structure Assay or SCSA®

The SCSA® is a test that looks at the quality of the sperm. If you have had successive unsuccessful IVF attempts, your doctor may use this test to determine if the sperm is fragmented, which makes it nonviable. The SCSA® is a very specialized test. To conduct the test, your partner's sperm sample will be frozen and then sent to a laboratory off site. There, the sperm sample will be thawed and then analyzed with an instrument called a flow cytometer. This instrument uses dye and a beam of light to see if the sperm DNA is fragmented. The results for this test are measured on the DNA Fragmentation Index or DFI, which gives results in the form of a percentage. The higher the percentage, the more fragmented the sperm.

According to research studies, the SCSA® is considered to be the most accurate and reliable DNA fragmentation assay available today. It is the only DNA fragmentation assay that is clinically accepted as an indication of a man's risk of infertility. SCSA® data is more predictive of male factor infertility than classical semen analyses.

Hysterosalpingogram (HSG)

A hysterosalpingogram or HSG is an X-ray of the uterus and fallopian tubes which allows your doctor to make sure there are no blockages in the fallopian tubes or abnormalities of the uterus. This is important because your fallopian tubes must be open to allow the sperm to swim from the vaginal canal, through the uterus, and down the fallopian tube. The ovaries release the egg into the fallopian tube, which is the most common site of fertilization. The sperm must have a clear path to reach the egg. Once this happens, the dividing embryo can implant in the uterus for successful conception. Generally, the HSG procedure helps to open the fallopian tubes and may enhance your ability to conceive for about two months after the HSG.

Clomid Challenge Test (CCT)

The use of clomid, also known as clomiphene citrate, in the Clomid Challenge test (CCT) is somewhat outdated as other drugs with less side effects may be used in its place. However, some doctors still use Clomid Challenge testing. Clomid is a medication that blocks estrogen receptors at the hypothalamus, which is like a hormone control center in the body. This stimulates the release of FSH and LH. The Clomid Challenge test helps determine how well the ovaries are functioning. For this test, you will likely take 100 milligrams of Clomid from Day 5 through Day 9 of your menstrual cycle. Your doctor will test your FSH levels on Day 3 before you begin taking Clomid and on Day 10 after you finish. The results of this test can give an idea of the responsiveness of your ovaries and can correlate to ovarian reserve. Because of this, the test is commonly used to tell whether or not you can induce ovulation and would be a good candidate for IVF. Clomid can also be used in men with male factor infertility.

ADDITIONAL LABS I RECOMMEND TO ASSESS YOUR FERTILITY

Progesterone (Luteal Phase Labs)

Progesterone levels are an important indicator of luteal phase defects. After the egg is released from the dominant follicle during ovulation, the follicle that remains is known as the corpus luteum. The corpus luteum produces progesterone, which vascularizes the endometrial lining. This process nourishes and prepares the uterine lining for implantation of the fertilized egg, or embryo. Adequate progesterone levels are important in preparing and maintaining a healthy uterine lining and vascular supply to feed the growing embryo after implantation and during pregnancy. Doctors typically check progesterone levels on Day 26 when the period occurs every 28 days between cycles. However, progesterone levels can be checked anywhere from Day 21 to Day 26 to assess if there are adequate levels of progesterone. Luteal phase defects can occur when progesterone levels are low or deficient.

Labs to Rule Out Polycystic Ovarian Syndrome (PCOS)

Polycystic ovarian syndrome or PCOS is a condition where multiple follicles develop during the follicular phase. The excess in follicular development increases estrogen levels and creates a disparity in hormone levels. Common symptoms of PCOS are hair growth where you don't want it (e.g. a mustache), elevated prolactin and testosterone levels, painful periods, cramps, and high blood sugar. PCOS is a known cause of infertility. We will discuss PCOS in greater detail in later chapters.

Prolactin

Prolactin is a hormone produced by the body in large quantities during breast-feeding. High levels of prolactin are most often associated with PCOS, and can inhibit ovulation and affect fertility.

Testosterone

Testosterone is an androgen or steroid hormone that controls the development and maturation of masculine characteristics. Elevated testosterone and conditions such as polycystic ovarian syndrome can inhibit ovulation. The free or active form of testosterone is a better marker than total testosterone when assessing PCOS, but both free and total testosterone should be checked.

DHEA Sulfate (DHEA-S)

Studies have shown that low levels of DHEA are associated with infertility. In addition, DHEA sulfate, an androgenic hormone like testosterone, can inhibit ovulation or prevent it from happening if levels are too high. This happens most commonly in patients with PCOS.

Hemoglobin A1C

Hemoglobin A1C is the glucose or sugar portion of a red blood cell. Since a red blood cell's lifespan is about 90 days or three months, when you draw your blood at any given time, some of the red blood cells are at the beginning of their lifecycle, while others are in the middle, and some are at the end. This means that you are taking an average reading of all of the blood cells. For the A1C test, an average of these red blood cells represents average blood glucose over the last three months. A1C levels that are elevated indicate insulin resistance, which can affect fertility negatively. This is common with PCOS.

LABS TO RULE OUT THYROID DYSFUNCTION

Assessing thyroid function is critical in helping with fertility, because an optimally functioning thyroid increases your chance of conception. Your doctor may order thyroid hormone levels as well as tests to rule out autoimmune related thyroid disorders, such as Hashimoto's thyroiditis or Graves' disease.

Thyroid Stimulating Hormone (TSH)

Thyroid stimulating hormone (TSH) serves as a messenger from the pituitary gland to your thyroid gland. When TSH levels are high, it indicates a sluggish or under-acting thyroid. When TSH levels are low, it signals hyper- or overactive thyroid function. Normal TSH levels in the blood have a wide range. Optimal levels are essential for maintaining hormone balance between the pituitary and ovaries. Whether you have an underactive or hyperactive thyroid, both conditions can interfere equally with healthy hormone balance, ovulation, and the ability to conceive and maintain a healthy pregnancy. Abnormal levels can even lead to miscarriage. The optimal TSH level when you are trying to conceive is 1.0.

Free T4

TSH tells the thyroid gland to produce more or less thyroid hormone. Free T4 is the inactive form of thyroid hormone, which is produced and stored in the thyroid gland. T4 is then converted to T3, which is the active form of thyroid hormone.

Free T3

Free T3 levels represent the active form of thyroid hormone. Low levels indicate a sluggish or low acting thyroid and high levels represent a hyper- or overactive thyroid. Optimal levels of T4 and T3 are essential in maintaining proper thyroid function. TSH is equally important, but not in the absence of both T3 and T4. All values give you an in-depth look at thyroid function and are necessary when you're trying to ensure that your thyroid is functioning optimally to improve your fertility.

Microsomal Thyroid Peroxidase Antibodies (TPO Ab)

Microsomal thyroid peroxidase antibodies or TPO Ab is an autoimmune marker associated with Hashimoto's autoimmune thyroiditis. This condition is quite common and can add an immunological element to the regulation of the thyroid, which can directly affect fertility. Hashimoto's can also be triggered by pregnancy and/or hormone changes. This can occur after having a baby or after being pregnant and miscarrying. This is why TPO antibodies should be tested before and after each pregnancy.

Thyroid Globulin Antibodies (TG Ab)

Thyroid globulin antibodies are another autoimmune marker associated with Hashimoto's autoimmune thyroiditis. This is one of the most common causes of low thyroid function in women.

Many doctors routinely skip testing for TPO and TG antibodies, running the risk of missing the diagnosis of autoimmune Hashimoto's. It is important to check for Hashimoto's because it is estimated that 40% of unexplained infertility relates to an immune modulated mechanism. It's important to rule out any autoimmune disorders when improving fertility.

Thyroid Stimulating Immunoglobulins (TSI)

Thyroid stimulating immunoglobulins or TSI is an autoimmune marker strongly associated with Graves' disease. This condition can directly affect your fertility and must be addressed when you have abnormal labs and/or clinical symptoms are present.

General Blood Work

General lab work is important to rule out anemia, nutritional deficiencies, and other disease processes that may affect your fertility as well as your general health and well-being. I recommend the following tests:

- Complete blood count — looks at red blood cells and white blood cells to assess anemia and immune issues
- Comprehensive metabolic panel — looks at multiple organ systems to rule out systemic health conditions
- Lipid panel — looks at cholesterol and triglycerides to see if you have adequate levels for hormone production
- Iron, total iron binding capacity (TIBC), and ferritin — these are markers for anemia, which can influence menses and affect your energy levels, and may reflect an underlying health condition
- Vitamin D3 25-Hydroxy — used to determine if you have a deficiency in vitamin D3, which is associated with increased miscarriage rates and immune dysfunction

Immune Factors

I find that some people are battling viral or immune related disorders that may affect their fertility. When testing for any of these viruses, a positive IgM result means that you have an active infection. If the results show a positive IgG result, it indicates a past infection or a reactivated infection in some cases. If a virus is active, it can wreak havoc on the immune system, affecting your fertility.

I routinely check for the following viruses to properly identify and treat them when appropriate. Your doctor might test for additional viruses when appropriate.

- CMV IgG and IgM — cytomegalovirus
- EBV IgG and IgM — Epstein-Barr virus
- HHN 6 IgG and IgM — herpes simplex six virus
- Parvovirus B 19 IgG and IgM — parvovirus, different than that in dogs

LABS RELATED TO RECURRENT PREGNANCY LOSS DUE TO CLOTTING DISORDERS

The American Society of Reproductive Medicine (ASRM) has redefined recurrent pregnancy loss as two or more pregnancy losses. Previously, it was classified as three or more losses. If you have had more than one miscarriage, you may have an undiagnosed issue that is contributing to your inability to maintain a pregnancy. A clotting disorder is one of the possible causes for recurrent pregnancy loss. One such disorder called Antiphospholipid Antibody Syndrome (APS) often goes undetected. It's important to do a panel related to clotting disorders to rule out any conditions that would directly impair your ability to carry a pregnancy.

Antiphospholipid Antibody Syndrome (APS) occurs if the body's immune system makes antibodies or proteins that attack phospholipids, which results in abnormal blood clotting. The following blood tests are used to rule out the immunological mediated clotting disorder call APS.

- Lupus Anticoagulant
- Anticardiolipin
- Beta-2 Glycoprotein I (β2GPI)

In order to be diagnosed with APS you need to test positive for two or more of these tests twice, at least twelve weeks apart. This is because a single positive test can result from a short-term infection. The tests above are generally used to rule out APS. However, there are individualized tests of different phospholipids including Anti-phosphatidyl-serine, phosphatidyl-choline, phosphatidyl-ethanolamine, phosphatidic acid, phosphatidyl-glycerol and phosphatidyl-inositol antibodies

Other labs that are associated with congenital clotting disorders and recurrent pregnancy loss are listed below.

- Factor V Leiden Mutation
- Protein C / Protein S Deficiency
- Prothrombin Gene Mutation
- Methylenetetrahydrofolate Reductase (MTHFR) — homocysteine
- Antithrombin III

OTHER FACTORS TO ASSESS RECURRENT PREGNANCY LOSS

Other factors may be related to pregnancy loss, including: infection, anatomical or structure factors, genetic testing, male factor DNA fragmentation and abnormal thyroid and prolactin levels. That is why if you have had more than one miscarriage, you need to seek an evaluation with a gynecologist, obstetrician, or reproductive endocrinologist to assess the possible factors contributing to your pregnancy loss, so that they can be addressed moving forward.

Tracking Your Menstrual Cycle

There are many apps that can help you chart your menstrual cycle. Once you choose one and start tracking, remember to describe the flow. Is it light, moderate, or heavy? How many days does it last? Did you have cramping on Day 1 and/or before the onset of bleeding? Apps can help you understand your pattern and determine when you are ovulating. You can also use over-the-counter ovulation tests. Start on Day 9 and stop when you get a positive result. A positive result means that you are ovulating. If you do not get a positive result, it may be that you are not ovulating. This test can help you determine if this is a factor that you need to address. Another way to track your fertile window is by using your basal body temperature or BBT.

Basal Body Temperature (BBT)

The easiest way to track your BBT is to use an app to help you graph your results, but you can also find a paper chart online and write down your values manually. Every morning when you wake up, which should be around the same time every day, take your temperature before you get up to urinate, drink, eat, have sex, or even sit up in bed. You can choose an oral thermometer or an axillary BBT thermometer, which you place in your under arm. Make sure you know which type of thermometer you are using, because the normal temperature for each thermometer type will be different. Each day, you will enter the thermometer reading in the app or mark a dot on the paper chart where your temperature is on that day of the cycle.

Connect the dots and look for a rise in temperature, which usually occurs when you ovulate. You can also corelate this rise to an increase in cervical mucus. If you are unsure of how to interpret the results of your BBT chart, bring it to your doctor to help you assess when you are ovulating. Charts can vary with many ups and downs or no rise at all, which indicates some abnormality with the cycle. In Traditional Chinese Medicine, both a lack of a rise and up-and-down zig zags indicate a deficiency pattern that needs to be addressed to restore proper hormone balance. Use your BBT chart as a way to get information about your cycle, and then go to a skilled practitioner who can help you address any abnormalities that the graph reveals.

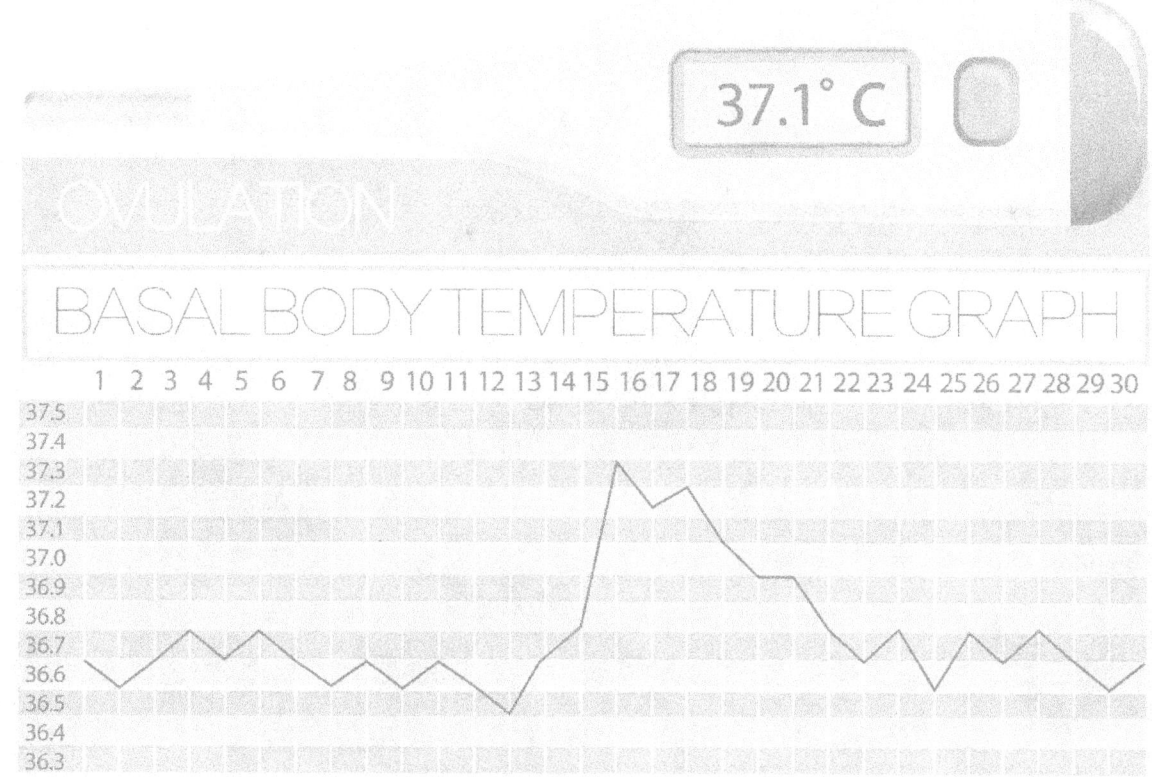

USE YOUR NEW KNOWLEDGE TO TALK WITH YOUR DOCTOR ABOUT YOUR LABS

Understanding labs related to your fertility is essential to interpreting your doctor's recommendations, and the reasons for the advice your doctor gives you. Now that you know more about the labs available for assessing fertility, you may want to request that your doctor includes additional labs in order to get enough information to make the appropriate decision on how to proceed on your fertility journey. No one expects you to know what a doctor who has studied for years knows, but understanding the basics will go far in helping you have a knowledgeable conversation with your doctor about the best path to take to conceive successfully.

CLEARING EMOTIONAL BLOCKS IS ESSENTIAL TO THE JOURNEY OF CONCEPTION.

CLEARING EMOTIONAL BLOCKS

Clearing emotional blocks is essential to the journey of conception. The mind and body are integrally connected, and the mind processes much quicker than the body. This means that it can take the body longer to release fear, stress, anger, and sadness. Many times, the body takes on the emotional stresses of life, a traumatic event, loss, or pain. I am by no means saying that your blocked emotions are the cause of your infertility. Infertility is a complex phenomenon that makes it challenging to conceive whether naturally or with artificial reproductive technologies (ART). What I can tell you after nineteen years of helping women conceive, both naturally and with ART, is that emotional well-being is essential to optimal functioning of the body and could be a cause of your stalled progress.

As the product of a psychotherapist mother and psychologist father, I know that emotions have a direct effect on our health. Observing the challenges and journeys of many women, I have seen the emotional toll that it takes on them and the emotional blocks that, when shifted, allow them to achieve success. Having my daughter conceived via IVF with integrative therapies including acupuncture, and then carried by a gestational carrier, I implicitly understand that this journey affects you on more than the physical level. It is quite personal to me. Each hurdle big or small is emotionally draining and can leave you feeling a deep sense of disappointment, sadness, and pain. However, it is hard to stay in those emotions, so most of my patients "power through it" as I did and don't realize the emotional impact that it has on their body and well-being.

Many times, when women come to see me they may need to have small changes made to support their physiological function, restore their menses, and to bring their FSH, LH, and other ovarian function markers into balance. In my perspective, it is absolutely possible for these women to get pregnant, and yet something is preventing this from happening. Fixing physiology is vital to health and effective fertility, but never overlook the emotional scars that need to be lifted.

Some of the most significant emotional factors that I see in women are the effects of grief. We all experience grief and loss in our lifetimes. This grief may be due to their own failed attempts to conceive, or to the loss of someone close to them. It could be grief over the loss of a loved one, a friend, or a miscarriage. Or it could be the loss of the life we thought we would have, the relationship we wanted but don't have, the baby we feel should be here but isn't, the job or support we don't have, or the loss of each month that conception is possible but does not happen. Women who are dealing with fertility struggles experience loss each month when they don't get pregnant, and these losses build and grow over time, creating a cloud of heaviness and an ever-present stress. Where does all this emotion go? It has to go somewhere, and the body tries to assist us by storing these emotions deep inside. Our bodies often take on these burdens and stresses without us realizing it, leading to disruption in physiology and the flow of energy.

RECOGNIZING LOSS

Some people don't recognize loss in their lives. Loss is not just the death of a person. Loss can be related to a move, the passing of youth, the end of a friendship, a lost job, a failed marriage or relationship, or other difficult events in your life. You may have had a miscarriage. You may have encountered one or many losses before your infertility struggles. You have likely experienced the loss of not getting pregnant when you get your period each month. When we perceive loss, for example, thinking, "I will never have children," we experience this loss in the current moment. Losses large or small build up and get internalized in our bodies.

In addition to the inevitable losses of life, we live in a more technically advanced, digital, and computerized society. We have begun to have relationships with technology rather than people and, as a result, we have become more disconnected from the support systems, friends, and family who once assisted us through the natural process of grief. Many of my patients struggling with infertility feel isolated and alone. Even with online chat groups, there is some sharing of information, but there is less personal connection, which makes women feel isolated and alone. That feeling further amplifies the loss of not having the support you need.

Many women and couples are dealing with loss and grief. To understand our emotions and how to clear these emotional blocks, you first need to understand grief. You can get "stuck" in one of the stages of grief and become depressed. Depression can be slowly insidious in this process of trying to conceive, especially after many failed attempts at conception. It is important to look for signs and symptoms of depression, so that it can be identified and properly addressed. Grief is different from depression. Grieving is a natural process of feeling loss and sadness that reduces over time in severity and frequency. Depression is when there is a constant level of deep disappointment with a sense of hopelessness, changes in appetite and weight, sleep irregularities, loss of interest or pleasure in activities, irritability, anxiety, guilt, general discontent, and lack of energy, along with an inability to get out of those feelings. Many people think of clinical depression as a state where you can't get out of bed and just want to sleep, but there are many functional people who are depressed. The main thing to remember is that if your depression stems from grief or loss, addressing the loss can help your depression.

SYMPTOMS OF DEPRESSION

Some of the symptoms of depression are listed below. Remember, you may experience a few of the symptoms or many of the symptoms. These symptoms could be mild and persistent or severe and debilitating.

Mood Changes: Anger, irritability, anxiety, apathy, guilt, hopelessness, loss of interest, lack of pleasure in activities, mood swings, sadness, despair, general discontent

Sleep: Restless sleep, waking early, trouble falling asleep, sleeping too much, insomnia, or restless sleep

General: Weight loss or weight gain, excessive hunger, fatigue, loss of appetite, emotional eating or stress eating

Behavioral Changes: Irritability, agitation, excessive crying, or social isolation

Mind: Lack of focus, lack of interest in things that used to fulfill you, lack of motivation, lack of concentration, slowness in activity, or thoughts of suicide

Now that you understand the symptoms of depression, you may have a new awareness that you might be depressed. However, not everybody who is experiencing loss is depressed. You may be experiencing the natural stages of grief and loss.

Grief is a natural process of accepting loss by going through the five stages of grief. To better understand this let's talk about the Kübler-Ross model of the five stages of grief. Remember, this applies to big, small, and perceived losses that relate to not conceiving, miscarriages, and other losses or disappointments related to infertility and in other areas of your life. Understanding the stages of grief is helpful for understanding your emotions and creating a level of normality around loss. Keep in mind that the brain cannot process significant and traumatic losses as well as constant repetitive losses in a short manner. The brain is designed to process loss over time. This allows the brain time to come to acceptance and resolution. Much like a computer, if the brain receives too much input or is asked to process too much at once, a short circuit of the brain may occur. To avoid this, the brain is designed to go through the five steps to process things in a manner that will resolve the grief over time. What changes over time is the frequency and intensity of the feelings of grief. As the old adage says, time is the greatest healer.

UNDERSTANDING GRIEF

The Kübler-Ross model, commonly known as The Five Stages of Grief, was first introduced by Elisabeth Kübler-Ross in her 1969 book, *On Death and Dying*. Elisabeth Kübler-Ross describes, in five discrete stages, a process by which people cope and deal with grief and tragedy. These stages do not necessarily have to be complete or in order. You can bounce back and forth from one stage to the other weekly, daily, or even hourly. Not everyone who has loss will feel all five stages; some people will miss one stage entirely.

The framework Elisabeth Kübler-Ross created is important for understanding how loss affects us emotionally. It gives us an understanding of the inner workings of grief, so we don't feel out of control with loss. This understanding also creates a normalcy. Depression can occur when you get stuck in one of these stages and experience hopelessness and despair for a prolonged period of time. When this happens, you can't move back and forth between the stages to fully process the loss or grief. When this happen, the depression needs to be addressed medically and/or with counseling so that the process of accepting and processing the loss can continue.

Let's look at the stages of grief to understand more about the inner workings of how our brain and mind work through these losses to create acceptance and balance once again.

Below are the five distinct stages that Kübler-Ross set in relation to death and dying. These are important to know in life as we will all experience significant losses in our lives related to someone dying. Remember these stages apply not only to death but also loss and disappointment related to miscarriage, infertility and the loss of the family and child you hoped to have.

THE STAGES OF GRIEF

1. Denial

"I feel fine."
"This can't be happening—not to me."

Denial is usually only a temporary defense for the individual. For example, you may tell everybody and yourself that you are fine, but inside you are feeling tired, resigned, apathetic, and sad. You might deny these emotions and experience the change only within your physical body, feeling exhausted and tired.

2. Anger

"Why me? It's not fair!"
"How can this happen to me?"
"Who is to blame?"

Once in the second stage, the individual recognizes that denial cannot continue. Because of anger, the person is very difficult to care for due to misplaced feelings of rage and envy.

You may be irritable and angry with those trying to help you. You may not want support from your spouse, friends, and family. You may be angry with yourself and everyone around you.

3. Bargaining

"If I would have done that diet, seen that doctor or listened to my friend maybe I could have gotten pregnant."
"I would give my life savings if I could only have a baby."

In relation to infertility, we may be thinking if I only got acupuncture treatment, I could have conceived. If I only did IVF with Femara and the other new drug I could have conceived. If I only had less stress in my life I could have conceived. If I only exercised and my weight was less I could have gotten pregnant. "Should of, Could of, Would of" thinking is what this stage is all about. "I'll do anything for a few more years." "I will give my life savings if..."

4. Depression

"I'm so sad, why bother to try with anything?"
"What's the point?"
"Nothing is going to change and I will never have the child(ren) and family I want."

You may just want to be left alone. You may become more withdrawn and isolated. You may want time to be by yourself, and to cry, grieve, and be sad. This is a natural stage of loss and grieving that allows you to clear your emotions and make space for grieving to occur. However some individuals may get stuck in this phase and not be able to bounce back into the other ones. When this happens, it creates a situation for depression that needs to be addressed and treated by a physician.

5. Acceptance

"It's going to be okay."
"I accept my struggle and I am going to do what I can to prepare for a better outcome."

We come to a place of accepting that there is some possible purpose or understanding that it's okay with what has happened in the past. We become hopeful and refocused in creating the family that we desire by being able to have a mindset to continue forward and continue to try to conceive. In this stage, you become more hopeful, focused and clear with your intent for positive outcome is in the future.

Understanding that you can experience different stages of loss can help you understand why you may feel angry, irritable, sad, hopeless, or fatigued. Removing this cloud of heaviness is essential to removing blocks and improving conception.

I have found that the best way to remove the emotional weight that may be causing blocks is with homeopathic medicines. To understand how this works, I will tell you a little bit more about what homeopathic medicines are and what they can do for you.

HOMEOPATHY TO RELEASE EMOTIONS

Homeopathy is the use of a diluted plant, substance or mineral that creates homeostasis in the body. Homeopathy was discovered in the mid 19th century by Dr. Samuel Hahnemann. He was a medical doctor at a time when medicine was fairly barbaric. For example, arsenic was given to sick patients and while some of them lived, a lot of them died. Giving patients more medicine was the trend at the time, even though patients died anyway.

Dr. Hahnemann felt that there was a different way to address disease and illness. Instead of giving his patients more medicine or stronger medicine as other doctors did, he took a substance and diluted it, making it less strong. This concept of using something diluted or in a small amount was not used at the time. For the sake of understanding how homeopathy was discovered, let's imagine that Dr. Hahnemann started with an onion. He took one drop of onion and diluted it in a glass of water. He then took a drop of that dilution and put it in another glass of water. After he had diluted the original substance over one hundred times, he had a homeopathic dilution of onion. This homeopathic solution of onion was then given to a healthy person and it created symptoms in that person as if they had just cut an onion. Their eyes burned, their nose ran, and they were irritable. Dr. Hahnemann then gave the homeopathic solution of onion to a patient who presented with the exact same symptoms of someone who had just cut an onion--the same burning eyes, runny nose, and irritability. This patient's symptoms resolved and homeostasis and balance, was achieved. Dr. Hahnemann had discovered the "Law of Similars," which is based on the theory that like cures like. That is, he found that giving a homeopathic substance to a person whose symptoms have the same qualities as that substance resolves their symptoms and creates homeostasis in their body once again.

Homeopathic medicine is diluted past Avogadro's number, which means that there is none of the original substance present in the diluted solution. So if you take homeopathic onion and homeopathic arsenic and look at those solutions under a microscope, you will just see water molecules. Homeopathy is energized water that gives a message to the body, telling it to create balance. Because of this extreme dilution, if you start with a toxic substance such as arsenic and create a homeopathic solution from it, it is no longer toxic and, instead, takes on new properties as a homeopathic medicine. Because of this, many substances that should typically be avoided are okay to take as a homeopathic preparation. This also means that homeopathic solutions do not interfere with other medications and can be taken concurrently with prescription medications. Homeopathy is used by many skilled practitioners in patients who are pregnant, and in kids and infants, as it is a very benign medicine that can be very powerful. Of course, it is best to consult with your own physician before taking any of these homeopathic medicines.

Again, in homeopathy, the symptoms of the patient are matched to the symptoms of the remedy. When the dilution is given to the person, it releases the discord and creates a balanced state once again. The body is always looking to be balanced. It wants to be balanced, work properly, and work in a way that serves you, however sometimes the body needs help. Homeopathy is a very benign and gentle but powerful way to assist the body in releasing trapped emotions and regaining physiological function once again.

Homeopathy is widely used in Europe, India, and other countries. It has been used in the United States for over 200 years and was a part of the medical education before the 1930s. It has also had a resurgence in the United States in the last 50 years. Although homeopathy is not part of the education in medical school for allopathic medical doctors, it is an integral part of Naturopathic education. There are also other types of doctors and practitioners who practice homeopathy. I use homeopathic medicines for emotional blocks often with my patients because it is such an important and integral part of creating balance within. It is necessary to clear those blocks, so that those internal emotions can be released. Clearing the emotional burdens not only helps conception, but also supports a healthy and happy pregnancy. It can help to create a flow and a sense of hope and balance, so that a woman's body can do what it is meant to do.

I want to give you some examples of patients who I have treated using homeopathic medicine to remove these emotional blocks. Of course, their names have been changed. I want you to understand the amazing impact that homeopathic medicine has on treating loss and grief. Homeopathy treats the way you have manifested and exemplified the grief. Whether you're angry, sad, withdrawn, or anxious because you did not get pregnant or had a miscarriage; you're angry that people don't understand; you feel isolated in the process; or you are sad that your parent or loved one has passed and is not here to support you; homeopathy treats the differentiation of those patterns unlike anything that I know. Outside of acupuncture and Chinese medicine, which we will discuss in another chapter, homeopathy is one of the best tools to release emotional burdens and blocks.

There are many reasons why homeopathy is easily accessible and a great option for clearing emotional blockages.

Advantages of Homeopathy

- It is noninvasive
- It doesn't interact with medications
- It is inexpensive
- It can be used short-term
- It has little to no side effects

HOMEOPATHY AT WORK

Tiffany's Story

Take for example Tiffany who is a 32-year-old patient who came to see me with an FSH level of 32. We all know what she was told. She was told she would absolutely not be able to conceive on her own or with IVF, and the only possibility that she would have for conception was with a donor egg. She was devastated as she wanted a child of her own, and her husband longed to have a child that was biologically related to him. There is not anything wrong with using a donor egg, but it was not what Tiffany wanted.

As I spoke with her about her trials and tribulations, I asked her about how she was feeling. She explained to me that prior to trying to get pregnant there were some stressors in her life. She had lost her father who she was very close to. He had passed away suddenly, and she had struggled with her loss. As she approached creating a family of her own, it became more important for her to have both of her parents with her, and she missed him terribly. As she looked forward to creating a family of her own, she looked back at what she did not have and wanted the cohesiveness of having the generations of her family together. This loss affected her deeply and had occurred within the year prior to starting her conception journey.

She was 32 years old and there was no reason for her FSH to be 32, but nonetheless, she was told she was in premature ovarian failure. She explained that in the next year following her father's passing, her menstrual cycle had changed. She had more PMS symptoms and was very tired. She would have some hot flashes before the onset of her period. Her periods were irregular and the flow was not consistent. She had gained weight, had low energy, and lacked motivation to get on a regular exercise program. She denied being depressed.

When she talked about this loss, you could see the energy and emotion attached to it. It was hard for her to not cry when talking about it. She was not overly focused on it, but when it was brought up, she would get emotional. I listened to her story and her journey with infertility; she had been struggling for two years to conceive. I thought, yes, she has premature ovarian failure at 32, but why? Her estrogen and progesterone levels were okay and she was having regular periods two years prior to all of the emotional stressors. The only thing that seemed to stand out was the profound loss that she felt. It makes sense to think that such a loss would cause stress, loss of sleep, and changes in the menstrual cycle, but—even knowing this—could we really say that grief was a major cause of her infertility? I could not be sure, but it seemed plausible that this had a large impact on her physiology. Her sadness and the despair were palpable; they cast a shadow on her and rested on her shoulders. There was a constant stress that lingered over her. At this point, it was important for me to address this with her and allow her to talk about her sadness. Equally, it was important to clear the grief from her body. How could I do this? With homeopathic medicines. As I have explained, homeopathy has the unique ability to release emotional blocks and heaviness from the body. I have found that this is especially effective to release grief and loss. It was clear that Tiffany needed to release this grief even to just make her feel better by releasing the stress within her body.

I gave her homeopathic Ignatia Amara 1M for grief and she took it for two days only. Four weeks later, I saw her for a follow-up visit and she told me that she felt lighter and happier. And, although her FSH levels were still at 32, she called me three weeks later to tell me she was pregnant. Even though she had started on supplements to support adrenal function and reproductive health, she had been taking them for less than 30 days. It would take much longer for these natural substances to help her conceive within a month if she was in ovarian failure. I believe that in her situation, medically speaking, she was not supposed to get pregnant yet, but once the grief was cleared, there was no longer a psychological disruption and her body was able to function normally. She did go on to bring the pregnancy to full term, and she gave birth to a beautiful and healthy baby boy. More than just being able to conceive, she was able to feel lighter, happier, and more at peace with her loss so that she could move forward in her own life.

Kim's Story

Kim had been a patient of mine for a number of years. She and her husband had decided to start a family and Kim was 37. They did conceive within the first year of trying, but unfortunately Kim had a miscarriage at about eleven weeks. She was devastated from this loss and it took her a long time to feel that she could try again to have another baby. She didn't really talk about her emotions and internalized them. When I would broach the subject of the loss of the miscarriage, I could see the sadness in her eyes, but she had the majority of her emotions on lock down. She decided that she would not think about trying to conceive again because it was too stressful, emotionally draining, and difficult to think about. So, she shelved her emotions and her fertility. Two years passed, and she was approaching forty. She started to think more and more about having a family. At this point, her FSH levels were 12 and her LH was 26; she was definitely in the phase of declining ovarian function. Feeling the biological clock ticking louder and louder, it became apparent she could no longer shelve her desire to try again to get pregnant. It was at that point that she wanted to try again to conceive and asked about focusing on fertility. Although I had given her remedies in the past, she did not want to focus on the loss. When she was able to talk about it in more detail, she told me that she had felt like she had failed and that somehow her body was not capable of carrying a pregnancy. She felt inadequate and sad, but resigned to the fact that she probably would never have a child. She was constantly reminded of this loss by her peers who had children and it was intensified because she knew her husband really wanted to have a biological child of their own. She longed to be a mother, and the biological clock inside started to tick louder.

Kim's way of dealing with her loss was to internalize her stress and not cry in front of anybody. She was someone who went by the adage of "pull yourself up by the bootstraps," and "buck up" and "power through it." Her sadness was hidden deep inside, but clearly present. She had a deep sadness, but didn't want to share this with others. She was comforted by her pets, and she would sometimes cry alone, but this was rare. Her distinct manifestation of her grief correlates to the nature and qualities of homeopathic Natrum Muriaticum. I gave her Natrum Muriaticum Homeopathic medicine in a two-day dose once per month for about three months to clear the grief. After that, she reporting feeling lighter, happier, and less sad and weighed down. Although she was older, had high LH, and was told by doctors she could not conceive, within three months of taking her supplements and having unprotected intercourse she conceived and was pregnant. With a beautiful twist of fate, she naturally conceived twins and went on to have a healthy pregnancy and normal birth. She is now the mother of two beautiful girls.

She was also on supportive supplements, which she had continued to take after her miscarriage, but she was also forty years old—three years older than she was the first time she conceived and miscarried. These supplements were minimal as she specifically said she did not want to focus on fertility. I encouraged her to take minimal support over that time, just so she did not become deficient. Even with that support, her FSH and LH increased over those three years. What was unique was that, when she was ready to release those emotions of grief and loss, homeopathy was able to help her to do this and improve physiological function in spite of her biological age. I believe the homeopathic prescription was instrumental in removing her emotional blocks so that things could progress, her physiological function could be restored, and she could conceive.

Many times, I see women who have an unaddressed factor in their fertility journey that relates to their emotions. The journey women take in working toward the ability to conceive may be a long, winding road. It may have hurdles to climb including examinations, laboratory testing, procedures, and surgeries. Their hopes and dreams will rise and fall again and again. What is it about this path that leads to women feeling like they failed, feeling alone, feeling sad and burdened? It's the little losses of not conceiving each month, the big losses of miscarriages, and the perceived loss of not having the child or family they so desire. In the United States, roughly 20% of all pregnancies before the twentieth week result in a miscarriage. Most of these happen around week seven. The cause is unknown, which can result in emotional turmoil, trying to understand the cause and how to prevent any future losses.

What many people don't realize is that each month that you do not conceive, each failed IVF cycle, each failed IUI there is an accumulative and progressive buildup of grief and loss. Each baby shower, every pregnant woman you see, each family with kids, and every friend or co-worker who seems like they sneezed and got pregnant is a reminder of your disappointment and inability to conceive. Many women feel they have failed. Each month there is hope and when the period comes their dreams are crushed. Unless they've gone through fertility struggles, it can be hard for others to understand, which can leave women feeling alone. I always talk with my patients about their emotions and want to know how they're feeling because it's very important to me. You must clear the sadness and grief yourself, or have tools to help you do that, or else the grief and disappointment can become a block to forward progress.

In homeopathy and Chinese Medicine, the emotional distress creates a blockage of Qi that then affects the function of organs and in turn affects the physiology. Constant disappointment and loss build up and become an ongoing source of stress, acting as a hormone disrupter that affects a woman's ability to conceive. It is not enough to take the right vitamins and supplements. It's so much more. Clearing emotional blocks is necessary to eliminate obstacles for conception to happen in an organic way.

HOMEOPATHY TO THE RESCUE: TOP 5 REMEDIES TO CLEAR EMOTIONS

I'm going to give you the top remedies for grief and loss that can be used before, after, and during IVF cycles or with natural conception. Homeopathic remedies or medicines represent a picture of a person or circumstance. Along with the other tools that I provide in this book, this is one that should not be ignored. *Complete Fertility* is about releasing the past to create space for the future. It's also about having tools to help you through the ups and downs and disappointments that may happen in your fertility journey. It's hard to say how that journey will be for a specific woman. Some women can conceive quickly. Others struggle through failed attempts numerous times before they conceive. Others have repetitive disappointments with unsuccessful outcomes. I understand the strong desire to have your own biological child, though this is not essential to becoming an amazing parent and having a healthy and wonderful child and family. There are now many viable options for women, men, and couples who are struggling with fertility to have families, including adoption, surrogacy, and embryo adoption. Luckily, we live in a time where there are multiple viable options to expand your family.

TOP 5 HOMEOPATHIC REMEDIES RELATED TO THE PROGRESSION OF GRIEF

Below are the top five remedies for grief. It is important to understand each remedy and its qualities as if you're describing a person. It is equally important to understand that there is a progression where initial grief can go deeper in the body. As the person becomes more withdrawn, they exhibit different symptoms. The schematic below shows initial grief starting with Ignatia Amara and, as the person becomes more withdrawn and the grief goes untreated and gets deeper, it progresses to the next remedy. The deeper the grief goes, the more withdrawn the person becomes. That is, Ignatia Amara can transform into Natrum Muriaticum, which can transform into Sepia, which can transform in to Phosporicum Acidum, which can then transform into Aurum Metallicum.

As the grief goes to a deeper level, a new remedy is needed.

Ignatia Amara
↓
Natrum Muriaticum
↓
Sepia
↓
Phosporicum Acidum
↓
Aurum Metallicum

HOMEOPATHIC IGNATIA AMARA

Ignatia Amara is the initial state we have talked about that comes about from sudden loss and grief, with the person wanting to be consoled and unable to control their tears. They are sensitive to what others say and can be silently brooding, irritable, sad, sensitive, and have an aversion to cigarette smoke. As the grief goes deeper for a multitude of reasons, Ignatia state turns to Natrum Muriaticum.

HOMEOPATHIC NATRUM MURIATICUM

In the Natrum Muriaticum state, the person is sad and feels sensitive, but they have become more withdrawn. They retreat a bit more, so they no longer like to be consoled and, in fact consolation aggravates and irritates them. One of the biggest indications of this homeopathic state is that they prefer to cry alone. They are sensitive, but they put up a wall of protection, so even though they are sad, they will hold back their tears until they are alone. They generally do not cry even in front of their spouse. Their reasons may be that they don't want to burden others, they feel people don't understand their pain, or they fear they will fall apart if they allow someone to hug or comfort them and won't be able to stop the tears. This happens because their sadness is too overwhelming to deal with and/or because they have had multiple losses and there is just too much to process at once. They confide in only a very select few and, although they are in pain, they don't like to talk about it. They do, however, feel safe with animals, so they have a great love of animals. They will cry in front of their pets because they know they are unconditionally loving and therefore it is safe to do so with them.

HOMEOPATHIC SEPIA

If the grief remains untreated and goes deeper, the person progresses to the Sepia state. In the Sepia state, the person withdraws even more and becomes very sad. They begin to reflect more of the appearance of a depressed person, not wanting to participate in social events, wanting to be left alone, crying and feeling very sad. At this point, they can no longer hold back their tears even if they want to, because the sadness runs too deep. They generally cry when talking about the events or feelings associated with their loss. They feel physically heavy and tired, and don't want to interact much with others. They like having someone around, like having their spouse in the house, because they don't want to be alone. But at the same time, they don't want to interact. They are irritable with those they love best, like their family. This state is not catatonic. The person in Sepia goes through their day-to-day life, but has deep sadness and, if given the choice, would decline invitations for social outings and gatherings. Those things that were once enjoyable with family and friends seem effortful. So, they are functional but decline invitations for extra-curricular functions and would rather be left alone. In this state, the woman's period tends to be heavy, as if she can't hold up the uterus anymore; she can also have a heavy sensation in the pelvis. She likes to cross her legs as if to hold things up. The physical sensation that she can't hold things in anymore correlates to the emotional plane as well. Sepia is very sensitive, so they need understanding and a trusted person to confide in. If the grief goes deeper than Sepia state, it moves to Phosphoricum Acidum.

HOMEOPATHIC PHOSPHORICUM ACIDUM

In this state, the person is more withdrawn; they are not only emotionally withdrawn, but also are physically and mentally withdrawn. They talk in monotone and are flat on all levels. No more are they teary and crying; it is like they are emotionless. There is no excitement, no joy—they will say they are sad, but without tears or any inflection in their voice. They just go through the motions of life. They may or may not be functional in everyday life. If untreated, Phosphoricum Acidum progresses to Aurum Metallicum.

HOMEOPATHIC AURUM METALLICUM

Once the person has become withdrawn to the Aurum Metallicum level, they have suicidal thoughts and may have even tried to commit suicide. The pain has gone too deep and they feel they must withdraw in the most ultimate way, by taking their life. They have ideations about suicide or feel like they don't want to be here anymore.

At any of these stages, intervention by a physician may be needed, but in a Aurum Metallicum state where a person is having suicidal thoughts, intervention is needed immediately. This may include, in-patient or out-patient treatment with a psychiatrist, therapist, or social worker; medication; access to an emergency hotline; homeopathic medicine and other integrative therapies, including drug therapy.

HOMEOPATHIC PRESCRIBING

The idea of homeopathy is to match the qualities of the remedy with the qualities within yourself. The homeopathic remedies or medicines can clear the emotion, as if you took a big sigh and an emotional weight has been lifted off your shoulders. Homeopathic remedies have the ability to work quickly to help improve your emotional state. Homeopathic remedies or medicines can serve as one of many important tools to release internalized emotions, grief, and disappointment. If you haven't looked at the emotional impact your infertility struggles have on you, it should be something you consider.

Homeopathic medicines come in many potencies. X potencies are very weak, while c potencies are little stronger, but still very gentle. Commercially available homeopathic strengths don't go in linear order. For example, the next dose after 6x is 12x, 30x, then 6c, 30c, 200c then M doses, such as 1M, 10M, then 50M. To avoid confusion, a general rule of thumb is that 200c and M doses are used for emotions. However, those doses will be given by a practitioner trained in homeopathy. Generally, you will have access to 30c doses at natural-oriented stores. Lower potencies can be used, but will need to be used more frequently.

For remedies for grief and loss, a good place to start is with an available potency like 30c. There many ways to take homeopathic medicines. You can take them as pellets or as a liquid; generally, pellets will be the easiest to get in a store. Homeopathic remedies should be taken at least ten minutes away from food or drink as they are absorbed sublingually, under the tongue. In my professional experience, if the remedy is right for you, whatever dose you take will help. However, a higher potency will generally last longer. I give homeopathic medicine at a higher dose for only two days in my clinic and the effects can last for one to two months. If you are taking pellets at a lower dose, you may want to take them daily for two weeks or more. You may need to take homeopathic medicine every month when you don't conceive and you feel disappointment, or you may need it every few months when your emotions build up inside over time. It is best to follow the manufacturer's recommended dosing since, in the context of this book, I cannot make individualized recommendations. However, if you feel you need to clear grief at a very deep level and you are not successful in doing so after following manufacture's recommendation for dosing, you should consult a physician or practitioner trained in homeopathy. They will be able to individualize a homeopathic remedy and select the one that is right for you, in the correct potency.

Although homeopathy is not the only method for clearing loss and grief, I find it to be an effective way to energetically clear the grief from the physical body, allowing these disruptions to be removed and restore natural physiological function. This does not discount or limit the other therapies, techniques, modalities or treatments that may clear loss and grief. This also does not limit the body's natural ability to process grief over time to restore the body, mind, and spirit to balance once again.

Use the top five homeopathic remedies as tools to clear your emotional blocks and restore physiological function. Remember, homeopathic remedies do not generally interact with medications, but ask your healthcare provider before starting anything new. Using homeopathy and other integrative therapies allows you to support your body, mind, and spirit in totality for release of old blocks and improved conception and well-being.

MORE AND MORE WOMEN ARE HAVING CHILDREN AT A LATER REPRODUCTIVE AGE.

ADVANCED MATERNAL AGE:

CAN I REALLY REVERSE THE HANDS OF TIME?

More and more women are having children at a later reproductive age. It has become common place for women to start families later in life compared to just a decade ago. Why is this the case? There are many factors including women having careers and being the bread winners of their families, caring for aging parents, health issues, economic factors, chronic stress in people's lives, changes in relationships like waiting longer to marry, and other external factors that play a role in waiting to have children until your thirties or forties. In addition, many women think that once they are ready to conceive, they will be successful immediately. This is no longer the case. We live in a busy, stressful world that is increasingly more toxic and, many times, lifestyle habits like inactivity and poor diet tend to contribute to women being in a depleted state that affects their physiology, making them unable to conceive easily. Many women start trying in their thirties and find themselves approaching forty without having been successful in getting pregnant. Then they begin a race against time. With their FSH levels rising and AMH levels declining, the pressure to have a baby before it's too late becomes palpable.

You may find yourself at the age of thirty-five or older, which is considered "advanced maternal age." I know that sounds crazy, but in the fertility world, thirty-five is old. Yes, there are valid risks with being an older mother, including increased rates of Downs' syndrome and other genetic disorders. There are more risks with an older mother because her eggs are older.

Complete Fertility

However, many women today are just starting to try to get pregnant in their thirties. If you are just starting to try getting pregnant at thirty-two years old, you may find yourself at thirty-five or older before you realize that you may have an issue with infertility. Just because a woman is thirty-five or even forty years old does not mean she can't start a family. And if she and her partner find themselves older and trying to have kids, it's not like they can turn back the hands of time.

If you are in this situation, you need help navigating through conceiving at an advanced maternal age. The good news is that women of advanced maternal age are able to have healthy babies if they can provide their bodies with the proper support and create a nutritive environment for healthy cell division, potentially reducing the risk associated with advanced maternal age.

Likewise, sperm parameters are reduced in men who are forty and older. However, many people fail to talk about the fact that the conditions and environment that a dividing egg, sperm, or fertilized egg grows in have a great impact on supporting cell division and the development of a healthy child. What I am saying is that there are things you can do to optimize the environment in which an embryo grows to support healthy fetal development and, possibly, to lower the risk associated with advanced maternal age. In some cases, although my older fertility patients have older eggs, they are generally healthier than my younger patients and have a more supportive environment for fetal development. I believe that if you are on the journey of trying to have a baby, then your heart has led you down this path and you deserve the tools to make your best effort at success.

Obviously, if a woman is past reproductive age, then it may not be possible to have a baby even with the help of ART. On the other hand, I see a lot of patients in their late thirties and early forties who are told that they cannot conceive naturally, and then I work with them and they get pregnant. I see it all the time. So what about those women; what is different about them and their ability to succeed?

These women are optimizing their physiology and hormone balance, and taking supportive nutrients that are shown to influence healthy cell division in a dividing embryo. These women might be taking CoQ10 supplements to help egg quality and to combat mitochondrial dysfunction in order to support energy production. Or, they might be using acupuncture and Chinese herbs to support blood flow, circulation, hormone balance, and healthy cell division to create a supportive environment for an embryo to grow and develop. These women are supporting their bodies and, as a side effect of these integrative tools, they are feeling more energetic, sleeping better, having better periods, experiencing improved mood, and feeling more vibrant and renewed. They are helping their bodies, so they have energy and are not going into pregnancy completely depleted. Rather, they are giving themselves the opportunity for fertility success. They are optimizing their adrenal function—a missing link in infertility, utilizing acupuncture to boost their fertility, and using other integrative tools such as nutritional and thyroid support. They are also addressing underlying genetic issues, MTHFR genetic mutations that may be factors in infertility, and other underlying health issues to create an environment that any egg or embryo would grow and flourish in.

Everyone wants to get pregnant yesterday. Some women with the right support get pregnant relatively quickly, within three to six months. Others take a longer amount of time to regain optimal physiology, but eventually conceive naturally. It is possible? I see patients who have not gotten pregnant with IUI or even IVF and then conceive naturally. I work with many patients who see me as their last resort. Sometimes these cases can be challenging, and not everyone I work with gets pregnant, but I have a lot of success with the tools I use to restore function in women at any reproductive age who otherwise have been told they will not have children. So can we turn back the hands of time? No, not technically; but we can create a healthier, better oiled, fine-tuned body, and a healthier version of ourselves that lends itself to conception and healthy babies. So, you may feel like you have turned back the hands of time, feeling healthier and more vibrant at forty than you did at thirty. I tell my patients that there is no guarantee that utilizing the tools provided to overcome roadblocks will lead to conceiving, but you can at least give yourself the best chance at success, and as a side effect, you will generally feel better than you do right now. If what you are doing is not helping, then you must do something different. Repeating the same unsuccessful route will get you nowhere.

Let's refocus on understanding the parameters that your doctor evaluates to assess if you have a reserve of eggs and what the quality of those egg might be. This information basically directs your doctor to give you the ultimate judgement of whether or not they think you can have a baby. Remember that many reproductive endocrinologists are not in the business of improving physiological function, so they are looking at these parameters as static things that cannot change. They are amazing at what they do, but they do not work on physiological function. For example, if your FSH is high, reflecting low ovarian reserve, their solution is IVF rather than herbs and supplements to help restore your natural physiological function and lower your FSH level. Understanding this, let's look at the parameters these doctors use to evaluate your potential for success of having a baby.

MARKERS TO ASSESS IF YOU CAN HAVE A BABY

In addition to FSH levels, there are two important markers generally used to assess ovarian reserve. Ovarian reserve refers to the eggs you have left in your ovaries. The first marker is called the antral follicle count and the second is called anti-Müllerian hormone (AMH). Antral follicle count reflects ovarian reserve and is also a predictor of IVF success (1). AMH reflects ovarian reserve (1) and is a major contributor to whether or not a fertility expert tells you that you will be able to conceive naturally, with our own eggs. If your AMH is too low, you might find your doctor telling you that your only choice to have a baby is to use donor eggs or a donor embryo. Let's take a closer look at antral follicle count and AMH and how these markers reflect your potential fertility success.

Antral Follicle Count—A Physical Marker for Ovarian Reserve

Pelvic and intravaginal ultrasound is used to asses antral follicle count. Antral follicles are growing follicles that produce AMH. Antral follicles are small, resting follicles that are visible on ultrasound and are a physical marker that allows doctors to assess ovarian reserve. Their size is about two to nine millimeters in diameter (2). As the follicles grow, they inhibit the growth of additional eggs from the primordial pool (resting eggs) so one egg can become dominant (2). As a follicle matures, AMH production declines, which allows the follicles to complete their developmental stage of growth as a result of stimulation by FSH (2).

The antral follicle count is used to assess ovarian reserve, especially by reproductive endocrinologists, as it reflects an expected response to ovarian stimulation drugs during in vitro fertilization. The number of antral follicles visible on ultrasound is indicative of the number of microscopic or resting primordial follicles remaining in the ovary. Each primordial follicle contains an immature egg that can potentially develop, mature, and ovulate in the future. When there are fewer antral follicles visible, there are fewer remaining eggs. In relationship to IVF, when there is an average or high number of antral follicles, a good number of eggs can be retrieved with IVF, and pregnancy rates are expected to be higher than average. When there are few antral follicles, there tends to be a poor response with mature follicles as well as lower pregnancy rates with IVF. When the number of antral follicles is intermediate, the response is not as predictable with IVF.

Anti-Müllerian Hormone (AMH)—A Marker for Ovarian Reserve

AMH is a marker for a woman's reproductive potential known as her ovarian reserve (1, 3). Anti-Müllerian hormone is produced by granulosa cells in the ovarian follicles. AMH is first made in primary follicles that have advanced from the primordial follicle stage. At this stage, follicles are microscopic and cannot be seen by ultrasound. AMH production is highest in pre-antral and small antral (about two to six millimeters in diameter) stages. Research studies show that the size of the pool of growing follicles is heavily influenced by the size of the pool of the remaining primordial follicles, which are like microscopic follicles that are sleeping (4, 5).

Production of AMH decreases and then stops as follicles grow. Follicles over eight millimeters make almost no AMH. AMH testing can be done at any day of the menstrual cycle, as it reflects the eggs you have on reserve. Ovarian reserve basically tells how many eggs you have left. Remember, you are born with all the eggs you will ever have in embryo state, and these eggs remain on reserve until they are used up during each menstrual cycle until menopause. AMH reflects the quantity of the ovarian follicle pool at any given time. AMH is produced only in small ovarian follicles, so AMH blood levels reflect the size of the pool of growing follicles in women.

So to simplify, from birth, women's ovaries contain immature eggs known as primordial follicles. At puberty, these follicles begin to change and mature with the menstrual cycle. During the first half of the menstrual cycle, known as the follicular phase, these primordial follicles undergo a series of changes both structurally and hormonally. First, the primary follicles turn into secondary follicles and then transition to tertiary or antral follicles. Once they are antral follicles, they become dependent on other sex hormones, especially FSH, to continue their development and growth until they are mature and are released during ovulation. AMH levels reflect microscopic follicles that are resting and waiting to be used, which reflects the pool of eggs you have left. AMH levels are higher in women with PCOS (6). AMH is considered to be an indicator of fertility in women who are in late reproductive age (thirty-five or older) and pregnancy outcomes in assisted reproductive technologies (IVF) as AMH levels can strongly predict poor response in the controlled ovarian stimulation (7).

AMH is thought to be the best available test to reflect ovarian reserve (3); however, one study suggests that antral follicle count may be a superior predictor of ovarian reserve compared to AMH levels (8). In addition, AMH is not a direct measure because we are not actually counting sleeping or unused eggs. Because it is an indirect measure, some studies suggest that other factors may influence AMH levels. That being said, in the reproductive world, AMH, along with FSH, LH, and antral follicle count is the standard to assess ovarian reserve and reproductive potential, as well as candidacy of IVF.

DOES A LOW AMH LEVEL SHATTER YOUR DREAMS OF HAVING A BABY?

It's important to understand that AMH, a marker for ovarian reserve, along with FSH and LH levels equate to your ability to have your own biological child or to become a candidate for IVF or donor eggs. AMH in particular is the number that most of my patients are very concerned about. When they find out that their level is low, they equate that with the inability to ever have a child. What's important to understand is that AMH is our best measure, but there are other factors affecting its interpretation. Let's look at the standard interpretation of AMH levels in the blood. Remember that AMH levels are a reflection of the eggs that are left, but not the quality of those eggs.

Interpretation of AMH Blood Levels for Women Under 35

AMH BLOOD LEVELS	INTERPRETATION OF WOMEN UNDER 35
Greater than 4.0 ng/ml	High (often with PCOS)
1.5–4.0 ng/ml	Normal
1.0–1.5 ng/ml	Low Normal
0.5–1.0 ng/ml	Low
Below 0.5 ng/ml	Very Low

Remember, it only takes one good egg. Keeping this in mind, we must understand that AMH is an important marker, but it is not a definitive marker that disables you from having a baby. If a woman is in complete ovarian failure, with a very low AMH paired with other factors such as high FSH and poor antral follicle count, or if she has an AMH of zero, then it may be impossible for her to have a child. However, even with a low AMH level, there is hope for a woman to conceive.

What if you could change your AMH levels? Would that mean your fertility potential had increased? How would that affect what your doctor tells you about having your own baby? Aren't these parameters static? These are good questions to answer. We will start with what may change AMH levels and improve them. No one ever tells you that you might be able to change your AMH levels. Research studies show that there are many factors that may affect AMH levels. In fact, it has been suggested that AMH levels can be altered by environmental factors, including vitamin D deficiency, obesity, smoking, and genetic factors including having the BRCA1 and BRCA2 tumor suppressor genes, having MTHFR C677T genotype methylation mutation, and possibly other factors. (We will examine these factors in more detail in this chapter.)

So, while AMH is our best indicator of a woman's ovarian reserve, it is an indirect measure that may be influenced by other variables. We need to take this into account as we survey the entire landscape of advanced maternal age and come to a conclusion about what your ability may truly be to naturally conceive.

FACTORS AFFECTING AMH

Vitamin D Deficiency

Vitamin D is not just a vitamin. Vitamin D is a steroid hormone that has an effect on fertility through a nuclear gene transcription factor, the vitamin D receptor (VDR). The presence of VDR and enzymes that are involved in both vitamin D metabolism and female reproduction suggests that vitamin D acts less like a nutrient and more like a hormone that modulates reproductive processes. In fact, vitamin D may act as a positive regulator of AMH production (9) and may influence ovarian reserve (10). In studies with animals, vitamin D deficiency is correlated with reducing fertility and also reducing pregnancy rates (11). Studies on humans suggest that vitamin D correlates with ovarian reserve and IVF outcomes (12). Some studies examined vitamin D in the serum of blood and other studies looked at the cellular level. One study found that low vitamin D levels have a negative impact on ovarian reserve and predispose women to early menopause (10). Another study confirmed that Vitamin D supplementation appears to normalize serum AMH levels in Vitamin D deficient premenopausal women (13). In another study, Vitamin D did not appear to have an effect on AMH levels in women under forty years old. More studies on vitamin D are needed, but it appears that there is a correlation with vitamin D levels and AMH levels, especially in women who are advanced maternal age. A recent study in Gynecological Endocrinology in 2017 evaluated the effects of the administration of 25 hydroxy vitamin D supplement on serum anti-malaria hormone levels in infertile women. The women were given 50,000 IUs weekly for up to three months and both Vitamin 25(OH) D and AMH increased significantly after treatment with 25(OH) D. The study concluded that administrating hydroxy vitamin D and increasing the vitamin D serum levels, the serum levels of AMH increased (14). In addition, young women between the ages of 18–25 years of age who were given 50,000 IU of Vitamin D3 for one week showed increased AMH levels, supporting the hypothesis that Vitamin D3 has a positive effect on the fertility of young women and that it may involve the regulation of ovarian AMH levels (15).

Basically, optimizing your Vitamin D levels has the potential to increase your AMH levels, reflecting an increase in ovarian reserve and fertility. So if you have all the eggs you are ever going to have from birth and AMH is a measure of ovarian reserve, or how many eggs you have in the bank, how does your vitamin D level increase the number of eggs you have in reserve? The answer is that it is complicated and other hormone-like factors, in this case Vitamin D, affect AMH levels. This means that AMH is dynamic rather than constant. We can surmise from this that AMH numbers alone are not a marker for ability to successfully conceive. There are a lot of cellular mechanisms that we don't fully understand at play. Nutrients and other factors can influence cellular function and your ability to conceive. So the take-home message is that numbers alone, although they give you a ballpark idea of where you are starting from, are not set in stone and may not reflect all there is to know about your ability to conceive.

I believe that these studies indicate that there is more to your ability to conceive than just the number of eggs you have, including the function of those eggs. And since vitamin D acts more like a hormone, it effects the function of the ovaries. This means that it is important to check for vitamin D3 deficiencies. If you are low in serum Vitamin D3 levels, increasing those levels via supplementation is essential for proper hormone function and helps to improve ovarian function, AMH levels, and ovarian reserve.

DHEA

Dehydroepiandrosterone (DHEA) has been used to improve the pregnancy rate in women with diminished ovarian reserve (DOR) during in vitro fertilization (16). Women with diminished ovarian reserve have lower levels of estradiol and, as expected, lower levels of AMH. However, one study showed that women with DOR who received supplementation with DHEA reversed their low levels of estradiol and AMH and in fact improved their levels. The study supports the theory that DHEA might play a role in regulating ovarian reserve functions (16), illustrating that some parameters may not be as static as we think.

Smoking

Do you really need a study to know that smoking is bad for you? It's kind of a no-brainer, and we have evidence that suggests that cigarette smoke acts as a disruptor of female fertility. Particularly in women who are undergoing assisted reproductive technology treatment, smoking is associated with the risk of premature ovarian failure, which leads to an earlier onset of menopause (17). Cigarettes contain thousands of chemicals such as oxidants, free radicals, carcinogens, and a whole bunch of bad stuff that basically disrupts biological processes and interferes with follicular development. In addition, studies have shown that women who smoke have significantly lower AMH levels compared with non-smokers. Cigarette smoking has been acknowledged as a factor for early ovarian aging, and women undergoing IVF who were smoking saw reduced success rates of pregnancy.

In short, if you're trying to conceive, you need to stop smoking. That includes other types of smoking too. There are no studies on marijuana use and AMH levels or egg quality, but there is a study that shows that marijuana use in men reduces sperm parameters (18). Common sense says that anything that's foreign to the body and contains chemicals should not be taken while trying to conceive. In addition, some medications may also influence AMH or other hormone levels and, for that reason, you and your partner/spouse should always check with your physician before trying to conceive. Smoking is an example of a foreign agent that disrupts the natural hormone balance in reproductive processes. This illustrates the effects that environmental influences have, and we can extrapolate that the air we breathe, the water we drink, the food we eat that contains chemicals, dyes, and pesticides may also act like hormone disruptors. Because of this, it is really important to support liver function as discussed in the "Detoxing Your Way to Fertility" chapter.

In addition, in Chinese medicine, cigarette smoke depletes the Yin of the body. The body is made of Yin and Yang. Yin and Yang are contained in all organs of the body. Yin is cool, moist, nourishing, and rejuvenating. Yang is hot, energizing, and moving. The kidney Yin is specifically what you need to improve fertility and what you pass on to have a healthy baby. So if you smoke, you are depleting the vital Yin energy or Qi of the body, including the kidney Qi, which is needed for reproductive success and health. If you have been a smoker in the past, what's important is to avoid any cigarette smoking moving forward and to work on restoring the Yin with acupuncture and Chinese herbs with a focus on the kidney Yin to support fertility.

Acupuncture

One of the first studies on acupuncture and its effect on AMH levels and ovarian volume was promising. This study demonstrated that acupuncture reduces serum AMH levels and ovarian volume in women with PCOS. Women with PCOS have abnormally elevated levels of AMH and increased ovarian volume. In essence, acupuncture helped normalize these parameters. In this study, they also determined that physical exercise did not influence AMH levels or ovarian volume, whereas acupuncture did have a positive effect of AMH levels (19). Another study of perimenopausal women looked at moxibustion, which is often used in combination with acupuncture. It involves heat therapy where a dried plant material called "moxa" is burned near the surface of the skin at an acupuncture point. Moxibustion treatment appears to improve AMH levels and ovarian reserve function and delay ovarian aging (20). It appears that acupuncture and moxibustion may have a positive influence on AMH levels in some women. Again, this shows that AMH levels may not be static.

Obesity

Some studies correlate obesity to low AMH levels in both infertility patients undergoing IVF and in women on oral contraception (21). Both groups of women had lower AMH levels related to obesity. On the other hand, there are studies that do not correlate obesity and low AMH levels. This suggests that obesity may play a role in AMH levels, and that there is some physiological shift that may be taking place with obesity that we have yet to understand completely. In addition, obesity does increase your chances of creating insulin resistance in the body, possibly causing prediabetes and diabetes. Insulin resistance raises cortisol levels, which in turn negatively affects the adrenal function. This works against your ability to optimize ovarian function. So, getting closer to your optimal Body Mass Index (BMI) and your optimal weight based on age and height is your goal. Insulin resistance is a common symptom of women with Polycystic Ovarian Syndrome (PCOS). So getting in a normal weight range can help normalize insulin and glucose levels, which avoids stressing adrenal function and improves fertility success and possibly AMH levels.

Genetics

It appears that genetic factors may lead to AMH variability from woman to woman (22). Other genetic factors may also be at play influencing AMH levels.

BRCA1 and BRCA2

BRCA1 and BRCA2 are tumor suppressor genes involved in the maintenance and repair of DNA. Mutations in these genes are most associated with the increased risk of developing breast and ovarian cancer. These genes are also regarded as factors that affect the formation and development of the embryo, ovarian function, and female fertility. People who have BRCA mutations may have decreased fertility, ovarian sufficiency, and a smaller egg reserve (23, 24).

MTHFR C667T Mutations

MTHFR C667T is a gene that provides the instructions for making an enzyme known as methylenetetrahydrofolate reductase. This enzyme is vital for cell division, DNA repair, and the regulation of normal embryo development. It helps methylate folic acid into 5-methyltetrahydrofolate (5-MTHF), the active and useable form of folate the body needs for cell division. If you have mutations with the MTHFR gene, you reduce your ability to convert folic acid to 5-MTHF. Having a mutation with this gene can interfere with crucial cell functions and, in addition, lead to increases in homocysteine levels that impair the development of follicles by increasing oxidative stress. Elevated homocysteine levels also increased cardiovascular risk. Some studies suggest that the heterozygous mutation of MTHFR C677T correlates with higher AMH levels, yet results in less egg retrievals with stimulation with IVF (25). These studies show that there is some interaction between the gene and AMH levels. Working with somebody familiar with MTHFR genotyping in mutations is an important step in fertility preparation. If you have an MTHFR mutation, it's important to address those mutations with the correct support to assist the body with proper cell division and DNA repair, and to support a growing embryo. This is something that you cannot ignore, as it could have detrimental effects on cell division leading to increased risk of infertility, miscarriage, spina bifida and other negative effects.

So can we really say with certainty that you will not get pregnant based on testing your AMH levels as a reflection of ovarian reserve? No. It is apparent that the body markers are dynamic and influenced by many changing factors. Although AMH gives us a baseline for assessing ovarian reserve and is our best measure, it is not the only factor that influences your ability to conceive successfully. Age clearly makes a difference, but is not the ultimate deciding factor of whether you can or cannot have a baby. What can you do to optimize AMH levels?

OPTIMIZE YOUR AMH LEVELS

To optimize your AMH levels, your goal is to make sure your vitamin D levels are optimal, reach the ideal body weight range for your age and height, quit smoking if you are a smoker, test for MTHFR and other methylation mutations, and support methylation with appropriate supplements. (For more information on methylation, refer to Chapter 12.) These factors may influence your AMH levels and have a direct impact on the recommendations your doctor gives you.

The fact that AMH seems to be influenced by outside factors suggests environment makes a difference. The environment in which your eggs grow is ultimately one of the most important factors is supporting your fertility. Most importantly, AMH is not a marker of the quality of your eggs. Therefore, supporting your body before conception and during conception is pivotal in creating opportunities for increased fertility and a healthy baby.

Research is ever changing and new discoveries are made each day, which allows the medical community to get more insight into the intricacies of how nutrients, lifestyle, and other factors affect not only AMH and ovarian reserve, but your fertility overall. This should provide hope that new things are always on the horizon, helping us understand infertility and how to address it to help women conceive.

Additionally, as discussed in the previous chapter, the decline in adrenal function is one major missing link unaddressed by reproductive endocrinologists that is creating a pattern of defeat. As a practicing physician who has been helping women conceive for over nineteen years, it does not take rocket science to see that my patients are stressed out. They might be working full-time jobs, be busy full-time stay at home moms, or be working part- or full-time and caring for the kids, the home, and the family. They are going 24/7. They are eating on the run, not getting adequate sleep, and not taking care of themselves while they take care of everyone else. They're running from place to place, activity to activity, and are exhausted. If they don't have kids, then they are generally working long crazy hours for years, under the invisible yet palpable stress looming over them of starting a family later. Basically, they are taking care of everybody except themselves, they lack time and energy, have poor eating habits, and lack regular exercise and proper self-care. Stress depletes the adrenal, leading to a negative effect on hormones and reduced fertility. This chronic stress over time negatively affects FSH levels and ovarian function. Optimizing adrenal function and FSH levels also impacts how we look at ovarian reserves. Since we can improve FSH levels with the proper integrative support, you can improve your numbers, which improves your doctor's outlook on your ability to conceive as well as the recommendations and options they give to you. Supporting adrenals helps improve your fertility, energy, and your ability to deal with stress. Optimizing normal reproductive function and physiology is the key to repairing your infertility blocks.

There is hope for women in their later reproductive years, and I don't believe that age is the deciding factor on whether someone has the possibility of conceiving naturally, or of having a healthy pregnancy and a healthy baby. I've even had a patient get pregnant naturally at forty-seven and welcome a healthy baby into the world without any complications. That's unusual, but just goes to show you that anything is possible with the right support. The bottom line is that there are options for you that you need to explore regardless of your age. You may not be able to change the hands of time, but you can create a healthier body and environment to nourish your eggs, and to improve cell division and the growth of an egg or embryo, regardless of biological age.

HAVE YOU BEEN TOLD THERE IS ABSOLUTELY NO HOPE TO HAVE YOUR OWN CHILD?

HOW TO NATURALLY RESTORE OVARIAN FUNCTION:

LEARNING ABOUT THE MISSING LINK TO IMPROVING FSH AND LH LEVELS

Have you been told there is absolutely no hope to have your own child because your FSH levels are too high? Have you been told your only option for having a baby is with in vitro fertilization (IVF) using your eggs, a donor egg, or embryo adoption? Have your dreams of having your own child or expanding your family been shattered by your ovarian function markers? Did you know that you can optimize your ovarian function?

Too many doctors judge your FSH levels as the end-all, be-all of being able to get pregnant. FSH is an important marker of ovarian function and reserve, as are luteinizing hormone (LH), anti-Müllerian hormone (AMH) and antral follicle count. Luckily, these are some of the markers that can be changed with integrative therapies. Generally, high levels of FSH and LH are most associated with ovarian decline and premature ovarian failure. Doctors routinely use FSH and LH levels to tell you if you are likely to conceive naturally, or if you are a candidate for IUI, IVF, a donor egg, or embryo adoption. However, there are ways to optimize ovarian function and improve FSH and LH levels to improve fertility. First, let's start by understanding what markers are used and how they are interpreted to predict your ability to get pregnant. Ovarian function is different than ovarian reserve which refers to the number of eggs you have left. While ovarian function can be changed with the right support and intervention, ovarian reserve can be harder to change. The good news is that one healthy egg is all you need. So if you can improve ovarian function, then conception might not be out of reach for you. Let's examine the markers for ovarian function.

FOLLICLE STIMULATING HORMONE (FSH)

The primary role of follicle stimulating hormone (FSH) is egg maturation. You create all the eggs that you are ever going to have in embryonic stage, when you are in your mother's womb. You are born with eggs for a lifetime of reproductive years, and these eggs are stored in follicles. Once puberty hits, your period starts, and you release an egg each month during ovulation. Each month, sleeping, or primordial, follicles wake up. A few of these become larger. The job of FSH is to mature the egg. This means that the influence of FSH on the follicles helps small antral follicles (a few of the sleeping follicles that are still small, but that awaken and grow in the beginning of your menstrual cycle) grow and mature. One lucky follicle that holds an egg becomes dominant. This egg will mature and be released during ovulation, so that it can be fertilized. Each follicle generally holds one egg. In the case of fraternal twins, however, two eggs could become dominant, mature, and be released and fertilized.

Interestingly, the process of determining which follicle and egg will become dominant each month is predetermined up to three months prior when the pituitary releases FSH and stimulates the follicles. In a regular twenty-eight-day cycle, FSH exerts its affect the first half of the cycle, which generally encompasses the first fourteen days. Day 1 being the first day of red blood flow. This is why the first half of the cycle is called the follicular phase, meaning that this phase is all about follicle stimulation and egg maturation. FSH and estradiol work together to ensure egg maturation. If the stimulation of FSH is not adequate, then the egg will not reach maturity and conception will not happen. An immature egg cannot be fertilized. This is why doctors keep a magnifying glass on FSH levels. If your FSH level is low, it will not exert a strong enough effect to stimulate the follicle, and the egg will not mature.

It would be logical to think that, when FSH levels are high, they exert a stronger effect. Right? Wrong! FSH has an optimal window in which it works best to stimulate and mature an egg. An FSH greater than ten indicates a down regulation of the ovarian function and inadequate stimulation of the follicle and egg. In fact, FSH levels of 30 or higher are generally associated with premature ovarian decline. They can also indicate perimenopause (a hormonal shift that begins the transition into the cessation of the menstrual periods, which can occur up to ten years before menopause) or the onset of menopause (the cessation of menstrual periods) when ovaries start to shut down. In the world of reproductive female health, an FSH level of ten or lower is desirable. An FSH between ten and fifteen may warrant a reproductive endocrinologist to recommend IUI and/or IVF. An FSH greater than fifteen may precipitate a reproductive endocrinologist to recommend donor embryo adoption. In addition, from a Western model, low numbers (an FSH level between two and three) don't seem to be negatively associated with fertility. However, in Chinese Medicine, a low FSH level (between one and three) indicates a deficiency pattern that can also be associated with infertility. Clinically, I see women who have low FSH levels of two or three not responding well to IUI or other ART protocols. This is because, in Chinese Medicine, the low FSH levels are telling you that your body is deficient and is not capable of responding appropriately to external messages; in other words, the body is on empty.

It would be like asking a car to drive without gas—not going to happen! Optimizing FSH levels to between five and six is the goal to create the best stimulation of the follicle and to ensure egg maturation.

ESTRADIOL

Estradiol (E2) is a form of estrogen that is dominant the first half of the reproductive cycle. Estradiol is primarily produced by the ovaries. FSH stimulates the ovarian production of estrogen by the granulosa cell of the ovarian follicles and the corpus luteum (a structure that forms once a mature egg has been released from a follicle). Some estrogen is also produced in much smaller amounts by other tissue, such as the adrenal glands and liver. Estrogen is important in conception, as it helps to grow and maintain the endometrial lining (the inner lining of the uterus) to help sustain a pregnancy. Estradiol also contributes to the vascularization of and the blood supply to the growing embryo by starting to build the uterine lining in the first half on the menstrual cycle. It can also help the placenta to boost blood flow to your uterus, and can prime your body for breastfeeding. Estradiol is commonly used in IVF cycles, along with progesterone to thicken the uterine lining and increase blood flow to the area. This helps to preserve the thickness of the lining and improves support for a pregnancy.

A normal level of estrogen on Day 3 testing can range from 25–75 picograms per milliliter (pg/ml) where levels greater than 100 pg/ml can be associated with cysts and diminished ovarian reserve. Lower levels on this normal range can be better for stimulating in an IVF or IUI cycle. However, when it comes to natural fertility where we are not using medications to alter hormone levels but rather supporting natural physiological function, we may want E2 levels to be around 70 pg/ml. Even a value of fifty shows some sign of deficiency according to Chinese medicine, but this value is still workable and can be optimized by taking supplements, bio-identical estrogen, Chinese herbs, and/or acupuncture treatment. However, an estradiol level of thirty or lower is too low to thicken the endometrial lining in preparation for implantation of the embryo and to supply a supportive vascular supply to a growing embryo. Remember that estradiol starts to build the endometrial lining in the first half of the cycle, and, during the second half of the cycle, progesterone is responsible for vascularizing the endometrial lining and building on that blood supply to the uterine lining. However, if progesterone levels are low, or even at the low end of normal, and estradiol is either low or deficient, the uterine lining may not be able to supply adequate blood supply to a growing embryo. Keep in mind that if you are on oral birth control pills (OBCPs), your estradiol levels may seem artificially low. Don't let that scare you. You cannot see your true level of estradiol until you are off OBCPs for at least two cycles.

Many times I see women who have decent FSH and LH levels, but their E2 levels are very low, which could be a roadblock to their fertility success. Optimizing estradiol levels can be a useful tool in conception and should not be overlooked.

LUTEINIZING HORMONE (LH)

In addition, Luteinizing Hormone (LH) is a very crucial hormone that acts as a trigger for the body to release the egg in hopes of it being fertilized. In a normal cycle, the surge of LH is the trigger that releases the egg. In IVF, LH-like drugs are used to carefully help mature the egg, getting it ready to be released. Before that happens, the egg is captured through a surgical procedure during which a needle extracts the eggs from the ovaries so that they can be used in IVF. In nature, if LH levels are not optimal, the trigger may be too weak to release the egg, and no ovulation occurs. Ovulation generally occurs midcycle, around Day 12 to Day 14, but the timing can vary from woman to woman. Once the egg is released from the follicle, its structure changes and it is known as the corpus luteum. The corpus luteum starts to secrete progesterone, which further vascularizes the endometrial lining of the uterus and prepares the lining for implantation. Once the egg is released, it can travel through the fallopian tube and make its way toward the uterine lining. The sperm must find the egg either in the fallopian tube or in the uterus and fertilize it. Once this happens, an embryo forms and implants in the endometrial lining of the uterus, where cell division continues and the embryo is fed by the blood supplied by the uterine lining.

CAN WE CHANGE MARKERS OF OVARIAN FUNCTION TO CREATE A SUPPORTIVE ENVIRONMENT?

The question, then, is can we change markers for ovarian function, including FSH and LH, to create an environment where optimal stimulation of the follicle and egg occurs. The answer is that yes, we can.

In my practice, I have seen FSH levels reduce and create an opportunity for natural conception to occur time and time again. If you look at the body as a finely tuned instrument, you can understand that an instrument that is not well tuned is not in harmony, and certainly is not working optimally. Much like an orchestra group working together to make beautiful and harmonious music, tuning an instrument or fine tuning the body's physiology is important in creating optimal levels of FSH.

Many fertility specialists do not focus on maximizing physiological function, they primarily rely on medications to supersede the body's own physiological triggers and mechanisms. They are asking, and sometimes pushing, the body to do what they ask it to do no matter how many times the body does not want to listen. How well do you think the body responds to these medications? The answer lies in the function of the body. When put under stress with medications, the body sometimes does not respond in the desired manner. This is because the body is in a deficient state and function is declining. So when asked to perform in a certain way, the body cannot do it. How do we help the body respond in an advantageous way? The key lies in restoring function and, in doing so, restoring FSH levels to normal ranges. Not everyone can reverse their FSH levels, especially if they're in menopause and their levels have dropped so significantly that changing them would be very difficult. However, for many women who are stressed out, deficient, and showing signs of this with rising FSH levels, it is possible to restore normal physiology to create optimal FSH levels and increase fertility.

Most of my patients come to me after seeing many fertility doctors, gynecologists and other health practitioners without success. Their FSH levels have maybe improved slightly, but not significantly enough to create the proper follicular stimulation for egg maturation. I have treated many women with elevated FSH levels who, after a period of treatment, have had their FSH levels fall below ten, allowing them to become pregnant with natural conception. In addition, if you think of your FSH level as a way of your body telling you, "Hey, I am deficient; I need support," then it makes sense that your body needs some additional boosting before it can do what you want it to do. This includes the proper outcomes with IUI and IVF. Having repetitive IUI and/or IVF without success is a sign that something in the body is not working in the first place and must be corrected before these procedures can succeed. A finely tuned body with normal physiological function can respond to the chemical messages during IVF and IUI appropriately.

Improving FSH levels is not a conversation that your RE will have with you, because their focus is to override your body's own physiology to make a baby. Don't get me wrong. IVF and IUI are important tools that can be used to conceive if needed, but you must prepare your body for this with natural integrative tools. As a practitioner who looks at things in an integrated manner, I advocate and support my patients who choose to do IUI and IVF. I also feel it's important to prepare your body so that you have a more successful outcome doing IVF or IUI. It's also important to understand that you do have the ability to optimize ovarian function and reduce your FSH levels naturally.

ADRENAL FUNCTION: THE MISSING LINK TO GOOD OVARIAN FUNCTION AND LOWERING YOUR FSH AND LH LEVELS

One of the biggest missing links to infertility is poor adrenal function or adrenal fatigue. High FSH levels are linked to poor adrenal function. You may be asking, "My adrenal glands are linked to my infertility?" I get it. It sounds strange. But hear me out; what I'm about to tell you may just help you get pregnant!

The adrenal glands sit on top of your kidneys on both sides of your body, and their job is to modulate stress. They are part of the endocrine system and are connected with your fight or flight system and with making hormones that drive almost every bodily function. Essential for life, the adrenal glands work closely with the hypothalamus and the pituitary gland in the brain, in a system known as the hypothalamic-pituitary-adrenal axis (HPA axis).

The adrenal glands make a variety of hormones including:

- Glucocorticoids or cortisol, which is your natural steroid hormone that helps with stress response, inflammation, pain, and energy, and sleep cycles.
- Mineralocorticoids, which maintain healthy blood pressure
- Adrenaline and epinephrine, which are part of your fight or flight response
- They also package your DHEA, a precursor to other sex hormones.

The adrenals respond to stress and, while they are designed to help us in an acute stress or threat, they are not designed for the long-term stress that most of us endure in day-to-day lives in the 21st century. Interesting enough, whether stress is chemical, physical, emotional, or perceived (thinking about the stress), it affects you in a similar manner. The body still needs cortisol to function and maneuver through life's good and bad stressors. Believe it or not, both good and bad stressors command the body to make cortisol. Marriage and divorce are both in the top five stressors in people's lives, yet one is good and the other is viewed as bad. Nonetheless, both can deplete your adrenals, forcing the constant production of cortisol to manage the stress. Unfortunately, you can't avoid all stress, and some stress is healthy and essential for daily living. What happens if your stress level is abundantly high and you have no way to counter balance it over a long period of time?

Chronic stress leads to adrenal decline or adrenal fatigue. This dramatically affects your ability to recover from illness and causes low energy, impaired sleep, and the inability to conceive.

One of the biggest reasons why ovarian function is affected by adrenal decline or fatigue is that we have not adapted as a species to deal with the constant bombardment of stress in our environment. Yet, we expect our bodies to somehow work optimally in a state of chronic stress and depletion. In addition, women in general are having babies later in life than we used to. Many women are postponing having children until their mid to late thirties and forties. Top this off with poor diet and lifestyle habits, along with toxic environmental exposure, and you have a formula that equals deficiency rather than a bountiful abundance of energy and hormones.

Long term stress depletes your adrenals and their function over time, which can lead to adrenal fatigue. Adrenal fatigue is a term that refers to a chronic stimulation of the adrenal glands over time by chronic stress, which leads to low cortisol levels in the blood.

SYMPTOMS OF ADRENAL DECLINE AND ADRENAL FATIGUE

To summarize, the adrenals, which sit on top of your kidneys on both sides of the body, are the cornerstone of balancing both physical and emotional stress and are vital to survival. Our bodies have a complete set of stress modulation systems in place, and the adrenal glands are the control center for these systems. When these glands become dysfunctional, our bodies' ability to handle stress, fatigue, hormone dysregulation, conception challenges, and ability to fight infections decreases. We can experience an array of symptoms with adrenal decline.

Do you have symptoms of adrenal fatigue? Or maybe you have symptoms of adrenal decline, which is not as severe as adrenal fatigue, but still impacts your life and your fertility?

Symptoms of Adrenal Decline

- Infertility
- Irregular periods
- Fatigue
- React to stress easily
- Low blood sugar
- Brain Fog
- Low mood
- Anxiety
- Allergies and food sensitivities
- Low blood pressure
- Low body temperature
- Lack of energy and motivation
- Increased effort required to perform daily tasks
- Get sick frequently
- Tired after exercise
- Weight gain, especially belly fat
- Crave stimulants like coffee and chocolate

Symptoms of Adrenal Fatigue

- Infertility
- Irregular periods
- Extreme fatigue
- Brain fog
- Difficulty getting up in the morning
- Anxiety
- Asthma, allergies, food sensitivities, and depressed immunity
- Dizziness
- Depression
- Extreme tiredness an hour after exercise
- Insomnia
- Joint pain
- Low blood pressure
- Blood sugar imbalances, prediabetes or diabetes
- Low sex drive
- Weight gain, especially belly fat

- Inability to handle stress
- Live on stimulants such as coffee
- Cravings for salt and sugar

If you are not in adrenal fatigue, but have a dysregulation of cortisol, meaning that your cortisol level is high or low, this can lead to HPA axis dysfunction and affect hormone levels. Decline of adrenal function can also result in reduced levels of dehydroepiandrosterone (DHEA). DHEA is known as a parent hormone because it helps to make other androgenic hormones, such as testosterone and estrogen. DHEA production can be reduced with adrenal fatigue or decline and can lower overall sex hormones, negatively affecting fertility. Low DHEA levels are known to be linked to infertility.

UNDERSTAND THE CONNECTION BETWEEN ADRENAL FUNCTION AND FERTILITY

To better understand the relationship between adrenal function and fertility, we need to look at a bigger picture of physiological relationship and the function of adrenals related to other organs and glands in the body. If we look at the body as a hierarchy, we can better understand physiology as a whole. At the top of the hierarchy is the hypothalamus in the brain. The hypothalamus directs the pituitary gland on the next tier down. The pituitary then directs the adrenal glands. This dynamic and complex intertwining connection of the central nervous system and endocrine system is known as the hypothalamic-pituitary-adrenal axis (HPA axis) and is involved in your ability to deal with stress. On the same tier as the adrenal glands, there are two other important organs to keep balanced—the thyroid and ovaries. The pituitary influences all of these organs as they strive to stay in balance. This tier is like a three-legged chair or triangle that needs to be balanced to create stable energy, hormone regulation, proper sleep cycles and optimal fertility.

Let's look at this triangle in more depth to understand how adrenal decline and adrenal fatigue creates a roadblock to optimal fertility.

HYPOTHALAMUS PITUITARY ADRENAL AXIS

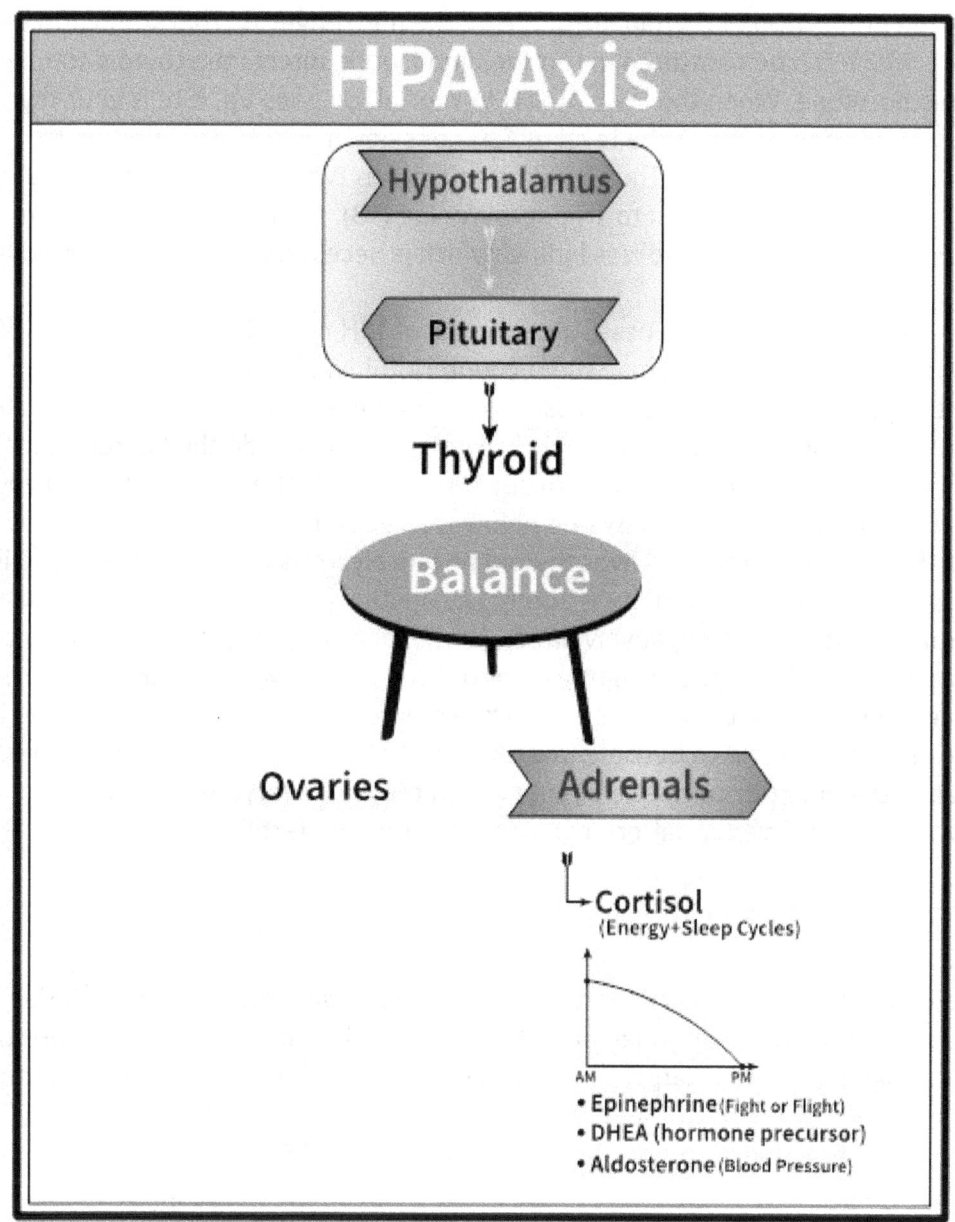

THYROID

The thyroid is a butterfly-shaped endocrine gland located at the base of your neck. It regulates metabolism, body weight and temperature, mood, appetite, and fertility. The pituitary regulates the production of thyroid hormone by the messenger thyroid stimulating hormone (TSH). TSH, which can be measured in routine blood work, directs the thyroid to make more or less thyroid hormone. When the level of TSH in your blood goes up, it tells your thyroid to make more thyroid hormones. When the level of TSH goes down, it tells your thyroid that it can stop making more thyroid hormone. The thyroid gland makes two hormones, thyroxine (T4), the inactive form, which is converted to Triiodothyronine (T3), the more bioactive form. In addition, the thyroid gland absorbs and utilizes iodine, which is necessary for normal thyroid function.

Depending on the lab that is used, blood levels of TSH range from about 0.45 to 4.5 milli-international units per liter. This may seem counterintuitive, but when you look at your TSH levels, the higher your levels are (the closer the TSH comes to 4.5), the more tired and sluggish your thyroid function is. If you have a high TSH level that is outside the lab reference range, you have a hypothyroid condition. The lower your TSH levels are, the more revved up your thyroid function is. If your TSH levels are low and below the reference range, you have a hyperthyroid condition. Both hyperthyroid and hypothyroid negatively impact your fertility. Keep in mind that an optimal TSH level for fertility is about 1.0. Anything above a 3.0 might cause sub-acute hypothyroid symptoms and negatively affect your fertility. Hypothyroid and low-normal thyroid symptoms may include fatigue, weight gain or difficulty losing weight, constipation, dry skin, low mood, and infertility. If you are in a chronic state of stress and have low functioning adrenals, this can cause your thyroid to become low functioning as well. A tug-of-war can occur when the adrenals and thyroid both compete for support. In the end, everyone loses because the tug-of-war is a result of a deficiency pattern that leads to impaired fertility.

OVARIES

The ovaries are explained in Chapter One, "Understanding the Menstrual Cycle." We know that the ovaries hold the primordial, or resting, follicles that are awakened via the stimulation of FSH and estrogen to become larger antral follicles. Of these follicles, one will become dominant, mature, and be released for ovulation under the influence of FSH, LH, and estradiol. If there is reduced adrenal function, there will be a negative effect on FSH, LH, and estradiol levels.

The HPA axis, which modulates our stress response, directly affect our hypothalamic-pituitary-ovarian (HPO) axis. Creating balance within the HPO axis is important for normal ovarian function. When others say, "Maybe stress is changing your menstrual cycles," they are correct. When the HPA axis is highly imbalanced it will cause change in the HPO axis, affecting your cycle length and function. This relationship is illustrated in the following diagram.

HYPOTHALAMUS PITUITARY OVARIAN AXIS

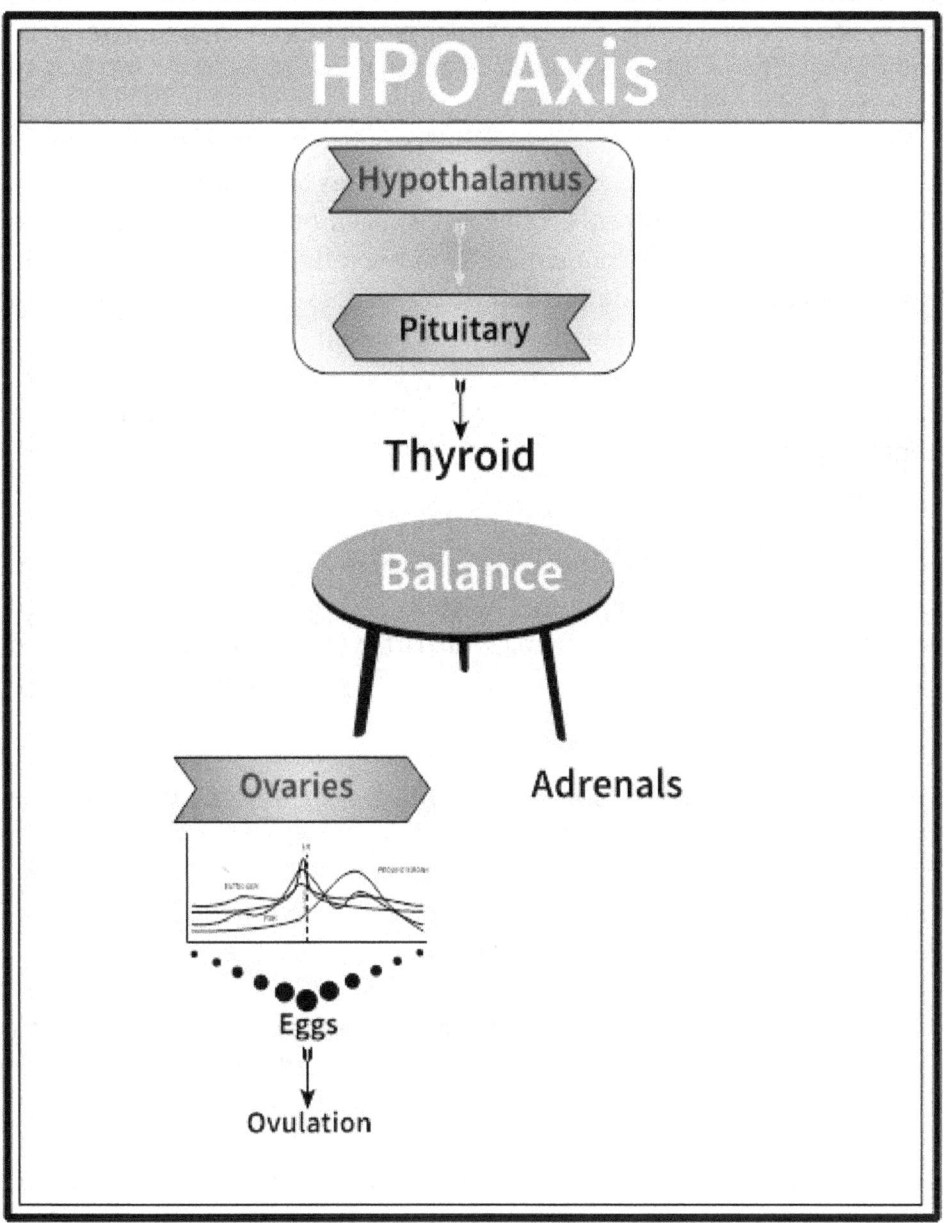

Therefore, creating balance and stability within both the HPO axis and the HPA axis is an important element to successful fertility. Understanding this relationship will help you better understand how to maximize your ability to conceive.

ADRENALS

Depleted adrenal function will create a pull for the body's support in the adrenal direction and will inadvertently cause a possible decline in thyroid function. In addition, this will negatively affect FHS, LH, and estradiol levels. There is basically a fight on this tier between the adrenals, ovaries, and thyroid. The problem is that, since adrenals are needed for survival, they will always win and everything else will take a back seat.

When reduced function of your adrenal glands crosses the line into a disease state, that is a different situation. A lack of cortisol production is called Addison's disease, which is a very serious condition that needs immediate medical intervention. In the reverse situation, highly elevated cortisol levels are associated with Cushing's disease, which is caused most commonly by a tumor and also requires immediate medical intervention.

Let's be clear, we are not talking Addison's disease or Cushing's disease when we are talking about adrenal fatigue or decline. Adrenal fatigue and adrenal decline are considered conditions, or down regulations of function, rather than disease.

However, these conditions affect how you feel day to day and impact your hormone levels and ability to conceive. When your adrenal function is declined, you feel like an old Chevy, not a new Mustang. There is nothing wrong with a Chevy; but if you feel exhausted, tired, and depleted all the time, it is going to be hard for your body to have the energy to get through your day and leave you with little left to make a baby.

The best way to determine cortisol levels is by testing saliva over a twelve-hour period. This includes samples taken in early morning, mid-morning, afternoon, and evening, allowing doctors to see a pattern of cortisol levels over time. When you have low, low-normal, high, or high-normal cortisol, or a mixture of these levels over a twelve-hour period, your adrenal function is abnormal. (This test is discussed in more detail later in this chapter.)

Now that we understand the interconnection between the adrenals and thyroid and ovarian function, we know four things that happen when you have adrenal fatigue or adrenal decline.

1. You lack the Qi to mature an egg and ovulate, which leads to an inability to conceive.
2. Since progesterone and cortisol are almost identical biochemical structures, your body steals progesterone to make cortisol for fuel to get you through your day. This shortens your luteal phase and reduces the blood supply available to nourish a growing embryo that has implanted in the uterine lining, or that is trying to implant in the lining.
3. You create a movement and focus for survival in your body that directs energy to adrenal function rather than ovarian function, since energy and survival supersede hormone regulation. Over time, this increases FSH and LH levels, negatively affecting egg maturation and ovulation.

4. You decrease dehydroepiandrosterone (DHEA) levels since the adrenal glands make DHEA. DHEA helps produce other hormones such as estrogen. Low DHEA levels are associated with infertility.

So why don't all doctors address, identify, and treat adrenal fatigue and low functioning adrenals? That's a good question that my patients often ask when they understand the relationship between adrenal function and hormone regulation. Our Western model looks at disease management, but is not focused on function. The intervention for adrenal fatigue is not a drug, rather, it is the therapeutic use of supplements, botanicals, specific nutrients, and other integrative modalities to restore adrenal function. In our Western healthcare model of disease management, you won't find a functional medical approach that aims to restore normal function. Instead, you will wait until you have a treatable disease. No one teaches medical students how to treat the grey areas or how to treat patients from a functional medical perspective. Doctors do not learn this unless they are a Naturopathic Medical Doctor or Integrative Practitioner who has taken further education in Function Medicine to learn this type of approach. I guess you can say that this approach is like working on the old Chevy so it can become a new Mustang once again. As a Naturopathic Medical Doctor and an Acupuncturist, I have been trained in integrative modalities. However, not all integrative practitioners work on restoring function, which is really important when it comes to fertility. If you can restore proper function, you increase your ability to conceive naturally, as well as to have your body respond in an appropriate and positive way during IUI and IVF. Most doctors are probably not going to work to improve your adrenal function or even discuss it with you as a possible roadblock. You can't fix what you don't know about. You also can't fix a problem if you don't have the right tools.

Listen to your body, because it is talking to you. You may not know what to do to help it, but the initial step is to pay attention and listen. If you suspect that you have signs of adrenal decline or adrenal fatigue, then address it. As we have discussed, adrenal fatigue or decline is about a down regulation of adrenal function. It is not a disease. Nonetheless, when you have this condition, it greatly affects the way you feel and has a significant impact on your fertility. In fact, one study done with Israeli women that addressed the issue of stress on fertility concluded, "from the studies presented in this review, it can be hypothesized that stress can induce altered cortisol-excretion patterns along the menstrual cycle, which ultimately affect the hormonal profile in critical stages of the fertilization process" (1).

Researchers have studied the unique stress that results from infertility and the continued impact of this stress on your fertility. They hypothesize that there are three additional stressors that occur in women who suffer from infertility:

1. your emotional state could be a risk factor for infertility;
2. the diagnosis of infertility causes psychological stress to you; and,
3. there is a reciprocal relationship with stress and infertility, meaning that suffering from infertility causes stress and changes in mood, and if you are always stressed out, it may affect your fertility outcome (2).

Do you feel trapped and stressed just reading that? I do too! Yes, of course you are stressed when you are trying with all that you have to have a baby and it has not been successful up to this point. And yes, the stress affects your mood and can trigger anxiety and depression, and create negative physiological changes in your body. Anyone going through this does not need a research study to prove this point. You are living it!

So back to your adrenals. They modulate stress and need to be regulated to help you maneuver through the stresses you encounter during your fertility journey. This will help you feel more energetic and vibrant so that your quality of life is better and your fertility improves.

CAN YOU TEST ADRENAL FUNCTION?

Yes, as discussed above, you can test adrenal function using saliva samples taken over a twelve-hour period. The test involves collecting four saliva samples in the morning, mid-morning, afternoon, and evening, to see what your pattern of cortisol levels is and how it compares to a normal curve. Blood levels of cortisol give a snap shot in time; because they are not generally tested four times in a day, they do not allow doctors to see cortisol level patterns.

Therefore, salivary cortisol testing is the preferred method for addressing adrenal function. This simple, noninvasive, functional, medical test can determine if you have an elevation of cortisol in the day or night, causing insulin resistance or adrenal fatigue. If you have elevated cortisol, low cortisol, or a mixed-level pattern, any of these three situations represents a dysregulation of cortisol and impaired adrenal function that needs to be addressed. In this case, proper function must be restored to help you feel better and improve your fertility.

WHAT IF MY DOCTOR TELLS ME THAT I CAN'T CHANGE MY FSH LEVELS?

Sara, a thirty-nine--year-old female patient had an FSH level of twenty-eight and an LH level of thirteen. She was told that she was in premature ovarian failure. She looked to me for any hope that she could change her FSH and LH levels. With the support of adaptogen herbs, Chinese herbs, and nutrients, she was able to bring both her FSH and LH levels under ten, and she did get pregnant. Sometimes, we assume that nothing can be done. But what if something can be done? You won't know if you don't try. In Sara's case, like many women, she had been under prolonged stress. She was so burnt out that her cortisol levels declined and she was in adrenal fatigue, which compromised her ability to makes FSH and LH. This, in turn, diminished her ovarian function and ability to conceive. In this case, her infertility roadblock was related to adrenals and due to chronic stress, not some unknown reason for premature ovarian failure. I see this all the time. Living in the 21st century is innately stressful and has an impact on our bodies and our fertility.

I find that the most successful outcomes include adrenal support, in addition to Chinese herbs, acupuncture, nutrients, proper diet, and stress management. Supporting the adrenals is the missing link, or special factor, that really expedites a woman's ability to conceive. Generally, if a woman has tried integrative therapies including acupuncture and Chinese herbs, which are so supportive for fertility, and she has not been able to get pregnant, I usually find that there are two other factors at play. Those two factors are MTHFR mutations, which we will discuss in a later chapter, and lack of adrenal support. Addressing these concerns can change the game. This is not to say that other practitioners are not comprehensive in their approach, but that if conception is not happening, then something is being missed and needs to be addressed. It could be emotional, genetic, or some other unknown variable, but adrenals are a likely suspect when a woman feels tired, burnt out, and has not been able to get pregnant.

WHY HAVEN'T REPETITIVE IUI OR IVF CYCLES SUCCEEDED? IT SEEMS LIKE THE MEDICATIONS SHOULD WORK.

Maybe your body is being asked to do something that it cannot do. Think about a person who is completely exhausted and drained, and you tell them to run a marathon right now. There is a point when the body says, "Sorry, no more. I can't and won't do it." If we can get the body working better and running like a new Mustang rather than an old Chevy, then the body might say, "Okay I think I can work with and not against you. Let's try this again."

HOW DO WE IMPROVE ADRENAL FUNCTION?

We improve adrenal function through natural interventions which will, in turn, restore FSH, LH, and estradiol levels over time. There are three categories of natural interventions that can help improve low adrenal function. These include nutrients, a category of botanicals called adaptogens, and glandulars. The adrenals are very nutrient dependent. For example, they need Vitamin C, Vitamin B5 (pantothenic acid), and other nutrients to make cortisol. If you have a poor diet and are not getting adequate nutrients, then your adrenal glands will not be functioning well. In addition, adaptogen herbs help your body adapt to stress and modulate cortisol levels whether they are high or low. Unlike drugs that have one action, adaptogen herbs can bring excess cortisol levels down and bring reduced cortisol levels to normal. This unique property is very helpful to restore adrenal function. Glandular supplements which generally come from a bovine source, contain cortisol and can increase low cortisol levels.

C

Let's look at some of the best ways that you can start to support your adrenals to improve their function and, in turn, skyrocket your fertility.

Adrenal Supportive Diet

- Whole foods (foods that you have to cook), non-processed, non-boxed foods without sugar
- A high vegetable intake that includes all of the colors of the rainbow– red (tomatoes, red peppers, etc.), orange (yams, oranges, orange peppers, etc.), green (spinach, broccoli, chard, green beans, Brussel sprouts, etc.), purple (blueberries, eggplant, etc.)
- No coffee or other sources of caffeine, which depletes adrenal glands
- Adequate lean protein (fish, chicken, turkey, pork, grass fed beef—all hormone free) to stabilize blood sugar and help stabilize cortisol levels

Nutrient Support for the Adrenals

Pantothenic Acid (Vitamin B5): an integral nutrient involved in adrenal function that supports cortisol synthesis, hormone production, and many other cellular activities. In fact, research has demonstrated that a deficiency of Vitamin B5 causes a decrease in adrenocortical function (3). In one study, animals that were given Vitamin B5 had higher levels of corticosterone (natural steroid) and progesterone (4). People who are under stress are more prone toward a deficiency of this important vitamin.

Methylcobalamin (active form of Vitamin B12): this active form of Vitamin B12 is a great energy booster. Vitamin B12 plays an important role in adrenal function, hormone regulation, cellular metabolism, energy production, cellular repair, and methylation. It is also an important nutrient in the building of red blood cells. Vitamin B12 is used with adrenal formulations to support adrenal and hormone production.

Vitamin B Complex: other B vitamins play an important role in energy production, cellular metabolism, hormone production, and adrenal function. A high-quality B Complex supplement can fill in the gaps of needed B vitamins needed to restore adrenal health.

Vitamin C: one of the most important nutrients that support adrenal function and the production of cortisol. Vitamin C is also an antioxidant that is protecting you from free-radical damage. It is important in the production of collagen and is involved in immune support and so many other important metabolic reactions in the body. When you're under stress, your need for Vitamin C increases. Vitamin C can be found in green leafy vegetables, orange juice, and citrus as well as in supplements.

Adaptogen Herbs for Adrenal Support

Adaptogens are a category of botanical medicines that help the body adapt to stress and support the immune system. Stress is managed by two physiological systems: the HPA system and the sympathoadrenal system (SAS), which is the interface between the sympathetic nervous system and the adrenal system (5). Stress triggers responses in both the HPA and SAS systems. Adaptogens are mainly associated with the HPA axis, which is important in hormone regulation. The HPA axis is part of the stress system that is believed to play a primary role in the body's reactions to repeated stress and adaptation (6). Studies show that when mice are exposed to environmental stress and given adaptogen herbs, the SAS helps the mice to adapt to the stress and control the acute reaction to the stressor (6). I think we can all use adaptogens, as we are bombarded with stress in our daily lives. A side effect of taking adaptogen herbs to help your fertility is that you are calmer, less reactive to stress, and more resilient to life's changes. Adaptogens have a stimulating and balancing effect, helping to increase energy and vitality. Unlike drug stimulants, they typically generate little to no side effects, and have no addictive, tolerance, or abuse potential (6).

In addition, adaptogens have the unique ability to balance cortisol levels whether they are high are low. Adaptogens normalize cortisol function and allow your body the ability to modulate stress. This has a result of helping mood, energy, and sleep cycles. Adaptogens create support for the HPA axis, which supports hormone production and normalizes FSH, LH, and estradiol levels. This, in turn, improves follicle stimulation, egg maturation, and the trigger for ovulation. Not every adaptogen is the same, with the exact same properties. Some adaptogens are more stimulating while some are more calming, and others have a balancing effect. Supporting adrenal function with adaptogens is one of the missing links I see for the success of both natural fertility and ART outcomes. While adaptogen herbs are supportive for conception, they cannot be taken during pregnancy.

Let's meet some of my favorite adaptogens herbs that could be used alone or in combination for improved fertility and vitality.

"The Balancer" – Ashwagandha

Ashwagandha (Latin name, Withania somnifera), commonly known as Indian Ginseng or Winter Cherry, is a traditional herb used in Ayurvedic medicine. Ashwagandha is an adaptogenic herb that belongs to the pepper family and contains active ingredients known as withanolides. Withanolides are key constituents thought to have calming properties that can support the body during times of emotional and physical stress. In animal studies, ashwagandha has been shown to support the activity of lymphocytes and macrophages (parts of the immune system), moderate occasional stress, enhance memory and cognitive function, provide neuroprotection by scavenging free radicals, and support thyroid function. Ashwagandha has a balancing effect and can be used for high or low cortisol imbalances. Research findings show a reduction of elevated cortisol levels and suggest that Ashwagandha root extract safely and effectively improves an individual's resistance toward stress, and thereby improving quality of life (7).

"The Energizer" - Ginseng

The most common types of ginseng are Chinese ginseng (Panax ginseng) and American ginseng (Panax quinquefolius). Siberian "ginseng" (Eleutherococcus senticosus) is not actually a ginseng because it contains different chemical constituents than Chinese and American ginseng, but it has similar properties. Ginseng is an adaptogen, balances cortisol levels, modulates stress, supports female and male reproductive health, promotes memory and learning, and supports immune function. Both ginsengs and another supplement called eleutherococcus encourage adrenal gland health in times of stress by maintaining healthy levels of cortisol. In Traditional Chinese Medicine (TCM), Eleutherococcus senticosus is used for general weakness and debility, lassitude, anorexia, insomnia, and dream-disturbed sleep. Pharmacologic studies have suggested that Eleutherococcus senticosus' effects are at least equal to, and perhaps superior to, those of Chinese ginseng (8). Eleutherococcus's actions, much like ginseng's, are considered to support the immune system, reduce stress, enhance performance and energy (8). The herb has demonstrated the ability to improve adrenal function and stress tolerance, enhance immune function and resistance to infections including influenza, and enhance selective memory.

"The Uplifter" - Licorice Root

Licorice root (Glycyrrhiza glabra) also know by the names sweet root, Chinese licorice, and gan cao or gan-zao (9), is an adaptogenic herb that uplifts energy and supports the immune system. It has gastrointestinal supportive effects and prevents the body from inactivating cortisol production, which allows for more availability of cortisol in the body, supports adrenal function, and enhances stress resistance. Licorice and its natural compounds have demonstrated anti-inflammatory activities (10). It is reported that licorice extract inhibits the growth of viruses, including herpes simplex, varicella zoster, Japanese encephalitis, vesicular stomatitis virus, influenza virus, and type A influenza virus. (11) Licorice root should be avoided or used with caution in people with high blood pressure, as it could worsen their condition.

"The Qi Builder" - Astragalus Root

Astragalus (Astragalus membranaceus) is widely used in Traditional Chinese Medicine because it tonifies Qi, or vital energy, including spleen Qi, which builds blood to help your period. it also contains trace mineral and micronutrients to support adrenal function and assist in restoring hormone balance. In addition to the typical adaptogenic action of modulating the immune system and cortisol levels, astragalus also contains the following high oxidative constituents: astragalosides, pterocarpans, isoflavones, flavanol aglycones (12). These protect cells from damage and inflammation, including DNA and protein damage done to ovaries and sperm caused by oxidative stress.

"The Old Sage" - Schizandra

Schizandra, (Schizandra Chinesis) made from the seeds of a berry, is an adaptogenic botanical that has been used in Chinese medicine for thousands of years. It is known for its ability to improve energy, endurance, and response to stress. It has protective effects of the liver due to its high lignan content, exerts a balancing effect on cortisol levels, and can lower blood sugar (13). It has shown potential for lowering blood pressure (14), helps with fatigue, increases endurance with exercise (15), and research studies have shown that it has no toxic effects (15). Because Schizandra has been used for thousands of years for so many conditions, and because of its gentle yet powerful adaptogenic properties, I like to call it the old sage—having thousands of years of wisdom and healing properties.

"The Sacred One" - Holy Basil

Holy basil, (Ocimum tenuiflorum) is an indigenous plant in India and Southeast Asia and has been used as a scared plant. The plant is used in the Ayurvedic tradition and is called Tulsi, which translates to "incomparable one" (17). In India, it is considered sacred anywhere it grows (16). Holy Basil has a very nice, calming and balancing effect on cortisol and energy. For stressed patients who are anxious and depleted, holy basil can make a big difference in how they feel. In one study, male mice who were given holy basil demonstrated lower concentrations of cortisol and glucose in the blood (18). Another study showed a reduction in blood sugar levels in diabetic rats who had holy basil leaf powder added to their diets (19).

"The Anxiety Reducer" – Rhodiola

Rhodiola (Rhodiola rosea), also known as golden root, has been used traditionally for hundreds of years to help lessen mental and physical stress and to promote endurance. Research suggests that rhodiola's adaptogenic effects may help physical exercise performance as well as mental fatigue and memory in healthy people (20). It also may be involved with the transport of neurotransmitters, chemicals in the brain that affect mood and may help release endorphins (21). Rhodiola is unique in that studies have shown it to lower stress response to physical, mental, and chemical stress. This means that whatever type of stress you are under, rhodiola is likely to help control cortisol from going too high and it may help brain chemistry in addition to helping with blood sugar. Rhodiola has an overall calming and balancing effect on cortisol, and is one of my favorites for someone under high emotional stress who might tend toward anxiety.

"The Memory Enhancer"

Gotu kola (Centella asiatica) is known for its anti-inflammatory, anti-epileptic, anticonvulsant, antioxidant, anti-depressant, cognitive enhancement, and wound healing properties (22, 24). It also has been shown to increase levels of GABA, which is a calming neurotransmitter in the brain that has an anxiety-lowering property. Gotu kola has a revitalizing effect on the brain and nervous system. It can increase attention span and concentration, and combat signs of aging. I like to use gotu kola in my patients who are having memory issues along with being burnt out and depleted to build adrenal function and help memory at the same time. One study showed that using gotu kola extract therapy of 750–1000 mg per day improved cognitive impairment after a stroke and was well tolerated with minimal side effects (23).

"Kidney Qi Builder" - Cordyceps

Cordyceps (Cordyceps sinensis) comes from a fungus and is known as the Chinese caterpillar fungus. It is naturally distributed across the Tibetan Plateau of Asia and the Himalayas. You might be thinking, "What, a fungus? Oh no!" But, cordyceps has been used in Chinese medicine for thousands of years as a tonic. It tonifies both the kidney Yin and Yang Qi and the lung Qi. In fertility, tonifying the kidney Qi is paramount, as this is the foundation Qi that you will pass to your baby and is needed to conceive. So you can see that building kidney Qi is really important. Cordyceps is used in many Traditional Chinese Medicine (TCM) formulas. Cordyceps is widely used as a tonic because research confirms Cordyceps had adaptogenic, aphrodisiac, antioxidant, antiaging, neuroprotective, immune balancing, and anticancer properties; it also protects the liver (25). If you are taking Chinese herbs then cordyceps is most likely one of those herbs, due to its wide support for the body.

"The Hormone Balancer" - Maca

Maca (Lepidium peruvianum) is well-known for its hormone balancing properties (26) and is discussed in further details in later chapters. Maca also has adaptogenic properties and can be used in combination with other adaptogenic herbs to enhance hormone balance and adrenal function.

GLANDULARS

Glandulars contain actual adrenal gland tissue either from bovine (cow) or porcine (pig) sources and can be used to provide natural cortisol to support adrenal function. Glandulars are generally stronger than herbs alone and can be used alone or in combination with adrenal supportive herbs and vitamins, for those with more severe adrenal decline or fatigue. Although glandular supplements do not require a prescription, you should have a licensed healthcare practitioner guide you in choosing the highest quality commercially available extract and the appropriate dosage. They also need to supervise its use, so that you do not overstimulate the SAS system, which can create symptoms such as heart palpitations, anxiety, and insomnia.

Taking botanicals (herbs), glandulars, and vitamins, in addition to healthy eating, acupuncture, meditation, and yoga are some of the modalities that can be helpful in restoring adrenal function to support your fertility. Regardless of whether you use one or a combination of these tools, it will positivity impact your adrenal function. Time and time again, I have seen this approach help women improve hormone balance and succeed in getting pregnant naturally, as well as helping women be more successful with IVF and IUI. Make sure you ask your physician to test your adrenal function with a salivary cortisol test and treat any underlying adrenal decline to maximize your fertility. The impact is vital to your success.

IT ONLY
TAKES
ONE
GOOD
EGG.

OPTIMIZING EGG QUALITY:

IT ONLY TAKES ONE GOOD EGG

It only takes one good egg. Is that true? I believe it is true. It takes one good egg that has good chromosomal makeup. What we are finding out more and more is that we can improve egg quality. The quality of the egg depends a lot on its growth as it matures and develops, as well as when sperm meets egg and cell division begins. We already know that many things influence egg development and that the environment is critical to egg maturation. Specific nutrients and modalities can help and nourish the body to feed and support the egg and its development. This, in turn, directly affects the egg quality and the maturation of the egg as well as cell division after fertilization of the egg. Can you imagine this? You have an egg, but it can actually develop into a stronger egg and more vibrant egg, and you can influence that development by taking certain supplements. Most GYNs rarely tell you that you can improve your egg quality. I think it's really important to know, especially as we age, that many studies support the idea that taking just a few supplements can actually change the outcome of egg development and quality. That means that you have an amazing opportunity to influence your eggs in a positive way by just simply supporting the development of your eggs as they grow with diet, lifestyle, supplements, acupuncture, and Chinese herbs. This allows you to take control. You have the power to improve your chances of natural conception and a positive outcome with IUI and IVF. In the world of reproductive health, doctors look toward research studies to guide their recommendations for women, especially women of advanced maternal age. Many REs recommend CoQ10 and melatonin supplementation because research shows this improves

IVF and IUI outcomes. There may be other things that, though they have yet to be researched, can positively influence your fertility. So, take charge and create the best possible environment to improve egg quality and outcomes with ART and natural conception.

WHAT CAN IMPROVE EGG QUALITY?

CoQ10 - THE NUTRIENT INVOLVED IN ENERGY PRODUCTION

Let's start by talking about CoQ10, the nutrient that is best known for its support in the area of egg quality. CoQ10 is a nutrient that is synthesized naturally in the body within the membranes of human cells. It acts as a strong antioxidant and is required for mitochondrial ATP synthesis, or the creation of energy in your cells. There are two forms of CoQ10, ubiquinone and ubiquinol. Ubiquinol is the active and most powerful form of CoQ10. When CoQ10 levels in the cells are low, energy production may be reduced and oxidative stress increases as a result.

Since the egg houses the chromosomal DNA and it is preparing for the sperm to fertilize the egg and then for cell division to rapidly start occurring, it makes sense that the egg would require more CoQ10 to make more ATP and energy to fuel cell division.

CoQ10 can be found in organ meats; dark leafy green vegetables such as spinach, kale and broccoli as well as nuts, seafood, and meat. It would be hard to get the amount of CoQ10 required to work as a strong antioxidant and aid in fertility; therefore, a supplement of CoQ10 is generally required.

CoQ10 in Women

CoQ10 has gained a lot of attention due to its significant role in mitochondrial energy production, which reduces with age. It is hypothesized that the role of mitochondrial dysfunction in reproductive health plays a role in infertility (1). Because of this, supplementation with CoQ10 is beneficial. As an egg matures, it depends on its environment for full and optimal growth and development. Once an egg is fertilized, the genetic matter is not active until around Day 3 after fertilization, when blastulation occurs. This is when the sixteen-cell blastocyst, which is the early dividing embryo filled evenly with cells, relies on the production of new mitochondria and CoQ10 is needed to continue cell division (2). Adverse environmental factors include aging, oxidative stress, obesity, smoking, alcohol, and psychologic stress can negatively impact egg quality. Whereas positive environmental factors like a healthy diet, exercise, antioxidants and other nutritional supplements, and psychologic interventions have a positive effect (2).

The mitochondria of the egg is the energy center and powerhouse that helps with production of energy that can deteriorate with age adversely affecting egg growth and cell division. Mitochondrial function and energy production deteriorate with age, adversely affecting ovarian reserve, chromosome segregation, and embryo competence. In studies with aging mice, the mitochondrial cofactor CoQ10 reverses most of these changes (2).

There are more animal studies than human studies on CoQ10 and egg quality. In studies with aging mice, the mitochondrial cofactor CoQ10 has a positive influence on egg quality. One smaller study in humans, which used a shorter duration of CoQ10 supplementation compared to studies done in mice, did show evidence suggesting that CoQ10 enhances egg quality and energy via the mitochondria. The study also suggested that CoQ10 shows promise in fueling proper cell division, enhancing egg quality, and raising overall pregnancy rates. Another study on CoQ10 supplementation was done on 483 patients and live birth rates in poor prognosis patients who were poor responders of IVF. They were given about 1,000 mg of CoQ10 per day along with their other IVF protocols. With the addition of CoQ10 supplementation, these women who had previously been classified as poor responders to IVF could achieve pregnancy rates even in their mid-forties. This is especially notable because egg donation is generally recommended in women of advanced maternal age who are poor responders to IVF. These studies on supplementation of CoQ10 imply that it may serve as powerhouse to the mitochondria and help cell division in women of advanced maternal age, when natural levels of CoQ10 would be low. With the extra boost provided by CoQ10, these women who had a poor prognosis for their fertility were able to achieve pregnancy (3).

One study looked into the effect of CoQ10 as a supplement for the invitro culture of bovine embryos and found a significantly higher rate of early embryo cleavage, blastocyst formation, and hatching, along with an increased percentage of expanding blastocysts, and a larger size of the inner cell mass (3). In addition, there was an increased ATP content in the group of embryos cultured with CoQ10 (3). All of those parameters suggest better quality embryos (3). Although the number of studies with CoQ10 in women is small, they provide another outstanding insight into the workings of the human egg and cell division. We know that mitochondria are very important in a lot of different illnesses including fibromyalgia and chronic fatigue, and others where mitochondrial function has declined. If you have all the right parts, yet you can't fuel the cell division, the cell division gets arrested, and then you can't get pregnant.

One study that looked at a compilation of studies on CoQ10 and egg quality reported that "in light of the prior literature and our preliminary animal data, we believe that supplementing the diets of older women with mitochondrial nutrients may result in an improvement of oocyte and embryo quality, and subsequently, better pregnancy outcome. Mitochondrial nutrients are naturally occurring vitamins that have been used successfully to treat conditions associated with diminished energy production from mitochondria and appear to be very safe in the doses studied" (4).

Understanding that CoQ10 is a very important nutrient required for rapid cell division, it makes sense that CoQ10 could offer benefits in all women, but especially in women of advanced maternal age. CoQ10 supplementation in research studies were given in the range of anywhere from 300 to 450 mg two to three times per day. There is no data that tells us if CoQ10 is safe during pregnancy or not. Therefore, supplementation during preconception as well as in pregnancy must be discussed with your doctor. The evidence points to a very positive direction of research with the benefits of CoQ10 related to egg quality and cell division. Some doctors might say there's not enough data to support the supplementation of CoQ10. However, based on the physiological reasoning of why CoQ10 might be important, it just makes sense to take CoQ10 in a preconception plan for women, especially women who are thirty-five or older. I suggest this to all my patients as a potential way to enhance the quality of cell division and improve pregnancy rates. In addition, I find that CoQ10 is well-tolerated and the benefits certainly outweigh the risks for many of my patients.

CoQ10 in Men

Let's talk about CoQ10 supplementation in men. There is actually more research to support CoQ10 supplementation for men and sperm quality. Yes, your better half is important, and what they eat, their stress levels, and their nutrients (or lack thereof) absolutely affect sperm production. We can't ignore the other side of the equation, can we? Absolutely not. So, let's talk about CoQ10 and men. It is well documented that excessive production of reactive oxygen species (ROS), also called free radicals, decreases sperm motility, impairs sperm function, and damages the morphology of spermatozoa (5). Reactive oxygen species play a key pathogenetic role in male infertility, besides having a well-recognized physiological function (6).

Studies show that CoQ10 supplementation in men with unknown low sperm count (idiopathic oligoasthenoteratozoospermia) increases sperm concentration, motility, and morphology (7). CoQ10 increases the level of ubiquinol (CoQ10) in semen and is effective in improving sperm movement in patients affected by low sperm motility (idiopathic asthenozoospermia) (8, 9). Because improved parameters of sperm quality were achieved using CoQ10 supplementation, this in turn had a beneficial effect on pregnancy rates. The studies with men suggest oral supplementation of about 300 mg of CoQ10 daily for about a year. Oxidative stress and reactive oxygen species play a role in male infertility as well as female. Oxidative stress ages our skin, our cells, our eggs and sperm. Because CoQ10 is a strong antioxidant and CoQ10 plays a significant role in mitochondrial functioning and energy production in men and women, numerous studies show that CoQ10 in fact improves sperm motility and sperm quality. Therefore, I routinely recommend CoQ10 supplementation for male patients to assist them in increasing semen quality and helping to increase the chances of natural conception.

It is important to know that not all CoQ10 supplements are alike and CoQ10 is not readily absorbed. Therefore, it's really important to check with your healthcare provider to know what type of CoQ10 you should be taking to have the most positive beneficial effect for conception.

MYOINOSITOL

Myoinositol is one of nine chemical structures, or shapes, of inositol. Inositol, sometimes referred to as vitamin B8, is a vitamin-like substance that occurs naturally. The best sources of inositol include whole grain breads, citrus fruits, meats, and dairy products. Inositol helps with metabolism and is an important building block for healthy cell membranes. Inositol promotes proper utilization of the hormone insulin, which in turn supports hormone balance and ovarian function. Studies show it has a positive effect on egg quality.

Inositol is actually best known for helping women with polycystic ovarian syndrome who have insulin resistance (PCOS) (10, 16). Research studies demonstrate that myoinositol has a normalizing effect on insulin levels in PCOS patients and is able to improve egg and embryo quality during ovarian stimulation protocols. Another study in 2011 looked at the effects of administering myoinositol and melatonin supplements. The study looked at a small subset of women who were treated with 4 g per day of myoinositol and 3 mg per day of melatonin for three months prior to IVF treatment. The outcome was that the treatment with myoinositol and melatonin improved ovarian stimulation protocols and pregnancy outcomes in women with poor egg quality (11). This was a significant study to illustrate that the presence of compounds in the follicular fluid could be altered to influence egg quality and growth. A more recent study in 2017 looked at using myoinositol to manage poor ovarian response in assisted reproduction. In looking at the efficacy of using myoinositol supplementation in women undergoing ovulation induction for intracytoplasmic sperm injection (ICSI) or IVF embryo transfer, the study concluded that myoinositol supplementation increased clinical pregnancy rates in both groups, and it may improve the quality of the embryos as well as require lesser amounts of stimulation drugs (12).

Another study used myoinositol plus folic acid and melatonin to compare treatment with and without the supplementation on pregnancy rates in IVF cycles. The studies show that melatonin helps the activity of myoinositol and folic acid by improving egg quality and pregnancy outcome in women with low egg quality history (13). This research regarding myoinositol in the last three years has been significant in having a tool to help improve egg quality. This may be especially important in women over thirty-five who have more chance of poor egg quality or poor response to IVF. In a nutshell taking myoinositol alone may be helpful in improving egg quality. More recent studies show that there may be a better affect with a combination of myoinositol and D-Chiro inositol in the right ratios to improve egg quality and embryo quality (14). Therefore, it's important to discuss the use of myoinositol with your doctor or medical practitioner to improve your egg quality.

Myoinositol Verses D-Chiro Inositol

There is still some debate on the best form of inositol to use to assist in improving egg quality. D-chiro in previous studies did not seem to have a positive outcome on improving egg quality compared to myoinositol during ovarian stimulation protocols with IVF. Another study showed high concentration of myoinositol in human follicular fluid improved egg quality and embryo quality. Whereas, D-chiro inositol seemed to worsen egg quality and ovarian response in PCOS patients (15, 16). However, in a more recent study in 2017, it appears that there may be a specific ratio of using both myoinositol and D-chiro inositol to best influence follicular fluid and help egg quality as well as embryo quality.

Using myoinositol, which has repetitive studies that show a positive influence on egg quality, seems to be the best approach to supplementation. But it is important to keep reading more about D-chiro inositol, as a combination of both forms of inositol may provide an even more effective way to influence egg quality in the future.

DHEA

DHEA (dehydroepiandrosterone) is a hormone produced by your body's adrenal glands. DHEA serves as a precursor to other steroid hormones including testosterone and estrogen. DHEA is commonly used by reproductive endocrinologists to improve fertility pregnancy outcomes and egg quality. The standard dosing to be used in IVF protocols is around 75 mg daily, which has been shown to improve egg quality and pregnancy outcomes in women who have been classified as poor responders to IVF stimulation medication (17, 20, 21). DHEA studies postulate that DHEA can improve egg and embryo quality, increase pregnancy rates, reduce time to conceive, reduce miscarriage rates and treat women with decreased ovarian reserve (18) and may be used to slow down ovarian aging (19). DHEA levels can be checked in the blood with standard medical testing. I generally test my patients at their first initial consult to see what their levels are. I base supplementation based on their serum levels, rather than giving them a one-size-fits-all supplementation. It is important to understand that DHEA is a precursor to other sex hormones. Because of that, you can have an excess of it, which can increase levels of other sex hormones such as testosterone. This can work against you and inhibit ovulation in natural conception. That's why it's important to have bloodwork before supplementation in addition to testing testosterone prolactin levels. Women with PCOS already have high androgenic levels that would contraindicate DHEA supplementation. DHEA supplementation is common with IVF protocols at a one-size-fits-all dose. If you have PCOS, whether or not you take DHEA will be decided between you and your doctor, but it is important to understand that it can aggravate your symptoms. Remember, dosing recommendations for DHEA supplementation can be different when trying to conceive naturally compared to supplementation during an IVF protocol. That is why it is important to consult your doctor to determine how much DHEA is needed for you, individually.

DHEA creates an anabolic or excitatory affect and gives you energy, which is a great benefit. However, if you take too much you can become agitated, have breast tenderness, acne, irritability, weight gain, and other negative side effects. DHEA should be taken in the morning because it has the potential to disrupt your sleep. Although DHEA is a supplement, it is also a powerful hormone precursor and has a significant impact on your hormone levels. Therefore, it's important to use DHEA with caution as it has a profound effect on your body, your hormones, and your moods, as well as your fertility.

MELATONIN

Melatonin is a hormone that is secreted by the pineal gland. Melatonin is best known for its effect on sleep-wake cycles as well as an influence on hormones of the female reproductive cycle. Melatonin can be found in small amounts in vegetables, grains and meat. It is also used as a supplement for sleep, jet lag, and improving egg quality for women undergoing ART. Melatonin protects against aging-induced fertility decline and maintains mitochondrial redox balance, lending to improved egg quality (22, 24) and the induction of egg maturation and fertilization potential (25).

Melatonin has been studied in relation to IVF in egg quality and egg retrieval. Melatonin does improve the quality of eggs and significantly accelerates the developmental ability of IVF embryos (26, 27, 28). In one study of sixty-five women undergoing IVF cycles, patients were randomized into groups with one group receiving myoinositol, folic acid and melatonin, and the other group receiving only myoinositol and folic acid. They found that embryo quality and the morphology of mature eggs retrieved, and pregnancy rates were all increased with the addition of melatonin (13). The study concluded that melatonin improves egg quality and pregnancy outcome in women with low egg quality history. In these studies, melatonin had no effect on sleep. In addition, in these studies, melatonin levels were not checked prior to supplementation, so we don't know if they started with low melatonin or not. You can test melatonin with saliva. However, in the traditional Western community, melatonin levels are generally not checked on a routine basis. It appears that melatonin does have a positive effect on egg quality and therefore may be a supplement that could benefit you in your journey to conceive. Other studies confirm that melatonin improves egg quality in ART. Generally, the dose used is about 3 mg. It's important not to take too high of a dose, which may end up affecting hormones negatively. It is also important to understand that the studies done with melatonin were done with women undergoing IVF, not trying to conceive during a natural cycle. It's important to discuss with your doctor if this might be of benefit to you, especially if you are doing IVF. Melatonin should not be taken while pregnant or nursing and can also cause drowsiness, so it is generally taken at bedtime. It's important to check with your doctor to see if the supplement is appropriate for you before starting.

OMEGA-3 FATTY ACIDS

As women age, so do their eggs; therefore, ovarian aging is an important issue in improving the egg quality. Omega-3 fatty acids contain eicosapentaenoic acid (EPA), which reduces inflammation in our body and also serves to support the health of our cell membranes and docosahexaenoic acid (DHA), which is different from DHEA (a hormone precursor) and is important for brain health and cognition. It is important to take omega-3 fatty acids for conception as well as in pregnancy. Fetal development requires omega-3 fatty acids for early cognitive development and optimal cell function. When taking a supplement for omega-3 fatty acids, check the label to make sure that the supplement is free of mercury, PCBs, pesticides, and other toxic elements. If it does not say this on the label, then the supplement has not been tested and that product should not be used. Inquire about the purity of the product you are taking on a regular basis. A high-quality omega-3 fatty acid supplement can be an important supplement in your daily routine for conception, egg quality, and overall health. A poor product could be of detriment, so make sure that you understand what you are taking.

It is important to include omega-3 fatty acids into your diet as it helps with egg quality, especially in women of advanced maternal age (thirty-five years and older). Studies even indicate that short-term dietary treatment of omega-3 fatty acids results in improving egg quality and delaying the aging of your ovaries (28, 30). In addition, serum levels of long-chain omega-3 fatty acids were positively associated with the probability of live birth among women undergoing ART (29). This may be due to the protective antioxidant effects of the omega-3 fatty acids, which fuel and nourish the cells of your body to diminish the aging process. Omega-3 fatty acids come from fish. So if you are vegetarian, it is difficult to get omega-3 fatty acids in your diet, and supplementation is generally required. Omega-6 fatty acids come from eating vegetables and vegetable oils. Omega-6 fatty acids do not need to be supplemented in addition to your diet. In fact, studies show that omega-6 fatty acid supplementation had a negative effect on egg quality (31). That does not mean that getting a high amount of vegetables from your diet is not good for you, but you do not need a supplement of omega-6 fatty acids. Rather you need omega-3 fatty acid supplementation that is of high quality because of its beneficial effect on egg quality, as well as its benefits for cardiovascular disease, anti-inflammatory action, protection of free radicals, support of brain cognition, and anti-aging properties.

FOLIC ACID

Folic acid, better known as vitamin B9, is part of the B vitamin family. This important nutrient is involved in DNA synthesis and repair. It is also involved in the production of nucleic acids that are part of our genetic material. Folic acid is well known to prevent birth defects and is recommended by all obstetricians for women who are pregnant. Did you know that folic acid can also affect egg quality? We associate folic acid with preventing birth defects, but not really affecting egg quality and embryo quality.

Folic acid must be converted to its active form called, methylenetetrahydrofolate (MTHF) to be useable by the body. It's estimated that fifty to sixty percent of the population have methylation defects or mutations that can reduce the conversion to active folate anywhere from mildly to significantly. The extent of the effects depends on the specific mutations a person has, which can impair cell division and DNA repair, which can result in possible miscarriage or genetic abnormalities. Therefore, it is important to use the active form of methylenetetrahydrofolate in your prenatal supplementation as well as in any additional folate supplement. Methylation mutations, or MTHFR mutations, will be further discussed in another chapter. For now, let's focus on what studies show about the association with folic acid supplementation and egg quality.

Does research that illustrates the link between folic acid supplementation and egg quality exist? In fact, it does.

MTHFR mutations can lead to increased homocysteine levels. Homocysteine is an amino acid and a breakdown product of protein metabolism (it's an intermediate in the metabolism of amino acids methionine and cysteine). In high levels, homocysteine is linked to increased risk of heart attacks and strokes. Homocysteine acts as an irritant in the arteries, causing an inflammatory response that increases plaque formation. Homocysteine levels can be elevated with several variants of MTHFR mutations. High levels of homocysteine not only increase cardiac risk, but can also diminish egg quality. Studies show that low levels of homocysteine (rather than high levels), are associated with improved egg quality (32). In one study looking at in vitro fertilization embryo transfer patients, supplementation of folic acid reduced homocysteine levels in the follicle fluid where the egg is growing. Those eggs were better quality and had a higher degree of maturation (32). Why would these eggs have better egg quality? One possible reason is that if you have an undiagnosed MTHFR mutation, which about fifty percent of the population has, then DNA repair may be negatively affected. When cells are rapidly dividing early in fetal development, mistakes in DNA replication can be easily made. Normally, you can correct this, but if you have MTHFR mutations, then your body's ability to correct mistakes can be thwarted, resulting in abnormal cell division affecting egg quality.

Another study looked at elevated concentrations of homocysteine associated with poor egg quality in women with PCOS who were undergoing assisted reproduction. This study concluded that high homocysteine levels in PCOS patient may be a useful marker of fertilization rates, as well as egg and embryo quality, in women who are undergoing assisted reproductive treatment (33). This demonstrated yet another possible correlation with PCOS and MTHFR mutations. If MTHF can lower homocysteine levels, then it could possibly improve egg quality.

In another study, myoinositol was used in addition to folic acid and melatonin, and the combination of these three supplements did have improvement in egg quality and increased the chance of pregnancy in women with poor egg quality history (13). Again, since three nutrients were used in this study, it's hard to know what part folic acid played. However, we know the folic acid affects DNA synthesis and repair, so it has a definite impact on egg growth and quality.

Another study, acknowledging that follicular fluid folate affects follicular metabolism and egg and embryo quality, showed some additional benefits of folic acid. They concluded that folic acid supplementation is correlated with reducing inflammation, specifically C-Reactive Protein (an inflammatory marker), and increasing the HDL (the good cholesterol) pathway preferred in hormone synthesis (34).

Although more studies are needed to illustrate the effect that folic acid has on egg quality and the specific way it works, we do have studies that say, yes, folic acid is important in egg quality. In addition, folic acid is vital for cell division and embryo development. When an egg is growing and developing in the follicle, it is dividing and needs to have proper repair of DNA for proper growth. When egg meets sperm cell, division gets ramped up and occurs rapidly, which is problematic if you have any kind of MTHFR mutation because your repair mechanism may be impaired. Just by understanding folic acid's role in creating healthy DNA and cell division, we can conclude that MTHF should be used in all prenatal supplementation regiments. Remember, folic acid should be in the active form, methylenetetrahydrofolate or MTHF, to ensure that the proper active amount of folic acid can be utilized by the body. Any doctor who tells you it is not necessary to have MTHF rather than folate or folic acid is doing a disservice to you by not giving you the tools to support healthy cell division. This may even cause you harm. The moral of this story is that taking MTHF as part of our prenatal supplementation regiment, as well as an additional supplement for preconception and during the entire pregnancy can help lead to healthy conception and a healthy baby.

ANTIOXIDANTS

We all know that antioxidants are important to us because they protect us against free radical damage. Free radicals are unstable oxygen species that create damage to our cells and lead to disruptions in physiological function. The more we age, the more damage that occurs through our exposure to the pro-oxidants in the environment as well as from food. Having a diet that is pro-oxidative means that it promotes free radicals, leading to oxidative damage to your cells and causes them to age more rapidly. Oxidative stress is one of the most detrimental factors affecting egg growth and maturation of eggs during aging (35). Reactive oxygen species (ROS), known as free radicals, have been shown to have an important role in the normal functioning of the reproductive system and in the cause of infertility in females (36, 41). Reactive oxygen species (ROS), or free radicals, form during normal metabolism of oxygen and are produced as by-products of aerobic metabolism. A certain amount of ROS production is necessary for gene expression. It is suggested that oxidative stress is involved in the age-related decline of fertility and that it plays a role during pregnancy, childbirth, and the initiation of preterm labor (37). An increase in ROS is indicated with a deterioration of egg quantity, embryonic development disorders, gynecological disease, and infertility (38). In addition, free radicals play an important role in the aging of the ovaries and are linked to female conditions such as endometriosis and polycystic ovary syndrome (PCOS) (39). Studies confirm that antioxidants play a significant role in the ovaries. Enzymatic and non-enzymatic antioxidants, namely vitamins and minerals, are present in the follicles of the ovaries to protect the eggs from the damaging effects of free radicals (40). The overproduction of free radicals leads to oxidative stress, which negatively affects the quality of the eggs and the maturation or growth of those eggs. Oxidative stress in females is a likely middle man in the success of conception and may influence the timing and maintenance of a viable pregnancy, as well as have links to early pregnancy loss (41). Antioxidant supplementation is indicated as a possible strategy for treating reproductive disease and infertility by controlling oxidative stress (42). More studies are needed, but evidence suggests that antioxidants play a vital role in egg quality and infertility.

An animal study looking at antioxidants' effect on egg aging shows that pre-maturation aging is detrimental to eggs' ability to undergo maturation and other cellular activities, and that antioxidants can protect eggs from damages to DNA shape and integrity, as well as other damages caused by aging (35). Another study that looked at women undergoing assisted reproduction showed that using certain types of antioxidants is promising for the prevention of oxidative damage to embryos, which helps improve their quality. However, more studies are needed (39). In another study, women with PCOS who supplemented with myoinositol and antioxidants after five months showed a significant increase in the number of eggs and antioxidant activity in their follicular fluid (43). Studies looking at invitro maturation (IVM) combined with IVF show that antioxidants are important for the maintenance of eggs to develop into the blastocyst stage influencing maturing of the egg and embryo development (44).

Bottom line, if you are trying to conceive and protect your ovaries against aging, you need antioxidants as part of your support. So increase the amount of full-spectrum colorful fruits and vegetables and reduce your consumption of fast foods, processed foods, and deep-fried foods. Increase your intake of whole foods that are healthy, nutrient dense, and full of antioxidants. In addition, an antioxidant formula that includes many different types of antioxidants, such as vitamin C, vitamin E, selenium, beta-carotene and other carotenoids, and glutathione, may also provide additional support to help egg quality.

The most superior types of antioxidants and the best regimen for taking them is still unclear from research studies. That is why I recommend an antioxidant formula that has a variety of high-quality antioxidants that contain at least vitamin E, which shows protective promise in research studies. Since studies on antioxidants varied in length, but the range for a positive effect with antioxidant supplementation was around three to five months, I recommend support for at least this amount of time to benefit egg quality. If you are of advanced maternal age, being thirty-five or older, then taking an additional antioxidant supplement in addition to a prenatal supplement would be very important in preserving egg quality and ovarian aging.

A LUTEAL PHASE DEFECT (LPD) REFERS TO AN ABNORMALITY IN THE LUTEAL PHASE THAT IMPEDES FERTILITY SUCCESS.

CORRECTING LUTEAL PHASE DEFECTS

WHAT IS A LUTEAL PHASE DEFECT?

Luteal Phase Defect (LPD) was first defined in 1949 as a corpus luteum defective in progesterone secretion, which in turn was a cause of infertility or early spontaneous abortion (1). Further investigation led to broadening the definition to include a short luteal phase interval (less than twelve days between ovulation and menses) with relatively normal progesterone concentrations, a normal-length luteal phase with inadequate progesterone production, or inadequate endometrial response to otherwise normal progesterone concentrations (1). In any of these situations, a luteal phase defect (LPD) refers to an abnormality in the luteal phase that results, generally, in suboptimal levels of progesterone, which interferes with the action of vascularization of the endometrial lining and impedes fertility success.

The luteal phase refers to the second half of the menstrual cycle. The luteal phase occurs after the Luteinizing Hormone (LH) surge causes ovulation around Day 14 and refers to the second half of the cycle, approximately between Days 14 and 28, or until the period starts again. The egg is released from the follicle during ovulation and the resulting structure is known as the corpus luteum. Hence, we call this part of the menstrual cycle the "luteal phase." The formation of the corpus luteum is complex. Multiple factors contribute to a healthy luteal phase, including: mitochondrial function (the power house of the cell that makes energy or ATP), amounts of cholesterol and pregnenolone which act as precursors to other sex hormones, LH levels which trigger ovulation, growth hormone (GH), insulin-like growth factor 1, prostaglandin E, prostacyclin and thyroid function(2). However, the resulting consequence of a luteal phase defect is an abnormal production of progesterone. Progesterone is a steroid hormone produced primarily by the corpus luteum in non-pregnant women, and by the placenta beginning in the second trimester of pregnancy. Progesterone is important for fertility because it helps to vascularize the endometrial lining of the uterus to prepare a fertilized egg to implant. This rich, nutritive, vascular supply of the lining feeds and grows an embryo. If you have an undernourished lining, then it will be difficult to get pregnant as well as to maintain a pregnancy.

HOW TO KNOW IF YOU HAVE A LUTEAL PHASE DEFECT?

An LPD can generally be confirmed with irregular periods and testing of progesterone levels in the blood on Day 21 of your menstrual cycle, or about seven days after ovulation. Low serum progesterone coupled with a generally short luteal phase, defined as less than twelve days between ovulation and menses, or abnormal basal body temperature (BBT) indicate an LPD. Generally, progesterone levels are low, at about 1–3 ng/ml in the follicular phase. They start to increase after the LH surge at the time of ovulation. In a natural cycle of a fertile woman, progesterone levels would likely reach 10–20 ng/ml after ovulation.

Your goal for progesterone levels during the luteal phase will vary, depending on the doctor interpreting them and what type of treatment you are undergoing. For example, a woman having natural cycles and trying to conceive may have a progesterone level of 10–20 ng/ml. When taking progesterone injections for IVF, or if you are pregnant, your target level of progesterone is 20 ng/ml. If you are undergoing a Clomid cycle you may have a progesterone goal of 15 ng/ml. Serum levels of progesterone may reach a peak at 20 ng/ml and then gradually decrease prior to onset of the period if you do not get pregnant. An optimal level of progesterone is 20 ng/ml. Therefore, a progesterone level of less than 10 ng/ml on Day 21 of your menses may not support conception and could mean that you have an LPD.

Do you have any of the common symptoms of a luteal phase defect? Take the quiz below to find out.

Luteal Phase Defect Quiz

If you answer yes to the following questions, you may have a luteal phase defect.
1. Are your periods irregular?
2. Do your periods come in cycles longer or shorter than twenty-eight days?
3. Is your luteal phase less than fourteen days?
4. Do you have spotting before the onset of your period?
5. Have you had a miscarriage for an unknown reason?

6. Have you been under chronic stress coupled with irregular periods?
7. Have you been on repeated months of clomiphene (Clomid) which has thinned your endometrial lining?
8. Do you have low serum progesterone levels (less than 20 ng/ml) tested in the luteal phase?
9. Have you had a vaginal ultrasound just prior to ovulation that revealed a reduced endometrial lining measurement?
10. Do you have an irregular basal body temperature (BBT) drop in luteal phase?

If you answered yes to any of the questions above, talk with your doctor about your concerns to determine if you have an LPD and if this is a roadblock in your fertility success.

HOW DO YOU DIAGNOSE A LUTEAL PHASE DEFECT?

There are several ways to diagnose a luteal phase defect that range from the least invasive to most invasive. Your history of the menstrual cycle plays a big role in diagnosing an LPD, as it provides a pattern that is most consistent with this disorder. The following are ways to diagnose an LPD from least to most invasive.

1) Basal body temperature (BBT) charting can pinpoint a luteal phase defect. This involves charting your temperature when you first awake every morning and tracking the change in temperatures to show when you ovulate, and when you are in the luteal phase. BBT should rise after ovulation and should be maintained for about twelve to fourteen days. With this rise, you will generally see an increase in cervical mucus. When a premature drop in BBT occurs, it illustrates an instability of the luteal phase temperature, reflecting premature degeneration of the corpus luteum.

2) Low serum progesterone level (less than 20 ng/ml) taken seven days after ovulation indicates a luteal phase defect. Very low levels of serum progesterone in the blood (measured without fasting), such as a 3 to 5 ng/ml indicate a more severe LPD.

3) Vaginal ultrasound can be used during the luteal phase to evaluate the thickness of the endometrial lining. A healthy, thick lining results from a normal progesterone level, reflecting a healthy luteal phase. On the other hand, a thin endometrial lining can reflect an LPD. This is because the LPD leads to low progesterone and results in a thin lining.

4) The most invasive testing for diagnosis of LPD is with an endometrial biopsy. Generally, two out-of-phase biopsies are done. The endometrial biopsy accurately reflects the functional state of both the ovarian cycle and the endometrial cycle and can be used to determine adequacy of therapy, thereby improving conception rates in patients with LPD (3).

HOW TO TREAT LUTEAL PHASE DEFECTS?

We can divide treatment into two categories: a conventional approach, often used by OBGYNs and reproductive endocrinologists (REs), and an integrative approach. The main objective is to increase progesterone levels either directly or indirectly. It is vital to understand the importance of creating a nurturing environment for an embryo's growth and development. Although you may have additional roadblock areas, do not underestimate the importance of addressing LPDs. You would never plant a tomato seed, for example, in a dry and unwelcoming environment and expect it to flourish. Although I have many patients who wish to increase progesterone levels naturally, it takes longer to do so. Therefore, it is recommended to avail yourself of herbal, nutritional, and hormonal support together to create the best support and possible outcome.

CONVENTIONAL APPROACHES TO TREAT LUTEAL PHASE DEFECTS

The three most common conventional methods linked to LPD are the following:
1. Give additional progesterone after ovulation orally, with injection, or by vaginal suppositories.
2. Give supplemental human chorionic gonadotropin (HCG), which is the pregnancy hormone that over-the-counter pregnancy tests react to, to improve corpus luteum secretion of progesterone.
3. Give clomiphene citrate (Clomid) or human menopausal gonadotropins (HMG) to stimulate follicular growth. Clomid is a less expensive option that blocks estrogen receptors at the hypothalamus, the hormone control center, to stimulate follicle stimulating hormone (FSH) and luteinizing hormone (LH). This triggers ovulation, in an effort to improve corpus luteum function and subsequent progesterone production.

INTEGRATIVE APPROACHES FOR LUTEAL PHASE DEFECTS

Integrative approaches to treating LPD also may include supplementation with progesterone, but focus on methods to improve the function of the corpus luteum, working with your own body's regulatory systems rather than using a drug to trigger natural hormonal responses. Medication is always an option to assist your body in these normal processes; however, a body that is not at optimal hormonal regulation may not react to medication in the desired manner. Therefore, it is important to work on developing optimal physiological functioning.

1. Optimize Thyroid Function

One of the first foundational pieces to help with luteal phase defects is to optimize thyroid function to support growth and development of the follicle. Thyroid hormones have also been found to alter hormone production (steroidogenesis) from granulosa and large luteal cells (4,23).

Thyroid hormones work synergistically with follicle-stimulating hormone to develop healthy granulosa cells. After release of the ovum or egg, the remaining cells of the granulosa and theca interna form the corpus luteum, which synthesizes progesterone (5). Optimizing thyroid function with a goal of TSH = 1.0 can work naturally to promote ovulation and support hormone production in luteal phase defects.

2. Support Adrenal Function to Optimize Cortisol Levels

The adrenal glands produce some progesterone, which they use mainly in the synthesis of cortisol. More importantly, cortisol is involved in regulation of progesterone. Though the process is multidimensional, it appears that cortisol and stress response affect progesterone levels and are also thought to influence the HPA axis essential in hormone regulation (6). In situations of stress, where high levels of cortisol are produced by the adrenals, more progesterone is also needed. The adrenals will then shunt additional pregnenolone, which is a steroidal hormone precursor found principally in the adrenal glands, down the cortisol pathway, reducing the amount available for progesterone. Progesterone can also be converted to cortisol under long-term stress for survival. You need cortisol to live and get through your day, and if you have very low levels, your body can steal progesterone and convert it into cortisol, depleting your progesterone levels over time. Supporting adrenal function through Chinese and Western herbs, nutritional support, and beneficial lifestyle choices is key. Nutrients like vitamin C, vitamin B5 (pantothenic acid), and many of the B vitamins contained in the Vitamin B complex, support adrenal health and stress responses. Herbs like ashwagandha modulate cortisol levels. Chinese herbs can effectively modulate cortisol levels and create better hormonal control.

3. Provide Nutrients to Improve Luteal Phase

Vitamin B6

Vitamin B6, known as pyridoxine or Pyridoxal-5-phosphate (P5P), has been used clinically to treat luteal phase defect. It modulates expression of receptors to hormones and progesterone (7). Generally, pyridoxal-5-phosphate is used at about 100 mg per day of vitamin B6 to support luteal phase defects. It is important to use the P5P form in case you have a CBS mutation associated with methylation defects.

Vitamin C

Vitamin C in the amount of 750 mg per day improves progesterone levels and increases fertility in women with luteal phase defect (8). It also enhances cellular health, and supports adrenal function and stress modulation.

Magnesium

Increased magnesium glycinate is required during the luteal phase because of increased progesterone synthesis (9). About 400 mg per day is sufficient to support progesterone production.

Omega-3 fatty acids

Omega-3 fatty acids (approximately 1200 mg of eicosapentaenoic acid and 800 mg of docosapentaenoic acid daily) are essential for follicle structure and function, and for hormone production (10,11). They have been found to directly increase progesterone secretion. They also enhance uterine and ovarian blood flow by increasing the ratio of prostacyclin to thromboxane (12).

Zinc

Zinc picolinate in the amount of 30 mg per day increases insulin-like growth factor 1 and growth hormone (13,14). Insulin-like growth factor 1 plays a significant role in the production of vascular endothelial growth factor in luteal cells and hormone production (15). Research in mice show that zinc deficiency impairs formation of the corpus luteum (16).

Melatonin

Melatonin protects granulosa cells undergoing luteinization from free radical damage in the follicle and contributes to luteinization for progesterone production during ovulation (7). Studies have shown that taking 3 mg of melatonin at bedtime during the luteal phase can increase serum-level production. Melatonin supports progesterone production and growth hormone secretion (17–19).

4. Acupuncture and Chinese Herbs

Acupuncture and Chinese herbs are underutilized modalities to restore proper luteal phase function and normalize the function of the hypothalamic-pituitary-ovarian (HPO) axis, which helps to resolve normal hormone production and function. When you improve follicular function, you improve corpus luteum function, which supports progesterone production. Acupuncture can also modulate stress and cortisol levels, creating better hormone regulation and control.

In Traditional Chinese Medicine, we focus on balances of the opposing forces Yin and Yang of the organs to help restore hormone balance. In the follicular phase, Qi, blood (a component of Yin), and Kidney Qi are required to promote hormones in the second half of the cycle. At ovulation, the Yang Qi must be strong enough to support ovulation, and a transition from Yin to Yang is required for proper hormone production. Disruption in this process can cause luteal phase defects. The most common patterns related to luteal phase defects involve Yin and blood deficiency, Qi and blood stagnation, and Yang and Qi deficiency. These patterns are outlined below by Sami S. David, MD, and Jill Blakeway, LAc, in their book, *Making Babies: A Proven 3-Month Program for Maximum Fertility*.

Pattern 1 – Yin and/or blood deficiency

If Yin Qi is deficient in the follicular phase of the cycle, it can lead to too little Yang in the second half of the cycle, which will impair ovulation and formation of the corpus luteum

Pattern 2 – Qi and/or blood stagnation

Stagnation of the Qi at ovulation can affect the hormonal transition and thus the transition from Yin to Yang.

Pattern 3 – Yang and/or Qi deficiency

Too little Yang Qi can negatively affect both the hormonal transition at ovulation and the quality of the luteal phase, creating abnormality in the luteal phase, such as a short luteal phase cycle.

Acupuncture, which is over 6,000 years old, has a long history of helping hormonal regulation and fertility. Current research is slowly legitimizing the positive effect acupuncture has on fertility. One such study demonstrated that both acupuncture and Clomiphene can substantially improve the luteal function; however, acupuncture can improve the endometrium and effect a lower miscarriage rate than Clomiphene can (20). This suggests that acupuncture may be superior in regulating luteal phase defects than medications, and that it may offer additional benefits in hormone production and regulation, as well as stress modulation.

Chinese herbs serve as a significant tool to improve luteal function. Chinese herbs can nourish the Qi, blood, Yin, and Yang that improve hormone levels and hypothalamic-pituitary-ovarian (HPO) axis control to improve follicular growth and better corpus luteum development. Herbs can also nourish key organs involved in supporting luteal phase and reproductive health, including the spleen, liver, and kidney. One study of fifty-three patients with luteal phase defects (LPDs) were treated with different Chinese medicinal herbs at different phases of the menstrual cycle. On the fifth day of the menstrual cycle, the treatment was implemented with the rationale of "nourishing the kidney Yin, invigorating the spleen and replenishing the Qi, promoting the blood circulation and enriching the blood," which might promote follicular development. The patients were treated for three menstrual cycles. There was significant improvement of the endometrium in the luteal phase, and prolonged basal body temperature elevation in the progestational stage, with a tendency for normalization of the wave forms and their amplitude after the treatment. In the mid-progestational stage, the levels of serum luteinizing hormone and prolactin were reduced and serum progesterone levels increased, compared with those before the treatment (21). The finding suggested that Chinese herbal medicines are capable of replenishing the Kidney Qi and Yin, and could help to regulate the hypothalamic-pituitary-ovarian axis, and thus improve the luteal function.

5. Progesterone support

Increased serum progesterone levels improve blood flow to the corpus luteum (22), which improves vascularization of the endometrial lining to support implantation of the fertilized embryo. We know that working with the body to restore natural hormone regulation improves natural progesterone production and supports the luteal phase. But what if you can't do this fast enough? Progesterone supplementation may be indicated in some women to support the luteal phase while simultaneously restoring function. Generally, a bioidentical progesterone source (in other words, a plant-based progesterone identical in chemical structure to the human form of the hormone) can be used orally, vaginally, or topically for further support of low or deficient progesterone levels due to luteal phase defects.

ESTROGEN DOMINANCE AND LIVER FUNCTION:

HOW THIS MAY BE IMPEDING YOUR FERTILITY SUCCESS & YOUR 7-STEP DETOX TOOLKIT TO CORRECT IT

Estrogen is a hormone needed to support the menstrual cycle and mature the developing follicle in the follicular phase of the menstrual cycle. It serves to build the uterine lining in the first half of your menstrual cycle and is responsible for female sex characteristics. Circulating estrogen produced in the first part of your menstrual cycle balances with progesterone, which is produced in the second, or luteal, phase of the menstrual cycle. Estrogen and progesterone are needed in a delicate balance to support the menstrual cycle and fertility. When estrogen levels become too high relative to progesterone, the balance is disrupted and estrogen dominance prevails. This is not always reflected in blood work, but is more expressed in symptoms. Common conditions related to estrogen dominance may include acne, menstrual cramps, heavy periods, premenstrual syndrome, fibroids, ovarian cysts, cysts in the breast, the liver, or other organs, polycystic ovarian syndrome (PCOS), migraine headaches, and endometriosis.

Why is there such a high prevalence of estrogen dominance? Unfortunately, we are living in a toxic environment. Toxins in our air, water, and food supply have bombarded our bodies, creating hormonal imbalance in many women, and causing havoc when it comes to creating optimal fertility. Where in our environment is estrogen coming from? A majority of estrogen dominance comes from xenoestrogens. Xenoestrogens are a type of xenohormone that imitates estrogen. They can be either synthetic or natural chemical compounds.

Complete Fertility

Xenoestrogens bind to hormone receptors, blocking true estrogen from binding to those receptors, and creating an excess of circulating estrogen in the blood stream. Xenoestrogens are not easy for the body to process, so they get stored in fatty tissue and continue to build up, causing weight gain, acne, and other estrogen dominant symptoms and conditions over time. Let's look at the sources of estrogen that can lead to an excess of estrogen in the body.

SOURCES OF ESTROGEN

- Endogenous estrogen (produced inside the body)
- Plastics and other xenoestrogen (estrogen-mimicking substances) that disrupt estrogen balance
- Meat and poultry treated with hormones leads to hormones in your food, which can create estrogen
- Pesticides, herbicides, and insecticides can promote estrogen by serving as xenoestrogens
- Oral birth control pill, which is an added source of estrogen that your body has to break down
- Genetically modified soy-based foods can act as xenoestrogen
- Household cleaning products that contain chemicals that serve as xenoestrogens
- Plastic water bottles that leach chemicals that act as xenoestrogens
- Toxins and chemicals in your drinking water that act as xenoestrogens
- Toxins and chemicals in the air you breathe that act as xenoestrogens

We are exposed to so many estrogen-mimicking substances on a daily basis that they can build up in our bodies over months and years, creating hormonal imbalance. Sound depressing? I know, it is a little depressing if you really think about it, but the good news is that there are very important steps that you can take to eliminate estrogen dominance and restore hormone balance. The answer lies in the liver. You have to support the liver detoxification pathway, so you can rid your body of toxins, xenoestrogens, and excess estrogen in order to create an optimal level of hormones (1). I can't tell you enough how important this is for your own health and a healthy pregnancy.

You see, your liver is consistently filtering everything you ingest, breathe, and absorb into your skin on a regular basis. The job of the liver is to break down things like hormones and to make things like enzymes, and to package cholesterol and other important molecules. Your liver is like a big manufacturing plant that needs to be running 24/7. The detoxification pathway is an actual biochemical pathway that is on all the time, helping to break down chemicals and hormones, and eliminate them. However, if the liver can't process chemicals and hormones fast enough, you will not eliminate them from your body. Instead, your body will store them in fatty tissue. That is why I always start my fertility patients on some sort of liver detoxification support for the first six to eight weeks before they try to conceive. There are times when I skip this step if a patient is going directly into an IVF or IUI cycle. Supporting detoxification in the liver could possibly alter the metabolism of fertility medications and affect the outcome or success. It is best to take some time to prep the body before doing IUI and IVF, if time permits. I give information to my patients and let them decide what they want to do with their bodies in the time they have.

However, I routinely encourage my patients to detox the liver prior to starting trying to conceive naturally or with Assisted Reproductive Technology (ART), when time permits. Once you are pregnant or breast feeding, you should not detox as you could expose fetal circulation and/or the baby to toxins that are harmful. Therefore, it is best to start off with detoxifying your body in the beginning of your fertility prep, so that you start the process of conception with less toxic overload, fewer hormone disrupters, and better hormone balance. Estrogen dominance becomes crucial in women with PCOS, endometriosis, ovarian cysts, and uterine fibroids. It must be addressed to help fertility. Endometriosis and fibroids may require surgical intervention, but the underlying pattern of estrogen dominance is present even after a fibroid is removed or a surgery is completed for endometriosis. Therefore, it is vital to support the detoxification pathway in the liver with these conditions prior to conceiving. So, let's learn more about the liver detoxification pathway and the role it plays specifically in your fertility.

THE LIVER DETOXIFICATION PATHWAY – WHAT IS IT AND WHY IS IT IMPORTANT?

The liver is a vital organ essential for life. The liver plays an important role in metabolism, energy storage, digestion, hormone production and detoxification. The detoxification pathway is an actual biochemical pathway in the liver. This pathway breaks down toxins, chemicals, and medications, as well as hormones. If the detoxification pathway is not working properly it will create hormone imbalance. Some of the factors that can overburden the liver detoxification pathway include: poor diet lacking in colorful vegetables and essential nutrients, excess alcohol intake, smoking, drug use, excess caffeine intake , processed food that contains preservatives and chemicals, pesticides in produce, and chemicals in cleaning supplies, makeup, skin care, and fragrance. The detoxification pathway is a continual involuntary cycle that is occurring all the time. However, if you are making hormones faster than you can break them down, a backup of hormones will result in creating estrogen dominance.

When the focus is on fertility, everyone is focused on hormone production. What is your FSH level? What is your estrogen level? These factors are important, but what about hormone breakdown on the other side of the equation? Liver detoxification is all about hormone breakdown. There needs to be a balance between both production and breakdown. It is important to understand that simply making the hormones is not enough; you must break hormones down in order for things to work efficiently and hormone balance to be possible.

In addition, the liver detoxification pathway utilizes enzymes that help break down medications, chemicals, toxins, and hormones (1). Genes direct the production of these enzymes. Some women have another complicating factor called single nucleotide polymorphism (SNP). This means they have mutations affecting the genes that direct you to make enzymes.

Meaning, the more SNPs you have related to the liver, the less enzymes you produce to support the liver detoxification pathway, making it that much harder for your body to do what it is supposed to do to break down hormones. You might be thinking that this is good because your hormone levels would then be higher. However, while this condition may lead to higher hormone levels, contributing to PCOS and other imbalanced hormone conditions, it does not benefit fertility. In fact, it hinders your fertility. Therefore, the liver must be working at an optimal level to support your fertility. How would you know if you have an SNP? Genetic testing. It is pretty easy these days to swab your cheek and send in a sample for analysis. Genetic tests looking at SNPs are widely available, fairly cost effective, and could give you vital information about how to harness your fertility.

How would you know that you might have an SNP in the liver pathway if you have not tested this? Usually, if you have estrogen dominant signs and symptoms show up early in your reproductive years, before you've had a lot of exposure to xenoestrogens that would occur over time, it's a sign that you might have an SNP. Take for example a woman who is diagnosed with PCOS at seventeen years old. She is pretty young to have had enough exposure to chemicals, toxins, and hormones for them to build up in her body. Her period started at age twelve with bad cramps, clots, heavy periods, bad PMS, and migraine headaches. Is this normal? No. She has not had enough years of exposure to cause this significant hormone imbalanced condition. It is more likely that this young woman has had estrogen dominant and dysfunctional hormone balance from the beginning, due to genetic factors or SNPs. These SNPs have affected her ability to clear hormones from her body, expediting estrogen dominance in her system. We would expect this woman to have difficulty with fertility as she ages because, if not treated, her hormone imbalances will likely become more severe with time. Depending on when she starts trying to have children, the problem could make it difficult to conceive. Supporting the liver detoxification pathway is key to reclaiming hormone balance.

The liver detoxification pathway is broken down into two phases. Phase 1 starts the breakdown of large fat-soluble molecules such as estrogen into smaller intermediate size molecule via the action of enzymes. Those intermediate molecules go through Phase 2 to be further broken down. It's like driving on freeway A and then merging onto freeway B to get to your final destination. Problems can arise when you get stuck between freeway A and B, or you never get to the end of freeway B. Intermediate molecules get stuck in the middle of Phase 1 and 2 where they are then recirculated back in the blood and get stored in fatty tissue creating more estrogen dominance along with other negative side effects.

Another thing to consider is that liver detoxification support becomes very important in preparation for taking IVF drugs. The body will be overwhelmed with medications to metabolize and if you don't breakdown hormones very well, you will further burden the body with an additional load of drugs to metabolize. If you are unsuccessful with IVF and have to do repeated cycles, hormones will build up at an accelerated rate, causing many symptoms now or in the near future. Even if you are not estrogen dominant, these medications—although they are a means to an end—may create estrogen dominance. That is why detoxifying your liver prior to IVF is a good idea.

To better understand the essential role of the liver and the two phases of the detoxification pathway, let's talk about each pathway and its job of metabolism and hormone breakdown.

PHASE 1 LIVER DETOXIFICATION

Phase 1 liver detoxification is where toxins and chemicals that are generally fat soluble and harmful are broken down into less harmful chemicals by an enzyme family called cytochrome P450. Cytochrome P450 enzymes help to neutralize substances and offer protection by converting toxic elements into less harmful substances. One of the important chemicals that use up enzymes in this phase is caffeine. So all you coffee drinkers are doing yourselves a disservice by using up valuable enzymes to break down coffee, tea, and other caffeine-related substances in Phase 1 of the detoxification pathway. In addition, alcohol will bombard this pathway and use up the enzymes in Phase 1. Each phase requires co-factors or helpers that assist with the breakdown. This usually includes necessary vitamins and minerals. For example, some of the nutrients that Phase 1 requires are folic acid, Vitamins B3, B2, B6, B12, A, C, and D3. In addition, other nutrients are needed to support and help this pathway run, such as, N-acetyl cysteine, calcium, bioflavonoids, quercetin and magnesium. If you don't have enough nutrients, you don't break the hormones down. Additionally, some people have SNP, a mutation in the enzyme systems discussed earlier in the chapter, which further hinder the breakdown of substances in this pathway. If all goes well and you do have adequate enzymes, nutrients, and co-factors to break substances down in Phase 1, then those substances move on into Phase 2 of the detoxification pathway.

LIVER DETOXIFICATION

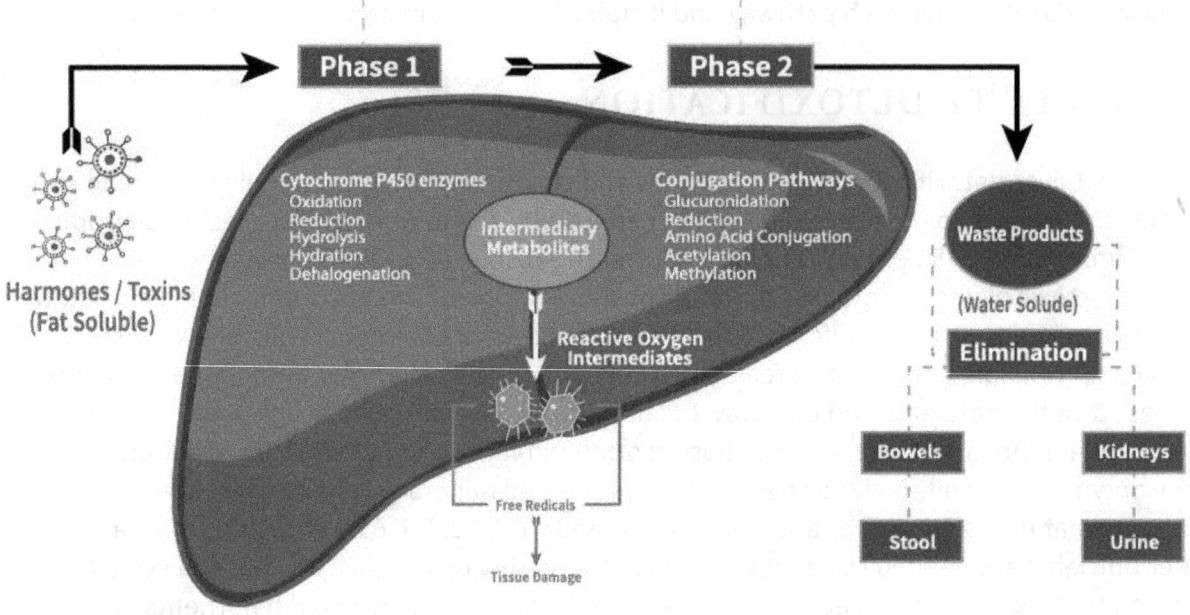

PHASE 2 LIVER DETOXIFICATION

Phase 2 detoxification provides a final breakdown and neutralization of toxins and hormones so that they can be removed from the body and either be eliminated through the bowels or through the urine. Phase 2 generally takes a fat-soluble substance and then converts it to a water-soluble substance that can then be processed through the body. Phase 2 liver detoxification consists of several processes within this phase to break down hormones and molecules. Think about Phase 2 having several off ramps off of a freeway. These off ramps include glutathione conjugation, sulfation, peptide conjugation, glucuronidation, acetylation and methylation. The problem is that if you're a chemical or hormone, you have to go to the off ramp you belong to. No tricking the body and going to a different off ramp. Sorry! The body won't break down that chemical or hormone. In fact, one of the most important off ramps of Phase 2 detoxification is the sulfation pathway (nothing to do with sulfa drug or sulfa drug allergies). This is because most hormones have to go through this specific pathway. If it's not working, you don't break down your hormones. Certain nutrients and minerals are also needed for this pathway to work efficiently. If you do not have these nutrients readily available, then you will not break down hormones.

Estrogen dominance is often addressed incorrectly. A common approach to estrogen dominant conditions such as PCOS is to take birth control to control hormone levels, add progesterone to balance out estrogen and progesterone, or give drugs like spirolactone for elevated hormones such as testosterone. All of these remedies do not fix the underlying cause of the body's ineffectiveness at breaking down excess hormones. This just creates additional hormones for the body to metabolize and puts an additional workload on the liver. The key is to support hormone breakdown, treating the root cause of the imbalance. This is not to say that medications cannot be used for symptom control concurrently with detoxifying the liver, but the underlying issue of impaired hormone breakdown needs to be addressed.

It is important not to do any detoxification while pregnant. While detoxification is important, it can create metabolites that can get into fetal circulation. Because of this, you do not detox while pregnant or breast feeding. Instead, you do prep your body before trying to conceive. I generally recommend my patients to do at least six weeks of supporting the biochemical pathways of detoxification prior to trying to conceive.

Many people think that all detox programs are alike. This is not true. Detoxification programs can contain elements for detoxifying the gastrointestinal tract, kidneys, lungs, skin, and liver. All can be helpful, but what is most vital is supporting the actual biochemical detoxification pathway of the liver to address hormone imbalances. Part of this support may contain dietary elements to clean the diet and allow less toxins into the body by avoiding and taking breaks from toxic food elements. Essential to detoxifying is having regular bowel movements so that when you do break down toxins and hormones, they can be eliminated through the bowels. If you are constipated, then you will recirculate toxic waste and hormones and store them in fatty tissue in the body. Some of the substances that support the Phase 2 detoxification pathway are calcium d-glucarate; the amino acids L-glutamine, L-lysine, glycine, carnitine, taurine; the nutrients methylsulfonylmethane (MSM) and N-acetyl cysteine; and cruciferous vegetables.

Another way of looking at the liver is from a Traditional Chinese Medicine perspective. When there is estrogen dominance, there is Qi in the liver that becomes stagnant. The liver relates to the emotion anger. So when you feel frustrated, your liver Qi is stagnant. When your liver Qi is flowing, you feel calm. When stagnant Qi builds up, it is likely that the detoxification pathway in the liver is on overload and needs support. Remember that the liver can have stagnant Qi and be over burdened with toxins, but this does not necessarily equate to any pathology or condition in the liver. Your liver test in standard bloodwork could be normal; having "normal" standard bloodwork results does not mean that your liver is not taxed or does not have stagnant Qi. The stagnant Qi, in turn, creates irritability, mood changes and hormonal symptoms like PMS, cramps and depression. Moving the liver Qi can assist with hormone balance from an energetic perspective as well as support the actual liver detoxification pathway with Chinese herbal formulas. Acupuncture is amazing at moving Qi which creates a calm and balancing effect on both mind and body.

We have established that we need to restore hormone balance in all women, especially in estrogen dominant women. Keep in mind, there are varying degrees of estrogen dominance. One woman might have started having PMS or acne more recently, whereas another woman has had a diagnosis and symptoms of PCOS for nine years, with irregular periods and elevated testosterone levels in her blood. They both have estrogen dominance, but the latter condition is a more severe version of estrogen dominance. We also have established that the liver is key to restoring hormone balance and enhancing fertility. Supporting Phases 1 and 2 of the detoxification pathway is essential to this balance. Since it can be a bit overwhelming figuring out where to start to support the liver detoxification pathway, I have created these seven simple steps to detox your way to fertility success.

7-STEP PROGRAM TO LIVER DETOXIFICATION

Step 1 – Elimination

This step is about removing toxic elements from your diet, your home, and any other sources that could be causing your liver to be overwhelmed with toxins and hormones, or causing your liver Qi to be stagnated due to frustration and irritations in your daily life.

- Avoid toxins, pesticides, and insecticides by eating organic food
- Avoid excess hormones by eating hormone-free meat, poultry, and eggs
- Avoid toxins in household products by buying natural and chemical-free cleaners and household goods
- Avoid solvents, which are chemicals that are used in the yard, in painting, and in some lines of work (e.g. chemical engineering, or aviation maintenance)
- Avoid toxic people and situations that create frustration and anger. Eliminate that which no longer serves you—any draining friendships, the job you hate, and unwelcome obligations—and replace them with people and things that support you.
- Avoid additives that are commonly in processed foods
- Avoid alcohol
- Avoid caffeine

Step 2 – Regulation

Step two is to regulate your bowel movements and eliminate constipation. Even if you do a successful liver detox program but are habitually constipated, you will not eliminate excess hormones and toxins from your body. Instead, you will recirculate them back into the body and will be back at square one with more toxicity. Not only do regular bowel movements help eliminate toxins, but increasing the fiber in your diet will help bind excess hormones and aid in your elimination. How do you do this?

- Increase soluble fiber such as oatmeal, applesauce, and prunes to add moisture to the stool and help support regular bowel movements
- Take digestive enzymes to aid digestion and help relieve constipation
- Increase water intake and exercise
- Take a probiotic to increase healthy gut microbiome
- Eat whole foods and avoid processed foods

Step 3 – Vital Nutrient Support

This is probably the MOST important step. Supporting Phases 1 and 2 of the biochemical detoxification pathway is vital to getting rid of excess hormones and toxins. The enzymatic biochemical reactions in Phase 1 change toxins like pesticides, medications, and hormones into small water-soluble molecules. While Phase 2 changes Phase 1 metabolites into more protective compounds such as in glucuronides, glutathione, sulfonates, and amino acids through its chemical pathways, making them less harmful and easier to eliminate. Getting metabolites stuck between Phases 1 and 2 can leave more toxic compounds circulating in your system; unable to get eliminated, they can be stored in fatty tissue leading to more estrogen dominance. Providing your body with vitamins and nutrient support to help it process waste completely, so that the waste can be eliminated, is vital to your health and fertility.

You need comprehensive support for both phases of the liver detoxificaiton. Would you prepare for half of a presentation for work or school? No, you would study all the material, so that you are fully and completely prepared. The liver needs complete support as well to function optimally. Here is a list that breaks down the individual nutrients needed in each phase of liver detoxification.

Phase 1
- Vitamins B2, B3, B6, B12, D, A, E, and C
- Folic acid
- Calcium
- N-acetyl cysteine
- Quercetin
- Citrus bioflavinoids
- CoQ10
- Minerals: selenium, calcium, zinc, manganese, copper, and molybdenum
- Green tea
- Glutathione
- Milk thistle

Phase 2
- Garlic
- Glycine
- Glutathione
- N-acetyl cysteine (NAC)
- Taurine
- High-quality protein
- Folic acid
- Vitamin B complex
- Magnesium
- Manganese
- Molybdenum
- Selenium
- Sulphur containing compounds such as MSM, garlic, onions, broccoli, cabbage, Brussels sprouts, cauliflower, leaks, and shallots
- Zinc
- Cruciferous vegetables like cauliflower, cabbage, kale, garden cress, bok choy, broccoli, Brussels sprouts, radish, etc.
- Amino Acids: L-lysine HCL, glycine, taurine, L-carnitine, L-glutamine
- Calcium-D-glucarate
- Ornithine aspartate
- Artichoke
- Curcumin
- Wasabi

It is important to support both Phases 1 and 2 of the liver detoxification pathway to completely break down and eliminate hormones and toxins. There are many products on the market that use a combination of Phase 1 and Phase 2 liver detoxification factors to support the liver. These nutrients are effective in detoxifying the liver and restoring both hormone balance and your fertility.

Step 4 – Diet Fit for a Liver

A diet free from hormones, pesticides, and herbicides are important to reduce estrogen dominance (2). In fact, an article in the Journal of American Medical Association of Internal Medicine, published a study showing that higher consumption of fruits and vegetables with high-pesticide residue were associated with lower probabilities of pregnancy and live birth following infertility treatment with assisted reproductive technology (ART) (3). The data suggested that dietary pesticide exposure within the range of typical and routine human consumption may be associated with adverse reproductive consequences—in other words, infertility. We know this because these chemicals act like xenoestrogen, mimicking estrogen and causing hormonal imbalance that negatively affects your ability to get pregnant. So you need a diet that can keep you healthy and minimize your exposure to additional toxins, hormones, and pesticides. Follow these dietary guidelines to optimize your fertility.

- Avoid hydrogenated oils that can increase inflammation in the body.
- Avoid refined sugar that provides empty calories and depresses your immune system.
- Avoid convenience, packaged, and fast-foods laced with chemicals, additives, and hormones.
- Avoid nitrates and nitrites, commonly found in hot dogs and lunch meats.
- Avoid genetically modified foods.
- Roast your own organic chicken and turkey breast to replace deli meats.
- Add fresh green leafy vegetables to all your meals.
- Replace processed snacks with fresh organic fruit, carrot sticks, or granola.
- Eat gluten-free and dairy free to eliminate inflammation.
- Avoid the Dirty Dozen (4), which are conventionally grown foods with the highest pesticide residues. In descending order from highest residue, these are: strawberries, spinach, nectarines, apples, grapes, peaches, cherries, pears, tomatoes, celery, potatoes, and sweet bell peppers.
- Include the "Clean Fifteen," which tend to have the lowest pesticide residues. These include avocados, sweet corn, pineapples, cabbages, onions, frozen sweet peas, papayas, asparagus, mangoes, eggplants, honeydews, kiwis, cantaloupes, cauliflower, and broccoli.
- Add liver supportive foods to your diet. Add artichoke to dishes and salads. Eat beets as a side dish or snack, or add them to salad. Enhance your salad by adding dandelion greens, eat plenty of organic spinach, add garlic and onions to your dishes, and use turmeric, ginger, cardamom seed, and curry to spice your food.

Step 5 – Juicing

There is a reason you hear so much about juicing in the media, and why the stars talk about juicing as a tool for anti-aging, radiant skin, and detoxing. Juicing is an excellent and effective way to provide available nutrients needed in both Phase 1 and Phase 2 of the detoxification pathway. It can help to provide the co-factors, or helpers, for this pathway to run more effectively. This, in turn, helps to break down toxins and hormones. When it comes to juicing, I generally recommend applying the 60/40 rule. That is at least sixty percent vegetables to forty percent or less of fruits. This way, you are getting more of the dark green vegetables like kale, parsley, and spinach relative to sugary fruit juice from carrot and apple. If you have issues with digestion or dysbiosis (an imbalance of bacteria in your digestive tract, affecting the gut microbiome) you are more apt not to absorb nutrients from your food as readily. Juicing provides available vitamins and minerals in a way that is easier for your body to absorb. Using organic fruits and vegetables ensures not over-taxing the body with more pesticides and herbicides. There are so many juice combinations for detox. The sky is the limit. Listed below are two of Dr. Oz's Ingredient lists for juices that are perfect for aiding the body in detoxing. Visit the links in the references section at the back of the book for more specific   directions on how make these nutrient dense ingredients into a great tasting juice. Add these or other combinations of ingredients for the perfect juicing recipes for supporting detoxification. Add this to your daily routine.

Dr. Oz's Green Juice Ingredient List (5)
- Spinach
- Cucumber
- Celery
- Parsley
- Mint
- Carrot
- Apple
- Orange
- Lime
- Lemon
- Pineapple

Dr. Oz's Kale, Pineapple and Ginger Detox, Drink Ingredient List (6)
- Pineapple
- Cucumber
- Kale without stems
- Lemon, squeezed
- Ginger
- Mint

Step 6 – Castor Oil packs

Castor oil is obtained from the seeds of the castor plant (Ricinus communis). The oil has been used for therapeutic purposes since ancient times, both orally and topically. A castor oil pack refers to a topical application of castor oil over the liver, in the upper right portion of the abdomen. This should not be used in pregnancy, or if you think you are pregnant. This is a tool for prior to conception. If you are unsure if you are pregnant, then do not use castor oil packs from ovulation until you get your period, or in the follicular phase of your cycle. The fatty acid structure of castor oil is absorbed into the skin and into the lymphatic circulation, which stimulates the flow of lymph and aids in cleansing the body. Along with lymph supporting qualities, castor oil has mild analgesic (pain relieving) and anti-inflammatory properties. We believe castor oil packs can aid in liver detoxification because they are thought to cause mechanical contraction of the liver (where bile is made, which binds other fats) and possibly gallbladder (where bile is stored), releasing fatty acids to bind toxins and help to move and process toxins so that they can be eliminated in the bowels. In addition, castor oil moves the

Qi of the liver, reducing stagnant Qi and reducing irritability. Castor oil packs provide a gentle way to support liver function. It is best to use organic castor oil that is cold pressed and free of preservatives and additives. The castor oil is applied to a wool flannel sheet about twelve-inches by ten-inches and placed over the liver, in the upper-right abdomen. A heat source like a hot water bottle or warm rice bag can be placed over the area to simulate movement of Qi in the liver and aid in its ability to help bind toxins. Castor oil covered by a piece of cloth should be kept on the skin for anywhere from thirty to sixty minutes. Be careful because castor oil can stain your clothes, so the wool flannel sheet should be cleaned separately from other clothes. Don't use castor oil on open cuts or infections. Consult with your doctor before using castor oil packs to make sure it is safe for you to use.

Step 7 – Lifestyles of the Wealthy and Healthy

This step is about creating prosperity of health. How do you look at wealth? I guess some would say health is everything. If you are wealthy in health, then anything is possible. Health is your basic denominator to success in every aspect of your life. This, of course, includes fertility. How can you become wealthier in health? Follow these suggestions.

- Regular exercise helps increase circulation and blood flow, delivers oxygen to cells, and increases sweating to aid in the elimination of toxins.
- Sweating through exercise or with the help of an infra-red, dry, or wet sauna can help to eliminate toxins from the body.
- Adequate sleep and rest will help all of your biochemical processes to work more efficiently.
- Increase water intake to stay hydrated, which will help flush and eliminate toxins from the body.
- Deep breathing through yoga or mediation can aid in releasing waste products. Lungs are an organ of elimination and aid in detoxifying your body.
- Dry skin brushing is a process of taking a brush with natural bristles and brushing your feet up to your torso and your arms down to your torso, or center. This should be done before you shower to move lymph and encourage sweating in order to aid in detoxifying your body.

Now you have a 7-Step Detox Toolkit to give your body what it needs to work naturally. The detoxification pathway is always on, no matter what you do or don't do. So it is better to eat healthy and support this pathway, allowing it to do its job more efficiently and, in turn, create better hormone balance and improve your fertility. The side effect is reducing toxins in the body and feeling and looking your best.

PCOS AFFECTS APPROXIMATELY FIVE TO TWENTY PERCENT OF REPRODUCTIVE AGE WOMEN.

PCOS IMPACTS FERTILITY:

HOW TO IDENTIFY IF YOU HAVE IT AND HOW TO IMPROVE YOUR FERTILITY SUCCESS

Polycystic ovarian syndrome, or PCOS, is a common female disorder that directly impairs fertility. PCOS affects approximately five to twenty percent of reproductive age women (1). There are several important characteristics of PCOS that affect fertility. First, PCOS is associated with women who have ovaries that produce multiple follicles at the same time, which elicits an increased production of estrogen along with other hormones. PCOS is considered an estrogen dominant condition. Not only does PCOS increase ovarian function in a hyperactive way, it can also impair adrenal function and increase levels of hormones like prolactin and other androgens, such as testosterone and DHEA. These imbalances disrupt the menstrual cycle and often block the body's ability to ovulate. PCOS tends to cause increased body weight and fat composition, and is associated with insulin resistance, prediabetes, and/or increased risk of diabetes and elevated blood sugar. Insulin is a hormone that is needed to transport sugar from the blood to the cells of our body to feed and nourish them with glucose, a type of sugar. Insulin resistance is a condition where the insulin is not working properly, causing elevated blood sugar levels. Insulin resistance is a common feature of PCOS and the reason why one key feature of treatment is the management of insulin resistance. Having elevated blood sugar levels over time has a myriad of negative consequences. Insulin resistance disrupts your ability for healthy hormone cycles, which negatively affects fertility. PCOS results in neuroendocrine dysfunction and hormone imbalance. This hormone disruption can stop follicle development and maturation of the egg, preventing ovulation, making it almost impossible to conceive, and crushing your baby dreams.

PCOS is said to have only ten percent heritability (1). However, PCOS belongs to a category of estrogen dominant conditions. I would say that if you look at the broader aspect of estrogen dominant conditions, you will see a familial trend from grandmother, to mother, to daughter. If we look at estrogen dominance conditions including PCOS, endometriosis, acne, PMS, ovarian cysts, fibroids, and dysmenorrhea, they all fit within the collective basket of estrogen dominant conditions. Clinically, you will see this type of condition in families passed on from generation to generation. Maybe your mother didn't have PCOS, but she had uterine fibroids. Maybe your sister has migraine headaches and acne, but you have PCOS. Estrogen dominance can manifest in many different ways, and that depends on each individual's genetic makeup, propensities, lifestyle, and additional known and unknown factors. This is most likely the work of genetic mutations that affect hormone breakdown in the liver and proper hormone metabolism. If you happen to manifest PCOS as one distinct estrogen dominant condition, then it can definitely create a barrier to your fertility success. Although there are many manifestations of estrogen dominant conditions with many integrative interventions, PCOS is most commonly linked to infertility. Understanding and addressing PCOS in a comprehensive and integrative manner will yield the best results when it comes to your fertility.

WHAT CAUSES PCOS?

Like I have stated, one factor of developing PCOS is estrogen dominance, which can be caused by environmental factors in addition to having something to do with genetic mutations called a single nucleotide polymorphism (SNP) pronounced "snip" in the liver (where hormone breakdown occurs). Having a SNP affects your ability to break down excess hormones creating an estrogen dominant environment in your body, which can manifest as PCOS. Studies show that PCOS has genetic origins and there may be multifactorial causes for developing this disorder. It has also been associated with inflammatory conditions, abnormal steroid regulation, and is thought to be associated with autoimmune diseases. PCOS is not only well documented to be a cause of infertility in women of reproductive age due to blocking ovulation, it also increases risk for cardiovascular disease and type II diabetes in women (2). Research has looked at women who have Hashimoto's thyroiditis (HT), an autoimmune condition where the body attacks its own thyroid, and found that they have some genetic links to women with PCOS. Studies like this indicate that there may be some common factors between autoimmune regulation and PCOS. There are several genes that play a role in their connection with fertility problems. Research studies have identified three genetic polymorphisms that might play a role in PCOS as well as in HT. They are polymorphism of the gene for fibrillin 3 (FBN3), regulating the activity of transforming growth factor-b (TGF-b) and regulatory T cell levels; gonadotropin-releasing hormone receptor (GnRHR) polymorphism; and CYP1B1 polymorphism standing for estradiol hydroxylation. High estrogen-to-progesterone ratios owing to anovulatory cycles (menstrual cycles during which ovulation does not occur), as well as high estrogen levels during prenatal life, disrupt development of the thymus and its function in maintaining immune tolerance, and are suspected to enhance autoimmune response in PCOS (1). Vitamin D may also be connected with development of Hashimoto's and PCOS (1).

COMMON SYMPTOMS OF PCOS

- Lack of a menstrual cycle, short or irregular menstrual cycle
- Presence of ovarian cysts
- Oily skin
- Hair loss
- Insulin resistance
- Obesity
- Acne
- Increased body or facial hair
- Elevated androgens (especially, high testosterone)
- Hair loss or abnormal hair growth (hirsutism)
- Infertility
- Mood Swings

CONVENTIONAL TREATMENT OF PCOS

Conventional treatment of PCOS can include diet, exercise, weight management, birth control bills, hormone therapy, and administration of Metformin, an oral hypoglycemic medication to reduce insulin resistance and blood sugar. One drug that is used frequently by OBs and GYNs to induce ovulation is Femara, or the generic letrozole, which is an aromatase inhibitor. Clomid, another common drug used to induce ovulation, is a selective estrogen receptor modulator and has many more side effects. It is still used, but Femara is the drug of choice to induce ovulation in women with PCOS. According to conventional approaches and studies that look at Femara to treat anovulating women, Femara is the most effective treatment and targets the hypothalamic-pituitary-ovarian (HPO) axis to induce ovulation (3). Other conventional interventions for PCOS include synthetic FSH and LH medications, IVF and laparoscopic ovarian diathermy. Laparoscopic ovarian diathermy, or drilling, is a surgical treatment that can trigger ovulation in women who have PCOS. During this procedure, (a laser is used to destroy parts of the ovaries in a process called electrocautery. This surgery is not commonly used, as there are less invasive options to treat PCOS. Let's look at conventional treatment protocols used to induce ovulation in women with PCOS.

CONVENTIONAL PROTOCOLS TO INDUCE OVULATION IN WOMEN WITH PCOS

A recent study conducted in part by Professor Adam Balen, a world-renowned expert in reproductive medicine and surgery, explains the conventional protocols used to induce ovulation in women with PCOS (64). The study notes that, in conventional diagnosis and treatment of PCOS where ovulation is not detected, lifestyle changes and weight loss will be considered first. If ovulation occurs after these changes are made, but the patient does not become pregnant for six to nine cycles, then IVF is recommended.

If no ovulation is detected after lifestyle changes and weight loss, then clomiphene citrate (CC) or Letrozole is used to induce ovulation. If that works to induce ovulation, but no pregnancy occurs for six to nine cycles, then IVF is recommended.

If no ovulation is detected after the use of CC or Letrozole, then several drugs may be used to induce ovulation, including gonadotropins or CC with metformin. Laparoscopic ovarian diathermy might also be considered. If these methods induce ovulation, but the patient does not become pregnancy within six cycles, IVF is recommended.

If no ovulation is detected after those treatments, then doctors may recommend IVF gonadotropin releasing hormone (GnRH) antagonist protocol, which would be a more aggressive drug treatment approach than previously described medications with IVF. This approach may or may not work. If it does not, then IVF may not be a viable option for conception.

Conventional approaches to treating PCOS can sometimes be successful. However, successive cycles using Femara, Clomid, or other drugs to induce ovulation can quickly deplete the Qi needed for natural conception, according to Chinese medicine. The woman becomes more deficient with conventional drugs and needs more support to build her system back up after unsuccessful cycles to conceive naturally and/or to have future successful IUI and IVF cycles. This is where you have to weigh the pros and cons of using conventional medications alone, integrative approaches alone, or a combination. The good news is there are many proven integrative tools to treating PCOS and induce ovulation so that natural conception can occur. Let's look at what natural interventions can help improve your chances to conceive if you have PCOS.

PCOS INTEGRATIVE TREATMENTS AND YOUR BABY DREAMS

Many women who have PCOS assume that they are never going to have a baby. Not true! PCOS and conventional approaches may be helpful, but there are a multitude of integrative support options that are just waiting to create balance in your body and help realize your baby dreams.

It is really important to have additional tools not only to address the symptoms of PCOS and maximize your ability to conceive, but also—and more critically, to restore normal hormone balance and menstrual regulation. How can you maneuver through PCOS to create the best chance at conception? Let's talk about the tools that you have to regain control of your fertility.

THE IMPORTANCE OF IDEAL BODY WEIGHT ON SYMPTOMS OF PCOS

According to the Centers for Disease Control and Prevention, weight that is higher than what is considered healthy for a given height is described as overweight or obese. Body Mass Index, or BMI, is used as a screening tool for obesity. The National Institutes of Health (NIH) defines being overweight as a BMI of 25–29.9 and being obese as a BMI of 30 or greater. Your BMI can be calculated by taking your weight in kilograms and dividing it by the square of your height in meters (4–6). Plugging in your height and current weight in a BMI chart is also an easy way to figure out your BMI number.

Why does being overweight matter when it comes to PCOS? Being overweight or obese disrupts the hypothalamic-pituitary-ovarian axis, which basically means that you have menstrual dysfunction, abnormal and irregular periods, lack of ovulation and inability to get pregnant. Hormone disorders and subfertility are common in PCOS. PCOS is commonly associated with insulin resistance, which contributes to obesity. It is a viscous cycle. Your weight leads to insulin resistance, which leads to gaining more weight, which leads to more impaired hormone dysregulation. In addition, obesity increases your risk for developing diabetes, a metabolic syndrome that affects blood sugar, and cardiovascular disease (7).

When it comes to fertility, extra weight and obesity may disrupt implantation of the embryo and other reproductive functions, resulting in delayed conception, increased miscarriage rates, and reduced pregnancy rates (8, 9). The good news is that weight loss programs with exercise and diet modifications have proven to restore menstrual cycles and ovulation to improve the likelihood of getting pregnant in women with PCOS. Even just a five percent reduction in weight can improve insulin resistance, reduce androgens like testosterone, and improve reproductive function (10). In addition, healthy diet and lifestyle habits generally reduce insulin resistance as well to improve fertility. Research shows that adopting a diet with low glycemic foods for three months combined with regular physical activity has reduced body weight and increased fertility in women with PCOS. I have treated many patients with PCOS who are taking the right supplements and getting the right nutrients, but are still not conceiving until they lose weight. If you have PCOS, weight loss is essential to restore hormone balance. Your weight does not define you, and it may not be a true reflection of your health, but when it comes to fertility and PCOS, weight does matter. With PCOS, you have a disorder that is affecting blood sugar and hormones, so weight loss is a vital component to your ability to conceive. Plant-based anti-inflammatory diets are an important tool to help get control of blood sugar and weight for women with PCOS. Cutting out sugar, simple carbs, process foods, and eating only lean and hormone-free protein sources helps, but a plant-based diet abundant in vegetables and fruits becomes pivotal in women with PCOS. Diet and exercise can help you achieve your ideal BMI and dramatically improve your fertility. This is a must and cannot be overlooked if you suffer from PCOS and have been struggling to conceive. If you need a more structured plan for weight loss, then you can follow a weight loss program that can assist you with monitoring and motivating you to achieve your goal and remove weight-related roadblocks to successful conception.

LIFESTYLE FACTORS

Let's face it, stress adds another layer that works against your physiology. Stress leads to increased cortisol, which leads to insulin resistance and hormone imbalance. We can't escape stress, as it is deeply rooted in our society and possibly more inherent in women, who act as the caretakers of many households. Women are exposed to psychological, physical, and physiological stressors that affect them daily. We live in a stressful world with the demands of family, work, financial responsibilities, commitments, relationships, and friendships. Being in the primary role of caretaker combined with struggling with fertility can be a little overwhelming at times, and— let's face it—stressful!

How does stress really affect our bodies? Stress raises cortisol and blood sugar levels, disrupts menstruation, and impacts reproductive health by inducing the generation of reactive oxygen species. These free radicals lead to oxidative stress that may affect the function of the ovary and the quality of your eggs, as well as cause female reproductive health disorders (11). So what can we do to reduce stress? Having a stress reduction plan can help manage stress in your life. This could include exercise, meditation, prayer, or arts like painting, journaling, and writing.

Anything that creates a sense of well-being and calmness can help. One research study looked at women with PCOS who practiced yoga. It found that yoga was efficient at bringing beneficial changes in polycystic ovarian morphology, meaning that the appearance of the ovaries was more normal after doing yoga (12). We don't necessarily need studies to know that reducing stress helps our bodies, but it is nice to know that research can prove there is a correlation. Other stress-reducing activities could include exercise (walking, biking, swimming, running, using an elliptical machine, tai qi, qi gong, etc.), talking to someone you trust (a counselor, support group, or close friend(s)), and spiritual and mindfulness activities like prayer, meditation, or deep breathing exercises.

Take ten minutes per day to meditate, breathe deeply, or do something else that calms your system and brings tranquility into your being. Writing down stress management strategies into your weekly calendar and creating the space for these activities is an important part of healthy living and creating a supportive environment, both in body and mind, so that you can be ready for conception.

LIVER DETOXIFICATION IS A KEY COMPONENT TO IMPROVING HORMONE BALANCE IN WOMEN WITH PCOS

We have established that PCOS is an estrogen dominant condition. Estrogen dominant conditions such as acne, menstrual cramps, heavy periods, premenstrual syndrome, fibroids, ovarian cysts, cysts in the breast, cysts in other organs, migraine headaches, endometriosis, and PCOS can benefit from addressing the common denomination—estrogen dominance. Each estrogen dominant condition has its own pathology and treatment approaches that can be determined by you and your doctor, but when we look at those conditions, there is an inherent issue with hormone breakdown. We know that PCOS causes excess hormone production, so we need to aid the body in breaking down those hormones as fast as we can. It's really important to regain this function, and one of the best ways you can do this is to support the liver detoxification pathway. How do we do this? Refer to the discussion on liver detoxification in the previous chapter for specific tools to help you take back your fertility.

THE IMPORTANCE OF ADDRESSING INSULIN RESISTANCE IN WOMEN WITH PCOS

One of the key elements of PCOS is insulin resistance. This leads to high cortisol levels negatively affecting hormones. Attaining normal blood sugar levels and reducing insulin resistance is essential in getting pregnant if you have PCOS. High blood sugar can disrupt endocrine hormonal regulation, which affects hormone balance. Metformin is a common oral hypoglycemic medication used in the treatment of polycystic ovarian syndrome to lower blood sugars in women with insulin resistance associated with PCOS.

Metformin

Metformin has some proven positive effects on insulin resistance by decreasing blood sugar and decreasing body weight. It also has been shown to improve menstrual patterns and to result in a significant decrease in luteinizing hormone androgens like testosterone (13). Although metformin can be helpful to women with PCOS, its common side effects include gastrointestinal upset, diarrhea, stomach pain, and nausea. In addition, studies show that metformin, over the course of six months of use, depletes vitamin B12 levels and increases homocysteine levels. Vitamin B12 is necessary for adrenal function in hormone balance, while increased homocysteine levels associated with low B12 increases cardiovascular risk (14). There are effective alternatives to metformin including: losing weight to reduce insulin resistance, and administration of myoinositol, berberine, bitter melon, and more. Of these options, myoinositol has been the most widely studied nutrient for blood sugar control in women with PCOS.

NUTRIENTS CAN HELP INCREASE FERTILITY IN WOMEN WITH PCOS

Vitamins, minerals, and other nutrients can act more like medicines, especially when it comes to PCOS. Supporting the body with the proper nutrients can support hormone balance and function, improve blood sugar, and help fertility. Research indicates there are viable nutrient interventions to help manage PCOS symptoms in a natural way to restore balance in the body. Let's look at nutrients that have been studied and shown to be beneficial in the regulation of hormones and insulin resistance in the treatment of PCOS. Keep in mind, there might be additional nutrients that may be beneficial in the treatment of PCOS.

Myoinositol

Inositol is a vitamin-like substance that is part of the B vitamin family. It is used to help the proper utilization of the hormone insulin which affects blood sugar. The two most common forms of inositol are myoinositol and D-chiro-inositol. Most of the research on the use of inositol with patients with PCOS is focused on myoinositol. Myoinositol helps to promote the proper utilization of insulin, which in turn supports healthy blood sugar, hormone balance, ovarian function, and menstrual cycle regularity.

What do we know about using myoinositol to help fertility? Treatment with myoinositol has been proven to a be a treatment option for patients with PCOS and infertility. Pregnancy rates after treatment are equivalent or even superior to those reported for women using metformin as an insulin sensitizer (15). Studies using 4000 mg of myoinositol per day in women with PCOS leads to better fertilization rates and a clear trend to better embryo quality without the moderate to severe side effects of metformin (15). The oocytes in this study showed the ovaries were smaller (meaning they were not enlarged due to multiple cysts) with myoinositol compared to Metformin . Since ovarian hyperstimulation syndrome is a risk for IVF, myoinositol can be used to reduce associated risk inherent with IVF (16). In addition, women using myoinositol showed an increased number of eggs with IVF (17). Myoinositol therapy in women with PCOS results in better fertilization rates and a clear trend to better embryo quality (18). In addition, myoinositol administration increases clinical pregnancy rates, lowers total FSH dose and the duration of the ovulation induction (19). Myoinositol also has been shown to increase pregnancy rates in women undergoing ovulation induction for ICSI or IVF-ET and studies indicate that it may improve the quality of embryos and reduce the number of poor-quality eggs (20). Recently, studies on inositol supplementation during in vitro fertilization programs (IVF) have gained particular importance due to the effect of this molecule on reducing insulin resistance, thereby improving ovarian function, egg quality, and embryo and pregnancy rates (21). Therefore, myoinositol should be considered as an alternative to Metformin in women with insulin resistance and PCOS.

Myoinositol, L-methyl Folate, and Gymnemic Acid

A comparison study was done supplementing a combination of L-methyl folate with myoinositol compared to the trifecta effect of combining L-methyl folate, myoinositol, and gymnemic acid. This trifecta combination showed an antidiabetic effect of lowering blood sugar and had an anti-inflammatory effect as well. L-methyl folate, myoinositol, and gymnemic acid together increased peripheral sensitivity to insulin. The combination had a greater effect after six months of supplementation, showing a more significant reduction in BMI and testosterone levels, as well as improved menstrual regularity than just using L-methyl folate and myoinositol alone (22).

Myoinositol and Alpha Lipoic Acid

We already know that myoinositol can be used as an alternative to metformin in helping to reduce insulin resistance and improve fertility. Alpha lipoic acid is a water-and-fat soluble nutrient that acts as an antioxidant. It plays a role in energy metabolism and healthy blood sugar control, and supports nerve health due to its role in the nitric oxide cycle. In patients with PCOS, studies show that combining alpha lipoic acid with myoinositol for six months helped to increase the number of menstrual cycles and number of eggs, reduce DHEA levels and other androgens, reduce androstenedione, decrease BMI, decrease AMH, decrease ovarian volume, decrease total antral follicle count, restore menstrual patterns, and improve hormone balance (23). This action of alpha lipoic acid may be due to its support of the detoxification pathway, which assists the breakdown of excess hormones related to PCOS to restore normal hormone balance.

Berberine

Another nutrient called berberine, a plant-based supplement used to lower blood sugar, has been shown to improve some of the metabolic and hormonal parameters in women with PCOS (24). Proper supplementation, a healthy diet that is high in fiber and protein but low in simple carbohydrates and processed foods, along with exercise, can help lower blood sugar and reduce androgens like testosterone to restore ovulation. The potential benefits of berberine supplementation should not be overlooked in women with PCOS.

Vitamins and Minerals

We cannot underestimate the role that vitamins and minerals have on the body's normal metabolic functions. It makes sense that some nutrients play a larger role than others. Although there may not be research on every nutrient and its relationship to PCOS, some studies suggest that the effects of nutrients are important. One such study looked at magnesium, zinc, calcium and vitamin D co-supplementations for twelve weeks among women with PCOS. It showed beneficial effects on insulin metabolism and markers of cardio-metabolic risk by reducing triglycerides, VLDL cholesterol, total cholesterol, and the ratio of total cholesterol to HDL cholesterol (25). This goes to prove that a healthy diet with proper nutrients as supplements can benefit your baby dreams.

Vitamin D

Vitamin D is a fat-soluble vitamin that is involved in many body functions, including: immune regulation, anti-inflammation, autoimmunity, cancer prevention, and healthy DNA. For example, deficiency of vitamin D may be linked to certain types of cancer and damage to DNA (26).

Animal and human studies suggest that vitamin D is also involved in many functions of the reproductive system in both men and women (27). Having low levels of active vitamin D3 in the blood, called 25-hydroxy-vitamin D (25OHD), is associated with PCOS (28). Vitamin D deficiency may also be linked to the endometriosis immune and anti-inflammatory effects (31) and associated with early pregnancy loss (32). Supplementation with vitamin D in women who are vitamin D deficient improves fasting blood sugar, visceral (organ) fat or adipose tissue, and adiponectin (a protein suggested to play a role in insulin resistance). It also increases serum vitamin D levels (30).

One study looking at vitamin D supplementation of insulin-resistant patients with PCOS showed that taking 4000 iu per day for twelve weeks had a beneficial effect on total testosterone, free androgens, serum CRP high sensitivity (or CRPhs, which is related to heart disease), and total antioxidant capacity, compared to patients taking a lower dose of 1000 iu per day (30). A study that considered other studies on vitamin D supplementation showed that vitamin D is associated with a reduction in total testosterone, but not free testosterone (30, 34). Free testosterone is associated with available testosterone the body can utilize, whereas total testosterone is a measure of free plus bound testosterone. In PCOS, free testosterone is generally elevated and total testosterone may be elevated. Based on this study, supplementing with vitamin D may help lower total testosterone levels, which is a benefit in women with PCOS.

Moderate weight loss can increase vitamin D levels and is correlated with a beneficial effect on insulin sensitivity (35). Taking vitamin D3 with omega-3 fatty acid from fish oil has a beneficial effect on total testosterone, CRPhs, inflammation, and antioxidant activity in women with PCOS (36).

So it is important to get testing before you conceive to see if you are deficient in vitamin D3, and to take the right amount of supplementation if you are. This will help your PCOS symptoms and pattern, to help create more hormonal balance. If you live in a sunny climate, you might think that you are making plenty of vitamin D, but that may not be the case. It's best to get your vitamin D and 25-hydroxy-vitamin D (25OHD) levels checked with bloodwork, and supplement vitamin D3 according to your lab results, thereby improving symptoms and/or patterns associated with PCOS.

Quercetin

Quercetin is a polyphenolic compound that is a pigment or flavonoid found in plants. Animal studies suggest that quercetin causes a reduction in insulin resistance and reduces a gene expression that relates to glucose transport and blood sugar (36). Quercetin has also been shown to suppress genes that promote inflammation, thereby reducing inflammation in ovarian tissue in women with PCOS (37). Quercetin not only addresses insulin resistance, but also decreases testosterone and LH concentration in overweight and obese women with PCOS (39). Quercetin supplementation can be beneficial in helping women with PCOS, and since it is a relatively benign plant compound, it can be considered a safe alternative to other medications for blood sugar control. How does quercetin help blood sugar? Studies show that quercetin upregulates the expression of adiponectin receptions which regulate glucose and fatty acid metabolism by activating AMP- activated protein kinase (AMPK). So basically, quercetin affects the receptors that regulate blood sugar and fat metabolism associated with PCOS (39). Another study confirmed that quercetin has the potential to alleviate hormonal and metabolic disturbances occurring in PCOS and found that its effects were moderately parallel to Metformin (40). For women who cannot tolerate Metformin, quercetin provides another great alternative to manage symptoms of PCOS and help fertility.

Chromium

Research studies have shown that chromium supplementation seems to have a positive effect on BMI and free testosterone concentration in the blood (41). It doesn't seem to help total testosterone or DHEA, but a study looking at an overview of multiple studies on chromium suggests that it has a beneficial effect on decreasing body weight, helping to improve fasting insulin, and lowering free testosterone in PCOS patients (41).

Cinnamon

Cinnamon is not just a delicious spice; it has therapeutic properties for women with PCOS. Studies show that cinnamon can be used as a supplement to reduce blood glucose and insulin, cholesterol, and triglycerides in women with PCOS (42). In Chinese medicine, cinnamon also can expel pathogens (viruses) by mobilizing the body's own immune response, aid weak digestion by warming digestive function to help process food, and help in removing painful obstructions in the body to treat painful menstruation.

CoQ10

The nutrient coenzyme Q10, or CoQ10, which studies show can improve egg quality, can also be used to reduce inflammation in the body. Inflammation is related to immune regulation. In fact, in one study, women given CoQ10 supplementation of 100 mg daily for twelve weeks reduced inflammatory and immune markers in their blood (43), showing a positive effect of

CoQ10 on immune regulation. This nutrient becomes pivotal, since it improves egg quality and provides support for women who are affected by the 40% of unexplained infertility that is thought to be related to immune dysfunction.

Probiotics

Probiotics regulate immune function and help to support a healthy gastrointestinal tract. We think of probiotics in relation to healthy elimination, but probiotics also have beneficial effects on fertility for both men and women. Taking probiotics can reduce DNA fragmentation in men as well as help women who have PCOS. Studies have shown that probiotic supplementation for eight to twelve weeks in PCOS patients resulted in lowered fasting blood insulin, triglycerides (44, 45), and VLDL cholesterol (46). Additionally, probiotics given with selenium lowered total testosterone levels, elevated mood, and reduced hirsutism (excessive hair growth) (47).

Omega-3 Fatty Acids with Vitamin E

There are three main omega-3 fatty acids. Alpha-linolenic acid (ALA) is found mainly in plant oils such as flaxseed, soybean, and canola oils. Eicosapentaenoic acid (EPA) and docosahexaenoic acid (DHA) are found in fish and other seafood. Research studies show that giving omega-3 fatty acids combined with vitamin E supplementation helped reduce depression, anxiety, and inflammation in women with PCOS (48). Omega-3 fatty acids are needed for basic prenatal health anyway, so it offers additional benefit for women with PCOS. Omega-3 fatty acid supplementation has also been associated with increased implantation rates (49) in mice. Additionally, low levels of DHA were associated with male infertility and supplementation of DHA improved testis function and sperm quality parameters (50).

Zinc

Giving zinc supplementation at 50 mg per day for eight weeks to women with PCOS had beneficial effects on alopecia and hirsutism, but not on hormone profiles in blood (51). In addition, studies show that magnesium-zinc-calcium-vitamin D co-supplementation for twelve weeks among PCOS women had beneficial effects on hormonal profiles, biomarkers of inflammation, and oxidative stress (52).

Many nutrients studied in the treatment of PCOS can be found in a whole-foods diet that is clean and healthy; high in fruits and vegetables, lean protein, and fiber; low in fat; and void of sugar, processed foods and junk food. Prenatal health is pivotal to restoring hormone balance and conceiving. At the most basic level, a healthy diet is required for women with PCOS who are trying to get pregnant. There may be other nutrients that have yet to be studied in the treatment of PCOS. Different foods contain a multitude of varied nutrients. Therefore, it is very important to have a high-quality prenatal vitamin with highly bioavailable forms of nutrients along with a healthy diet.

THE ROLE OF ACUPUNCTURE AND CHINESE HERBS IN TREATING PCOS AND CREATING HORMONE BALANCE

Traditional Chinese Medicine (TCM) and acupuncture is rooted in the philosophy of balance of yin and yang, or opposing forces, to create homeostasis in the body. In TCM Qi, pronounced "chee," or energy, can be deficient, excess, stuck, stagnant, or trapped in what is called "phlegm or damp conditions." All of these situations create layers of imbalances in the body. When we look at PCOS from a TCM perspective, we can see a TCM pattern of disharmony or imbalance. Once the TCM pattern is identified, we can then treat it with acupuncture and Chinese herbs to restore the flow of Qi and create balance in both body and mind.

We know that correcting these imbalances with acupuncture and Chinese herbs can restore physiological function. Although Chinese medicine and acupuncture are over 6,000 years old and have been recognized in many countries as a leading system of medicine to address a multitude of ill conditions, it gained recognition in the United States in the 1970s and it is now being recognized as a viable and effective tool for many conditions. In fact, the National Center for Complementary and Integrative Health (NCCIH), which is the Federal Government's lead agency for scientific research on diverse medical and healthcare systems, practices, and products that are not generally considered part of conventional medicine (53), conducted extensive studies on acupuncture, proving its efficacy for the treatment of back and neck pain, osteoarthritis, knee pain, and headaches. More studies continue to support the expansive effect acupuncture and TCM can have on many health conditions, including women's health condition and fertility.

In fact, acupuncture has been shown in research studies to have a regulatory effect on the hypothalamic-pituitary-ovarian axis, which is vital to creating a physiological environment that leads to conception. Acupuncture can normalize the secretion of follicle stimulating hormone (FSH), luteinizing hormone (LH), estradiol (estrogen), and progestogen, and improve ovulatory function (54). Even adding acupuncture to medication protocol such as Clomid can have a greater positive benefit than medication alone (55, 56). Using acupuncture to treat PCOS has also shown to be effective in lowering elevated testosterone levels, reducing BMI, and improving menstrual cycle irregularities (57, 58).

Acupuncture also appears to have an important role in increasing blood flow to the ovaries, which can reduce ovarian volume and the number of ovarian cysts (59). Based on research studies and clinical practice, acupuncture seems like a highly beneficial and non-invasive tool in treating women with PCOS and infertility. Electroacupuncture is a procedure where a small electric current is passed between pairs of acupuncture needles to create a stimulating effect on certain points in order to regulate the body's physiology. Electroacupuncture has been studied in PCOS patients and shown to improve pregnancy rates and improve the number of blastocyst (embryo) implantations (60), lower insulin resistance, lower BMI, and improve blood hormone levels (61). In addition, the use of Chinese herbs and herbal formulae alone, or the use of Chinese herbs combined with acupuncture or medications (62) to enhance the therapeutic value of treating PCOS patients, gives added therapeutic tools to help women with PCOS to regain control of their hormones and enhance their fertility.

Using acupuncture, electroacupuncture and Chinese herbs alone, or together or in combination, starts with the basic understanding of diagnosing TCM patterns. To know how best to treat each woman, you have to determine the underlying TCM pattern they have. One woman with PCOS can have a different pattern than another women with PCOS. To understand the TCM perspective, let's look at the Qi of three organs that relate to the Western diagnosis of PCOS.

The Kidney Qi

The kidney Qi is a foundation Qi important in fertility. It is what is needed in abundance to pass on to the baby. The Yin (cool) and Yang (warm) must be balanced within this organ or it will create imbalances vital to being fertile. When the kidney Yin becomes deficient, you become short tempered, experience hot flashes or feel warm before the period, have cracked dry tongue, absent or heavy menstrual period, dry mouth and skin, light periods, and become tired and thin. When you become kidney Yang deficient, you may experience weight gain, water retention, insulin resistance, irregular menstrual cycles, become very chilly, and have more phlegm, such as sinus congestion in your body. The kidney Qi is integrally involved in creating new offspring, as it is connected to the Qi of inheritance or genetic origin. You have to have strong kidney Qi to conceive and pass this Qi on to help support a healthy pregnancy.

Symptoms Related to Kidney Qi Deficiencies

- Irregular or absent menstrual cycle
- No ovulation
- Fatigue
- Dry, cracked, or swollen tongue
- Low back and/or knee pain
- Night time urination
- Heat symptoms or feeling very chilly

How else can you tell if you have kidney Yin deficiency or kidney Yang deficiency, or a combination? This is based on your symptoms, your tongue, and your pulse, which are markers for determining your TCM patterns. In addition, bloodwork can also give a clue into the type of kidney deficiency pattern you may have, shown in the ranges below (63).

LH to FSH > 2.5 = Kidney Yang deficiency
LH to FSH < 2 = Kidney Yin deficiency (closer to normal range)

The Spleen Qi

The spleen Qi relates to separating "the pure from the turbid," or digesting thoughts as well as food, assimilating nutrients that can nourish you, and getting rid of wastes. The spleen Qi is important in helping to maintain a pregnancy. Spleen Qi that is deficient can result in miscarriage known as "spleen Qi sinking." It is important to have strong spleen Qi in order to hold the baby inside the body. Robust spleen Qi is also vital in order to conceive. In TCM, the spleen Qi plays an important role in making the blood needed to get pregnant, and is vital in maintaining a pregnancy and nourishing a growing embryo.

Symptoms Related to Spleen Qi Deficiencies
- Overweight
- Excess hair growth
- Fatigue
- Swollen tongue
- Abnormal menstrual cycles
- Digestive problems
- Insulin resistance
- Water retention
- Improper diet and excess of rich foods

The Liver Qi

According to TCM, the liver acts like a general, directing the proper flow of Qi and blood, and helps to create the balance and flow of emotions. When the Q gets stuck due to chronic stress, hidden emotions, or other reasons, it creates a multitude of issues. The stagnant liver Qi disrupts the female reproductive system causing PMS, painful periods, abnormal menstrual cycles, and other female-related health conditions. Liver Qi stagnation is a common pattern in PCOS.

Symptoms Related to Liver Qi Stagnation

- PMS symptoms
- Thin or normal weight
- Irritable and mood swings
- Irregular and/or painful periods
- Hirsutism (unwanted hair)
- Acne
- Emotional stress
- Depression and anxiety
- Sensation of lump in throat
- Sighing

Remember that there can be a combination of disharmonies that relate to PCOS, such as kidney and spleen Yang deficiency with phlegm accumulation, or kidney Yin deficiency with liver Qi stagnation. In addition, these imbalances can lead to further imbalances. For example, liver Qi stagnation can create stasis of the blood and heart, causing very painful periods. Likewise, spleen Qi and kidney Yang deficiency can lead to phlegm dampness and create other conditions such as fibroids. Finding a knowledgeable and licensed acupuncturist with a specialty in fertility can further assist you in determining your TCM pattern and the best therapeutic interventions to help symptoms of PCOS and dramatically improve your chances to conceive.

ESSENTIAL GUIDELINES FOR IMPROVED CONCEPTION OF WOMEN WITH PCOS

1. Lifestyle changes that support lowered stress
2. Proper nutrient supplementation to support hormone balance, reduce excess androgens, and restore normal ovulation
3. Detoxification support of the liver to support breakdown of hormones and excess androgens
4. Create blood sugar control and address insulin resistance through diet, exercise, and supplementation of specific nutrients, if needed
5. Achieve optimal BMI through exercise and diet
6. Reduce androgens (like testosterone) to regulate menstrual cycle and encourage ovulation
7. Utilize acupuncture and Chinese herbal medicines to support balanced hormones, regular menstrual cycles, and improve fertility

OPTIMIZING THYROID FUNCTION TO IMPROVE FERTILITY

Most patients find it surprising that the thyroid gland can directly affect your fertility. Thyroid hormones are vital for normal reproductive function. In fact, thyroid dysfunction is associated with infertility, miscarriage, preterm birth, and poor neurodevelopment of offspring (1).

The thyroid is a butterfly-shaped endocrine gland located at the base of your neck that regulates metabolism, body weight, temperature, mood, appetite, and hormones. The pituitary regulates the production of thyroid hormone via thyroid stimulating hormone (TSH). TSH serves as a messenger from the pituitary gland to your thyroid gland, telling it to make more or less thyroid hormone. The thyroid gland makes two hormones, thyroxine (T4) the inactive form, which is converted to triiodothyronine (T3) the bioactive form. When TSH levels are high, it indicates a sluggish or underactive thyroid (hypothyroidism). When TSH levels are low, it signals a hyper or overactive thyroid (hyperthyroidism). Thyroid hormones affect how FSH and LH work in regard to ovarian cells, which directly affects reproduction (2). So the thyroid gland has a direct effect on hormone balance and your fertility.

TSH can be measured in routine bloodwork. Normal TSH levels in the blood have a wide range of 0.45 to 4.5 milli-international units per liter (mIU/L) though the range may vary slightly from lab to lab. Optimal levels are essential for maintaining hormone balance between the pituitary and ovaries. Whether you have an underactive or hyperactive thyroid, both conditions can equally interfere with healthy hormone balance, ovulation, and the ability to conceive and maintain a healthy pregnancy. So this is one of the first things that should be checked when you are thinking about trying to have a baby. Even if your TSH is checked in bloodwork and you are told it is normal, or within the normal reference range, it may still be an issue affecting your fertility. So what is an optimal level to help conceive? When it comes to fertility, and frankly, just feeling good, a TSH level of 1.0 is optimal. For example, if your TSH is 2.5, that might be too high and you might feel a little sluggish, possibly constipated, and have some thinning of your hair. At 3.5, your TSH is too high, and you might notice more fatigue, weight gain, and irregular periods. At 4.2, your TSH is higher and closer to clinical hypothyroidism, where you might be tired, constipated, losing hair, have irregular periods, and be gaining weight in spite of eating well and exercising. The higher your TSH level goes in the normal range, there is an increased chance it will negatively affect your fertility. A TSH greater than 4.5 is considered clinical hypothyroid, which is a condition your doctor may diagnose that includes symptoms of depression, fatigue, weight gain, hair loss, constipation, brain fog, and irregular menses. At this stage of irregular thyroid function, your fertility is directly being affected. The higher the TSH, the higher degree of potential interference on hormone levels and a great negative impact on your fertility. The need for thyroid function screening with TSH in infertile women attempting to get pregnant is recognized by many international societies (3).

What do these specific levels mean for fertility? Technically, if your TSH is outside the reference range, starting at 4.6, you have clinical hypothyroidism. According to researchers and many doctors versed in integrative and functional medicine, if your TSH is 3.5, you may still have what is called subclinical hypothyroidism. That means that you have a sluggish thyroid, and although you do not yet have clinical hypothyroidism, you could have similar symptoms to hypothyroidism, like fatigue, low mood, hair loss, and constipation. A TSH in the high end of the normal reference range could indicate a disruption in hormone balance that is affecting your fertility. Studies indicate that a TSH level of less than 3.0 in infertility patients is associated with better functional ovarian reserve (higher AMH) than a TSH level of greater than 3.0. There is clearly a benefit in lowering TSH levels below 3.0 in women with infertility (4). Another study reports that when TSH exceeds 4.0 before IVF, thyroid medications should be used to improve thyroid function, and that women with TSH of more than 2.5 before IVF may also benefit from receiving thyroid medications (3). In the fertility world, a typical goal for TSH levels is less than 2.5. I like to get my patients' TSH close to 1.0 as a general rule, but always determine the optimal level with each person individually, based on all the factors that are presented to me during their consult.

Thyroid disease is the second-most common endocrine condition in women of childbearing age (2). That means that thyroid dysfunction is very common. Hypothyroidism is more common than hyperthyroidism, but either can negatively affect your fertility. In addition, thyroid autoimmunity, causing a condition known as Hashimoto's thyroiditis, is also prevalent among women struggling with infertility. In fact, Hashimoto's is the leading cause of thyroid dysfunction in women of reproductive age. Women with thyroid autoimmunity, even with normal thyroid function, appear to be at a higher risk for poor reproductive outcomes, including miscarriage and preterm birth (1). Hormone changes may be a trigger for the onset of Hashimoto's, along with hereditary disposition. Pregnancy is a time of great hormonal change, and these rapid hormone changes can serve as a trigger to the onset of Hashimoto's, which can show up after pregnancy and in subsequent pregnancies. Therefore, you cannot assume you do not have it if you had normal thyroid function with your first pregnancy, because the disease can often develop after pregnancy.

You may not recognize the symptoms of Hashimoto's, an autoimmune disorder where your body attacks your own thyroid, especially when you are a new mom and tired. This is because the symptoms might be subtle enough that you attribute your fatigue, mood changes, and hair loss to changing hormones post-partum. You may also have yet to be pregnant and have a hereditary tendency or other factors that lead to the development of Hashimoto's. You may not recognize common symptoms of the condition, and attribute them to something else. Hashimoto's often goes under the radar and can be missed. I cannot tell you how many women come to my office with a normal TSH level who were never screened for thyroid antibodies to rule out Hashimoto's, and in fact, they have it and have not been diagnosed or treated properly. Left untreated, this condition can greatly affect hormone balance and immune function, creating obstacles to conception.

What are the best labs to assess thyroid function and rule out thyroid conditions that could be affecting your fertility?

LABS TO RULE OUT THYROID DYSFUNCTION

Assessing thyroid function is critical in helping with fertility. Common thyroid lab tests used to rule out thyroid conditions such as hypothyroidism, hyperthyroidism, Graves' disease, Hashimoto's thyroiditis, and a subclinical hypothyroidism include a thyroid ultrasound and bloodwork, including labs for:

- TSH
- Free T3
- Free T4
- Total T3
- Reverse T3
- Thyroglobulin Antibodies (TG)
- Microsomal thyroid peroxidase (TPO) antibodies
- Thyroid stimulating immunoglobulins (TSI)

Let's look at these common tests to determine thyroid function and rule out thyroid diseases. This is important because an optimally functioning thyroid increases your chance of conception.

Thyroid Ultrasound

Thyroid ultrasound scanning is non-invasive, widely available, less expensive, and does not use any ionizing radiation (5). Hashimoto's causes inflammation and changes in the thyroid tissue over time. Someone with Hashimoto's will generally have an abnormal thyroid ultrasound showing the changes in the tissue. Common terminology found in the thyroid ultrasound of a person with Hashimoto's thyroiditis may include the following: enlargement of the thyroid gland, diffuse inflammatory tissue of the thyroid gland (seen as coarse heterogenous and hypoechoic parenchymal echo patterns), nodules (one or multiple discrete hypoechoic micronodules 1–6 mm), or lobulated appearance of tissue (5). Even if your antibodies are not elevated but you suspect Hashimoto's thyroiditis, an ultrasound can catch changes in the thyroid gland even before those changes are seen in the bloodwork.

There are additional reasons to have a thyroid ultrasound. According to the American Association of Clinical Endocrinologists, the indications for thyroid ultrasound can include any of the following reasons listed below (5):

1. To confirm presence of a thyroid nodule when physical examination is ambiguous.
2. To characterize a thyroid nodule(s), i.e. to measure the dimensions accurately and to identify internal structure and vascularization.
3. To differentiate between benign and malignant thyroid masses, based on their sonographic appearance.
4. To differentiate between thyroid nodules and other masses located in the surrounding area of the thyroid and neck.
5. To evaluate diffuse changes in thyroid tissue.
6. To detect post-operative residual or recurrent tumors in thyroid bed or metastases to neck or lymph nodes.
7. To screen high-risk patients for thyroid malignancy.
8. To guide diagnostic tissue or biopsy procedure and therapeutic interventional procedures.

TSH

Thyroid stimulating hormone (TSH) serves as a messenger from the pituitary gland to your thyroid gland. When TSH levels are high, it indicates a sluggish or under-acting thyroid. When TSH levels are low, it signals a hyper or overactive thyroid function. The optimal TSH level when trying to conceive is 1.0 mIU/L.

Free T4

TSH tells the thyroid gland to produce more or less thyroid hormone. Free T4 is the inactive form of thyroid hormone produced and stored in the thyroid gland. T4 is then converted to T3, which is the active form of thyroid hormone.

Free T3

Free T3 levels represent the active form of thyroid hormone. Low levels indicate a sluggish or low acting thyroid and high levels represent a hyper, overactive thyroid. Optimal levels of T4 and T3 are essential in maintaining proper thyroid function. TSH is equally important, but not in the absence of both T3 and T4. All values are needed to give you an in-depth look at thyroid function, which is necessary when trying to ensure optimal thyroid function to improve fertility.

Total T3

There are two types of T3. There is the free thyroid hormone called free T3 and there is also a portion of thyroid hormone bound to proteins in the blood. The free T3 is the bioactive form of thyroid hormone. Total T3 represents the summation of the bound plus the free forms of thyroid hormones. This can be useful when determining if you have a subclinical hypothyroid condition where your total T3 is at the low end of normal and you have many hypothyroid symptoms, but your TSH is in the "normal" range.

Reverse T3

Reverse T3 (rT3) is not the standard for routine thyroid screening by endocrinologists and primary care doctors, but it can be an additional tool to look at under-functioning thyroid glands. T4 is converted to active T3 form or to rT3 which is considered inactive. As rT3 rises, it means less active thyroid hormone is available to do its job. The ratio of active to inactive hormone can indicate low bioactive available thyroid hormone, resulting in a down regulation of the thyroid, which negatively affects fertility.

TPO Antibodies

Microsomal thyroid peroxidase antibodies (TPO Ab) is an autoimmune marker associated with Hashimoto's autoimmune thyroid disorder. As discussed earlier, this condition is quite common and can add an immunological element to the regulation of the thyroid, which can directly affect fertility. Hashimoto's can also be triggered by pregnancy and/or hormone changes, and can occur after having a baby or after being pregnant and miscarrying. That is why TPO antibodies should be tested before and after each pregnancy.

TG Antibodies

Thyroid globulin (TG) antibodies is another autoimmune marker associated with Hashimoto's autoimmune thyroid. This is one of the most common causes of low thyroid function in women.

TPO and TG antibody labs are routinely skipped by many reproductive endocrinologists. However, testing for these antibodies is important because their presence can indicate an autoimmune disorder, which relates to immune dysfunction that may play a significant role in women and couples suffering from unexplained infertility. Thyroid autoimmunity is the most prevalent autoimmune disease; it affects between five and twenty percent of women during reproductive age (6). Therefore, it is important to rule out and address any autoimmune disorders, especially disorders of the thyroid, to improve fertility.

TSI

Thyroid stimulating immunoglobulins or TSI is an autoimmune marker strongly associated with Graves' disease. Grave's disease is an autoimmune related condition that causes an overactive thyroid gland. Symptoms of Graves' can include weight loss, heart palpitations, anxiety, hand tremor, puffy eyes, enlarged thyroid, heat sensitivity, and increased heart rate. This condition can directly affect your fertility and must be ruled out and addressed when clinical symptoms are present.

THYROID TESTING

Based on a simple blood test that looks at thyroid hormones, you can rule out more serious thyroid conditions. In addition, you may find that your thyroid is "normal" to the extent that you have no thyroid disease, but it may be not functioning optimally. Or you may find that you have an autoimmune disorder that could be a roadblock to your fertility. Supporting thyroid function is one of the most significant and easiest things you can do to help improve your chances to conceive naturally. Step 1 is to get your thyroid tested through bloodwork. Step 2 is to diagnose any thyroid condition you have. Step 3 is to treat that condition to enhance your fertility. Let's look at thyroid conditions you are trying to rule out with bloodwork.

THYROID CONDITIONS AFFECTING YOUR FERTILITY

Hypothyroidism

Hypothyroidism is when TSH levels are high and outside the normal reference range, usually above 4.5. Many women and men have subclinical hypothyroid (TSH >3.5) symptoms and signs where they just don't feel right. They are tired, have low mood, and women experience irregular menses or menstrual disturbances. So what are the symptoms for a sluggish thyroid?

Symptoms of Low-functioning Thyroid and Hypothyroidism
- Fatigue, feeling of heaviness in limbs
- Weight gain or inability to lose weight
- Constipation
- Feeling cold and/or sensitivity to cold
- Dry skin
- Depression
- Muscle aches
- Irregular and or heavy periods

Subclinical Hypothyroidism

Subclinical hypothyroid symptoms can look a lot like those of hypothyroidism, where your TSH is between 3.0 and 4.5, which is considered normal, but you just don't feel normal. How many times do patients tell me they have gone to their doctor saying that they just don't feel good, and their doctor looks at their labs and says, "nothing is wrong, you are fine?" All the time. An absence of a disease does not mean you are healthy or that you feel great. Subclinical hypothyroid may be playing a bigger role than you think.

Symptoms of Subclinical Hypothyroid or Suboptimal Thyroid Function

- Fatigue, feeling of heaviness in limbs
- Weight gain or inability to lose weight
- Constipation
- Feeling cold and/or sensitivity to cold
- Dry skin
- Depression
- Muscle aches
- Irregular and or heavy period

Hyperthyroidism

Hyperthyroidism is an overactive thyroid gland. This may be due to an autoimmune condition known as Hashimoto's thyroiditis, discussed earlier in the chapter, or to heredity, overuse of iodine, overuse of medication, or other reasons. Graves' Disease is the most common form of hyperthyroidism. This disease may cause patients' eyes to look enlarged or bulging. Hyperthyroid presents with a low TSH (TSH < 0.45) and elevated T3 (Free T3 > 4.2, but may vary depending on the lab).

If hyperthyroid is due to Grave's disease, then TSI levels will also be elevated. Basically, everything tends to speed up in the body. So what are the symptoms of hyperthyroidism?

- Sweating
- Heart racing or rapid heart rate
- Nervousness, irritability, or anxiety
- Diarrhea or frequent bowel movements
- Changes in menstrual patterns, such as light flow or less frequent periods
- Unexplained weight loss
- Tremors or trembling of the hands and fingers
- Fatigue
- Enlarged thyroid gland (called a goiter) or swelling at base of neck
- Muscle weakness

Hashimoto's Thyroiditis or Thyroid Autoimmunity

Hashimoto's also known as Hashimoto's thyroiditis is an autoimmune condition where the body is attacking itself, and more specifically, attacking thyroid tissue. Autoimmune thyroid disease is characterized by the presence of autoantibodies including thyroid-peroxidase (TPO) and thyroglobulin (TG) antibodies, as well as cellular inflammation within the gland, which can be seen on a thyroid ultrasound.

Common Symptoms of Hashimoto's
- Anxiety, depression, or other mood changes
- Fatigue, heaviness, sluggish feeling
- Constipation and dry skin
- Puffy face
- Feeling cold
- Water retention
- Change in menstrual cycle
- Brittle nails, hair or eyebrow loss, or thinning of hair
- Joint pain and muscle aches and/or weakness
- Eczema
- Increased cholesterol

Thyroid autoimmunity is the leading cause of thyroid dysfunction in women of reproductive age (7). Hashimoto's is the most prevalent autoimmune disorder that affects five to twenty percent of women during reproductive age (7). Prevalence of Hashimoto's thyroid disease is significantly higher among infertile women, especially when the cause of infertility is endometriosis or polycystic ovary syndrome (7). Hashimoto's, which affects thyroid function, could be a cause of infertility (8). In many females, the diagnosis of Hashimoto's is missed or overlooked, and reproductive endocrinologists do not routinely check for it. It is important to check for this disease because it could be contributing to your infertility.

Inflammation is the foundation of autoimmune diseases like Hashimoto's. This inflammation causes dysregulation of the immune system, which can lead to problems with embryo implantation, and contribute to menstrual irregularities. Many people with Hashimoto's are initially hyperthyroid and then become hypothyroid, but thyroid levels can swing back and forth depending on the level of inflammation and dysregulation of the thyroid gland. Conventional treatment generally uses synthetic T4 medication to stabilize thyroid function and monitor thyroid levels. However, this protocol does not address the inflammatory element of the autoimmune disease or the immune dysregulation component. Addressing these elements is essential in order to fully stabilize thyroid function and regulate the immune system to help support your fertility.

The National Institutes of Health (NIH) estimates 23.5 million Americans have an autoimmune disease (9). Genetic predisposition, environmental factors, infections and gut dysbiosis play major roles in development of autoimmune diseases (9). There is a strong association to gluten as an irritant in the gut that may contribute in the development of Hashimoto's. Therefore, gluten should be removed from the diet when you have Hashimoto's, especially when trying to get pregnant.

Thyroid Disorders in Men

Thyroid conditions, although more common in women, also affect men's reproductive health. Hyperthyroid and hypothyroid both are associated with negative changes in sperm production, semen quality and hormone levels. Hyperthyroid reduces sperm motility (10, 11), whereas, hypothyroidism results in abnormal sperm morphology, or shape (10). Both hyper and hypothyroidism are associated with changes in sperm production, levels of sexual hormones, and erectile function (11). So screening your male counterpart for thyroid disorders is equally important when it comes to trying to have a baby. This is often overlooked, but should not be because this could be the issue that is preventing you from success.

TREATING THE THYROID TO MAXIMIZE YOUR FERTILITY

Conventional medications, Western herbs, Chinese herbs, acupuncture, glandulars, iodine, and nutrients are just some of the tools used to treat thyroid dysfunction. If someone does not tolerate medications, then acupuncture can be used to regulate thyroid function. The standard medical community uses a synthetic T4 medication to treat hypothyroid and Hashimoto's, but medications from porcine sources (pig) that contain active T3 and some T4 may be more effective in treating these conditions in some people. In addition, because iodine is a nutrient that is necessary for making thyroid hormones, having low iodine levels could be a factor with subclinical thyroid function or hypothyroidism. Supplemental iodine could help improve thyroid function, but excess iodine could work oppositely to create a hyperthyroid state. Because of this, it should be used only with the direct supervision of a licensed medical practitioner. Specific medications are also used in conventional medicine to treat hyperactive thyroid. However, botanical medicines, Chinese herbs, and acupuncture may also be effective modalities to treat, or provide integrative treatment for, hyperthyroidism.

Reducing inflammation in people with Hashimoto's is key to helping with fertility and embryo implantation. Avoidance of gluten and other food allergens is vital if you have Hashimoto's. In addition, an anti-inflammatory diet is key to reduce inflammation. Addressing gut dysbiosis and leaky gut may also improve immune function and reduce immune dysregulation. It is equally important to provide the proper thyroid co-factors including iron, zinc, iodine, and selenium needed for conversion of inactive T4 to active T3, as well as supplements to reduce inflammation. Of course, thyroid conditions should be addressed based on your individual parameters and needs, with the help of a skilled practitioner. Whether you have a subclinical low functioning thyroid or a thyroid disease, you have to be proactive and get ahead of this condition to optimize your fertility. Addressing underlying thyroid disorders is key to hormone balance.

Small changes can surprise you with big results. It starts with a simple blood test to rule out thyroid conditions and suboptimal thyroid function. If you do have a thyroid condition and your doctor is offering only one solution that does not work for you, know that there are many ways to support the thyroid that are effective and safe. Remember, small changes can yield big results so get your thyroid checked when you start trying to conceive.

IMMUNOLOGY AND UNEXPLAINED INFERTILITY:

WHAT NO ONE TALKS ABOUT

Once egg and sperm meet and fertilize, an embryo is formed and must implant into the nourished, rich lining of the uterus. It is believed that one mechanism responsible for unexplained infertility is the rejection of the embryo by the women's endometrial tissue, due to changes in immune regulatory agents in the uterine lining. This, in effect, causes a rejection of the embryo, leading to the inability to get pregnant, or potentially, to miscarriage.

One study published in Molecular Human Reproduction looked at key immune components associated with infertility. The study reported that "data indicates that unexplained infertility is linked with reduced expression of FOXP3 mRNA, the key fate-determining transcription factor for generating the Treg cells implicated as essential mediators of immune tolerance required to initiate pregnancy" (1). What does that mean? Transcription factor or FOXP3 mRNA assists with the natural development and production of Treg cells. Treg cells, or T cells, are part of the immune system and help to suppress other cells in the immune system. In this way, they keep the "checks and balances" in the immune system and affect how you respond to foreign particles called antigens. In one study, regulatory T cells were determined to be involved in modulation of the immune system, which plays a role in affecting antigen reactions involved in preventing autoimmune diseases, and was correlated with initiation of pregnancy. This means that if the Treg cells are not providing the proper regulatory action, then the body could perceive an embryo as a foreign particle, or antigen, and attack it. There may be unseen immunological actions that may cause rejection of the embryo in the endometrial lining, influencing your ability to get pregnant. This is not a theory; it is happening in many women. It is hard to know if this is happening to you, because you may not have any symptoms except infertility or miscarriage. We have to assume this may be a factor in your infertility and take preventative action in your fertility support plan to reduce inflammation and support a healthy immune system.

Another study looked at the complexities of endometriosis and the immune factors associated with this condition that may contribute to infertility. The study concluded that the revealed changes in the expression of transcription factors may indicate the imbalance between T helper cells of the Th1 and Th2 types, which are involved in cell-mediated immunity. It also found that changes in regulation of T cell function may be one of the causes of endometriosis, predisposing women with this condition to the development of infertility associated with this disease (2).

In addition, there may also be a link with FOXP3 and T regulatory cell (Treg) expression and endometriosis, which has immunologic factors associated with it (3). These studies provide a further indication that immunological factors may be at the root of your infertility. Women with endometriosis may have a hard time conceiving, and this may be due to immunologic factors. More research is needed to understand the complexity of the immune system and its regulation of the processes of fertility. However, we know that the immune system is intimately involved in the physiology of fertility, and perhaps, future studies will show that this role is more important than we ever thought. We know that the area of immunology in fertility should not be overlooked.

Let's think about this , you have gone through the long haul of getting hormones balanced, helping ovulation occur, raising sperm count high enough so that one strong sperm can swim to the egg, so fertilization can happen, and an embryo can form. The embryo, at last, makes its way to the uterine lining and finally implants, only to be rejected due to immunological factors. This seems so cruel; it is hard to understand why this would happen. You know you want to welcome that embryo with open arms and watch it grown with ease, well-nourished and cared for. Yet the body seems to have a different idea. Why would your body do this?

It is estimated that close to forty percent of unexplained infertility is due to immune factors. Though the exact cause is unknown, we know disruptions in the immune system may create a roadblock to your fertility success. One thing that we can focus on to support a healthy immune system and your fertility is to eliminate or significantly reduce inflammation in the body. Inflammation engages the immune system and can over tax it, causing it to behave abnormally and create a cascade of negative reactions in the body. Inflammation seems to cause havoc wherever it goes. Many immune related disorders share the common denominator of inflammation.

The normal healing process when you get a cut or sprained ankle involves an inflammatory reaction. Inflammatory agents go to the site of the injury to help fix or heal it and then subside once they are no longer needed. This process generally has a beginning, a middle, and an end. But when you have an insidious, chronic level of inflammation, it has no end. Long-term inflammation causes a disruption in the normal immune function. It also creates a pathway for chemical messengers in the body that promote the opposite of what you want, including free radicals that cause cell damage, and pro-inflammatory agents like leukotrienes that lead to an exhausted and chaotic immune system. What if on top of this, you have exposure to a virus like Epstein Barr that is causing a dysregulation in the immune system. What if on top of that, your genetics predispose you to Hashimoto's thyroiditis (an autoimmune condition of the thyroid) or rheumatoid arthritis (an autoimmune condition affecting the joints), both autoimmune disorders where the body attacks itself causing further disruption of the immune system and more inflammation. You can see that as you start adding causes, the outcome looks bleaker and bleaker. Add to this a poor diet and food allergies, creating more inflammation, and it is no wonder the immune system might see something like an embryo as foreign and reject it. It would be like trying to have a conversation with someone while getting so many messages and interruptions that you can't be clear what the person you are talking to is actually telling you.

Immune dysregulation with inflammation is linked to a plethora of other health conditions, but certainly seems to play a role in infertility. One significant place inflammation can be prevalent is in the gastrointestinal tract. Let's look as some of the possible players that affect inflammation and immune function and how to address them to improve your fertility.

Dysbiosis

Dysbiosis is the condition of abnormal balance of bacteria in your gastrointestinal tract (gut), which negatively impacts your immune system and creates inflammation. A healthy balance of gut bacteria is fundamental in establishing optimal gut health, which translates to overall health. About seventy percent of immune modulated activity occurs in the gut, and this is your first line of defense to fight off foreign invaders (4). The gastrointestinal (GI) system plays a central role in immune system homeostasis (4). It is the main route of contact with the external environment and is overloaded every day with external stimuli including bacteria, protozoa, fungi, viruses, and toxic substances (5). There are hundreds of bacteria, some of which are good for us and provide us with healthy immune function, and some that are not good for us and create a negative impact on our immune system. Some bacteria are what we would call opportunistic, meaning they will grow in large amounts or in excess when given the opportunity in an unhealthy gut environment. Think about your gut as an apartment complex. If there are nice, friendly, nondisruptive tenants then everyone gets along. However, when some of the tenants start having loud parties all night, littering and destroying property, then the balanced and serene environment is turned upside down, and the apartment complex becomes a potentially hostile place to live. Much like tenants in an apartment complex, good bacteria and some bad, or less desirable, bacteria could live in harmony. However, if the bad bacteria grow in excessive amounts, it creates an imbalanced environment called dysbiosis. In addition to bacteria, a poor diet, medications, stress, and other factors can also contribute to dysbiosis and cause harm to the gut microbiome (the gut environment), further creating damage to the GI tract and leading to inflammation that negatively impacts the immune system. Dysbiosis can occur both in the small and large intestines.

Small Intestinal Bacterial Overgrowth (SIBO) and Dysbiosis

Small intestinal bacterial overgrowth (SIBO) is a type of dysbiosis where there is an overabundance of bacteria in the small intestine. SIBO can cause intestinal cells that normally absorb nutrients not to create inflammation, and allow an environment for bacteria and even yeast to proliferate. Because the small intestine is where most of nutrient absorption occurs and the presence of excessive bacteria can lead to malabsorption of nutrients among other detrimental effects, it is important to have a healthy intestine.

Are you taking a lot of supplements that seem like they are having no effect? This may be due to poor absorption of nutrients caused by SIBO. Common symptoms of SIBO include bloating, belching, abdominal distention, abdominal pain or discomfort, diarrhea, fatigue, and weakness, as well as more severe symptoms like malabsorption. SIBO creates an imbalance that causes a cascade of immune factors. It is believed that SIBO causes low gastric acid secretion, abnormal intestinal motility (movement), and possible structural abnormalities through surgery or diverticulosis. These conditions may further encourage bacteria to grow, and possibly, to translocate from the large intestine to the small intestine (4). Stomach acid or gastric acid suppresses the growth of ingested bacteria, so if there is a reduction in gastric acid, some bacteria may not be eradicated, allowing them to proliferate in the gut. Normal movement or motility of the gut involves a complex, tightly coordinated series of events designed to move material through the GI tract. Something called the migrating motor complex (MMC) helps sweep bacteria along the mucosal tissue of the small intestine. SIBO impairs the MMC, allowing bacteria to overgrow in the gut. SIBO is strongly linked to irritable bowel syndrome, poor diet, uncontrolled diabetes, aging, and celiac disease (6).

Why is SIBO important in relationship to fertility? People with SIBO have abnormalities in their intestinal mucosal (lining) immunity. This reduced immune function in the gut can cause a cascade of immune-related actions that may create a suboptimal immune regulation and negatively affect fertility. There is no research regarding SIBO and infertility, however research does clearly show that if gut immunity is altered, then general immunity is altered. Because the small intestine is so long, we cannot test for SIBO with a biopsy because we can't reach it with a scope from mouth or anus. That is why testing is so important. To test for SIBO, you ingest a fiber that you don't digest but the bacteria does. You breathe in oxygen and breathe out carbon dioxide. Bacteria also breathe. They breathe out hydrogen or methane, which mixes with your breath and can be measured. SIBO is tested using a three-hour breath test that can reveal if you have hydrogen- or methane-dominant bacteria, or both. Diet changes, medication, and botanical medicine are used to treat SIBO.

More on Dysbiosis

Dysbiosis can refer to abnormal balance of bacteria in the small or large intestine. Abnormal or pathogenic (disease causing) bacteria can come from the large intestine in addition to the small intestine. This can also be a gateway for other organisms such as parasites, yeast, or candida to grow. Likewise, if you have candida or a parasite, it can allow bacteria to grow.

Nearly eighty percent of immune system cells are found in your gut, and changes to gut bacteria can weaken your defense against illness and disease (4). Research also shows a direct link between gut health and acne (7), skin conditions, autoimmune disorders (8), Type 1 diabetes (9), allergies, mood disorders (10), and autism (11).

Dysbiosis creates inflammation and immune mediated chemicals that could have a systemic effect on the body and create disharmony in the immune system. If the immune system is overtaxed, it may not perform normally. This could affect how you feel as well as your fertility.

Do You Have Dysbiosis?

There are common symptoms that may lead you to believe that you have dysbiosis of the gut. You don't have to be a debilitated person with a chronic illness to have dysbiosis. Some people don't have that many GI symptoms, though they may have gas and bloating. However, dysbiosis may be visible in only subtle ways while having a heavy impact on your immunity and your fertility.

Common Symptoms of Dysbiosis
1. Frequent gas, bloating, belching
2. Diarrhea, loose stool, or constipation
3. Bad breath (halitosis)
4. Present or past diagnosis of irritable bowel syndrome
5. Acid reflux or heartburn
6. Skin conditions such as eczema, psoriasis, rosacea, or acne
7. Low energy and chronic fatigue
8. Difficulty with focus and brain fog
9. Anxiety, depression, or other mood disorders
10. Little to no apparent symptoms

How Do I Test For Dysbiosis?

Think about dividing the intestine into two sections, the small and large intestines. We can test for bacteria, parasites and yeast with a stool test in the large intestine, while we use a breath test for detecting bacteria in the small intestine. The three-hour-breath test for overgrowth of bacteria in the small intestine requires a modification of your diet for twenty-four hours prior to the test. You ingest lactulose, which is a fiber that you cannot break down, but the bacteria in your gut can. As they do so, they off gas hydrogen or methane gas, which mixes with your breath. You collect samples of your breath every twenty minutes for three hours. The test will analyze these samples for the presence of hydrogen or methane gas, which can determine if you have an overgrowth of hydrogen bacteria, methane bacteria, or both. Each type as well as the combination of the two are treated differently. The treatment includes diet modification, herbs, medications, and other supportive supplements based on your individual test results. Hydrogen sulfide and small intestinal fungal overgrowth (SIFO) may also be present. These do not show up on a test, but can be determined from a combination of your test results, your symptoms, and your response to treatment. It is important to work with someone knowledgeable about the treatment of small intestinal bacterial overgrowth (SIBO). SIBO could be creating inflammation in the body and creating an over taxed and dysfunctional immune system that is negatively affecting your fertility.

Another test I often use is a stool test from a functional medicine lab that can identify candida, yeast, parasites, and bacteria. Unlike the test for SIBO, which focuses on the small intestine, this test reflects the bacteria of the large intestine and end of the small intestine. This test takes your stool and cultures it to see what grows. Then, the lab identifies the organisms that grow and tells you what medications or natural substances will kills those organisms. This comprehensive approach to identifying bacteria is important because most stool tests that are done at major routine laboratories test only for a specific organism. If the test is not set up for the right organism, you will miss identifying that bacteria, which means that it will go undiagnosed, and most importantly, untreated.

For example, say that a stool test from the lab where you get your annual blood work done is capable of testing for organisms A through F, but you have organisms G and Z. The lab will miss those organisms. Unlike those tests, the test that I am referring to cultures the stool to identify organisms A through Z so nothing is missed. It does not test for any specific bacteria; it just allows the culture to grow then they can identify what organisms are present. In addition, this type of stool test can identify bacteria as well as many strains of candida and parasites. It can also test for the good gut bacteria that should be colonized in a healthy gut to provide you with healthy immunity.

These tests are useful in identifying the specific organisms that you need to treat and help determine the treatment. Organisms A and G may need to be treated differently. There is no one-size-fits-all solution here . To establish a return to a healthy microbiome in the gut takes strategy. A healthy gut equals a healthy immune system, and our gut is our first line of defense in establishing a healthy environment to boost our immunity and improve fertility. An unhealthy microbiome leads to inflammation, impaired absorption, leaky gut, and possibly a dysfunctional or overactive immune system.

Leaky Gut

Dysbiosis causes leaky gut. Leaky gut creates inflammation and dysregulation of the immune system. Leaky gut refers to the increased permeability of the gastrointestinal lining, causing inflammation and damage to the absorptive surface of the small intestine. This allows large proteins, toxins, indigested food particles, and waste products to be absorbed into the blood system, causing an immunological reaction. Normally tight junctions at the brush border or intestinal surface of the small intestine do not allow large foreign molecules to pass through the cells, preventing them from getting into the systemic circulation. However, leaky gut allows large proteins and particles to get into the blood system, where your body recognizes this as foreign.

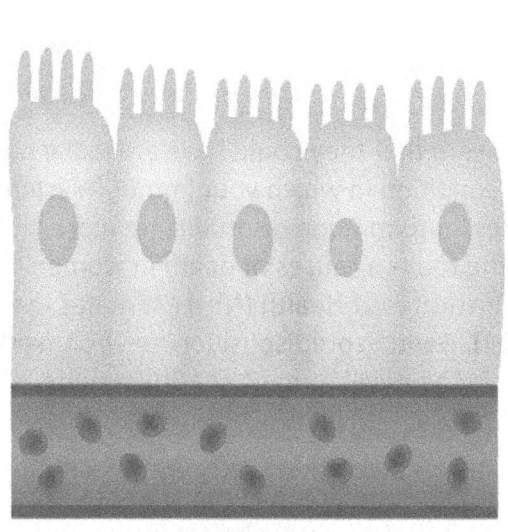
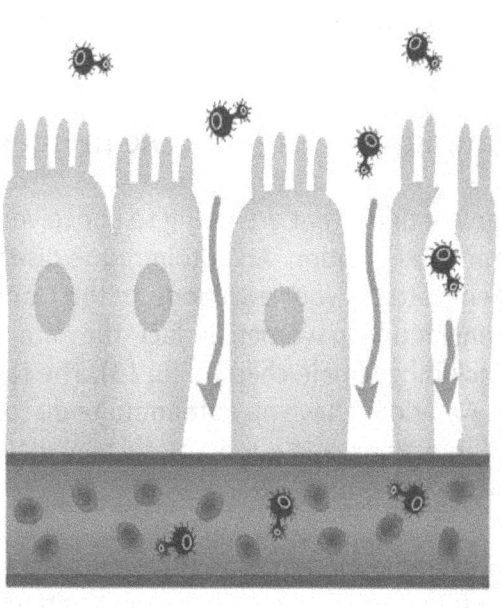

Normal Tight Junction **Leaky and Inflamed**

This creates a cascade of immune-mediated reactions that puts your body in a state of high immunological alert and compromises your immune system. A research article published in the Frontiers of Bioscience journal in 2018 stated, "The intestine plays an important role in systemic inflammation. Disturbances in the intestinal microcirculation due to infiltration of immune cells during systemic inflammation can increase bacterial translocation from the gut to the circulation and aggravate the pathological condition" (5). Leaky gut is linked to inflammation in the gut, which may lead to systemic inflammation, which could potentially affect any part of the body, including the uterine lining where implantation occurs. Leaky gut is not a disease, rather it is a condition of the body. Leaky gut can be caused by a variety of factors including a poor diet, food allergies, bacteria, or infection by parasites or yeast. Organisms that don't belong in the gut will damage the cells and cause leaky gut. In addition, long term use of steroids and repeated use of antibiotics can contribute to leaky gut and create immunological imbalance. The gastrointestinal microbiome must be in balance, and when it is not, it causes multiple negative reactions that affect your general immune system.

Intestinal permeability plays a role in certain gastrointestinal conditions such as celiac disease, Crohn's disease, and irritable bowel syndrome because there is damage to the cells in the GI tract in these disorders, affecting permeability. Intestinal permeability affects the microbiome of the GI tract, or it may be that changes in the microbiome incite increased intestinal permeability. Research shows that obesity, type 1 diabetes mellitus, rheumatoid arthritis, and systemic lupus erythematosus are linked to chronic inflammation, and people with these disorders have characteristic shifts in their gut microbiome composition (12). These shifts can create an unhealthy microbial environment in the gut that can lead to damage to the cells and increased permeability or leaky gut. Leaky gut causes inflammation and immune dysregulation.

Autoimmune Disorders' Role in Infertility

Many patients that are trying to conceive are unaware that they could have an undiagnosed autoimmune condition. An autoimmune disease is a condition in which your immune system mistakenly attacks your own body. In the United States, autoimmune disorders are more commonly found in women. In fact, they are one of the top ten causes of death in women of all ages, including female children (8, 13). The National Institutes of Health (NIH) estimates that 23.5 million Americans have an autoimmune disease (8, 14). Genetic predisposition, environmental factors, infections, and gut dysbiosis play major roles in the development of autoimmune diseases.

For example, Hashimoto's thyroiditis is an autoimmune condition where your body attacks your own thyroid. This causes changes in thyroid function and produces inflammation in the body. This disease can be diagnosed with a simple blood test. Commonly, I see patients in my practice who have seen other specialists and have not been tested for Hashimoto's or other autoimmune conditions. Standard fertility bloodwork testing on Days 3 and 21, along with antral follicle count with ultrasound are common basics for REs and other specialists, but not in the absence of testing and evaluation of other systemic conditions that may influence fertility. Hashimoto's thyroiditis is often triggered after pregnancy or other hormone-changing events. It is also hereditary. If undiagnosed, you have an abnormal function of the immune system, which negatively influences your fertility. Your immune system is overtaxed dealing with this disorder and cannot have a normal immunological reaction to a newly implanted embryo. For example, take endometriosis, a condition where the tissue that normally lines the inside of your uterus grows outside your uterus and commonly involves your ovaries, fallopian tubes, and the tissue lining your pelvis. Endometriosis is associated with immune dysregulation. This condition can cause pain and studies have shown that it is linked to immunological changes in the endometrial lining that may affect implantation and fertility. In addition, autoimmune conditions, such as rheumatoid arthritis, Lupus, Sjogren's syndrome, anti-phospholipid antibody syndrome, type 1 diabetes, and conditions with strong links to autoimmune etiology like irritable bowel syndrome, lichen sclerosus, and psoriasis are telling you there is an abnormal function of the immune system. If your immune system is not working appropriately, how does it respond to a new implanted embryo in the lining? Does it accept it? Reject it? Support it? For how long? Does your immune system play a role in accepting an embryo that has been implanted?

The answer to this last question appears YES. The immune system affects fertility. For one, we have different immune factors that influence inflammation and implantation. For example, research published in The American Journal of Reproductive Immunology showed that leukemia inhibiting factor (LIF), which is not just associated with leukemia but also plays a role in inflammatory response, implantation, and cell growth, is associated with a down regulation in both the follicular and luteal phases of the menstrual cycle in infertile women. Moreover, the abnormal regulation of agents that promote inflammation in the body is more profound in women with multiple failures of implantation (15–17). What does this mean? This study concluded that the immune system is directly involved in infertility.

In addition, studies show that the presence of anti-phospholipid (APL) and/or anti-nuclear antibodies (ANA) seems to be more frequent in the population of infertile women (13). Blood markers for autoimmune antibodies are associated with early ovarian failure. The study reports "the direct pathogenesis of this auto-immunity is unknown, but therapeutic immunomodulators, prescribed on a case-by-case basis, could favor pregnancy even in cases of unexplained primary or secondary infertility" (18).

Then, there is the immune modulated rejection of sperm via antisperm antibodies (19). This is when a woman's body can make antibodies to her partner's sperm, disabling them or rejecting them when they get to the cervical mucus of the vagina. The antibodies, which are proteins, are used to protect against foreign invaders. Again, this demonstrates the immune system's innate involvement in the area of fertility.

In addition, there is research suggesting that women who go into premature ovarian failure, which means that their ovaries stop working before the age of forty, are more likely to have multiple autoimmune disorders (20, 21). Studies suggest that the environment and genetic triggers cause an immune reaction where the body recognizes the ovaries not as part of itself, but as a foreign invader. The level of ovarian antibodies measured in the serum of women with premature ovarian failure demonstrate that it may be an auto immune mediated condition (20).

Let's face it—the immune system is complex. However, screening for common immune related conditions is a good start to determine if you may have an autoimmune disorder, or can identify immune dysregulation with blood work. Once you do this, you can attempt to address any conditions that you identify, in order to regulate and balance the immune system and improve your fertility success.

How to Improve Immune Function

To improve immune function, you need to address underlying gut dysbiosis, leaky gut, food allergies, and autoimmune conditions; reduce inflammation by making changes in your diet; and supplement your body with specific nutrients that can improve immune regulation.

Food Allergies and Sensitives/ Gluten Intolerance

Many people suffer from food allergies and sensitivities. A true allergen will cause an immune reaction mediated by IgE immunoglobins. However, some people may experience a sensitivity, which can cause a reaction anywhere from twenty-four to seventy-two hours after exposure to a food. This is mediated by IgA and IgG immunoglobulins, which react within twenty-four and seventy-two hours respectively after the ingestion of a food. They can cause chronic inflammation that can tax and negatively affect the immune system. One such allergen is wheat, which contains gluten. Wheat is the most consumed cereal grain worldwide and makes up a substantial part of a typical American diet (22). The United States dietary guidelines promote the inclusion of grains in our diet. "Eat whole grains, not white flour." You have heard it before, so why would foods that contain whole wheat be bad for you? The truth is that wheat gluten and wheat lectin, both constituents of wheat, can contribute to chronic inflammation and autoimmune responses by increasing intestinal permeability and eliciting a proinflammatory immune response in some people (22, 23, 24). Gluten has also been linked to chronic fatigue syndrome (25). Gluten is the main structural protein complex of wheat. It consists of glutenins and gliadins. Gliadin has been researched, and studies show that it increases intestinal permeability, causing leaky gut by affecting tight junctions which are multi protein complexes that maintain the gut barrier (26). This releases zonulin, a protein that directly compromises the integrity of the junction complex on the mucosal cells of the intestine, causing permeability. If leaky gut occurs, it can allow other bacteria and microbes in, which then react with the immune system.

Celiac disease is a disorder where gluten starts a chain reaction that damages the small intestine, altering absorption of nutrients, causing inflammation, and resulting in injury to the gut. Infertility, miscarriage, stillbirth, obstetric complications, cesarean delivery, reduced duration of breastfeeding, menstrual irregularities, amenorrhea, and early menopause are found more frequently in women with celiac disease (27). Celiac disease is underdiagnosed, and doctors often test patients when they are already eating gluten-free, which gives a false negative diagnosis of the disorder. To have an accurate test for celiac disease, you must eat an equivalent of two pieces of wheat bread for two weeks before getting testing. If you are not positive for celiac, you still can have an immunological reaction to wheat, which is contained in bread, pasta, and many commercially available cereals, bars, and other packaged foods. People with celiac disease diagnosed after 10 years of age have a 7-fold higher rate of autoimmune disorders compared to celiac-free counterparts (27). It is suggested that "the entire span of reproductive life may be disrupted in women with undiagnosed celiac disease" (28).

We know that this is happening in people with celiac disease and gluten sensitive individuals, but what about apparently healthy people? Some individuals who experience distress when eating gluten-containing foods and show improvement when following a gluten-free diet may have what is commonly referred to as gluten sensitivity, instead of celiac disease (29, 30). Research suggests that gliadin does increase gut permeability and alter immune function in some "healthy" people, and more studies may show that this affects individuals on a wider scale than we currently think.

Eat wheat, and the result is impaired intestinal permeability, a burdened immune system, and a chronic inflammation pattern that can go undetected. This change in the immune function can directly affect immune function in the host. And that host? It's you! Women, do you really need that scone or whole wheat toast for breakfast? Probably not. When it comes to building healthy immune function and improving your fertility, it is better to avoid wheat and gluten in order to take chronic inflammation and gut permeability out of the equation. This could not only improve your chances of conceiving, but creates a healthier body needed during pregnancy and beyond.

In addition, studies show that leaky gut syndrome with subclinical inflammation is associated with cell autoimmunity (where your immune system attacks its own tissue) and type 1 juvenile onset diabetes (9). Animal studies suggest that leaky gut plays a key role in the destruction of insulin producing beta cells of the pancreas, while treating the leaky gut appears to modulate the development of juvenile onset diabetes (23). Probiotics seem to help prevent juvenile onset diabetes, illustrating the importance of good gut health in children. Gut health is important in all stages of life. So before starting your fertility journey may be the time to create a healthy microbiome in the gut and remove gluten from the diet to reduce an immune mediated reaction that feeds inflammation and creates immune dysregulation or immune dysfunction or negatively impacts the immune system.

Viruses and Fertility

Can viruses affect your fertility? Absolutely! If you have an active or acute viral infection, it can affect your body's ability to function normally and tax your immune system. Think about getting a viral cold in the winter and how bad you feel, and nothing seems to help until that virus is completely out of your system. The body is programmed to fight off viruses you may come into contact with, such as the rhinovirus associated with the common cold. However, some tricky viruses may have a devastating effect on the immune system, leaving it depleted and not working optimally.

In addition, you may have viruses affecting your immune system without knowing. You may think your fatigue is due to lack of sleep, but you actually have an undetected virus causing issues in your body. Viruses, such as cytomegalovirus (CMV), Epstein-Barr virus (EBV), and herpes simplex 6 (HHV-6), or a combination of these common viruses, may be affecting your immune system. Additionally, some virus that you had in the past or were exposed to unknowingly can reactivate like in the case of Epstein-Barr virus (EBV), which is the same virus that causes mononucleosis and is often linked to chronic fatigue syndrome. Viruses can alter immune function in small and large degrees, affecting thyroid function, immune function, and fertility. Viral exposures greatly influence immune function.

We can test blood for the presence of certain antibodies to see if you have a past or present infection. We find high levels of IgG antibodies to a certain virus in patients who have been infected by that virus in the past. When we find high levels of the IgM antibodies to a virus, it tells us that you have a current infection. Someone with many elevated IgG antibodies may still have impacted immune function. For example, one person with an Epstein-Barr virus IgG reading of 8 high shows a past infection, while another person has an Epstein-Barr virus IgG reading of 600 high. Is there a difference between these two elevated numbers? Yes, the extraordinarily elevated IgG antibodies to Epstein-Barr virus found in the second person may be an indicator that their immune system is overtaxed by this virus, or possibly has a reactivation of the virus, and that they may require intervention to help calm and regulate the immune system.

In addition to Epstein-Barr, the herpes virus family includes varicella-zoster virus, cytomegalovirus, and herpes simplex. Any of these viruses could be influencing your immune system. In fact, herpes viral infections are associated with reduced fertility in men and alter sperm production (31, 34). Cytomegalovirus (CMV) may also play a role in reduced fertility in males due to alteration in sperm production (32).

Research has also shown that the herpes simplex 6, or HHV-6A, infection might be an important factor in female unexplained infertility development, and that it might have a role in modifying endometrial natural killer cells' immune profile. Natural killer cells are a type of white blood cell that plays a role in taking care of viral infected cells. Having an HHV-6A infection can alter the activity of the natural killer cells that protect the endometrial tissue. HHV-6A causes an increase in cytokines, a substance that increases inflammation in the tissue altering endometrial tissue, causing negative changes in the healthy cell environment. These changes alter the lining of the endometrial lining causing immune dysfunction and affecting implantation and the ability to sustain a successful pregnancy (33). When researchers looked at samples of the uterine lining from endometrial biopsies, they found HHV-6A virus present in forty-three percent of the women with unexplained infertility (33). Again, this points to the role that viruses have in infertility.

These viruses may be compromising the immune system and creating inflammatory agents associated with infertility. I routinely test for viral infection in the initial fertility consult because you may or may not have symptoms related to these viruses, while they are negatively impacting your fertility. If you have not tested for common viruses, then you may be missing the chance to find and remove the roadblock to your success. I routinely test for the following viruses that can cause issues with fertility. Additional viruses can be tested based on individualized history.

Viruses to Test for in Blood Work

- Epstein-Barr (EBV) IgG and IgM
- Cytomegalovirus (CMV) IgG and IgM
- Parvovirus B19 IgG and IgM
- Herpes simplex 6 (HHV-6) IgG and IgM

It is important to address immune factors that might be contributing to your unexplained fertility. This is hard to assess without having a little camera that we can put in the uterus and see what happens during embryo implantation. We can't do that, so what you must do is optimize your health, address any known conditions you may have, create support for your body, reduce inflammation, and build immunity overall. Your body is yearning for your support, so just a little may go a long way in helping to turn the tides and create an environment beneficial for growth and development, which is needed to conceive and support a healthy pregnancy. Focusing on the uterus alone and not taking a broader look at factors that affect inflammation and immunity systemically may be causing you to miss a larger issue or pattern that is creating a non-hospitable environment for an embryo to flourish and grow.

Turning the Tides to Create Optimal Immunity

As previously discussed, your gut health is the core of your immunity. If you have bacteria in the small or large intestine, then you need to identify what type(s) of bacteria you have and treat them accordingly. A healthy diet is a great foundation, but it will not kill bacteria or address dysbiosis that is altering your immune function. Seek out a doctor who is familiar with the appropriate testing and treatment approach to address underlying issues of dysbiosis, SIBO, and/or gut permeability issues.

In addition to addressing gut health, one of the best ways you can reduce inflammation in your body is to optimize your diet. The food you eat dictates if inflammation will flourish or be quenched, and if your immune system will be disrupted or not.

Eat a Nutrient-Dense Healthy Diet Free of Sugar

One thing I see across the board with my patients is poor eating habits. Somehow, everyone has gotten too busy to prepare real food. Most people eat on the go, and choose prepared, boxed, or fast food. Moms who need extra energy and nutrients tend to be the worst, because they are too dedicated to their child's nutritional needs, but neglect their own, making themselves more depleted. Nutrient support becomes extra important for moms when preparing to conceive for the next pregnancy.

Even my patients who exercise regularly are generally missing a healthy whole foods diet component. Having studied clinical nutrition before becoming a doctor and working in multiple clinical settings, I have learned eating is about a lifestyle routine and habit. When we are stressed out, we tend to revert to fast food, foods that are prepared, comfort foods, and foods that give us quick energy. Unfortunately, that tends to be foods high in sugar. When we eat high amounts of refined sugar like cookies, cakes, chocolate, ice cream, sugary cereal, bars, and snacks, we displace good foods with essential nutrients to support hormone, thyroid, and adrenal production essential in fertility.

Many women have been on oral birth control pills for years, depleting their stores of vitamin B6. Maybe they are vegetarian and eating unhealthy food, which can lead to a lack of vitamin B12 and many essential amino acids—the building blocks of protein. Maybe their diet is just devoid of green leafy vegetables. This is not to say that there are not vegetarians who eat a healthy diet, or that none of my fertility patients have been diligent in eating a low inflammatory diet. However, the majority of women need to create a better support system with food. The biochemistry of the body needs nutrients that come from "colors of the rainbow" vegetables and fruits. Nutrients contained in these foods can literally turn metabolic processes in cells on or off. They can tell them to make things that reduce inflammation or increase inflammation to support or hinder hormone production.

Supporting your body with proper nutrients is essential when it comes to fertility. It is not an option to eat poorly. Your body cannot do what you ask it to do unless you supply it with the proper nutrients. So how do you change a habit with food? You target one or two goals and practice them until they become a habit, and then build in another healthy habit over time until your diet looks different. With making only small changes, you have created stability and a routine of eating a whole foods, low fat, high-quality protein, high vegetable, and gluten free diet. If you do nothing to change your diet, nothing changes inside your body in terms of inflammation and immune dysfunction. There are a few tips to follow. We will discuss diet and fertility in detail in another chapter. But for now, follow these basic guidelines.

Address:
- Gut dysbiosis in small intestine (SIBO) and large intestine
- Yeast and parasites affecting the gut microbiome
- Leaky gut

Avoid:
- Sugar that is void of nutrients, takes the place of healthy foods, and creates a glucose and cortisol roller coaster that adds to adrenal fatigue and insulin resistance
- Common allergens: gluten, soy, corn, dairy
- Chemical substances that overload the liver: caffeine, alcohol and recreational drugs

Eat:
- Whole unprocessed foods
- Omega-3-rich foods such as salmon, sardines, and tuna
- Healthy fats such as avocado, coconut oil, olive oil, and nuts

- Lean protein sources such as turkey, chicken, and beans
- 6 servings of green leafy vegetables per day
- Juice greens daily, if possible
- Three meals and two snacks per day

Include:
- Digestive enzymes to enhance digestion of nutrients
- Eat consciously and not on auto pilot, so you are aware of what you are eating
- Drink about ½ your body weight in ounces of water

To Make Diet Changes:
- Target one or two dietary goals at a time
- Add another goal only after you have mastered the first
- Start with a simple goal such as eating a well-balanced breakfast

Adding one new habit at a time, mastering it, and then choosing another will continue to shift and change your diet over time, creating a routine that allows you the foundation and stability to be sustained throughout time. Then, you can slowly start to re-energize your body with healthy habits for long-term support.

OTHER TOOLS TO REDUCE INFLAMMATION IN THE BODY

Gluten-Free Diet

Gluten may play a role in increasing immune-mediated reactions in the body that can increase inflammatory chemicals, creating a cascade of negative effects in the body. Rather than wonder if this is happening or going through testing that may not be comprehensive enough to thoroughly evaluate if you have an immune mediated reaction to gluten, it may be better to go gluten free. By doing this, you minimize the risk of this negative impact. There are many gluten-free alternatives today that are commercially available and restaurants with gluten-free menus, making is easier to eat gluten free at home and on the go.

Enzyme Therapy

Enzyme therapies can contain a combination of plant-based enzymes such as papain from papaya, bromelain from pineapple, and other proteolytic enzymes that are used to reduce inflammation and favorably modulate the immune response of the body. Enzymes have historically been used in the treatment of digestive conditions, cancer, and recovery from sports injuries and surgery. Enzyme therapy can be used in autoimmune disorders and inflammatory conditions to temper and calm the immune system by reducing inflammation. Systemic enzyme therapy has been shown to have favorable effects on inflammatory, metabolic, and immune markers when studied in exhaustive exercise recovery (35). Enzymes can also have blood-thinning properties and improve circulation, which may be helpful with implantation. Enzyme therapy is usually taken orally on an empty stomach. There are many types of enzymes, and having a healthcare practitioner help you to choose the best formula is a good idea.

Fish Oil

There is a multitude of studies on the anti-inflammatory effect of fish oil. Fish oil can serve to reduce inflammation and also has blood-thinning properties, which can benefit blood flow and implantation in addition to reducing inflammation.

Turmeric

Curcumin, a natural active ingredient derived from rhizoma of curcuma or turmeric, possesses antioxidant, antitumorigenic, and anti-inflammatory properties and has been shown to improve production of sperm in obese men suffering from infertility (36). Turmeric also had anti-inflammatory properties in women to reduce systemic inflammation in turn improving immune function.

Resveratrol

Resveratrol is a substance found in plants—specifically in grape, berries, and fermented wine—that may affect your health and fertility. Resveratrol has several benefits. It acts as an anti-inflammatory and antioxidant and can inhibit the growth of tumors (37). In animal models of endometriosis, resveratrol treatment in in-vitro studies suppressed the inflammatory responses of cells in the endometrium (it does this by reducing endometrial stromal cells) (37). Another study indicated that resveratrol has an effect on the immune system that leads to reduced inflammatory substances, which is essential for proper immune function. This is because resveratrol modulates several human immune cell functions related to its effects on cytokine production by both CD4+ and CD8+ T cells (38), thereby reducing inflammation and improving immune function. It has also been shown to protect against age-related diseases such as cancer, Alzheimer's, and diabetes in mammals (39), and has been used in combination with curcumin to improve cognitive disorders (40).

OTHER TOOLS TO SUPPORT A HEALTHY IMMUNE FUNCTION

Manage Stress

Stress is immunosuppressive and causes many other negative effects on the immune system. Studies show that both physical and psychological stress increase inflammatory proteins in tissues and blood in both humans and animals (41). This is not surprising, as we know stress can influence many chemical reactions in the body, leading to reduced immunity. Think about it. When you are stressed and over extended, you get sick. Right? Well, a body under chronic stress is impaired, and this can lead to changes in immune function. It is important to create short-term and long-term stress management strategies to keep your immune system functioning optimally. These strategies can be different for different people, but here are a few ideas that might help.

Short-Term Stress Management Strategies

1. Ten minutes of deep breathing per day
2. fifteen-minute relaxing yoga routine
3. Journaling for ten minutes to express your feelings
4. Talk to a friend for ten minutes
5. Get one more hour of sleep each night
6. Use homeopathic and other adaptogen herbs to modulate stress
7. Don't eat sugar, and eat a well-balanced meal
8. Exercise to reduce stress
9. Write a gratitude list to think of all the good in your life

Long-Term Stress Management Strategies

1. Join a support group
2. Get counseling to work out inner feelings and frustrations
3. Create a long, routine exercise program
4. Incorporate meditation daily into your routine
5. Create a support network of friends and family
6. Release stress, grief, anger, and resentments through many methods (homeopathics for grief are discussed in Chapter 3, including journaling, counseling, and other techniques)

Exercise Regularly

Studies have shown that long-term moderate aerobic exercise training improves sleep, reduces depression and cortisol levels, and promotes significant positive changes in the immune system (42). Exercise is a natural stress reducer. It appears that aerobic exercise has a positive impact on the immune system. Choose the best exercise routine for you. This could be swimming, walking, using an elliptical machine, riding your bike, or any activity that you can incorporate into your life while you are trying to conceive and beyond. Exercise that is mild to moderate can extend into pregnancy and has positive benefits for you and your baby.

Get Adequate Sleep

Lack of sleep further depletes the immune system, creating opportunities for dysregulation. Exercise is a good tool to counter-balance stress and improve sleep, immunity, and cortisol levels. If you are not sleeping or getting regular exercise and are under high stress, then you are not doing yourself any favors. Healthy lifestyle habits and stress reduction help immune function. Shoot for seven hours of sleep each night that is uninterrupted. If you are having problems with sleep, then address them with your healthcare provider. Sleep is your time for your body to repair. If you don't sleep enough, you are altering your immune system and its normal regulation.

Prebiotics

Prebiotics are indigestible plant-based foods that are high in fiber that the good gut bacteria eat to make protective probiotics to keep your gut healthy. Some prebiotics to include in your diet are sauerkraut, kefir, and high-fiber foods like Jerusalem artichoke, asparagus, and kimchi. Including them in your diet can help to support healthy gut flora and reduce inflammation.

Probiotics

Probiotics are the good gut bacteria that stabilize the gut environment, dissuading other bad bacteria from growing and proliferating. In fact, one study looked at the effect of the presence of the probiotic Lactobacillus plantarum in reducing inflammatory substances, which ameliorated inflammation-induced fertility (43). The results confirmed a reduction of proinflammatory agents, an increase in anti-inflammatory cytokines, and improved fertility. Another study showed preliminary evidence that supplementation of probiotic in men significantly improved sperm motility and decreased DNA fragmentation in men with reduced sperm motility (44). This is huge. Keeping a healthy gut biome is really important to the immunity and health of sperm, egg, and your entire body. Supporting immune function is vital to your fertility. Adding high-dose probiotics is an easy way to improve immune function, reduce inflammation, and increase fertility success. A high dose of probiotics can be 25 to 50 billion CFUs (colony-forming units) per day.

Vitamin D

Vitamin D acts more like a hormone in the body and plays a significant role in general immune function. Vitamin D is associated with increased autoimmunity and increased susceptibility to infection (45). This may be because vitamin D receptors are present on immune cells, such as B cells and T cells that help synthesize vitamin D, because it has such a critical role in the immune system (45). It can have a local or more systemic effect on immune function, so it is important to test for vitamin D in the serum and make sure your serum levels are in the optimal range. The reference range of the total 25(OH)D level in the serum is 20–100 ng/mL but an optimal range is 50–80 ng/ml. To get to this level, supplementation may be needed.

In addition, low vitamin D levels are associated with increased risk of miscarriage in the first trimester. So make sure you are taking the right amount of vitamin D and do not have a deficiency.

Colostrum

Colostrum, which comes from the mammary glands of cows, is like breast milk in humans but from a bovine source. It contains proline-rich polypeptide molecules, or immunoglobulins, that contain immune and growth factors. Colostrum has been shown to have a regulatory activity, stimulating or suppressing the immune response, which suggests that prostaglandins (related to inflammation) are involved in the activity of the colostrum (46). Immunoglobulins found in colostrum modulate chemical mediators that suppress cells and stimulate immune cells that favorably support immune function. Immune factors in colostrum protect against invading organisms, neutralize toxins, and help support a strong immune system. It is important to use a hormone-, pesticide-, and antibiotic-free source of colostrum that is the highest quality.

Adaptogens

Adaptogens are botanical medicines or herbs that help modulate the immune system. Examples of adaptogens include astragalus, ginseng, ashwagandha and other herbs with immune modulating properties. They also help to modulate cortisol, which is involved in stress response, pain, and inflammation. Adaptogens can be used alone or in combination with other adaptogen herbs to modulate the immune system. It is important to understand that if you have an autoimmune disorder, you may inadvertently overstimulate the immune system, so check with your doctor before starting any adaptogen herb.

MTHRF MUTATIONS CAUSE AN

ABNORMAL CHANGE IN GENE STRUCTURE THAT AFFECTS FUNCTION AND IMPACTS FERTILITY.

MTHFR AND INFERTILITY:

A POSSIBLE CAUSE OF INFERTILITY AND PREGNANCY LOSS

MTHFR AND INFERTILITY

We know infertility is on the rise and women are having babies older than they did ten years ago. We have established that in addition to advancing maternal age, there are several other potential causes of infertility: hormonal imbalances that affect ovulation, adrenal decline, thyroid dysfunction, inflammation, autoimmunity, and genetics, to name a few. Even with fertility treatments, some women have recurrent miscarriages or remain unable to conceive. One important piece of the puzzle that is too often overlooked, and which may be implicated in recurrent pregnancy loss (RPL) (1–4), repeated implantation failure (RIF) (1,4), and infertility (5) is MTHFR gene mutations or polymorphisms. MTHFR mutations cause an abnormal change in gene structure that affects function and impacts fertility.

WHAT IS MTHFR?

MTHFR is a gene that makes an enzyme that we all need in our cells to convert the inactive form of folate to its active form. Folate, also known as vitamin B9, is a naturally occurring nutrient in certain foods, most notably green leafy vegetables. In fact, folate got its name from green leafy vegetables or "foliage." Folic acid is a synthetic form of folate used in fortified foods

Complete Fertility

and most supplements. Mammals cannot synthesize folate and depend on supplementation through the diet or through vitamins to maintain normal levels (6). The body cannot use folic acid unless it is converted to its active form, 5-MTHF (5-methyltetrahydrofolate). This conversion requires the MTHFR enzyme and a lengthy series of complex biochemical reactions.

The MTHFR gene provides the instructions for converting folate to 5-MTHF, the active form of folic acid or folate. Folate is the same thing as folic acid, and both names imply the non-active or non-methylated form. 5-MTHF is the active form. 5-MTHF is the active form of folate that plays a vital role in cellular physiology by participating in nucleotide synthesis, DNA repair and methylation, and creating stability of genes (7). Mutations of the MTHFR gene may increase homocysteine levels (8) and affect DNA synthesis and methylation, leading to oxidative stress and the disruption of methylation reactions, thereby affecting reproductive function (5). If you have an MTHFR mutation, it means that the MTHFR pathway in the liver and other cells in the body are not able to make the MTHFR enzyme, so it cannot properly change inactive folate to 5-MTHF. With MTHFR mutations, there is reduced ability to make active useable 5-MTHF. This can lead to the body becoming deficient in 5-MTHF, leading to a whole host of problems, including contributing to infertility and birth defects.

MTHFR mutations are actually quite common. The two most common MTHFR mutations are the C677T and A1298C variants. The number and letter sequences refer to what is known as a single nucleotide polymorphism or SNP (pronounced "snip"). It is estimated that MTHFR mutations may occur in 50% of the population or higher, which means that an MTHFR mutation could be playing a subtle or significant role in your reproductive health.

The combination of SNPs you get from your mother and father will determine what mutations you have. DNA is a double helix and the mother and father each give one strand of the DNA helix to make the baby's DNA. So both the woman and spouse/partner have an influence on what MTHFR SNPs the baby will get. That is why both mother and father should be tested for MTHFR mutations. The test is a simple swab of the cheek; it's painless and easy to get results through certain labs. It should not be overlooked as it can be a major issue in infertility and recurrent pregnancy loss. The more SNPs, the less ability to makes active folate for healthy cell division. Both the maternal and paternal MTHFR results affect fertility.

C677T and A1298C MTHFR mutations can be expressed as "heterozygous," meaning different, or as "homozygous," meaning the same. The more mutations, the greater the reduction in your body's ability to make active 5-MTHF. MTHFR mutations can be written in several ways, but usually will include both letters and numbers (for example C677T = 677CT) or even just the letters with no numbers (for example CT or TT). The letter and number sequence refers to the gene and gene position. For example, if the prospective mother has a genetic test with a result of CT when she should have a normal result of CC, she has one mutation and her genes are heterozygous (different). If she has TT results from her genetic test when a normal result would be CC then she has a double mutation, or homozygous (same) mutation. The numbers relate to the location of the gene. What is important is to understand is that the more mutations you have, the more

MTHFR mutations could be an issue affecting your fertility. In addition, MTHFR mutations not only affect conversion of folate to 5-MTHF, they can result in higher levels of homocysteine, especially if you are homozygous for C677T with a double mutation, or heterozygous for both C677T and A1298C with a single mutation on each gene. Research shows that MTHFR mutations, specifically associated with C677T mutations result in high homocysteine levels causing oxidative stress, which can negatively affect egg quality, increase risk of cardiovascular disease (9,10), cause developmental delay of offspring, and cause a variety of neurological and vascular symptoms (11).

MTHFR mutations can be expressed in different language, which can be confusing. Dr. Ben Lynch, author of *Dirty Genes* and expert o MTHR mutations, reports that researchers present MTHFR mutations most commonly in the following language (49, 50):

- MTHFR 677CC = a normal MTHFR gene
- MTHFR 677CT = a heterozygous mutation, which is one mutation
- MTHFR 677TT = a homozygous mutation, which is two mutations
- MTHFR 1298AA = a normal MTHFR gene
- MTHFR 1298AC = a heterozygous mutation, which is one mutation
- MTHFR 1298CC = a homozygous mutation, which is two mutations
- MTHFR 677CT + MTHFR 1298AC = a compound heterozygous mutation, which is one mutation from two different parts of the gene

HOW IS THE MTHFR MUTATION RELATED TO INFERTILITY?

Folate is an incredibly important nutrient. It is involved in the formation of DNA that is required for cell division, DNA repair, and nucleotide synthesis. It facilitates energy production, regulates hormones, and creates neurotransmitters. Folate or folic acid is well known for the important role it plays in pregnancy, ensuring proper neurological development of the fetus, and preventing neural tube defects. Neural tube closure occurs in the first few weeks after conception, commonly before a woman even knows that she's pregnant. Low levels of folate in women have also been linked to low birth weight, preterm delivery, and abnormal fetal growth (12). So we know that you need adequate folic acid for a healthy baby. Cell division, even in the very early stages of embryo development, occurs rapidly with fetal development. Sperm penetrates an egg and cell division starts. Once a fertilized egg divides, cell division occurs rapidly to sixteen cells called a blastocyst. It is in this stage of cell division, which typically falls on Day 5 during IVF, that an embryo is frozen for later transfer to the uterus for implantation. Even in the first early stages of cell division, errors can occur when cells are rapidly dividing, whether you are doing IVF or conceiving naturally. Adequate folic acid is important in the formation of DNA required for cell division. This is huge and CANNOT be overlooked. Not only that, but your body needs the ACTIVE form of folic acid called 5-MTHF. What if your body can't make the active form of folate? Can your body protect against improper DNA synthesis? Can you prevent against neural tube defects? It appears that inadequate 5-MTHF is associated with many links to infertility.

There are conflicting studies on MTHFR mutations and their effects on fertility. A few studies that found no association between MTHFR mutations and fertility focused on retrospective data that looked at pregnancy outcomes and folic acid supplementation. However, these studies did not distinguish what type of supplement was given, and specifically, if it was the active 5-MTHF or regular folic acid supplementation. Clearly, the type of supplement would make an important impact, especially if it was not the active 5-MTHF form. In addition, these studies have focused on only one variant, such as C677T, alone and not in combination with other SNPs related to methylation and/or clotting factors. So what do the scientific studies say about MTHFR mutations and infertility?

It is believed that folate deficiency and high homocysteine can compromise fertility and lead to pregnancy complications by affecting the development of oocytes (eggs), preparation of endometrial receptivity of the uterine lining, implantation of the embryo, embryo quality, and egg maturation and pregnancy (13). MTHFR mutations have been associated with fetal malformations, spontaneous pregnancy loss, decreases in oocyte maturity, neural tube defects, negative pregnancy outcomes (14) and more recently linked to Down's syndrome (15).

Research studies have examined that MTHFR mutations may play a role in recurrent pregnancy loss (1–4) and repeated implantation failure (1, 4), increase early onset preeclampsia (16), neural tube defects (14), pregnancy complications (17), and may play a key role for prevention of preterm labor and low birth weight of babies (18). Additionally, it appears that MTHFR mutations paired with hereditary blood clotting disorders in women with infertility may increase spontaneous miscarriage (19). More research is needed to determine MTHFR's role in clotting disorders. Additionally, one study investigated anticoagulant treatment on pregnancy outcomes in patients with previous recurrent miscarriages who carry MTHFR gene mutations. They concluded that the most effective treatment was low-dose aspirin, heparin, and 5-MTHF, which helped reduce miscarriage rates (20).

In one recent study, a detailed analysis of two common MTHFR polymorphisms, C677T and 1298AC, was performed. The results demonstrated that maternal MTHFR 1298AC genotype strongly influences the likelihood of a pregnancy occurring, with the A1298C allele being significantly overrepresented amongst women who have undergone several unsuccessful assisted reproductive treatments (21). In addition, parental MTHFR genotypes are one of the few known human genes with the capacity to modulate rates of chromosome abnormality.

The study also revealed the dramatic impact of the MTHFR C677T allele on the capacity of chromosomally normal embryos to implant (21), which makes it evident that MTHFR testing is of important clinical value. Based on the MTHFR mutations identified, doctors could identify women at high risk of implantation failure and help to reveal the most viable embryos during IVF cycles (21).

One study reports that the low folate levels that result from MTHFR polymorphisms or mutations may be factors in nonoptimal egg maturation before conception, which may contribute to congenital abnormalities (22). Of course, the interaction with the environment, both due to external factors as well as factors inside the body, may play a role in epigenetics, the severity of how a mutation may manifest, and its effect or outcome on offspring.

MTHFR C677T mutation is associated with a negative effect on the numbers of eggs retrieved during IVF (23). There are few studies related to MTHFR mutations and IVF outcomes, but more studies are needed to determine the effects of MTHFR mutations on IVF outcomes.

In addition, women who are taking a prenatal vitamin with regular folic acid who have an undetected MTHFR mutation are at risk for unmetabolized folic acid (UMFA) syndrome. Women with this syndrome are unable to convert folic acid to 5-MTHF and they are receiving additional folic acid that they can't break down. This accumulates in the body and causes UMFA. UMFA is suspected to cause immune dysfunction and other adverse pathological effects such as cancer (colorectal cancer in both sexes and in prostate cancer in men) (24). Researchers suggest that the consequence of high folate and UMFA concentration in maternal and fetal circulation warrants additional investigation because excess folate may affect the long-term health outcomes of offspring (25). One study suggests that taking 800 mcg of 5-MTHF per day can bypass the MTHFR block and work as an effective treatment for couples with MTHFR mutations to take while trying to conceive (24).

The important thing to remember is that having 5-MTHF in a prenatal vitamin and men's vitamin could have a vital impact on cell division, immune function, and pregnancy outcomes by supporting methylation pathways.

HOW DO MTHFR MUTATIONS AFFECT INFERTILITY IN MALES?

Research suggest that polymorphisms of MTHFR C677T and A1298C have a close relationship with male infertility (26). This is really ground-breaking. More studies must be done to confirm this, but we can start supporting methylation in men now and work toward reducing defects in sperm to create healthier babies. In addition, the "Male Factor" which is the male genetic role in conception and fertility, is the cause of about 30% or more of infertility in couples. As men age, there is increased risk for developmental delays in offspring. This is probably due to prolonged oxidative stress exposure in men forty-years old and older, paired with methylation mutations and the resulting consequences over time. So since men are aging just like women, they need support as well to create healthy sperm. Let's look at studies that show that men with methylation mutations are making sperm with defects.

Sperm Structure and Quality and MTHFR-C677T Mutation

Sperm production involves cellular, genetic, and chromatin (material chromosomes are made from, composed of protein, RNA and DNA) changes during the production of sperm. Folate and normal activity of 1-Carbon metabolic pathway enzymes are central to nucleotide synthesis, methylation, maintenance of gene integrity, and protection of DNA against damage (27). Lacking folate and/or having a mutation that affects the DNA of the sperm can be detrimental to fertility.

A recent study looked at the association between MTHFR-C677T and the structure of sperm DNA. The study concluded that defective methylation linked to MTHFR may contribute to sperm that is abnormal due to increased sperm nucleus decondensation (28). What does that really mean?

Fertility and sperm quality are linked. Sperm take about three months to mature. When we talk about sperm analysis and quality, we are looking beyond the basics of motility (the ability to move), count (the number of sperm), and morphology (shape). Beyond these parameters, you want to have sperm DNA that is structured normally and mature. The more mature and intact the sperm, the better their overall quality.

As sperm mature during the course of their development, the chromatin or genetic material making up the DNA condenses. If the sperm is immature, however, then their chromatin will abnormally condense. Determining the extent of these structural defects in the DNA reveals the extent to which the sperm have successfully matured and remained intact, thereby evaluating their quality. This process of condensation of the sperm can be measured with the sperm nucleus decondensation index (SDI). The SDI measures DNA damage and sperm maturity.

The exact mechanism by which damaged or immature sperm DNA affects pregnancy outcomes is not known; however, the correlation is strong, making SDI a valuable test, especially for those undergoing fertility treatment such as IVF.

One study looked at two markers of men with MTHFR C677T heterozygous and homozygous mutations. The MTHFR C677T homozygous mutation was associated with a higher sperm nucleus decondensation index (SDI) but did not increase DNA fragmentation (29). A higher incidence of sperm nucleus decondensation index (SDI) was present with men with MTHFR C677T mutations compared to the general male population (29). These men produced sperm with DNA that could not fully condense and were immature, which impaired the DNA structure of their sperm (29).

In addition, DNA methylation is one important regulator in a number of biological processes, including spermatogenesis (the production of sperm). There is a direct influence of epigenetic mechanisms on the process of spermatogenesis (30). MTHFR mutations are one of several genetic factors that have been reported in association with poor semen parameters and male infertility. Men with infertility and severe low sperm count who had MTHFR C677T mutations had a higher incidence of alteration of sperm (31).

More MTHFR-C677T Studies

It appears that research points to MTHFR C677T mutations as the most likely mutations to be associated with male infertility. Several studies have seen a link with MTHFR C677T causing male infertility susceptibility in Asians (32) and concluded that this mutation is likely a risk and a contributing cause of male infertility (1, 26, 32–40). One study did link the presence of MTHFR A1298C mutations with increased risk of male infertility (41). Another study stated that mutations of MTHFR C677T and A1298C may have a close relationship with male infertility (26). Though there may not yet be enough research to say whether or not MTHFR A1298C has an effect on male fertility, it appears that MTHFR C677T mutations imply the most risk of male infertility.

A meta-analysis, which reviews the results of previous research studies, looked at MTHFR C677T polymorphism or mutations involving twenty-six studies and 5,575 cases, and concluded that the results indicate the MTHFR polymorphism is associated with an increased risk of male infertility (36). This does not account for gene-environment interaction with male infertility risk. You could have a mutation and also have sperm developed in a high-oxidative-stress environment, which can further damage DNA. A poor diet low in antioxidants or other factors could compound the results of these studies. MTHFR mutations affect healthy sperm production, but so do other factors that may negatively compound your risk for poor sperm quality.

It is reported that men with MTHFR C677T heterozygous mutations have a 35% reduction in conversion of folate to 5-MTHF, men with MTHFR C667T homozygous mutation have a 70% reduction (42). Five to ten percent of the general population is estimated to have an MTHFR C667T homozygous mutation (42), but those percentages may be higher in men with poor sperm parameters or couples struggling with infertility.

How to Support Men with MTHFR Mutations?

One study showed an increase in sperm count and motility after three months of treatment with folinic acid (43). Generally, 5-MTHF supplementation is needed to support methylation. However, studies also show that taking B12 with 5-MTHF also influences sperm parameters with MTHFR mutations (44). Additional nutrients such as vitamin B6 also support methylation.

What Other Gene Mutations are Related to the Methylation Pathway?

There are other gene mutations that can alter the methylation pathway in the body and further complicate or reduce the ability to methylate folic acid to 5-MTHF. I will just give you a brief description of other genes involved in the methylation process. When these mutations are present, this makes it even harder to get the body to use bio-active 5-MTHF.

WHAT IS CBS?

The CBS gene is involved in methylation. CBS (cystathionine beta synthase) catalyzes the amino acid homocysteine to a molecule called cystathionine with the help of vitamin B6, or pyridoxine. CBS can also convert homocysteine methionine or cysteine. Cysteine is a precursor to glutathione, while methionine is important for DNA methylation and the growth of new blood vessels. A mutation in the CBD gene causes an upregulation of the CBS enzyme, which may cause changes in neurotransmitter production and affect mood. It can also further impair your ability to methylate folic acid to 5-MTHF, causing further impact on fertility. This gene mutation may also contribute to possible mast cell activation disorder (MCAD).

WHAT ARE MTR AND MTRR?

MTR, or methionine synthase, and MTRR, or methionine synthase reductase, are genes that help recycle vitamin B12 (Cobalamin). The MTR gene provides instructions for making an enzyme called methionine synthase. This enzyme converts homocysteine back into methionine, preventing the negative build-up of homocysteine in the blood and supplying the methionine integral for DNA methylation to occur. The body then uses methionine to make proteins and other important compounds. Methionine is also necessary for utilization of methyl-groups from the folate cycle. MTR or methionine synthase needs methylcobalamin (active vitamin B12) and another enzyme called methionine synthase reductase, which is produced from the MTRR gene.

A mutation in one or both of these genes can deplete methylcobalamin and reduce methylation. In fact, a meta-analysis study looking at a compilation of thirty-seven studies concluded that MTR A2756G and MTRR A66G both play a significant role in the pathogenesis of male infertility (40). Remember, the body needs methylation to work in order to turn folate (folic acid) into the active 5-MTHF, so it can be used during DNA production and repair during fetal development. A mutation with MTR, MTRR, and MTHFR further reduces your ability to methylate, thus impairing your fertility. Generally, both 5-MTHF and methylcobalamin supplementation is required to support these mutations.

WHAT IS COMT?

COMT stands for catechol-O-methyltransferase and it is an enzyme that is responsible for the breakdown of substances in the body called catecholamines. Catecholamine based neurotransmitters (chemical messengers) include dopamine, norepinephrine, and epinephrine (adrenaline). COMT also functions to break down estrogens and is involved in toxin elimination in the body.

What is the COMT Gene Mutation?

With the COMT genetic mutation, there can be excess levels of dopamine, epinephrine and norepinephrine, which are excitatory (stimulating) neurotransmitters. Those excess levels can contribute to anxiety, aggression, and mood swings. The COMT mutation has also been correlated with panic disorder (45), bipolar disorder (45), ADHD (45, 46), and fibromyalgia (47). It may possibly play a role in some autoimmune disorders. Moreover, because the COMT mutation inhibits the proper breakdown of estrogens, it can contribute to PMS, hormonal migraines, painful menstrual cramps, and heavy bleeding.

How are COMT and MTHFR Related?

The MTHFR pathway is helping to produce neurotransmitters, and COMT helps to breakdown those neurotransmitters. So if the MTHFR pathway is enhanced, that can overload the COMT pathway, because it can't break down the neurotransmitters fast enough to keep up. Even if you don't have both mutations, both the MTHFR and COMT pathways need to be supported and balanced to optimize treatment outcomes.

What Nutrients are Involved in Methylation?

Other nutrients, such as methylcobalamin (vitamin B12 in its active form), riboflavin (vitamin B2), pyridoxal 5'-phosphate (P5P or vitamin B6) along with other nutrients are vital in the methylation process. Depending on your individual genetic mutations in this pathway, your doctor may recommend additional nutrients that act as helpers to support this pathway. These nutrients can act in both subtle or dramatic ways to help this pathway work properly and improve your health and well-being.

HOW DO WE TEST FOR THE MTHFR AND OTHER METHYLATION GENE MUTATIONS?

Testing for MTHFR mutations requires a simple DNA test, which is usually done as a saliva test or swab of the cheek. This can be completed at home or in a doctor's office. It is painless, quick, and easy to do. The MTHFR test is just one of several diagnostic approaches to investigate the cause of infertility, allowing for better outcomes. However, this often is overlooked and could be your roadblock and should be addressed. I find that supporting this pathway can get women pregnant, even if they had trouble conceiving previously or had miscarried. Remember not to overlook the testing of your partner or spouse, as we see there is a link between MTHFR mutations and quality of sperm.

WHAT NUTRIENTS ARE INVOLVED IN THE TREATMENT OF METHYLATION MUTATIONS?

Taking 5-MTHF supplementation as well as other nutrients, such as vitamin B12 (in its active form, methylcobalamin), vitamin B6 or pyridoxal 5'-phosphate (called P5P in its active form), vitamin B2 or riboflavin, and magnesium are vital in supporting the methylation pathways (49). What forms does folic acid come in? Folate or folic acid, folinic acid, and 5-MTHF. Folinic acid is a metabolically active form of folic acid that does not require enzymatic conversion into another form. Folinic acid, like folate, can be found naturally in foods we eat. However, folinic acid does not supply a methyl donor to the methylation pathway to support it, which you want if you have an MTHFR mutation and folinic acid does not seem to raise the 5-MTHF levels in the brain (48) with supplementation. This illustrates the fact that it may function differently than 5-MTHF. Therefore, 5-MTHF is the preferred source of supplementation for people with MTHFR mutations. Naturally occurring folate from food sources, such as kale, spinach, broccoli, and other green leafy vegetables seems to be tolerated well with people with MTHFR mutations, but enriched folate products generally in processed foods, such as boxed cereals, should be avoided.

Focus on taking added folic acid supplementation for conception in the form of 5-MTHF in a prenatal vitamin or as an additional supplement. Naturally occurring 5-MTHF has important advantages over synthetic folic acid because it is well absorbed, even when gastrointestinal pH is altered. Also its bioavailability is not affected by metabolic defects. Using 5-MTHF instead of folic acid reduces the potential for masking hematological symptoms of vitamin B12 deficiency, reduces interactions with drugs that inhibit dihydrofolate reductase, and overcomes metabolic defects caused by methylenetetrahydrofolate reductase polymorphism (7). It appears that B12, 5-MTHF, and B6 have a beneficial effect on pregnancy outcome with supplementation in women with recurrent pregnancy loss (2) as well as the effect that low folate levels have on reduced methylation to 5-MTHF and its negative effect on sperm quality, pregnancy loss, and multitude of other negative effects on fertility. Use of 5-MTHF also prevents the potential negative effects of unconverted folic acid in the peripheral circulation (7) and UMFA (24). Depending on your individual genetic mutations in this pathway, your doctor may recommend additional nutrients that act as helpers to support the methylation pathway. These nutrients can act in both dramatic and subtle ways to assist methylation, cell division and DNA, affecting your fertility and your ability to have a healthy pregnancy and offspring. Remember that supplementation depends a lot on the results of both you and your partner's MTHFR test results. So before starting to conceive or during the process, make sure you are checked for these mutations so you can provide the proper support. I find that some of my hardest cases are with patients who missed the MTHFR mutations that prevented them from achieving success. Once those MTHFR mutations were identified and supported, they were able to conceive, not miscarry, and have healthy babies.

MALE FACTOR:

MAYBE IT'S NOT JUST YOU

What is male factor, you may ask? It is simply the other part of the equation when we look at the puzzle of infertility. Women may naturally feel like it is their bodies that are the problem preventing them from getting pregnant. Sometimes it is, but the male factor accounts for an estimated thirty to fifty percent of infertility cases. We are missing something if we don't focus on what your partner contributes to the equation. No one likes a magnifying glass put upon their manhood, but discovering a roadblock that can be easily addressed is an important part of the puzzle that should not be overlooked.

Infertility is a serious social problem in advanced nations, with male factor infertility accounting for approximately half of all cases of infertility (1). About half of infertile couples have a male factor component of infertility, while almost thirty percent of infertility in couples is due to male factor alone (2). According to the National Infertility Association, thirty percent of infertility cases are related to male factor issues, a recent study showed that only forty-one percent of OB/GYN physicians even considered a urological evaluation of the male partner and only twenty-four percent would routinely refer men to the urologist before ordering a semen analysis (3). Considering that male factor may be up to fifty percent of the cause of infertility in couples struggling to conceive, the medical profession as a whole is not referring to or considering male factor in cases of infertility when they should. Research studying semen quality of over 1,400 men in a total of sixty-one papers published between 1938 and 1991 report there has been a genuine decline in semen quality over the past fifty years and an overall reduction in male fertility (4).

What is the cause of this rise in infertility and issues with male factor? It seems that poor sperm parameters are closely related to a male's overall health. So infertility reflects less than optimal health. Most men who have poor sperm quality may also have other health conditions at the time of their diagnosis. Are we just not as healthy as we used to be fifty years ago? There are probably many factors, including men having babies with their partner or spouse at forty years old or older, when sperm fragmentation increases. We also are living in high-stress times, eating a diet that is about convenience rather than health, exposed to more toxins in our environment, pesticides in our food, and other lifestyle factors all of which may be contributing to issues with male factor affecting fertility.

We can divide male factor infertility into two basic categories: obstructive and productive. Obstructive causes relate to conditions that obstruct the flow of sperm, which negatively impacts fertility. Productive causes relate to the actual production of sperm and how this can also negatively impact fertility. Let's look at the two categories that negatively affect male factor.

OBSTRUCTIVE CAUSES

According to the Urology Care Foundation and The Official Foundation of the American Urological Foundation, obstructive causes of male factor infertility can be due to several reasons (5). These can include the blockage of the vas deferens, which affects transport of sperm from the testicle to the urethra. Post-operative surgery in the region of the inguinal canal or pelvis, such as hernia repair and orchidopexy, may also cause obstruction of the transport of sperm. In some men, infections such as chlamydia, gonorrhea, or tuberculosis can result in blockage. Other bacterial or viral infections may also cause blockage of sperm transport. Congenital abnormalities or undescended testicles, which maybe present from birth, can cause obstruction of sperm transport. Lastly, a vasectomy can purposely obstruct the vas deferens, inhibiting the transport of sperm. In some men, this procedure can be reversed.

PRODUCTIVE CAUSES

Productive causes of male factor infertility may include: viruses causing inflammation in the testes, which may affect sperm production; mumps orchitis, which can destroy sperm-producing cells and may result in permanently low or even absent sperm count; hormone-related issues causing a down regulation in sperm production; varicocele, which is like varicose veins in the testes that could impair sperm production; erectile dysfunction; retrograde ejaculation (sperm move in a backward propulsion during orgasm); injury; cancer; and genetic or environmental exposure to toxins affecting sperm production (6). Another concern is immunological-related issues, which can prevent sperm from successfully penetrating the egg. This could be related to endocrine disorders or to antisperm antibodies.

In addition, medications including antihypertensives (spironolactone and calcium channel blockers), H2 blockers (cimetidine), and antiandrogen treatment for the prostate (flutamide), may adversely affect sperm function.

Furthermore, there are changes in sperm production and sperm parameters with aging (7). Changes in sperm parameters start around age forty, but could happen earlier depending on various factors. Changes in sperm parameters have a direct effect on impaired fertility.

Whatever the cause may be, male factor clearly should not be ignored in the equation of infertility. Since 1980, the fertility rate for men in their thirties has increased by twenty-one percent, and for men aged forty years and older, the rate has increased nearly thirty percent. Both men and women are having babies at an older age (7). While men's sperm parameters reduce starting at forty years old, they drastically decline at 45 years old. Older fathers pose a new challenge in addressing the complexity of male factor. Now that we have established how important healthy sperm are, let's understand how they are produced and what you can do to improve male factor.

HOW ARE SPERM PRODUCED?

The production of sperm takes place in the seminiferous tubules of the testes. Sperm cells divide in the seminiferous tubules until they are mature. Two cells that support this process are the spermatogenic cells that develop the spermatozoa, aka sperm, and the Sertoli cells, which support and provide nutrients to help the maturation of the sperm. Sertoli cells also produce testicular fluid, including a protein that binds testosterone (8). Leydig cells that are between the seminiferous tubules make and secrete testosterone. The production of testosterone is derived from a series of chemical signals exchanged within the brain, specifically between the hypothalamus and the pituitary gland. The production of gonadotropin-releasing hormone triggers the release of FSH (follicle-stimulating hormone) and LH (luteinizing hormone), both necessary to stimulate natural testosterone production. Testosterone is important because it promotes production of sperm.

Sperm production, from beginning to end, takes about three months. That means everything you do now to improve sperm count, motility, morphology, and quality will have an effect about three months from now. The good news is males can continuously make new sperm, whereas females are born with all the eggs they will have in their lifetime. This gives men an amazing opportunity to turn their infertility issues around in a relatively quick amount of time.

Complete Fertility

WHY IS SPERM COUNT AND MOTILITY ON THE DECLINE?

There are many reasons why sperm count and motility are on the decline. Environmental factors, oxidative stress, poor lifestyle habits such as smoking and drinking, genetics and older fathers (> forty years old) all play a role in the decline of sperm count and motility (9, 10). As we have noted, it is estimated that forty to fifty of all infertility cases may be due to male factor (9). That a big percentage, which definitely emphasizes that it "takes two to make a baby." It is important to have your partner checked out to assess his sperm parameters and start treatments that can help turn the tides in your direction for a successful pregnancy.

SEMEN ANALYSIS – WHAT IS NORMAL?

What is normal? Sperm analysis generally focuses on three core parameters: sperm concentration or count; sperm motility, which refers to the sperm's ability to move in a forward direction to find the egg; and sperm morphology, which relates to the shape of the sperm. Although sperm may have an abnormal shaped tail or head, it does not necessarily mean that the DNA is damaged. However, a sperm that is not shaped properly is most likely not going to be the one that can swim to the egg and fertilize it. Generally, we want all sperm parameters to be in the normal range, so that the concentration of sperm is high enough to ensure fertilization. This means that enough sperm are the right shape, can move in the proper direction at the proper speed, and can get to the egg in time to penetrate its outer layer and fertilize it.

Most men fall into three parameters that may be suboptimal or low, including: a low sperm count (oligospermia) or no sperm count (azoospermia), decreased sperm motility (asthenospermia), or abnormal morphology. You would be surprised that men under forty often have abnormal sperm parameters. Who thought getting normal values would be so hard at thirty-five, or even thirty-two years old? If, for example, sperm count is low but motility is normal, you may still have a fighting chance. But, if both count and motility are low, that poses a more significant barrier to conceiving.

The World Health Organization (WHO) in 2010 recruited a team of physicians and scientists to publish a manual describing in detail what the normal semen parameters of a fertile man should be and how to analyze semen in the laboratory (11). However, in 2017 researchers did a systematic review of the WHO semen analysis and identified limitations of semen analyses in the evaluation of infertility, as well as the disadvantages of using a single threshold value to distinguish abnormal and normal parameters (12–13). For example, the WHO semen analysis guidelines did not account for equal distribution of population, under- and over-representing different population groups. Additionally, only fertile couples were included in the study instead of comparing them to sperm analysis of infertile men. Even with the limitations of the WHO guidelines, it is still considered the gold standard for evaluating semen analysis and determining if sperm parameters are normal. What the 2017 study illustrated is that normal sperm analysis guidelines might be different for infertile men. Taking this into consideration, there may be sperm values that appear normal according to the WHO guidelines, that are actually too low for infertile men. And there may be a more optimal range that is superior for infertile men, rather than men in the general population. To understand the table below, you first need to understand that sperm can be described as non-motile, non-progressive motile, and progressive motile.

- Non-motile: refers to sperm that are not moving. On a semen analysis report, this will sometimes be abbreviated as IM for "immotile," or grade D.
- Non-progressive motile: refers to sperm that are moving, but not moving in the forward direction as they should. Also called "NP" for non-progressive, these sperm are slow and are labeled grade C.
- Progressive motile: refers to sperm that are moving in the correct direction. Called "PM" for progressive motile, these sperm are medium to fast, and are labeled grade B.

For an accurate semen analysis, it is recommended to avoid ejaculation for 2-5 days prior to the test. When interpreting semen parameters, "normal" may just not be good enough. The subfertile range is better than normal but you are striving for the fertile range, which is most optimal for conception.

Understanding Semen Analysis Results

SEMEN PARAMETERS	NORMAL RANGE (NEEDS IMPROVEMENT)	SUBFERTILE RANGE (BETTER BUT STILL NEEDS IMPROVEMENT)	FERTILE RANGE (OPTIMAL RANGE)
SPERM CONCENTRATION	≥ 15 million/ml	20-40 million/ml	> 40 million/ml
SPERM MOTILITY	> 32% PM or > 40% PM +NP	40-62% PM	> 63% PM
SPERM MORPHOLOGY (TYGERBERG STRICT CRITERIA)	≥ 4%	9-12%	> 12% or more
SEMEN VOLUME	≥ 1.5 ml	2-5 ml lower end of range	2-5 ml upper end of range

References for table (11, 14-16)

DOES AGE MATTER?

It appears that age does matters. In men, changes can start to appear in semen analysis by age forty, but the magic number for men is forty-five. If you are forty-five or older, there is a definitive decline in semen quality. Research shows that semen quality in healthy males will continue to decline as men progress in age from their late forties to mid-fifties. One study that looked at men between fifty and eighty-two years old showed that Sertoli cell population declines with age, resulting in a significant relationship between sperm production rates and number of Sertoli cells (17). There seems to be a decrease in semen volume, sperm motility, sperm morphology, and count, as men age (18–20). In addition, studies confirm that aged men have overall negative changes in sperm genetics (20–21). Studies continue to show an overall increased risk of health problems, particularly neuropsychiatric conditions, such as schizophrenia, bi-polar, and autism, in the offspring of older men (20). While men can often maintain fertility potential throughout a lifetime, increasing evidence indicates the worsening of semen parameters, including sperm genetics, and potentially worse reproductive success (18–22). Older men pose increased risk in their offspring for certain medical conditions. So what if you are fifty years old and ready to start a family? What do you do, then? Support healthy sperm production at any age to improve your odds for healthy sperm and a healthy baby.

IMPROVING SPERM PARAMETERS

Improving sperm parameters is important since the male provides half the DNA. Improving sperm parameters improves your chance to have a baby and create healthy sperm with healthy DNA. It is possible to change sperm parameters with integrative and natural substances. There is more research showing evidence of natural supplementation and specific nutrients that can improve sperm parameters. We know that sperm is produced about every seventy-two days (close to three months); therefore, males have the unique opportunity to create increased sperm count in addition to more viable sperm with healthier DNA every three months. Specific research has been done to see what nutrients positively impact sperm parameters. This means that by simply taking certain nutrients, you can improve sperm parameters in about three months.

Nutrients to Improve Sperm Parameters

- Vitamin D – Involved in hormone and sperm production. Supplementation increases sperm motility (23).
- Carnitine – Involved in sperm maturation. Supplementation increases motility and improves morphology (24).
- Vitamin E, C, and CoQ10 together – Increase sperm count (25).
- Antioxidants - Increase sperm motility, improve morphology, and sometimes improve DNA integrity. Studies cite vitamin C, vitamin E, glutathione, CoQ10 as beneficial antioxidants proven to benefit male infertility (25–28).
- Myoinositol – Improves insulin sensitivity, increases sperm concentration and motility, and improves sperm morphology in men with metabolic syndrome (29-32).
- CoQ10 – Improves sperm concentration and motility. Research does not show an increase in pregnancy rates or live births, but does show an increase in sperm parameters (33).

- DHA – Increases sperm quality and motility. In one specific study, after only one month of use of 1 –2 grams, or after three months use of a half gram per day, there was an increase in sperm quality and motility (34).
- Ginseng – Is currently being researched for its impact on sperm parameters, but it appears to have a beneficial effect (35, 36), and supplementation has been shown to protect sperm during chemotherapy (37).
- Zinc – low levels are seen in seminal plasma of infertile males and supplementation may increase sperm quality (38, 39).
- Selenium – may help protect DNA integrity and reduce DNA fragmentation (40).
- L-arginine with Pycnogenol® (41) and L-arginine with Pycnogenol®, French maritime pine bark extract, L-citrulline and roburins enhanced sperm volume, concentration, motility, vitality, and morphology (42).
- B-12 – improve sperm counts and motility (43).
- Lycopene – Improves sperm count, viability and may improve sperm morphology (44-45).

WHAT LIFESTYLE CHANGES CAN HELP SPERM PARAMETERS?

Making small lifestyle changes can impact the condition of sperm in a relatively short time. You have the power to positively impact sperm production with the following suggestions that you can start immediately.

- Wear loose underwear to reduce pressure and circulation to testes
- Avoid saunas, tubs, or spas that increase your body temperature
- Avoid toxins in your home, yard, and in your food supply
- Exercise and maintain ideal body weight (IBW) for your height
- Maintain a healthy diet with foods rich in antioxidants
- Don't smoke or use recreational drugs
- Eliminate alcohol or significantly reduce alcohol consumption to one drink per week
- Take a high-quality daily multivitamin
- Reduce stress with stress-management strategies

Avoid Toxins

Studies confirm that male sperm counts are declining, and that environmental factors, such as pesticides, exogenous estrogens, and heavy metals may negatively impact spermatogenesis (46). Do a survey of all possible environmental exposure that could be negatively influencing sperm production. Remember to consider exposure in the home, at work, and with recreational activities. This means you need to avoid or limit exposure to many household cleaning products, bug sprays, week killers, or other substances that may alter sperm production. In addition, if you think you have been exposed to heavy metals from the environment, such as old piping, or through mercury tooth fillings, or growing up on a farm with pesticide exposure, you need to be tested and treated appropriately. High levels of lead or mercury reduces sperm production. Make sure to eat an organic diet free from pesticides, herbicides, and fungicides, which can help you to avoid chemicals in your food supply that would otherwise have a negative impact on sperm parameters.

CAN ACUPUNCTURE HELP SPERM COUNT AND MOTILITY?

Acupuncture reduces inflammation, increases sperm motility, improves semen parameters, modulates the immune system, and improves sexual and ejaculatory dysfunction in male infertility (47–49). I have seen sperm parameters change drastically with acupuncture treatments. Even in the case of vasectomy reversal, regular weekly acupuncture treatments over a three-month period have dramatically increased sperm parameters. Not only are there clinical studies to show that acupuncture can help sperm parameters, but in Traditional Chinese Medicine (TCM) we know that acupuncture can help build the Qi, or vital force, of both the sperm and the person being treated. It can help stress, reduce low-back pain, and much more, while helping fertility. The beauty of acupuncture is that it treats the whole person, so by helping fertility, you also help other conditions and the body as a whole to create more balance and health. Based on research, the scientific explanation of what acupuncture does on the physiological level suggests that acupuncture enhances germ cells through improvement of Sertoli cells. This may facilitate sperm production and restore normal semen parameters in infertile men. Furthermore, studies conclude that acupuncture may be useful in nontraumatic treatment for males with very poor sperm density, especially those with a history of genital tract inflammation.

DOES TESTOSTERONE "T" USE HELP SPERM PRODUCTION?

You might think that testosterone supplementation would help sperm production, since testosterone is involved in the maturation of sperm. However, there is a difference between taking testosterone from an outside source and producing it internally. Contrary to what a lot of people might think, taking "T" supplementation will reduce sperm production and reduce your fertility (50). This is because the pituitary gland and hypothalamus in the brain tell the body how much testosterone to produce. Excess testosterone levels, which can result from taking some supplements or testosterone therapy, send a signal to the brain that there is enough testosterone in the body. This signal can result in less internal production of testosterone and lead to a lower sperm count.

DOES SPERM QUALITY MATTER?

Yes, quality matters, and it matters a lot. You can have all the sperm in the world, but if you have sperm with damaged DNA, then you are not going to be very successful in becoming pregnant and you risk increased incidence of other health problems in your offspring, including birth defects and chromosomal abnormalities. I don't like the sound of this. Do you?

The reality is that couples are having babies older than they used to, and that includes the male counterpart. There is a direct correlation with aging and reduction in sperm parameters, including sperm motility, concentration, count, and morphology. A male can have a good sperm count, good sperm motility, and normal sperm shape, but still exhibit a high degree of damage in the DNA, called DNA fragmentation. One of the most significant factors in aging is an increase of DNA fragmentation. One test that is used to determine if the quality of the sperm is good, is called a sperm chromatin structure assay. This diagnostic tool detects small breaks in the sperm chromosomes consistent with a high degree of DNA fragmentation. The test is used to distinguish normal sperm from those with DNA fragmentation. The test uses a series of stains, complex instrumentation, and laser beams to look at the percentage of sperm that are intact versus the ones that have breaks and fractured DNA. DNA fragmentation could be the root cause of repetitive failed IVF cycles, recurrent miscarriage, and infertility. In addition, sperm condensation index (SDI) is a measure that's used to look at the faulty compaction and abnormal structure of sperm. The SDI has not been a point of focus in the past, but recent research is looking at increased SDI as a factor related to failed IVF and infertility. Higher SDI levels are correlated with lower sperm concentration and some negative effect on sperm shape. Again, these changes are correlated with men as they age. This research focuses on men that are "aged," meaning men that are older than forty. I know you don't feel old and you don't look old, but according to the research, when you're forty, things start to change with your sperm, and when you are forty-five, sperm parameters start to rapidly decline. Are you getting down? Don't! The good news is that research is finding some tools that can help change and improve DNA fragmentation, which leads to higher incidence of pregnancy and healthier babies.

IMPROVING SPERM QUALITY

Many factors affect sperm quality. Therefore, it is important to know not only what things to avoid but also to learn what elements you can incorporate into your routine and lifestyle that can improve sperm quality. Let us survey the best researched-based nutrients and lifestyle habits to improve sperm quality.

Lifestyle

Lifestyle habits such as alcohol consumption, steroid use, and obesity are well known to increase sperm DNA fragmentation (51). Chemicals in a highly polluted environment can also have a negative impact on sperm DNA. Oxidative stress plays a role in DNA fragmentation, and oxidative stress increases with age. Some of the best things that you can do in terms of lifestyle modifications are related to your diet. Eat a diet rich in whole foods, healthy fats, and lean protein sources. Avoid sugar, simple carbohydrates, and processed foods. Eat food free of hormones, pesticides, herbicides and chemicals. Refrain from smoking, drinking, and recreational drugs, and minimize your use of medications to those that are medically needed. Avoid or minimize exposure to pollutants, chemicals, and toxins. Use chemical-free detergents, soaps, and cleaners in your home, and avoid chemicals at work or in your garden or while doing yard work. Consider a good water filtration system and air filters with a carbon layer to pull gases from the air in your home. Minimize chemical exposure with proper gear and precautions while painting or doing other activities where exposure could occur.

MTHFR Mutations

Methylenetetrahydrofolate reductase (MTHFR) is a gene that produces an enzyme that changes its structure through a chemical process called methylation by converting folic acid to its active form, called methyltetrahydrofolate, known as MTHF. There are two isoforms of the MTHFR gene: C677T and A1298C. Men with the isoform of MTHFR C677T appear to be at increased risk for infertility (52, 53), however, a recent study also links A1298C mutation with male infertility (54). Research has shown that if someone has a single mutation, called a heterozygous mutation on this gene, they are at risk. If they have a double mutation, known as a homozygous mutation, they have an increased risk of infertility, higher SDI, and significant abnormalities in sperm DNA and structure (55). It is estimated that about thirty to forty percent of the overall population carries the C667T and A1298C isoforms of MTHFR gene. That means it is possible that you have this mutation, giving you an increased risk of impaired condensation of the sperm, which results in decreased quality of sperm and infertility (56), and potential miscarriage (57).

Furthermore, hereditary hyperhomocysteinemia results from a mutation of the MTHFR gene. This condition reduces folate in men, which affects sperm quality and sperm DNA methylation, and causes epigenetic modifications that can result in fetal neural tube defects (58). Anyone who has a high SDI should be tested for mutation of the MTHFR gene. Really, every male should be tested, as this greatly impacts your ability to conceive with your partner and have a healthy baby.

Studies further suggest that taking supplementation of MTHF could decrease DNA fragmentation (59, 60). So if you have this mutation and/or you are a male over forty years old, and you are trying to conceive with your partner, you should be taking a supplement with MTHF and NOT folic acid or folate. Folic acid and folate are not the active forms your body needs if you have this mutation, and should be avoided in your vitamins and supplements. MTHF or L-methylfolate are the forms you should be supplementing with to improve DHA quality.

Probiotics

Probiotics are the good bacteria that reside in your gastrointestinal (GI) tract. Did you know that taking certain strains of probiotics could improve sperm DNA fragmentation? That is amazing! A recent study has shown that probiotics (specifically the two strains selected for the study, which were lactobacillus rhamnosus and bifidobacterium longum, did in fact improve sperm motility and decrease DNA fragmentation. Motility improved six-fold, and DNA fragmentation decreased one-and-a-half fold with only three to six weeks of supplementation (61). More studies are needed to understand the impact that probiotics have on sperm quality, including long-term use of probiotics (greater than three to six weeks), the impact of other strains of probiotics, the combination of different strains of probiotics, combinations of probiotics having a greater impact than others, and synergistic effects with other therapies concurrently. This is a great finding because it is easier to change sperm parameters such as count and motility, but it's much harder to find ways to improve sperm DNA. This is especially true for men who are forty or older, who are more at risk for increased DNA fragmentation. Most reproductive endocrinologists can identify that you have sperm DNA fragmentation, but offer few solutions to the problem, except using a sperm donor. This study begins to show that natural substances and nutrients can have a positive impact on DNA structure. We know that probiotics have a definitive impact on the quality of sperm. So in a nutshell, if you are male and trying to conceive, you should be taking probiotics!

Antioxidants

Oxidative stress has been implicated as a major cause of DNA fragmentation. Antioxidants seem to have a protective effect upon DNA integrity. Oxidative stress has been considered a major contributory factor to male infertility. Studies have demonstrated that lowering and controlling levels of oxidants known as reactive oxygen species plays a vital role in normal sperm production (62). Differences in oxidative damage may be involved in the cause of defective sperm production in some men but not in others (62).

Different studies have shown that antioxidants positively affect sperm concentration and motility. One study reported improvement after six-months of treatment with vitamin E alone (63), another saw positive changes after three-months of treatment with vitamin E and selenium (64), another study reported that sperm motility improved with supplementation of vitamin C with vitamin E (65), and one study showed that three-months of treatment with the combination of vitamins C and E (66) reduced DNA damage of sperm. Although antioxidants have been shown to improve sperm concentration and motility, DNA fragmentation is an entirely different issue.

One study showed that supplementation of vitamin C at 500 mg two times per day and vitamin E at 1000 iu per day for two months significantly reduced fragmented DNA (66). Research has shown previously that germ cells from men with different testiculopathies suffer altered DNA sperm concentration and decreased motility. However, increased motility has been described after six-months of treatment with vitamin E alone at 400 mg per day (67), and after fourteen weeks of treatment with vitamin E and selenium (68), while another group reported an improvement of sperm motility after a three-month treatment with a combination of selenium and vitamins A, C, and E (66). The discrepancies between these observations may also be due to different pathophysiological backgrounds predominating in each of these studies. It is possible that oxidative damage may be involved in the etiology of defective spermatogenesis in some patients and not in others. From the clinical point of view, the present findings open the question of whether male infertility associated with sperm DNA damage can be alleviated by antioxidant treatment. High levels of sperm DNA damage have been reported to decrease male fertility (69-71), and researchers concluded that it is reasonable to prescribe antioxidant treatment in some patients. In fact, some studies have reported an improvement of pregnancy rates in asthenozoospermic patients after combined oral antioxidant treatments (72–75).

Superoxide dismutase and Antioxidants

Superoxide dismutase is in antioxidant that can be used as a supplement. We already know that antioxidants improve sperm quality, but there haven't been many studies on the correlation with antioxidant supplementation and its effect on sperm DNA fragmentation. One recent study looked at men who were taking various oral antioxidant supplements in addition to specific SOD-based antioxidant supplementation, plus hydroxytyrosol (a natural phytochemical with high antioxidant properties from olive and olive leaf extract), and carnosol (carnosol is a naturally occurring phytopolyphenol found in rosemary). The study showed a fifty-six percent improvement in sperm DNA fragmentation (76). Interestingly enough, men taking various oral antioxidant supplementation that were not related to SOD showed a thirty-three percent improvement in their sperm DNA fragmentation (76). In addition, another study found that giving vitamin D and vitamin C together reduces sperm DNA damage (66). Pretty cool, right? Antioxidants helping your DNA fragmentation. Genius! So simple, yet potentially so helpful.

Selenium

Selenium is an essential trace mineral involved in many metabolic and physiological processes. Research suggests that selenium may help to maintain DNA integrity (78). Another study in mice showed that selenium supplementation in a test tube with sperm protected against damage from free radicals by keeping enzymatic and antioxidant process in optimum condition, helping to maintain DNA integrity (78). What these studies imply is that selenium has a protective effect on sperm DNA and may inhibit DNA fragmentation of sperm (79). Infertile men have lower serum selenium levels, which may further illustrate their need for selenium supplementation to improve sperm quality.

Varicocele

Infertility and sperm DNA fragmentation is generally elevated in men with a condition known as a varicocele. A varicocele is similar to varicose veins in the legs, but it applies to veins in the testicles. The valves in the veins no longer function properly and create varicosities in the testes. This may or may not cause changes in sperm production. However, this often is a condition that can reduce fertility in men. Just like with varicose veins, the veins in a varicocele often are not symptomatic, but they can cause reduced sperm production and quality, and could be a cause of infertility. This condition can be surgically repaired, and studies show that a repair of a varicocele can reduce oxidative stress-induced sperm DNA damage and potentially improve fertility. So if you are having issues with infertility, your male partner should be checked for a varicocele and, if he has one, he should be offered a surgical treatment option to potentially improve your fertility.

There are three grades or severities of a varicocele. Grade 1 varicoceles are the most minor and can be connected with increased DNA fragmentation. In one clinical study, grade one varicoceles were shown to improve by simply taking an oral antioxidant supplement. Antioxidants quench free radicals reducing oxidative stress and damage to cells, and serve as great protection when it comes to sperm quality. We don't know if supplementation with antioxidants in men without a varicocele improves DNA fragmentation, but we know it improves sperm quality. A recent study showed one particular antioxidant that can help DNA fragmentation (77). What we know from this study is that a varicocele changes the local environment of the testes, creating oxidative stress and increasing DNA fragmentation. And research shows that oxidative stress decreases sperm parameters. A varicocele, in essence, expedites the oxidative stress due to structure changes. What is the take-home message here? Males, both with varicocele and without, could benefit from antioxidant supplementation and potentially improve the quality of the DNA in their sperm.

THERE ARE NUMEROUS BENEFITS IN USING ACUPUNCTURE AND TCM IN TREATING INFERTILITY.

TRADITIONAL CHINESE MEDICINE (TCM) & ACUPUNCTURE:

HOW IT CAN IMPROVE YOUR FERTILITY

Research is slowly growing in the area of acupuncture and Traditional Chinese Medicine (TCM) to illustrate the efficacy of its use for health conditions including reproductive health and fertility. The National Center for Complementary and Integrative Health (NCCIH) at the National Institutes of Health (NIH) funds and conducts research to help answer important scientific and public health questions about complementary medicine. The NIH is part of the United States Department of Health and Human Services, which is the largest biomedical research agency in the world. According to the NCCIH, "Results from a number of studies suggest that acupuncture may help ease types of pain that are often chronic such as low-back pain, neck pain, osteoarthritis and knee pain. It also may help reduce the frequency of tension headaches and prevent migraine headaches. Therefore, acupuncture appears to be a reasonable option for people with chronic pain to consider. However, researchers are only beginning to understand whether acupuncture can be helpful for various health conditions and is generally considered safe when performed by an experienced, well-trained practitioner using sterile needles" (1).

Although the NCCIH is limited in support of the entire therapeutic scope of acupuncture and TCM including the area of fertility, a growing body of research using acupuncture and Chinese herbs in the area of reproductive health is helping to legitimize its use to benefit women, men, and families. Although it is important to have studies that support the use of acupuncture and Traditional Chinese Medicine, TCM has been in existence for over 6000 years. This ancient system of medicine uses sterilized fine needles that are inserted through the skin to stimulate the body's natural healing process, normalize physiologic function, and create balance in the body.

In China, acupuncture and Chinese herbs are routinely used to improve conception, combat infertility, and support and maintain pregnancy. In the United States, research is growing in the area of reproductive health, especially in the area of using IVF to increase pregnancy outcomes. The significant effect that acupuncture has in the area of fertility offers a unique tool to assist women to improve outcomes with ART, as well as to improve hormone balance, uterine circulation, and other factors that increase chances of natural conception.

WHAT YOU SHOULD KNOW ABOUT ACUPUNCTURE

It is important to understand that licensed acupuncturists are trained in depth in the practice of acupuncture and Chinese medicine. They also have specialized training to uniquely diagnose and treat patients from a TCM perspective. TCM uses pulse and tongue diagnosis along with clinical symptoms to identify TCM patterns that are imbalanced and need to be corrected with acupuncture and Chinese herbs to restore normal physiological function. In addition, some licensed acupuncturists have a specialty in the area of reproductive health and fertility.

Here are some facts about acupuncture and TCM related to fertility that might help you understand it better:

- Becoming a licensed acupuncturist requires advanced graduate training and certification. This means that licensed acupuncturists have completed and graduated from a master's or doctoral level degree program in Acupuncture and/or Oriental Medicine.
- All practitioners performing acupuncture must be licensed and will have the credentials L.Ac. listed after their name. This credential refers to a licensed acupuncturist who has passed state board licensing examinations.
- An acupuncturist certified by the National Certification Commission for Acupuncture and Oriental Medicine (NCCAOM) has passed rigorous national certification exams that go beyond state requirements. These acupuncturists will have the Diplomate of Acupuncture (Dipl. Ac.) or Diplomate in Oriental Medicine (Dipl.OM) after their name to show this certification. It is recommended that a licensed acupuncturist have this national certification, as it denotes that the recipients have attained a national standard of knowledge and care that is tested and certified.
- Some doctors, such as medical doctors or chiropractors, may have training in acupuncture, but may or may not have the same breadth of knowledge of TCM diagnosis and treatment procedures, or the same number of clinical training hours required for a licensed acupuncturist.
- Fellows of the American Board of Oriental Reproductive Medicine (FABORM) are licensed acupuncturists that have highly specialized training in the area of reproductive health and fertility, including all Western assisted reproductive technologies (IVF, IUI, etc.), procedures, and medications, in addition to TCM patterns, diagnoses, and treatment of infertility. They are

versed in treatment of infertility with acupuncture, herbs, medications, supplements, and lifestyle interventions. FABORM must have accumulated specialized training and knowledge in the area of fertility before being accepted to sit for a rigorous examination that covers TCM as well as traditional ART interventions. Fellows of ABORM have the unique knowledge base of both Western and Eastern approaches to addressing issues of reproductive health and infertility.

- The FDA regulates acupuncture needles as medical devices and requires that the needles be sterile, nontoxic, and labeled for single use by qualified practitioners only.
- Acupuncture treatments can be done fully clothed, and the acupuncture points used most commonly are located on the elbows and knees, hands and feet, the abdomen, and head. Auricular (ear) points are also quite common.
- Acupuncture can be used in fertility as well as pregnancy with a trained practitioner to support reproductive health and help to maintain a viable pregnancy.

There are numerous benefits in using acupuncture and TCM in treating infertility. Acupuncture alone and in conjunction with Chinese herbs is quite effective in helping hormone imbalances, such as, PCOS, endometriosis and other menstrual irregularities, and reduce the risk of ovarian hyperstimulation syndrome (OHSS) in women doing IVF. Some of the benefits of acupuncture in treating infertility are listed below.

- Balances hormones
- Improves cycle length
- Improves blood flow to the uterus
- Reduces clots, cramping, and painful periods
- Regulates blood flow or normalizes flow, whether it is heavy or scanty
- Improves thickness of endometrial lining
- Modulates side effects of fertility medications
- Improves the success of IVF and IUI outcomes
- Improves sperm count motility and morphology
- Improves ovulatory function and follicular stimulation
- Improves luteal phase defects
- Reduces anxiety stress and worry
- Decreases physical response to stress

TCM is based on the concept of balance. Traditional Chinese Medicine uses the pulse and tongue to diagnose disharmonies in the body that reflect either a deficiency or excess of Qi or life force. Qi or Chi, pronounced "Chee," is the vital energy that flows through the body and works to maintain health. Qi runs through channels in the body, much like rivers. These channels, called meridians, run on both sides of the body. In TCM, the Qi in these channels must be balanced for optimal health. TCM is based on the balance of five elements: water, fire, wood, metal, and earth. Each element is associated with an organ and channel, as well as other factors including a season, a color, a taste, a time of day or night, an orifice (opening) of the body, and an emotion. For example, the element wood corresponds with the organ liver. Liver corresponds with a sour taste, the color green, the season spring, the time period from 11:00 p.m. to 3:00 a.m., and the emotion anger. The liver channel opens to the eyes. Since TCM is very observation-focused, the color and coat of the tongue, along with the quality of the pulse can give information about what channels are imbalanced. So if a person had a sour taste in their mouth, was waking up at 2 a.m., was irritable, and had a wiry pulse with a purple tongue, it would indicate a disharmony in the liver channel. In TCM, we would use acupuncture and Chinese herbs to smooth the liver and balance the channel to restore health and resolve the symptoms of the disharmony.

Within each organ and corresponding meridian, there are opposing yet complementary forces of Yin and Yang. Disease or reduced function occurs when there is an imbalance of Yin and Yang. Yin is cool, relaxing, nourishing, and moist, where Yang is moving, invigorating, and warm. When checking the TCM pulse, the quality of the pulse reveals the deficiency or excess of Yin and Yang in the different channels. The observation of the tongue also gives information about Yin and Yang of different organs reflecting the balance of Qi. The balance of the channels has a physiological function on hormone regulation, ovarian function, and ovulation, and even helps to thicken the lining of the uterus. TCM and acupuncture can create improved balance, which will help reproductive health and increase your ability to conceive naturally. Acupuncture and TCM can support natural fertility and/or can be used as a transformative complement to intrauterine insemination (IUI), as well as in vitro fertilization (IVF).

In order to understand acupuncture and how it plays a role in fertility, it is important to look at what acupuncture does to create changes in the body's cascade of hormone control. How does inserting a small needle into acupuncture points affect ovulation or any physiological function in the body? In order to understand this from a scientific evidence-based model we can look at research that explains how acupuncture may be altering fertility.

RESEARCH PROPOSING THE MECHANISM OF HOW ACUPUNCTURE WORKS TO IMPROVE FERTILITY

According to an article by author Hesham Al-Inany, M.D., published in the Middle East Fertility Society Journal in 2008, there are three potential mechanisms postulated as to how acupuncture can help fertility. The first is that acupuncture may mediate the release of neurotransmitters, which in turn stimulate the secretion of gonadotrophin releasing hormone, thereby influencing the menstrual cycle, ovulation, and fertility (2). Second, acupuncture may stimulate blood flow to the uterus by inhibiting uterine central sympathetic nerve activity (1). Third, acupuncture may stimulate the production of endogenous opioids, which may inhibit the central nervous system outflow and the biological stress response (2). In addition, the author discusses the systemic review conducted with acupuncture given with embryo transfer to improve live birth rates among women undergoing IVF (2). Seven trials with 1,366 women undergoing IVF were included in the meta-analysis. Acupuncture used with embryo transfer was associated with significant and clinically relevant improvement in clinical pregnancy, ongoing pregnancy, and live birth. The author suggests the possible explanation that if acupuncture works by modulating the balance of endogenous opioids, it opens a gate to apply to fertility patients to improve outcomes by disinhibiting cyclic adenosine monophosphate (cAMP) involved in intracellular messaging, and perhaps also reducing stress felt by couples by disinhibiting dopamine release (2).

AN OVERVIEW OF ACUPUNCTURE AND FERTILITY RESEARCH

We know that acupuncture and TCM can assist both women and men in the area of reproductive health. In order to legitimize and more fully understand the important effects that acupuncture and Chinese herbs can have on your reproductive health, let's survey some of the scientific research into these integrative treatments. In the summaries of studies below, we will look at the growing evidence that acupuncture may increase your success in having a baby and the mechanism by which acupuncture may do this.

ACUPUNCTURE TO ASSIST WITH NATURAL REPRODUCTION

Clinical Studies on the Mechanism for Acupuncture Stimulation of Ovulation (3)

This study used acupuncture points Ganshu (UB 18), Shenshu (UB 23), Guanyuan (Ren 4), Zhongji (Ren 3), and Sanyinjiao (Sp 6) to treat women with ovulation dysfunction, which may contribute to infertility. The group was small, but did show promising results. Thirty-four women who were suffering from ovulatory dysfunction were treated with acupuncture approximately thirty times. The specific acupuncture points used in this study were chosen to strengthen liver and kidney Qi, and to nourish the uterus through the Chong and Ren channels. This, in turn, adjusted the patient's HPA axis function and recovered ovulation. The results showed that acupuncture may adjust FSH, LH, and E2 levels and raise the progesterone level, bringing hormone levels to normal. Animal experiments then confirmed these results. Results showed that acupuncture may adjust endocrine function of the generative and physiologic axis of women, thus stimulating ovulation. The results of this research provided some scientific basis for treating ovulatory dysfunction with acupuncture, and in turn, improving fertility.

Prior to Conception: The Role of an Acupuncture Protocol in Improving Women's Reproductive Functioning Assessed by a Pilot Pragmatic Randomized Controlled Trial (4)

This study was conducted to see if acupuncture had an influence on women's reproductive health prior to conception. The study was done by a pilot pragmatic randomized controlled trial; this type of study allows researchers to conduct new research with real people, in real time. Specifically, the study asked whether providing multiple rounds of fertility-focused acupuncture to women who have non-optimal fertility would increase their awareness of fertility and normalize their menstrual cycles. The treatment group's results were compared with a lifestyle control group in this randomized controlled study. Women were offered an intervention of acupuncture with lifestyle modification or just lifestyle modification alone. The lifestyle modification for both groups included adopting a healthy diet that supported fertility and an appropriate exercise routine (neither too intense, nor too soft), abstaining from smoking, and reducing or avoiding consumption of caffeine and alcohol. Those receiving acupuncture conceived within an average of 5.5 weeks compared to 10.67 weeks for the lifestyle-only group. In addition to conception occurring in half the time in the group receiving acupuncture, women also reported an increased sense of well-being. This is yet another study that supports the use of acupuncture to help with fertility. Moreover, it establishes that acupuncture is not only for improved IVF outcomes, but that it can also be used to expedite natural conception. Since the risks are low for acupuncture treatment, and the benefits are high, acupuncture should be a consideration of every preconception program.

Impact of whole-systems Traditional Chinese Medicine on in vitro fertilization outcomes (5)

This study showed that taking a whole-systems approach, which includes diet, lifestyle, stress reduction, Chinese herbs, and acupuncture nine to twelve weeks prior to starting IVF results in a marked increase in live birth rates compared to acupuncture alone on the day of embryo transfer. This is one of the first studies to evaluate the effect of acupuncture with other lifestyle variables. More research is needed, but this study suggests that taking a comprehensive approach to infertility looks like it is more effective than the benefits of acupuncture alone, without herbs, diet, and lifestyle intervention. This exemplifies the basics of a healthy lifestyle, including stress reduction and diet, which both play a pivotal role in healthy conception. In addition, research has shown a positive effect with the use of Chinese herbal medicines, and adding these medicines to your acupuncture treatment to enhance fertility might be just the ticket to success. Adding positive tools to your fertility toolkit adds up and generates greater support and overall success.

ACUPUNCTURE AND PREGNANCY OUTCOMES IN WOMEN WITH PCOS

Effects of electroacupuncture intervention on changes of quality of ovum and pregnancy outcome in patients with polycystic ovarian syndrome (6)

This study focused on 200 women with PCOS and looked at the effect of electroacupuncture treatment and pregnancy rates. Electroacupuncture is similar to traditional acupuncture in that the same points are stimulated during treatment. As with traditional acupuncture, needles are inserted at specific points along acupuncture meridians, or channels. The acupuncturist then uses small metal clips to attach the needles to a device that generates continuous electric pulses. Electroacupuncture uses two needles at a time so that the impulses can pass from one needle to the other (2). In this study, electroacupuncture was used on six points on both sides of the body for a total of thirty minutes. The study concluded that electroacupuncture can improve high-quality embryo rates, which may be related to the effect it has in increasing serum and follicular fluid stem cell factor levels (3). Higher quality embryos have greater potential to lead to healthy, normal cell division in a growing embryo, which in turn leads to healthy pregnancy and healthy babies.

Stem cells, as referenced in this study, are involved in egg growth and new egg development. There are some doors opening to the future of promoting the use or stimulation of stem cells to promote the growth of new eggs. Women are born with all the eggs they will have in embryo state, and while men produce sperm throughout their lifecycle, women cannot make new eggs in their lifetime. They are born with the eggs they will have and start releasing those egg after puberty hits and they have their first period. This process continues until menopause. Some researchers theorize that stem cells may be able to create new eggs or have regenerative properties that could impact infertility issues. Due to their regenerative ability, stem cells are looked at as a promising tool for improving infertility treatments in women (4). Although the promise of science may create new possibilities for conception in the future, the reality of now is that you have a certain finite number of eggs and you must protect and preserve these eggs to enhance your fertility. Because studies indicate that acupuncture can improve IVF success rates and embryo quality, while reducing OHSS during IVF in women who have PCOS, many fertility experts are incorporating acupuncture into their fertility programs.

Effect of electroacupuncture on oocyte quality and pregnancy for patients with PCOS undergoing in vitro fertilization and embryo transfervitro fertilization and embryo transfer (7)

This study looked at the effect of electroacupuncture on egg quality in pregnancy for patients with PCOS who were undergoing IVF and embryo transfer fertilization. The study concluded that electroacupuncture played an active role in pregnancy outcomes of PCOS patients undergoing IVF and embryo transfer. It also relieved symptoms of kidney deficiency. Kidney deficiency is a pattern in TCM of imbalance that is related to fertility. Kidney deficiency manifests in common symptoms, such as low back pain, memory loss, dry skin, constipation, and dry mouth. This study focused on sixty-six women with PCOS who were undergoing IVF and embryo transfer. The results are pretty impressive because they basically showed an improvement in egg quality with the use of electroacupuncture. Another study involving 200 women with PCOS who were undergoing IVF and embryo transfer concluded that electroacupuncture can improve the high-quality embryo rate. This may be related to its effect of increasing stem cell factor levels in the serum and follicular fluid that promotes egg development.

From these studies, we know that acupuncture has an impact on egg quality as well as other aspects of egg maturation, ovulation, and growth of the embryo. There's so much research to support the use of acupuncture, not just before and after the transfer of the embryo with IVF, but as a preparatory therapy to begin at least three months prior to trying to conceive. Although there are many reasons to use acupuncture as part of your fertility regimen, the effect it has on egg quality is a compelling reason to incorporate acupuncture in your treatment plan. Studies found that using five specific acupuncture points resulted in a rise in levels of stem cell factors in the serum of follicular fluid. This study's results showed an overall change in the endocrine system in the local microenvironment of the ovary, which shows without a doubt that acupuncture acts on the ovaries. The study also showed improved egg quality through the up regulation of stem cell factor in the serum and follicular fluid, resulting from Chinese herbs. Chinese herbs can be used as an adjunct treatment strategy with ART to improve success. And from a TCM perspective, treating the underlying TCM patterns that are not balanced benefits a woman in many ways, including follicular development, ovulation, thickening endometrial lining, reducing stress, improving egg quality, and many other things. Acupuncture is an impactful tool to assist you in your fertility quest and should not be overlooked.

ACUPUNCTURE AND IVF

Effectiveness of acupuncture in women with polycystic ovarian syndrome undergoing in vitro fertilization or intracytoplasmic sperm injection: a systematic review and meta-analysis (8)

This study looked at women who have polycystic ovarian syndrome (PCOS) undergoing IVF or intracytoplasmic injection (ICSI), a common procedure used in IVF. This study included women receiving traditional acupuncture or electroacupuncture compared to control groups. Based on this study of fifteen databases, it was concluded that acupuncture may increase clinical pregnancy rates and ongoing pregnancy rates, while decreasing risk of ovarian hyperstimulation syndrome (OHSS) as well as adverse events in women who have PCOS and are undergoing IVF and ICSI. The researchers concluded that further studies are needed. However, this study shows great promise for treatment of women with PCOS who are at higher risk of OHSS and may not be otherwise able to use IVF as a reproductive tool. If acupuncture can minimize the risk of negative side effects of IVF, decrease OHSS, improve hormone imbalances, and reduce elevated circulating androgen levels, then it opens the door for women with PCOS and infertility to pursue IVF with less overall risk and adverse side effects.

Effects of acupuncture on rates of pregnancy and live birth among women undergoing in vitro fertilization: systematic review and meta-analysis (9)

This study is a meta-analysis that looks at acupuncture's effect on IVF success. What is a meta-analysis? A meta-analysis is a study that looks at the combined results of multiple scientific studies that have already been done.

This study looked at data from seven previous trials (or studies) with 1,366 women undergoing in vitro fertilization (IVF). The author concluded that using acupuncture increased the pregnancy rate by sixty-five percent compared to those not getting acupuncture. The author of the study also discussed the cost of IVF, which in the United States costs an average of $12,400 per cycle. If acupuncture increased the likelihood of success of an individual cycle, the author suggested, then the need for a subsequent cycle would be reduced, and overall costs would be decreased. Although there were some limitations in this study, including baseline rates of pregnancy and other possible bias, the author made the comment that adding acupuncture to IVF improved pregnancy rates more than any other recent improvement or advance in IVF technology. This is a dramatic statement as there was a lot of resistance and debate by reproductive endocrinologists and other researchers who felt that the findings of this study were inaccurate. Because acupuncture is a great divergence from Western biomedical science, it is sometimes difficult to understand how acupuncture works. There was criticism about how the study was conducted and analyzed in addition to the size of the study. However, these studies do point toward growing evidence that acupuncture has a positive effect on pregnancy rates. This study was, of course, related to IVF because there are measurable variables you can control during IVF that you cannot control in natural conception. This meta-analysis was conducted on existing studies that point to the positive effect acupuncture has on IVF and pregnancy rates. This study suggests what we have known for thousands of years, that acupuncture helps fertility. Manheimer et al. concluded that current preliminary evidence suggests that acupuncture given with embryo transfer improves rates of pregnancy and live births amount women undergoing IVF.

Acupuncture and Good Prognosis IVF Patients: Synergy (10)

This study looked 114 infertile patients undergoing controlled ovarian hyperstimulation in a private practice IVF clinic. Traditional acupuncture combined with auricular (ear) acupuncture before and after embryo transfer protocols were used. Acupuncture was used for patients in the poor prognosis population and enhanced outcomes were observed. This was also the first publication of birth outcomes data in acupuncture treating IVF patients. Acupuncture increased live births, and decreased ectopic pregnancies and miscarriage rates. This study suggests that acupuncture can enhance and statistically improve the chance of getting pregnant when used in cooperation with IVF. This gives more evidence that if you are doing IVF you should be also be getting acupuncture to increase your success.

Influence of acupuncture on the outcomes of in vitro fertilization when embryo implantation has failed: a prospective randomized controlled clinical trial (11)

In this study, researchers looked at the influence of acupuncture and outcomes of IVF when embryo implantation had failed. This study demonstrated that acupuncture improved pregnancy rates in women who previously had a pregnancy fail after embryo transfer. The study included acupuncture on the first and seventh days of ovulation induction, on the day before ovarian puncture, and on the day after embryo transfer. The acupuncture group was treated with specific acupuncture points to improve fertility along with moxibustion. Their results were compared to sham groups (control groups who were not getting treatment at the correct acupuncture points) and control groups who received no acupuncture treatment. The clinical pregnancy rate in the acupuncture group was significantly higher than that in the control and sham groups. The study concluded that acupuncture and moxibustion increases pregnancy rates when used as an adjunct treatment in women undergoing IVF for whom previous embryo implantation had failed. This demonstrates the type of significant impact that acupuncture has, especially in a group of females that had prior unsuccessful embryo implantation. The study clearly demonstrated that the acupuncture had a physiological effect in improving the success of embryo transfer.

CHINESE HERBS AND FERTILITY

Hot off the presses, new studies confirm that traditional Chinese herbs improve egg quality, ovarian function, hormone balance, and sperm motility, and increase pregnancy rates in poor responders of ART. I'm not sure why every reproductive endocrinologist is not having a licensed acupuncturist doing acupuncture and giving herbs to their patients. It is clearly a tool that can increase conception success while improving egg quality and HPA axis function in women, and sperm parameters in men. If we were in China, it would be commonplace to use Chinese herbs to prepare for pregnancy, as well as during pregnancy, to keep mother and baby healthy and support proper development. However, in the United States, using Chinese herbs during pregnancy would not be an acceptable route, since there is not enough literature or studies to support their use during pregnancy. However, there are studies based on using Chinese herbs to improve natural fertility success as well as enhance the success of ART. So why is this approach a rarity and not the norm?

Part of the reason is that we have yet to integrate the best that Western and Eastern medicine has to offer. In the area of reproductive health, this integration can result in far better outcomes than using Western fertility approaches alone. In some ways, it is understandable that many REs do not want to interfere with their IVF protocol and may not understand the interaction between drugs and Chinese herbs. However, there are a few REs who also have training as an acupuncturist in the area of fertility who are combining the therapies to heighten their success rates and support the expansion of many happy families. Still, many fertility doctors cling to their own protocol and do not want herbs to interfere with their Western medications. As a physician, I understand that all doctors want to assist their patients in achieving the best possible outcomes. Doctors, therefore, do not want additional outside factors to influence the results of their recommendations, which is an understandable reason not to want Chinese herbs to be used in an IVF cycle, for example.

On the other hand, there are studies to support the use of Chinese herbs in improving fertility for natural conception, and especially for improving egg quality and pregnancy rates for women on medications during IVF. We know women are having babies at an older age, and that as we age, our ovarian function and the quality of our eggs decline. We need to have viable ways to improve this. If you get pregnant, but cell division can't continue because the quality of the egg and the environment in which the egg is developing is not supporting its growth, then you have a failed IVF cycle. If the support is not there, then cell division stops; resulting either in no pregnancy, or if there is a pregnancy, this can lead to a miscarriage. This can happen multiple times for some women, resulting in recurrent pregnancy loss.

Getting pregnant is only the first step in the process for success. Sustaining a pregnancy is paramount, and supporting healthy cell division for a healthy baby is part of the bigger picture of conception. We have to have ways to effectively manage declining egg quality with advanced maternal age. The studies highlight the benefits of Chinese herbs on fertility including lowering FSH levels, and improving a host of fertility-related issues, such as luteal phase defects, sperm and sperm quality, hormone regulation in women with PCOS, endometriosis and other hormone imbalances. These positive results show us the importance of not overlooking the benefits of Chinese herbal medicine.

In addition, some studies have been done with women taking IVF medications while on Chinese herbal medicines to increase pregnancy success. Let's look at some of the studies using Chinese Herbs to support fertility.

CHINESE HERBS AND EGG QUALITY

Oocyte quality improvement using a herbal medicine comprising 7 crude drugs (12)

Recent literature has reported that women who repeatedly failed to conceive by ART have become pregnant after using macrophage-activating Chinese mixed herbs. The studies showed improvement of egg quality and ovarian function using seven Chinese herbs. Those herbs included: Radix angelicae, Rehmanniae radix, Plantaginis semen, Lonicerae flos, Carthami flos, Ginseng radix, and Cucurbita moschata Duch. In addition to having improved egg quality and ovarian function, the women in this study also had an increase in successful pregnancy rates. One of the mechanisms that caused the beneficial effects seen in this study could be the improvement of blood flow, increasing the number of eggs, supporting the development of the early-stage embryo, and leading to successful pregnancy rates.

Clinical study on effect of Erzhi Tiangui Granule in improving the quality of oocytes and leukemia inhibitory factor in follicular fluid of women undergoing in vitro fertilization and embryo transfer (13)

Another study looked at the effects of Chinese Erzhi Tiangui granules or herbs. This study treated forty-two women with these herbs combined with Western medicines. The addition of the Chinese herbs increased the amount of eggs and the quality of the embryo, which raised rates of successful IVF and embryo transfer.

Clinical efficacy of macrophage-activating Chinese mixed herbs (MACH) in improvement of embryo qualities in women with long-term infertility of unknown etiology (14)

This was a small study, but significant. It looked at thirty women who were going through IVF and embryo transfer. These thirty women had long-term histories of infertility and they had significantly low rates of developing good quality embryos. They had unsuccessful pregnancies after three or more IVF embryo transfers. The women were given a combination of macrophage-activating Chinese herbs. Chinese herbs have the ability to enhance the nutritive and nourishing environment of a growing embryo. When these thirty women took these herbs orally, it significantly increased the percentage of early-stage embryo quality in all patients, and for 19 of the 30 women, there was a 52.6% increase in the percentage of late-stage embryo division. No participants dropped out and no side effects from the herbs were reported. This illustrated that the Chinese herbs improved embryo quality in women with difficult cases or unknown causes of infertility. This study demonstrated the potential to increase the possible success rate of IVF in women who otherwise had little hope of success.

Effect of Erzhi Tiangui Recipe on ovarian reactivity in elderly sterile women (15)

This study looked at Erzhi Tiangui Recipe (ETR), a traditional Chinese recipe for strengthening Shen and nourishing Tiangui, in improving the ovarian reactivity in women of advanced maternal age who are sterile. Sixty-six women receiving in vitro fertilization pre-embryo transfer (IVF-ET) were randomly divided into two groups. One group was given the Chinese herbal formula ETR plus follicle stimulating hormone (FSH), and the control group was treated with FSH alone. There were thirty-three women in each group. This is a small sample size, however, the study showed that adding Chinese herbs to the FSH reduced the dosage of FSH needed, improved ovarian reactivity, the pregnancy rate, and the quality of eggs. The authors propose that the mechanism related to ETR's ability to improve ovarian reactivity is that it elevates blood estradiol levels and regulates the hypothalamic-pituitary-ovarian axis.

CHINESE HERBS AND AUTOIMMUNE-RELATED OVARIAN FAILURE

Preventive and therapeutic effects of Bushen Huoxue Recipe on autoimmune premature ovarian failure in mice (16)

This study looked at the use of Bushen Huoxue Recipe (BSHXR), a traditional Chinese herbal medicine formula, on autoimmune-related premature ovarian failure in mice. The results showed that the Chinese herbal formula could reduce patients' high levels of FSH and LH, increase their level of estradiol and the number of growing and mature follicles in their ovaries. It also helped patients to recover ovarian function by regulating hormone levels, and had a preventive effect on autoimmune regulation. Therefore, Chinese herbal medicine can be a useful adjunct to ART and women who have repeatedly failed to conceive by infertility treatment.

COMBINED TREATMENT OF CHINESE HERBS AND IVF

Combined therapy of Chinese medicine with in vitro fertilization and embryo transplantation for treatment of polycystic ovarian syndrome (17)

This study looked at using Chinese herbs to reinforce the Shen and regulate the Chong meridians, which is important in fertility with women who have polycystic ovarian syndrome (PCOS) and are undergoing in vitro fertilization and embryo transplantation (IVF-ET). The study demonstrated that adding the Chinese herbal formula in IVF-ET can reduce the dosage of gonadotrophin that patients require and can raise the clinical pregnancy rate.

Effect of Chinese Herbs Combined DHEA Pretreatment on Pregnancy Outcomes of Elderly Patients with Normal Ovarian Reserve Undergoing IVF-ET (18)

This study looked at women between thirty-six and forty-two years old who had normal ovarian function and wanted to prepare their bodies for a more successful IVF embryo transfer (ET). Two hundred and thirty women in this study took dehydroepiandrosterone (DHEA) with Chinese herbs for eight weeks prior to IVF-ET. The women were randomly divided into three groups: women who took DHEA and Chinese herbs, women who took DHEA only, and women who took neither as a pretreatment before IVF-ET. The results from this study showed some improvement with DHEA alone, but the greatest benefit came from a combination of Chinese herbs and DHEA, which improved embryo quality and increased AMH levels. This study suggests that AMH may not be a static measure, and that it could be improved. This is important because higher embryo quality generally means a higher chance of success in a pregnancy.

Smoothing Gan Reinforcing Shen Method Adjuvantly Treated Poor Response of Diminished Ovarian Reserve Patients in in vitro Fertilization and Embryo Transfer: a Clinical Study (19)

This study looked at eighty-four women who had diminished ovarian reserve and who were undergoing IVF-ET. Part of the group was given the Chinese herbal formula Smoothing Gan Reinforcing Shen (SGRS) daily prior to IVF-ET, and the result was an increase in the number of eggs and improved quality of embryos. The study concluded that Chinese herbs could improve ovarian responsiveness in women with diminished ovarian reserve who are undergoing IVF-ET, increase the quality of their eggs, and the number of embryos. Again this evidence suggests that using Chinese herbs with IVF protocols including IVF medications may improve outcomes in women who have not been successful with IVF alone.

OVERVIEW OF CHINESE HERBAL MEDICINE AND FEMALE INFERTILITY

Traditional Chinese medicine and infertility (20)

This study reviewed the use of Chinese medicine in the treatment of infertility, including an evidence-based evaluation of its efficacy and how well patients tolerated it. The study found that Traditional Chinese Medicine could regulate the gonadotropin-releasing hormone to induce ovulation, and to improve the uterine blood flow and menstrual changes of the endometrium. It also demonstrated that TCM has a positive impact on patients with infertility, resulting from polycystic ovarian syndrome, anxiety, stress, and immunological disorders. The authors highlight the need to examine the pros and cons of both Western and Traditional Chinese Medicine approaches, and that the use of integrative medicine should become a trend in existing clinical practice and serve as a better methodology for treating infertility.

Measuring the effectiveness of Chinese Herbal Medicine in Improving Female Fertility (21)

This study looked at the relationship between female fertility indicators and the administration of Chinese herbal medicine. Fifty women with unexplained infertility were treated with Chinese herbal medicine to see if it could increase pregnancy rates. The results of the study showed that using Chinese herbal medicine results in higher success rates of pregnancy, with no patient side effects, and a reduction in the category of patients conventionally classified as having unexplained infertility.

The sample sizes of these studies were small, but nonetheless, demonstrated that Chinese herbal medicine can enhance the ability of women to conceive naturally and/or with ART. Combine the potential benefits from Chinese herbs with acupuncture, and you have the ability to improve your chances of success. If you are investing the time, money, and energy into IVF then you want the best possible outcome. If you are undergoing IVF, acupuncture at the least is a MUST before and after embryo transfer. These are proven protocols that increase success rates by as much as twenty-percent, or according to certain studies, even more.

SHOULD YOU USE ACUPUNCTURE AND CHINESE HERBS TO INCREASE YOUR FERTILITY?

There is not one good reason why you would not use acupuncture to improve your success rates, after going through the arduous process of IVF. If you are not doing acupuncture before and after embryo transfer, you are doing yourself a disservice. Some patients I've had tell me, "Well, I don't believe in acupuncture." I simply tell them you don't have to believe in it for it to work. Acupuncture and Traditional Chinese Medicine are not a belief system, but a medical system that has been used for thousands of years. Studies are clear that acupuncture does improve success rates of embryo transfer. In a perfect world, you would do one acupuncture treatment per week for twelve weeks prior to starting IVF, IUI, or even natural conception to improve your chances for a successful and healthy pregnancy. However, if weekly acupuncture is not available or feasible for you, then you should find a practitioner that follows proven research protocols that are used before and after embryo transfer to maximize your success with IVF.

In addition, once you have conceived, acupuncture can be very effective in helping during the early stages of pregnancy, to improve fatigue, treat morning sickness, reduce or eliminate nausea and vomiting, and support pregnancies to prevent miscarriage and reduce stress. Many women that have struggled with infertility and/or had pregnancy loss are fearful of miscarriage and have a pretty high level of operating stress in the first trimester. Acupuncture can physiologically support women in their pregnancy in addition to helping them to feel calmer and at peace. Acupuncture can be used for support of common ailments in the second trimester of pregnancy, such as low back pain, heartburn, stress, and fatigue. It can also be used in the third trimester for stress, anxiety, insomnia, back pain, heartburn, and prepping for a healthy birth process. Acupuncture can even be used to reduce signs and symptoms of post-partum depression and assist with lactation after your baby is born.

Although acupuncture is not necessary in order to conceive, it is a good idea to add it in to your complete fertility protocol. I have some patients who do weekly acupuncture and others who do not have access to acupuncture for various reasons. Even without it, many patients using the tools contained in this book can conceive naturally. However, acupuncture adds a significant supportive tool in conceiving naturally. In addition, I have observed many women and couples trying to conceive over more than nineteen years in clinical practice, and it appears that those couple having regular acupuncture get pregnant faster than those not doing acupuncture. So if this is an option for you, I recommend acupuncture as a supportive treatment for conceiving and an absolute must with IVF embryo transfer.

NUTRIENTS PLAY A PIVOTAL ROLE IN HORMONE PRODUCTION AND THE ABILITY TO CONCEIVE.

EATING FOR FERTILITY SUCCESS:

HOW DIET PLAYS AN IMPORTANT ROLE IN CONCEPTION

Essential for conception is a healthy lifestyle which involves stress modulation, supporting the physiology of the body, and providing vital nutrients. Nutrients play a pivotal role in hormone production and the ability to conceive. We know that folic acid is important for conception and in pregnancy for proper fetal development. Other nutrients play an integral role in cell division, energy production, and many physiological functions related to conception.

Many diets are effective, but what are they effective for? Is their purpose to lose weight? Is their purpose for cardiovascular health? Is their purpose for longevity? Many standard diets are not specifically designed for fertility. When you are focusing on fertility, your needs are different than those of someone who is on a weight-loss diet. Nutrients play a vital role in hormone regulation, energy production, and in hormone-related conditions such as polycystic ovarian syndrome (PCOS). One of the common denominators of disease and imbalance is inflammation. Inflammation disrupts immune regulation and can alter implantation, increase blood sugar, and worsen auto immune conditions in women trying to conceive. Where is most of this inflammation coming from? The diet.

Inflammation is a common denominator in degeneration diseases of aging. Studies show the importance of chronic low-grade inflammation in the pathology of numerous age-related chronic conditions (1, 2). Inflammation is also an underlying pathology of autoimmune diseases, such as Hashimoto's thyroiditis, that pose as a roadblock to successful conception. As we have discussed, environmental toxins, lifestyle, and of course, diet significantly contribute to inflammation. Although you may tell yourself that you have no control over what you eat, the reality is you DO have control of what you eat and can enhance or hinder your fertility success based on your food choices. No one expects perfection, but looking at removing inflammatory foods and enriching your diet with anti-inflammatory nutrients can change your trajectory toward success. No one said it was easy, but my fertility patients are generally willing to do whatever it takes to create a hospitable environment for conception to happen.

The standard American diet of burgers, fries, and food on the run just won't do. It provides little nutrition for hormone production or a growing baby, and is riddled with inflammatory promoting substances. Inflammation creates havoc on successful implantation at the uterine endometrium (lining) by altering immune factors and signaling a cascade of chemicals that may prevent implantation of the embryo. Think about it this way, do you want a hotel room that is clean, neat, and orderly, or one that is dirty, chaotic, and disorganized? I am pretty sure you will pick the clean, tidy, and orderly one. A chaotic, cluttered immune system is not the preferred environment for a rapidly dividing embryo. Our bodies are wise and want an optimal and supportive environment to flourish in from the very start of life. Remember that a growing and dividing embryo needs to be fed everything that is good and nutritive, not the opposite. A low-inflammatory environment fosters healthy physiology and a hospitable environment for implantation—the kind of environment that your body and any growing embryo, left to its own devices, would choose every time. So if you are trying to get pregnant, you MUST change your diet, moving in the direction of creating less inflammation and providing essential nutritive support for your body and a growing embryo.

Studies show that plant-based and anti-inflammatory diets reduce systemic inflammation and can prevent certain diseases, such as Type 2 diabetes, obesity, and cardiovascular disease, all of which share inflammation as a common denominator (3–6). An anti-inflammatory diet contains high amounts of antioxidants from vegetables and fruit. Antioxidants are effective in fighting free radical damage. Free radicals come from processed foods, oxidized fats, and environmental toxins. They create unstable molecules that cause cell damage, creating a high amount of oxidative stress. Oxidative stress promotes disease and reduces egg and sperm quality (7, 8). An anti-inflammatory diet is primarily a plant-based diet and a way of eating that helps prevent and/or manage disease, and creates better health. Most importantly, an anti-inflammatory diet improves fertility successes.

ANTI-INFLAMMATORY DIET 101

Inflammation comes from foods that are not good for you, but may taste good to you. Examples of pro-inflammatory foods include processed foods, high sugar foods, and fatty meats. The "meat and potatoes" diet, or the standard American diet of burgers and fries, is void of essential nutrients contained in fruits, vegetables, fish, and lean protein. Instead, this diet is loaded with animal fat, oxidized fats, and chemicals in processed, fast, and sugar-rich foods that act like pro-oxidants, causing increased oxidative stress in your body. In addition, red meat contains high amounts of arachidonic acid, which increases inflammation. Maybe you're not a meat-and-potatoes type of person, but you live on a diet of mac-n-cheese, frozen chicken alfredo, and cereal, for example. To some this might seem like a relatively healthy diet. But it is still lacking in nutrients and contains cheese, which contains unhealthy fats, can be pro-inflammatory, and is generally devoid of any significant amount of nutrients to support your fertility. You need a diet with a low inflammatory load when trying to conceive.

In fact, studies show that a diet containing green vegetables, beans, seasonal fruit, and probiotic yogurt is a good source of natural antioxidants and delivers anti-inflammatory effects. This type of diet is recommended for patients with the autoimmune disease rheumatoid arthritis (9), which is a disease rooted in inflammation. Inflammation is associated with prediabetes and diabetes, Hashimoto's thyroiditis, adrenal fatigue, and other conditions related to infertility. Eating a diet based on anti-inflammatory principles dramatically reduces inflammation in the body, helps autoimmune conditions, improves immune function, and improves your chances of success to conceive and to support a healthy pregnancy. It is a no-brainer to think that food can improve fertility. In fact, research shows that a diet high in trans-fatty acids, high glycemic-index foods that spike blood sugar, high carbs, and high animal protein negatively affects fertility (10, 11). On the other hand, a diet high is omega-3 fats from fish and omega-6 fats from vegetables, low glycemic-index food, low carbs; and a diet high in vegetable, proteins, and antioxidants improves fertility (10). Diets high in unsaturated fats, whole grains, vegetables, and fish have been associated with improved fertility in both women and men (12).

According to existing data, women trying to achieve pregnancy are encouraged to increase consumption of whole grains, omega-3 fatty acids, fish, and soy, and to reduce consumption of trans fats and red meat. In addition, a daily multivitamin that contains folic acid both before and during pregnancy may not only prevent birth defects, but also improve the chance of achieving and maintaining a pregnancy (13). The right food combats inflammation and supports proper immune regulation. Plant based diets reduce inflammatory markers such as interleukin-6, C-reactive protein (CRP), and white blood cell count (14, 15). In addition, a Mediterranean diet, which is a primarily plant-based diet with healthy fats and fish, has been shown to reduce inflammatory markers including CRP, interleukin-6, and tumor necrosis factor. Research suggests these benefits are due to the high content of choline and betaine rich foods in a Mediterranean diet (16). So what should you be eating on an anti-inflammatory diet?

What Foods Should I Eat on an Anti-Inflammatory Diet?

An anti-inflammatory diet should contain whole foods, green leafy vegetables, and colorful fruits and vegetables. It should be free of dairy, gluten, and saturated fats. It may contain some fish and some lean protein, though it is primarily a plant-based diet.

Foods to Include
- Organic green, leafy, and other "colors of the rainbow" vegetables and fruits
- Free-range and organic eggs
- Lean, skinless cuts of poultry and meat, with limited red meat
- Fish that live in the deep sea including wild pacific salmon and halibut, and short-lived small fish, such as mackerel and sardines
- Healthy fats like cold-pressed extra-virgin olive oil, flaxseed or hempseed oil, avocado oil, coconut oil, nuts, seeds, and avocados
- Low glycemic foods that do not spike blood sugar
- Whole grains and other unprocessed foods
- Gluten- and dairy-free products

Foods to Avoid
- Processed foods and genetically modified foods (GMO foods)
- Oxidized fats from oil used in restaurants and fast food preparation
- Trans-fatty acids in margarine
- Gluten and dairy
- Foods with high amounts of pesticide residue
- Red meat, fatty foods, and deep-fried foods
- Genetically modified soy, peanuts, and peanut butter (but NOT other nuts and nut butters)
- Sugar, alcohol, high-fructose corn syrup, dried fruits, and fruit juices
- Most grains except high-fiber gluten-free grains in small quantities
- Avoid artificial colors, flavors, preservatives, and sweeteners

How to Create Change

To better understand what to eat, we first need to start with looking at what you are eating right now. I encourage you to take a moment to write down what you have eaten in the last twenty-four hours to get a better idea of where you are starting right now. Write down what you ate for breakfast, lunch, and dinner yesterday. Take a hard look at what you are really eating. Are you eating vegetables? How many servings? Three or six servings in a day? One serving or none? Are you eating pre-prepared foods, or eating out? Are you eating things from a box? Food on the go? Sugar? A mocha latte every morning? I'm not judging you, and I certainly don't eat amazingly well 100% of the time, but take a good look at your list. Sometimes, you might think you are doing pretty well, but when you really think about it, there is much work to be done.

Let's look at an example of a twenty-four-hour recall of dietary intake for my patient Kathy, and consider what we notice about her diet.

Kathy's 24-Hour Food Diary

Name: Kathy

Age: 36

Breakfast: Honey O's cereal with milk, coffee with creamer and sugar

Lunch: Ham and cheese sandwich on white bread and chips

Snack: Two medium chocolate chip cookies at work

Afternoon: 1 cup coffee with sugar and cream

Dinner: Quesadilla with cheese and salsa, and a side salad with iceberg lettuce, tomato, cucumber, and ranch dressing

Snacks: Popcorn and three chocolate kisses

What do we can see from Kathy's diet? Many people might think she is eating pretty well because she is not eating fast food and has three meals per day. However, her diet lacks essential nutrients and includes items that are promoting inflammation. Let's take a closer look. Is her diet whole-foods based? Her cereal came from a box, but her sandwich and quesadilla was homemade. However, her sandwich was made with low-nutrient white bread, and her quesadilla was made with high-starch tortillas and high-fat, shredded, packaged cheese. So, while some of her diet is made from food in its natural state, the quality of foods she is choosing is low and devoid of nutrients. A whole-foods diet infers a diet high in fruits, vegetables, lean protein, and healthy fats that you prepare rather than buy ready-made. It is primarily plant-based, meaning that it has ample vegetables. Does Kathy's diet meet that goal? No, I don't think we can count salsa as a vegetable, and her diet lacks largely in green, leafy vegetables. Is she eating healthy fats? She is getting fat from sweets and cookies, which do not contain healthy fats. She is eating cheese, which has saturated fats. What about eating organic and hormone free? She has not described any food as organic. Does her diet contain sugar? Yes, she is eating sweets throughout the day during her snacks. Is her diet nutrient dense, which means loaded with vitamins and minerals? She is getting calcium in her milk and cheese, but her diet is void of many nutrients that can be found in purple, red, green, and yellow vegetables. Does her diet lean toward being primarily plant-based? No, she is eating a lot of carbohydrates, such as, bread, tortillas, cookies, and cereal, which goes in the opposite direction of a plant-based diet. Unfortunately, the saturated fat from the cheese and milk in her diet is pro-inflammatory. Her diet lacks the vegetables and antioxidant rich foods she desperately needs, she is lacking in healthy fats, and her diet is too high in sugar. Her diet is not helping her succeed at lowering systemic inflammation.

How might we change her diet to reduce inflammation? Let's take a look.

Kathy's Revised 24-Hour Food Plan

Breakfast: Egg white scramble with broccoli and onion cooked in olive oil with a small side of blueberries, and hot herbal tea

Lunch: Green, dark-leafy salad, peppers, peas, tomatoes, and chickpeas, with olive-oil based salad dressing, and three ounces of salmon, with a gluten-free tortilla

Snack: Ten Almonds and three organic strawberries

Afternoon: Hot water with lemon

Dinner: Quesadilla with gluten-free tortilla and dairy-free cheese, vegetarian refried beans, a side of steamed broccoli, and a small dark-green spring mix salad with Balsamic vinaigrette

Snack: Hummus and baby carrots

By making simple changes to her existing diet, we improve her fertility. By adding snacks that have healthy fats, such as almonds, choosing organic foods, adding low fat protein dense egg whites and adding broccoli, carrots, peppers, peas, dark green leafy lettuce and other nutrient-rich vegetables to her meal, Kathy transformed her diet into a low-inflammatory nourishing diet. Using dairy-free cheese helps eliminate saturated fats. Eating salmon increases omega-3 fatty acids. Eliminating sweets and treats, and replacing them with healthier options reduces her intake of sugar, unhealthy fats, and high glycemic-index foods. These changes now foster an anti-inflammatory diet, enhancing blood sugar control and providing more nutrients for hormone production.

As you can see, it is not difficult to shift your diet to a healthier and more supportive one to help your fertility. With a little planning and prep, you are on your way to better health and success.

HOW TO TRANSITION TO AN ANTI-INFLAMMATORY DIET

Replace Boxed Foods with Whole Foods

Eliminate foods that come in a box, such as frozen dinners, crackers, and other pre-prepared foods. Replace those foods with whole foods. What does a whole-foods diet mean? A whole-foods diet consists of foods that are non-processed, that lack additives, artificial colors, and preservatives, that grow in nature, that contain nutrient-dense vitamins and minerals, and that can be cooked and ready to serve. An example of a whole-foods dinner might consist of grilled chicken, steamed broccoli, and a garden salad. Whole foods provide maximum nutrients, enzymes, fiber, and antioxidants that are from natural sources. Think about foods that would come straight from Mother Nature when you think of whole foods.

Create a Foundation of Plant Based Foods in Your Diet

Plant based diets include eating a variety of fruits and vegetables, and may include beans, legumes, seeds, nuts, and whole grains. A plant-based diet discourages intake of meat, dairy products, and eggs, as well as added saturated and unhealthy fats and oils, and all refined foods and processed carbohydrates (17).

Studies show plant-based diets have additional benefits other than improving fertility. They reduce the number of medications needed to treat a variety of chronic conditions, lower body weight, decrease the risk of cancer and diabetes, and reduce the risk of death from ischemic heart disease (17). Research studies show that a Mediterranean diet, which is primarily a plant-based diet with limited eggs, fish, and dairy, promotes increased life expectancy (16). Plant-based diets are important for enhancing fertility, because they reduce systemic inflammation, normalize body weight, reduce blood sugar, and provide rich nutrients and other building blocks for conception and fetal development.

Although many true plant-based diets contain no animal proteins at all, when it comes to fertility, some animal products are important to include in the diet. This is because your body needs protein that provides amino acids, the building blocks for fetal development. If done correctly, a vegetarian or an ovo-lacto vegetarian diet (which includes eating eggs and milk), a pescatarian diet (which includes eating fish), or a vegan diet (which avoids all animal products including eggs, milk, dairy, and other animal proteins), could be supportive and helpful for conception, especially in the cause of PCOS. However, while it is possible to get all the building blocks needed for conception and fetal development without any animal products, doing so is unlikely for the average person. It would take a lot of planning, preparation, and food combining to ensure all nutrients are included in the diet. Therefore, I recommend a plant-based foundation for your diet with the addition of some lean proteins such as salmon, chicken, turkey, lamb, and organic beef (especially if you are blood-deficient and anemic).

I recommend the 70/30 plan. This means that, when looking at a plate, seventy percent of it should be plant derived or plant based and thirty percent of it should be lean protein, sourced from fish or another lean animal source (chicken, turkey, eggs, etc.). A plant-based diet is high in vitamins and nutrients that support hormone production, and rich in anti-oxidants that reduce oxidative stress on eggs and sperm, and reduce inflammation to help with implantation and proper immune function. Most of the plant-based foods should come from vegetables rather than fruits to stabilize blood sugar and help maintain ideal body weight. Think about eating the "colors of the rainbow" when you think of plant-based foods. Seek out dark green vegetables such as broccoli and spinach that are sources of B vitamins and calcium to support production of hormones and adrenal support. Consume rich purple foods like eggplant and blueberries for sources of antioxidants to fight free-radical damage. Include orange, yellow, and red foods, such as tomatoes, carrots, and butternut squash that contain carotenoids; these foods are abundant in antioxidants to help decrease aging of eggs and sperm by oxidative stress.

Choose Low-Glycemic "Good Carbs" over High-Glycemic "Bad Carbs"

Oh, those "bad carbs" taste so good! We associate bad carbs with refined sugar, sweets, cookies, candy, donuts, and other sugar-laced treats. Why are these sweet treats bad for you? They are bad because they cause a rapid rise in blood sugar, inhibiting insulin production, and causing a negative cascade of hormone- and endocrine-related activity. If you have PCOS, you are already struggling with insulin resistance, and eating bad carbs is making your condition worse. Even if you don't have PCOS, eating bad carbs is not helping you. Bad carbs can include pasta, bread, potato chips, ice cream, white potatoes, and refined sugar and sweets. Not all carbs are bad. In facts good carbs that have a low glycemic index reduce the rise of blood sugar, creating balanced blood sugar and hormone regulation. Good carbs include beans, such as black beans, pinto beans, lima beans, and lentils; non-starchy vegetables such as broccoli, Brussel sprouts, spinach, Swiss chard, zucchini, and squash; and small amounts of high-fiber grains such as quinoa, brown rice, chia, and flaxseeds. Eating low glycemic carbohydrates, or good carbs, leads to better control over insulin and blood sugar, enhancing fertility, helping insulin resistance related to PCOS, and preventing pre-diabetes and diabetes.

The Gluten-Free and Dairy-Free Edge

A lot of people ask, "Do I really need to be both dairy and gluten free?" And I always say, "What are you willing to do to get pregnant?" No one says you HAVE TO DO anything, but if you want the best chances of conception, then it's probably best to avoid gluten and dairy. Why, you ask? Let me explain. Gliadin, the protein in gluten, initiates intestinal permeability, causing gliadin and other glutenins to interact with the immune system and giving rise to inflammation (18). In many people, this inflammatory and immunological cascade in the body wreaks havoc on the immune system, which contributes to the manifestation of chronic inflammation and autoimmune disease (19). In addition, gluten from wheat may not be what it was even twenty years ago, let alone fifty years ago. Many wheat species have become genetically altered hybrids, in addition to the pesticides, herbicides, fungicides, and the many other chemicals used on wheat crops that then become a part of food production.

Keep in mind that, in the area of marketing and selling food and food products, the industry is not focused necessarily on nutrient content. You likely assume that foods are made to be nutritious, and that simply is not true. In the area of food science, the top concern is what sells and how long it will last on the shelf. They are focused on taste and sustainability. How long can that product stay on the shelf without going bad? The longer it is, the better chance it will be sold, and the company will profit. It is about profitability and sustainability, not nutrition. Call me a cynic, but that is the ugly truth. So what you think might be highly nutritious, might actually be riddled with chemicals and genetically altered DNA that creates toxic overload and inflammation in the body. If you get tested for celiac disease and the results say that you don't have it, that does not mean that there is not a local effect on the body tissue, causing a negative reaction to gluten consumption. If you go gluten-free, you sidestep any possible reaction you may or may not be aware of inside your body. It is best to eat a diet high in vegetables as your carbohydrates, but if you are going to add other grains, it is best to eat organic and gluten free. Alternatives to foods containing gluten include: gluten-free grains, such as amaranth, sweet and white rice, quinoa, chickpea flour, buckwheat, millet, corn, potatoes, ground chia seed, flaxseed meal, sorghum flour, mesquite flour, oat bran, coconut flour, almond flour, guar gum, locust bean gum, and xanthan gum.

Dairy has a high content of arachidonic acid, which promotes inflammation in the body. In addition, many people have an allergy to proteins in dairy (casein and whey), or the sugar in dairy (lactose), causing inflammation. Dairy-free alternatives may include dairy-free cheese, which does not include casein, made from vegetable sources or coconut oil. You can also try commercially available coconut, almond, cashew, oat, and hemp milk, as well as coconut yogurt. Many people can eat eggs because they do not contain casein or whey. They can be a good choice because they have a nearly complete array of useable amino acids and the yolk of the egg is a good source of vitamin B 12. However, you should avoid eggs if you have a known allergy to them. If you have had recurrent ear infections as a child, chronic mucus, colic, or eczema, these could be signs of subtle and chronic inflammatory conditions created by dairy intolerance. Even though dairy tastes so good, it increases the inflammatory load on the body that is working against successful fertility. Especially with autoimmune disorders like Hashimoto's, lupus, and rheumatoid arthritis, dairy should be avoided at all costs when trying to conceive.

Why Eating Organic Foods Is Essential to Your Fertility

Organic foods are free from chemicals, added antibiotics, and steroids, leaving food in its unadulterated state, like Mother Nature intended. According to the U.S. Department of Agriculture, organic farming practices preserve the environment and avoid most synthetic materials, including pesticides, genetically modified crops, and antibiotics. The organic standards describe the specific requirements that must be verified by a USDA-accredited certifying agent before products can be labeled USDA organic (20). Just because something is labeled organic does not mean it is inherently good for you, as in the case with organic cookies, but it does limit chemicals that act as hormone disrupters. Keep in mind that the practices behind the organic label might differ from state to state. For example, California might have stricter guidelines for a food to be labeled organic than Michigan. It is important to do what you can to limit exposure to pesticides and chemicals in your diet. Eating organic foods whenever possible is the most advantageous for fertility. If you are doing a combination of organic and non-organic foods, it is best to avoid the The Dirty Dozen, which is a list of the top twelve non-organic foods with the highest researched pesticide residue.

Avoid "The Dirty Dozen"
1. Strawberries
2. Spinach
3. Nectarines
4. Apples
5. Grapes
6. Peaches
7. Cherries
8. Pears
9. Tomatoes
10. Celery
11. Sweet bell peppers
12. Hot Peppers

The Dirty Dozen may change from year to year so it is important to check with research done by the Environmental Working Group (EWG) or other reputable sources to get up-to-date information from year to year. This will help you identify the foods that have the highest pesticides residue that can create toxicity in your body.

There have been a few studies looking at the best way to remove pesticides from fruits and vegetables. The studies suggest there are a few factors to consider, including the type and structure of the fruit and vegetables, as well as what pesticides, fungicides, and chemicals have been used on them. One study looked at tomatoes and another looked at pesticides on and inside of apples, but not all fruits and vegetables have been tested. Based on a few studies that are starting to look at the effectiveness of different agents in removing pesticides, it appears that the use of a baking soda solution (21) or the use of acetic acid contained in vinegar (22, 23) were most effective in removing some of the pesticides compared to water alone. However, they did not remove pesticides completely and were more effective when the fruit was peeled, such as in the case of an apple. Other commercially available detergents for fruits and vegetables may not be effective in removing pesticides. High heats may not remove chemicals, so cooking your vegetables may still expose you to pesticides and chemicals. That is why the best way to limit exposure is to buy and consume organic fruits and vegetables whenever possible. If you don't buy organic produce, research the best way to wash your fruits and vegetables to limit your exposure.

Proteins are the Building Blocks of Life

Protein is composed of smaller molecules called amino acids. Amino acids combine in different ways to make different types of proteins. Proteins serve as the building blocks of every cell in your body and are essential to a growing baby. Proteins make enzymes used for digestion, cellular activity, and communication with other cells in the body. Proteins are also used to make neurotransmitters, immunoglobulins, and hormones. They play a vital role in the immune system, and are involved in a multitude of other functions in the body. We need both essential and non-essential amino acids to make complete proteins. We need these complete proteins to support basic human physiology and to further support fertility, conception and fetal growth. Our body makes non-essential amino acids, but we must get essential amino acids from our diet.

Many people associate protein with animal sources like chicken or beef, but there are also plant sources of protein. Each food has a different compilation of amino acids, and that is why it is important to eat a variety of protein sources to get both essential and non-essential amino acids. Protein sources should be organic, free-range, antibiotic free, and pesticide free whenever possible. Although animal proteins contain needed amino acids, they should make up only thirty percent of your total diet. Instead, your diet should weigh heavily on plant-based whole foods to provide the nutrients needed for fertility support.

Is soy protein a good plant source? A small amount of non-genetically modified soy from tempeh, miso, and fresh sprouted soybean curd can be eaten a couple of times per week. Too much soy can cause hormone imbalances, so it should be eaten in small quantities and avoided completely if you have PCOS, endometriosis, or fibroids, which contribute to excess hormone levels. A majority of your vegetable-based proteins should come from high-quality sources like legumes, such as split peas, green peas (or pea protein powder), lentils, pinto beans, mung beans, kidney beans, adzuki beans, black beans, great white northern beans, garbanzo beans, lima beans, vegetarian refried beans; nuts such as walnuts, almonds, cashews, macadamia nuts, brazil nuts, walnuts, and pistachios; seeds, such as pumpkin, sunflower, sesame, chia, and flax seeds; and non-genetically-modified soy products, such as tofu, tempeh, and edamame (except in women with PCOS, where soy can be estrogenic and create more hormone imbalance).

High-quality protein sources from grains may include quinoa, amaranth, and other sprouted grains. High quality animal sources of protein include lean turkey and chicken; cold water fish, such as albacore tuna, mackerel, salmon, herring, lake trout, and sardines, (always choose wild fish over farmed fish because wild fish have a better fat compilation because they hunt for their own food). Organic eggs and bone broth can also be added to a plant-based diet to ensure adequate protein.

Is Plant Protein Superior to Animal Protein for Your Fertility?

The answer is yes. In one study, 18,555 married women without a history of infertility were followed as they attempted a pregnancy or became pregnant during an eight-year period. During the follow-up, 438 reported ovulatory infertility (lack of ovulation). Vegetable protein rather than animal was associated with a more than fifty-percent lower risk of ovulatory infertility (24).

In another large prospective cohort study called the Nurses' Health Study (NHS) II, women who had the highest intake of a "fertility diet," comprised of plant protein from vegetable sources, full-fat dairy foods, iron, and monounsaturated fats, during the preconception period, were found to have a sixty-six-percent lower risk of infertility related to ovulatory disorders and a twenty-seven-percent lower risk of infertility due to other causes (11).

In another study of college-educated women in Spain who followed a Mediterranean-style diet, which included a high intake of vegetables, fish, and polyunsaturated oils, had forty-four-percent lower odds of seeking medical help for difficulty getting pregnant compared to women not on a Mediterranean diet (25).

A Mediterranean-style diet consists primarily of plant-based foods with the addition of good fats and fish. It improves fertility in men, not just women. In one study men on a Mediterranean-style diet improved semen quality, including morphology, motility, and concentration (26).

Healthy Fats Boost Your Fertility

Healthy fats are essential for your fertility. We live in a world obsessed with weight. Don't get me wrong, having an ideal body weight and eating a whole-foods diet low in fat is vital for your fertility and general health. But in many cases, we sacrifice the nutrition and whole food choices for low-fat labels. What you need to be thinking is, "Is this healthy fat?" not, "Is this low fat?" Fat is not inherently bad. First, some cholesterol is essential as a precursor to the production of hormones such as estrogen and progesterone. A diet too low in fat will cause you to have no period or an irregular one. However, many unhealthy fats are contained in processed foods and the food we get in restaurants, which often use oxidized fats (oils used to fry foods over and over again), hydrogenated oils, saturated fats from beef and butter (used in many restaurant meals to make them taste good). These fats are unhealthy and work against your fertility. There are also other unhealthy ingredients, preservatives, and increased sugar used to substitute fats in lowfat products. All cells of our body contain a phospholipid bilayer as a protective barrier from the outside world. The word lipid means fat. When healthy fats are incorporated into the cells of our body, it makes them more fluid, allowing for nutrients to get into our cells and waste products to get out. Healthy fats positively affect hormone production, nutrient absorption, and utilization.

What are good sources of healthy fats? Some sources of healthy fat include: coconut oil, olives, cold-pressed virgin olive oil, almond and avocado oil, cold-pressed flaxseed and hempseed oil, sesame oil, avocados, unrefined black-currant oil; nut butters (except for peanut butter, which may contain aflatoxins which are known to be a carcinogen or cancer causing agent); nuts and seeds; fish rich in omega-3 fatty acids such as salmon, mackerel, halibut, sardines, and tuna; and plant sources of omega-3 fatty acids from flaxseeds (27).

Fertility Superfoods

Certain foods under the anti-inflammatory umbrella can further enhance your fertility success by tonifying, or building, your Qi from a Traditional Chinese Medicine (TCM) perspective. Think of these foods as your personal fertility superfood boosters that give you the fertility edge. Include these foods in their organic, whole-foods form as much as possible.

In TCM, it is vital to nourish and tonify the kidney Qi, Yin, Yang, and Jing, which provides foundational Qi to increase your fertility. Strong kidney Qi can be passed to the baby during development to help establish a strong constitution with abundant vitality for that growing baby. Foods that tonify the kidneys include most beans, blueberries, blackberries, grapes, mulberries, pumpkin seeds, sunflower seeds, flax seeds, lamb, eggs, black sesame seeds, millet, quinoa, string beans, corn, adzuki beans, cucumbers, watermelon, fish, seaweed, deep green leafy vegetables, melons, and bone broth. Tonics such as kelp, green algae, spirulina, and royal jelly can also nourish the kidney Qi (28).

Tonifying the spleen Qi is also important in fertility since, in TCM, the spleen Qi creates the blood to nourish the womb and a growing baby and helps to maintain a pregnancy. Deficient spleen Qi can result in impaired absorption of nutrients, fatigue, and an overactive mind, associated with hypothyroidism and miscarriage. Tonifying the spleen Qi is relevant and important to improve your fertility. Foods that tonify the spleen Qi include oats, spelt, sweet rice, winter squash, carrot, parsnip, turnip garbanzo beans, black beans, onion, leek, black pepper, ginger, cinnamon, fennel, garlic, nutmeg, dates, mackerel, halibut, anchovy, chicken, turkey, and lamb (28). These foods should be cooked rather than served raw, in the case of vegetables, or cold, in the case of animal protein, as this weakens the digestive energy, depleting the spleen Qi. Avoid cold and damp foods such as ice cream, cheese, dairy, and cold shakes, as well as rich foods, high-sugar foods, and processed foods. These foods must be avoided because they will also damage the spleen Qi.

Adding the fertility superfoods listed above further enhances your fertility. Diet sets the foundation for your physiology function and success, so make the necessary changes in your diet so you can have a chance at success.

Important Meal Preparation Tips

Keeping foods as close to what Mother Nature intended is a good rule of thumb to follow. Grilled, baked or sautéed food is better than highly processed food. In TCM, the way that you prepare your foods and the avoidance of certain foods drastically influences your fertility and your Qi. For example, foods that are too cold damage the spleen Qi, whereas, steamed vegetables tonify the spleen Qi.

Here are some guidelines to follow. Eat cooked foods rather than cold or raw foods to avoid depleting spleen Qi. Eat soups; stews; baked, steamed, or sautéed vegetables; and avoid overcooking your food, which diminishes nutrients. Add flavorful spices to make whole foods taste fresh, interesting, and appetizing. Avoid specific cold foods like yogurt, ice cream, shakes, and overly rich foods as they deplete the digestive energy and create damp, phlegm, and cold digestive energy that works against successful fertility. Drinking room-temperature drinks rather than cold drinks is also recommended. These small but profound tips can make a big difference when it comes to your diet and food preparation that can enhance your fertility.

Now we have learned why it is important to follow an anti-inflammatory and Qi-boosting diet. We know that an anti-inflammatory diet creates the foundation for an inviting environment that can increase fertility success. Let's take a look at these principles put into action in meal preparation.

SAMPLE ANTI-INFLAMMATORY MENU FOR A DAY

Breakfast
Egg-white scramble with spinach and onions, topped with avocado
Hot water with lemon
Or the vegetarian option of chia seed pudding with blueberries and almonds

Lunch
Three ounces of grilled chicken, a quarter cup cooked quinoa, and two cups steamed broccoli
Or the vegetarian option of black bean soup, a green salad, and half an avocado

Dinner
Three ounces sea bass with sautéed great white northern beans and kale prepared with garlic and olive oil, with a green salad
Or the vegetarian option of a veggie burger wrapped in lettuce with the same side of beans and kale

So now you see that an anti-inflammatory diet is needed to support your fertility. You know the major areas to start changing in your diet. It may seem overwhelming, so the best way to approach this shift is to change one element of your diet per week. Start with eating organic foods. The next week, start shifting your carbohydrates. The next week, work on eating the best protein sources. Last, add in healthy fats. Map out a week's worth of recipes or meals to help you stay on track. Remember to prep before you are starving to avoid grabbing a candy bar or other high sugar snack . Have available healthy snacks packed and ready to go. Team up with your spouse or family, supporting one another with healthy choices. It will be easier and more successful if you have the support of others. Diet changes are about lifestyle changes, and they are long lasting when done over time, step by step. Don't be afraid to make changes in your diet. Get started now. Your body will thank you for it.

REMEMBER THAT THE BODY NEEDS PREPARATION TO CEONCEIVE.

THE TOP FOUR REASONS IVF MAY NOT WORK AND WHAT TO DO DIFFERENTLY TO INCREASE YOUR SUCCESS

What happens when you have taken extraordinary measures and had IVF, and it turns out to be unsuccessful? It can be devastating after investing so much money, time, and emotion into the process, only to be disappointed. What if you have tried multiple IVF cycles and still not been able to conceive? Have you wondered why it is not working and if there was anything you could do to improve the success? My guess is that you have thought about this a lot and just don't have answers to guild you to the next step. Remember that the body needs preparation to conceive, whether you are trying to conceive naturally or with ART.

I have seen many patients in this scenario, and I am not going to say that I know the reason for every person's failed IVF cycle. Sometimes you do everything right and it still does not work. But remember that the body needs preparation, so the principles contained in this book apply to you whether you are conceiving naturally or using ART. The principles and tools contained in this book improve both natural and IVF outcomes. A body that is not prepared will not respond in a favorable manner. Over many years, I have seen trends in patients and would say there are four major reasons why IVF may not be working. The cause may be something other than the four that I discuss, but these four causes are common roadblocks to IVF success.

Over more than nineteen years, I have helped women successfully navigate failed IVF cycles and transform their bodies to respond in a normal manner and conceive during their next IVF cycle with success. Maybe you have already had one baby with IVF, but your attempts at IVF for baby number two have not been successful. Don't worry, it is not unusual for a mother to be worn out, tired, and in a depleted state after her first baby, which can lead to an unsuccessful IVF cycle when it's time for a second baby. While working with many women over many years, I have seen the best combination of support methods to transform their trajectory to success.

Sometimes my patients even conceive naturally after having their first child via IVF while preparing their body for baby number two. I know this is hard to believe, when it took IVF to have the first baby, but maybe that was because the roadblocks were never addressed during the first journey toward conception. Once those barriers were removed, natural conception was not as hard as it was before. Remember that the principles of preparing the body for natural conception are the same for IVF preparation—you want to prepare the body to have optimal physiological function. Once you do this, your body will respond appropriately to external stimuli like IVF medications, which tell the body what to do. Your body simply has to be willing to listen to those directives. The body is wise, so if you are not ready, nothing will happen. Let's discuss the four main reasons that your IVF may be failing.

1 – LOW ADRENAL FUNCTION OR ADRENAL FATIGUE

When your body is in a depleted state, asking your body to do IVF and respond the way you order it to is like asking a car to run without gasoline. It's not going to happen! Everything about infertility is stressful—the emotions, the expense, the worry, not to mention the everyday stressors, and bigger life and family stressors. We have an abundance of stress in our lives, so it is no wonder our bodies get depleted, and then we expect them to do exactly what we want, when we want it.

Your adrenal function, essential for life, can become depleted. When your adrenals become severely depleted (but before a disease like Addison's Disease has manifested), adrenal function can decline. The adrenal glands make glucocorticoids, including cortisol, which are your natural steroid hormones. They help with stress response, inflammation, pain, energy, and sleep cycles. The adrenals also make mineralocorticoids, which maintain healthy blood pressure, as well as adrenaline and epinephrine, which are part of your fight or flight response. Adrenal decline or fatigue causes a dysregulation of cortisol, meaning that your cortisol level can be high or low. These improper cortisol levels lead to HPA-axis dysfunction, affecting hormone levels.

Because the adrenal glands also package dehydroepiandrosterone (DHEA), which is a precursor to other sex hormones, decline of adrenal function can also result in reduced levels of DHEA. DHEA is known as a parent hormone because it helps to make other androgenic hormones, such as testosterone and estrogen. DHEA production can be reduced with adrenal fatigue or decline, which can lower overall sex hormones, negatively affecting fertility. Low DHEA levels are known to be linked to infertility. Low cortisol is related to an inability to deal with stress. IVF can be considered in these terms as a physiological stress. If the body has a dysregulated ability to deal with stress, then IVF is often not successful. By restoring adrenal function and the HPA-axis, you greatly improve your body's ability to respond the way you want it to during an IVF cycle in order to achieve your long-awaited successful outcome.

You can do a salivary twenty-four cortisol test to determine if your adrenals are operating like an old Chevy or a new Mustang, which makes a difference to you and your fertility success. Once you support the adrenals through lifestyle, diet, nutritional and botanical medicine interventions, you can generally restore their function in about three months, depending on the severity of the adrenal decline. Commonly, I see women who have gone through unsuccessful IVF cycles who, after proper adrenal support, went through another IVF cycle that worked well and gave them a positive outcome.

2 – MTHFR MUTATIONS

As previously discussed, methylation support is essential for DNA repair and proper DNA synthesis. The MTHFR gene, one of several genes involved in methylation reactions, may have a significant effect on fertility. It provides the instructions for converting folate to 5-MTHF, the active form of folic acid known as methyltetrahydrofolate. 5-MTHF plays a vital role in cellular physiology by participating in nucleotide synthesis, DNA repair, and methylation, as well as creating stability of genes (1). Mutations of the MTHFR gene may increase homocysteine levels (2) which negatively affects egg quality and DNA synthesis, leading to oxidative stress and disrupting methylation reactions, thereby affecting reproductive function (3). In addition, one study suggests that a MTHFR C677T mutation is associated with a negative effect on the numbers of eggs retrieved during IVF (4, 5). Folate or folic acid is well known for its important role in pregnancy for proper neurological development of the fetus and prevention of neural tube defects. Neural tube closure occurs in the first few weeks after conception, commonly before a woman even knows that she's pregnant. In addition, low levels of folate in women have also been linked to low birth weight, preterm delivery, and slowed fetal growth (4). One study reported that MTHFR mutations resulting in low folate levels may be considered a factor in non-optimally matured eggs before conception (6), which may contribute to congenital abnormalities.

Research suggests that MTHFR mutations impact male infertility significantly as well. Studies show mutations of MTHFR C677T and A1298C have a close relationship with male infertility (7). Folate and normal activity of 1-carbon metabolic pathway enzymes are central to nucleotide synthesis, methylation, maintenance of gene integrity, and protection against DNA damage (8). A recent study looked at the association between MTHFR-C677T and structure of sperm DNA. The study concluded that defective methylation linked to MTHFR may contribute to sperm that is abnormal due to increased sperm nucleus decondensation (9). There may not be hundreds of studies on MTHFR gene mutations yet, but there is a body of research that suggests this is an issue for sperm DNA integrity, or quality, and the ability to retrieve eggs in order to have a successful IVF outcome.

Complete Fertility

Although many doctors in the fertility community may differ with my opinion, I have seen a significant trend in women and men with MTHFR mutations and failed IVF outcomes. Think about it this way, you can get the eggs during egg retrieval and you can take a sperm to fertilize the egg with ICSI, but then it is up to proper cell division to take over. If proper cell division does not happen, you may not even have an embryo get to Day 3 to be frozen. Or maybe it gets to Day 5 to be frozen, or you use a fresh cycle, but after embryo transfer there is not proper support for cell division and repair beyond that. At that point, things break down and cell division stops. Somewhere along the way, if cells cannot be repaired and too many mistakes occur over time, this can lead to arrested cell division, resulting in no pregnancy and a failed IVF cycle, or possibly a miscarriage. I see this as a big contributor to fertility struggles and always provide support for methylation in both women and men. This generally results in better outcomes. I believe scientific research in the future will provide more support for this theory.

In addition, women who are taking a prenatal vitamin with regular folic acid who have an undetected MTHFR mutation are at risk for unmetabolized folic acid (UMFA) syndrome. This is because they are unable to convert folic acid to 5-MTHF. When they receive additional supplementation of folic acid, on top of what is already in their diet they can't break it down. The folic acid accumulates in the body and causes UMFA. UMFA is suspected of causing immune dysfunction and other adverse pathological effects (10).

Unfortunately, there is no way to test an embryo to see if MTHFR mutation is the cause of failed IVF cycles. A reproductive endocrinologist (RE) can do genetic testing on embryos to look at broader disease risk, while MTHFR relates to issues that might be going on at the cellular level, related to cell function. Again, the application of MTHFR genetic testing relates to the function of the body rather than an outcome of a disease. That is an important but different type of genetic testing. Testing both the male and female for MTHFR and other methylation genetic defects requires only a painless cheek swab, which is easy to obtain and can provide vital genetic information about how your methylation pathways work. Providing the proper methylation support in response to these test results can create the needed foundation for healthy cell division.

So what can you do to remove this roadblock to IVF success? Test both the female and male who are trying to conceive. See what type of mutations are occurring. Once you know what mutations you have, you will be able to provide your body with the proper support. You may need to seek professional help from someone familiar with MTHFR mutations and fertility. Based on genetic methylation test results, you can provide the proper methylation support with vitamins and nutrients to support healthy cell division in production of quality sperm, normal growth of a dividing embryo, and healthy fetal development in pregnancy.

Remember that support equals vitamins, so this is a very noninvasive and easy way to provide methylation support. Research suggests that taking a physiological dose of 5-MTHF at 800 mcg per day can bypass MTHFR blocks and is an effective treatment for couples to take while trying to conceive (10). This support can be individualized, but for basic methylation support, it should include 5-MTHF as well as other co-factors and methyl donors. A basic methylation support supplement should include 5-MTHF at 800 mcg, active vitamin B12 (called methylcobalamin) or a combination of methylcobalamin and adenosylcobalamin at 1000 mcg, active vitamin B6 (called pyridoxal 5' phosphate, or P5P) at 15 mg, and vitamin B1 (called Riboflavin 5' phosphate sodium) at 25 mg.

3 – MALE FACTOR/ DNA FRAGMENTATION

When there is repetitive failed IVF, a likely cause is the male factor. That means that even though there is enough sperm, and the sperm can swim, their DNA is fragmented. This means that the DNA is defective, and cell division will not be able to proceed. This is especially true for men who are forty years old or older, who are more at risk for increased DNA fragmentation. Most reproductive endocrinologists can identify that you have sperm DNA fragmentation, but offer few solutions to the problem except using a sperm donor. Research studies are beginning to show that natural substances and nutrients can have a positive impact on DNA structure. A recent study has shown that probiotics (specifically the two strengths selected for the study, Lactobacillus rhamnosus and Bifidobacterium longum) did in fact improve sperm motility by six-fold and decrease DNA fragmentation by one-and-a-half fold with only three to six weeks of supplementation (11). Another study showed that supplementation of vitamin C at 500 mg two times per day, and vitamin E at 1000 iu per day for two months significantly reduced fragmented DNA (12). High levels of sperm DNA damage have been reported to decrease male fertility (13–16), and researchers concluded that it is reasonable to prescribe antioxidant treatment in some patients. In fact, some studies have reported an improvement of pregnancy rates in asthenozoospermic patients (patients whose sperm have reduced motility) after combined oral antioxidant treatments (16–18). Consider testing for DNA fragmentation when you have had multiple failed attempts with IVF. Consider antioxidant and probiotic support to decrease DNA fragmentation in sperm for better IVF outcomes.

4 – IMMUNE DYSREGULATION

Why, after embryo transfer, would an embryo not become embedded in the uterine lining to grow and flourish? This question brings us to a large number of women who don't realize that the uterus has created a hostile environment riddled with inflammation, rather than a welcoming and hospitable place to grow a baby. It is estimated that up to forty percent of unexplained infertility may be due to immunological dysregulation. How do you test for this? And why would a body reject an embryo that you desperately want? Because of inflammation and immune dysregulation. To test for this, you must first rule out other diseases that have immune dysfunction with your doctor. You may also not have an autoimmune disease and have covered the other areas to support fertility, but still have failed IVF cycles. If all your other boxes are checked then, by process of elimination, you can surmise that you might be missing the inflammatory aspect of immune dysregulation.

If you do have a pre-existing autoimmune disorder like rheumatoid arthritis, or Hashimoto's thyroiditis, or inflammatory markers that show up on blood work such as high sedimentation rate and/or high CRP, you can be sure that you want to take extra steps to counterbalance the inflammation in the body and the immune dysfunction that already exists. How can you take out inflammation? The diet is one of the largest sources of inflammation. There are a few simple steps that you can take to reduce inflammation caused from your diet. Start with removing gluten, dairy, and known food allergens. Make sure to follow an anti-inflammatory diet that includes a high-quality probiotic that has 100-billion organisms per dose for immune support, and high-quality fish oils, which you should be taking as part of your prenatal care. You should also consider testing for gut bacteria, parasites, and yeast to identify sources of inflammation and then find an effective protocol to eradicate those sources in order to create better immune regulation in the body.

IS THAT ALL?

In addition to the four major roadblocks to unsuccessful IVF cycles, we are assuming that you have already met the other basics discussed in this book. In other words, you are eating a low-inflammatory diet, taking a good prenatal supplement, and taking basic supplements to improve the quality of your eggs, for example. If you are generally in good health and you adopt a relatively healthy lifestyle, then one of the four roadblocks that I've discussed could be the cause of your struggle to conceive. Let's look at the stories of four of my patients, all of whom had initial failed IVF cycles, but whose stories ended in success after they gave their bodies proper fertility support. The patients' names have been changed for the telling of their stories.

STORIES OF SUCCESS

Kim

Kim had done six failed IUIs and was very frustrated. She came to me asking what she could do, and intuitively knowing that her body was not responding the way it should. Though she had this intuitive understanding, she was not sure how to fix the problem. She had one child who was four years old, but was not able to conceive her second child with her husband. After discussing her history, it was clear that she had been under high stress for many years, and being a new mom, she was very depleted. She was tired, reacted to stress readily, and felt low mood and brain fog. We tested her adrenal function, and it was very low. After about three months of preparation, supporting her adrenals with botanical medicines, nutrients, and acupuncture, she had renewed energy and had improved her ability to respond.

Before she prepared, her body was saying, "I don't care how many drugs you throw at me, I won't participate." It was like asking a car with an empty gas tank to go. It simply could not. Her body could barely respond to IVF medication and increased IVF medications did not help. After supporting and restoring adrenal function, she was feeling energized and able to handle stress, and had a renewed sense of well-being. Once her adrenal function had normalized, she then responded to IVF medications with even less than in her previous IVF failed cycle and was able to conceive. She conceived and carried to term a healthy pregnancy and gave birth to a healthy baby girl.

Jen

Jen had come to me after having a successful IVF cycle that resulted in her daughter being born, but then having an unsuccessful embryo transfer for a second child. She was worried because she did not have many embryos left and was scared the next IVF cycle would be unsuccessful. She was forty-one years old, fatigued, depleted, and not dealing with stress well. Based on her evaluation, I concluded that her adrenal function was an issue. We supported her adrenals for three months, and before she was ready for embryo transfer, she got pregnant naturally. She went on to have a healthy baby.

Alice

Alice had been trying to conceive with her husband for three years. She had multiple failed IUIs and one failed IVF cycle. We began working on preparing her body well for natural conception. Her biggest roadblock was immune dysregulation. So when she decided to try IVF again, she knew that her focus had to be to reduce inflammation in her body through supplementation and diet. We applied the principles discussed in this book to regulate her immune dysfunction, and she did get pregnant with a healthy baby boy.

Sara

Sara, a thirty-two-year-old female had a hard time conceiving. She had a previous miscarriage and could not figure out the cause. She and her husband had gone through nine unsuccessful IUI cycles. Her husband was ten years older than her, at forty-two years old, which made me consider possible issues with DNA fragmentation and/or methylation. It turned out that Sara did have significant MTHFR mutations, so we supported her and her husband's system for methylation issues and supported her husband for sperm DNA fragmentation. They had decided they would do IVF but gave IUI one last try, and with support for about three months prior to doing anything, they gave one last go at IUI and were able to conceive. They had a healthy baby and did not have to do IVF.

CREATE THE CHANGE

If you are feeling like there is no resolution to your problem, like you have put in your sweat and tears to conceive naturally, and still had to take the steps to do IVF, only to be disappointed with an unsuccessful outcome, the time has come to create a better result.

You can increase your odds of creating a successful IVF outcome if you address the four major causes of unsuccessful IVF cycles. I cannot guarantee your results, but I can say through years of experience that you will be increasing your chances of success, that you can be an active participant, taking your power back, and being proactive in the IVF process to create fertility success.

ADVOCATING FOR YOURSELF & CHALLENGING YOUR DOCTOR

With changes in healthcare, it is no surprise that you have to be a true advocate for yourself and your own healthcare these days. Most patients are well educated and know a lot more than the average person when it comes to fertility. You have heard of FSH, LH, and AMH and have some idea what they are and how they are used to determine if your doctor thinks you will be able to have a baby. You have easy access to information (albeit not always creditable information) via the internet. You also have important questions and decisions on your mind regarding your fertility and the chosen route for addressing your fertility issues. In light of these things, it is totally appropriate to come to see your doctor with a list of questions, as well as to question your doctor's medical recommendations.

I am by no means saying to be adversarial with your doctor. What I mean is that true success is a collaboration between you and your doctor. Many times, my patients have gone to multiple doctors before I see them, and they have many questions that they are seeking real answers and solutions to. Understanding this, I am perfectly fine when a patient brings a spouse or mother with a large list of questions, because I understand that this terrain is difficult to navigate and my role is to listen and help. I understand that people get frustrated, so I don't generally take that personally. While many doctors ignore the emotional impact that this journey has on the women, husbands, partners, and the entire family, I honor the role emotions play in this process. Loss, disappointment, joy, excitement, fear, and worry are common emotional hurdles involved in the process of having difficulty conceiving. The act of being present, listening, and working together toward viable solutions is core when it comes to healthcare in general, and especially when it comes to fertility.

So understand that your doctor is there to help you, but some doctors have better skills than others. Some are more caring, some are more skillful, some are better technicians, some are better problem solvers. Some doctors also have different emphases in their practice and approaches. It can be a bit overwhelming deciding who to work with and what advice to act upon. Will you invest the time and money into IVF? Should you start with improving your chances of natural conception first? If so, for how long until you look at other options? Should you get another opinion? Which doctor is correct in their recommendations? It can be arduous making your way down the road of fertility decisions. To be honest, it is almost never easy. Doctors are people too; so they are ALL doing their best, but part of being an advocate for yourself is choosing the physician and/or practitioner(s) that is the right fit for you, so that you can work together to create the best outcome for your fertility success.

In the 1950s, it would be unheard of to question your doctor. Ever! But we are living in different times. We live in an age of technology information and education. So challenging or asking questions in the doctor-patient setting is absolutely appropriate. You may have concerns or fears that need to be addressed. You need to feel that your doctor is in your corner and can act as part of your supportive team. If your doctor is not receptive to answering your questions, then you need to evaluate if you want to work with that doctor or with someone else. Advocating for yourself means being okay with asking questions to empower your role in the process, seeking multiple options and routes for success, while figuring out the path that is right for your particular case.

Because I am a Naturopathic Medical Doctor and Acupuncturist, I talk with patients more than the average doctor. In my conversations with my patients, I hear all kinds of stories about their bad experiences with other doctors and practitioners. I am grateful my patients feel they are in a safe place to vent. Many times, they recollect their conversations with their previous or current doctors that make me understand why they feel so alone and disheartened. For example, one of my patients tells me she had a follow-up appointment with her very well-respected RE, who happens to be female. During her exam, she is undressed and in stirrups, and her doctor's head is down toward her genitalia. Without bothering to look her in the eyes, her doctor tells her, "Your test results show you will never get pregnant with your own eggs, and you need an egg donor." My patient said she was mortified and could not speak, not just because the information she had been given devastated her dreams of a biological child, but also because of the way in which the information was delivered. She thought a female RE would be more compassionate, but that was not that case in her experience.

Another patient revealed that her RE told her, "There is no way you will get pregnant on your own, ever," based on her FSH levels during her initial consult. This was also devasting to this patient, as this was her first visit to an RE to look at her options. She was just trying to see what might help her achieve her pregnancy dreams, and left feeling like her dreams were shattered and would never come to light. In her case, there were things that could be done to help her, so the statement her doctor made that she would never conceive was not accurate. Fortunately, both of these patients did get pregnant naturally and have healthy happy babies. So that goes to show you that your doctor is not always right. That includes me, by the way. I am not saying I have all the answers, but I do have a wealth of knowledge to share in order to help you advocate for yourself.

It is clear that how your doctor conveys information is as important as what they are conveying. No one wants to feel like they are on an assembly line, as may patients describe feeling in very busy RE offices. That is not to say that all REs operate this way. There are some amazing REs who are caring, skillful, and helpful. Generally, REs are not looking at improving the function of the body to help patients conceive naturally or to increase the success of IVF with integrative recommendations. Remember, if you are a doctor just looking at test result numbers that you think can't be changed, you may have a different conclusion than someone who knows you can change physiology and possible outcomes. I hear many frustrations in my office, but they generally are not communicated to their REs because the patients fear that the REs won't work with them. They think, "This is my only shot," or they think that challenging their doctors will alter their recommendations or chances for success.

Having personally used both natural tools and IVF to have a baby, I am well aware of the challenges involved. And although I can't understand my patients' unique experiences entirely, I do understand what it is like to be on the other side of the doctor's desk with many emotions, questions, and fears. Being a doctor who specializes in fertility certainly gave me the ability to ask good, educated questions. It also gave me insight as to how I might best approach my doctor and who I would choose as a doctor to collaborate with. However, even as a doctor, I had my own unique challenges. Things change when you are the patient, in a vulnerable situation trying to maneuver through the process. There are times you can feel alone, especially if you don't know anyone who has gone through this experience. If, for example, your friends never had fertility issues or did IVF, they can be understanding and compassionate, but they may not fully understand the magnitude of the journey. It might be in your best interest to ask other women, friends, and acquaintances in fertility support groups about their experiences with their doctor(s)—their approaches, bedside manner, knowledge, and successes. It is also a good idea to interview a couple of doctors you are thinking of working with to get an idea of who you want to proceed with. It is worth a few new patient consults to figure out the best team to work with. In addition, make sure you advocate for yourself and ask questions when appropriate.

Many patients tell me that they just don't know what questions to ask, or that they feel overwhelmed and find it hard to access information from the doctor during their visits, which tend to be brief. To help you get a sense of the right doctor for you, I've listed some questions that you can ask your doctor or the clinic you are considering working with. This is by no means a comprehensive list, but these are important questions that may provide you with better information to make the best decision for yourself and your family when it comes to your fertility journey.

Questions You May Want to Ask Your Reproductive Endocrinologist (RE) or Gynecologist Who Treats Infertility

- How long have you been helping women conceive?
- What is your success rate with natural conception, IUI, and/or IVF?
- Do you freeze your eggs on Day 3 or Day 5? (Well-trained embryologists will freeze when they are more mature—usually Day 4 or 5)
- Can I influence my AMH levels?
- Can I improve my FSH and LH levels?
- Can I improve my egg quality?
- What fertility options do you offer?
- Do you evaluate my spouse or partner's fertility?
- Do you look at MTHFR mutations and their influence on fertility?
- Do you use blood work, salivary testing, or additional tests to evaluate my fertility?
- Do you use other labs in addition to FSH, LH, estradiol, and progesterone? (For example, do they include thyroid, thyroid antibodies, autoimmune, and inflammatory marker labs?)
- What additional tests do you run for patients with a history of pregnancy loss? (They might add clotting disorder tests or other tests; the new standard for recurrent pregnancy losses is two miscarriages, rather than three)
- Do you use an integrative approach? If not, are you open to it?
- Can I take integrative supplements during IUI or IVF?
- If not, why?
- How do you feel about acupuncture before and/or with IVF protocol?
- How do you feel about working as a team with other providers?
- How can I communicate with you if I have a question?

Questions You May Want to Ask Your Naturopathic Doctor or Acupuncturist Who Specializes in Fertility

- How long have you been helping women conceive?
- What is your success rate with natural conception or helping with ART?
- How can you help me improve my FSH and LH levels?
- How can I improve my egg quality?
- What are my options, since I am forty or older?
- Do you evaluate my spouse or partner's fertility?
- Do you look at MTHFR mutations and their influence on fertility?
- Do you used blood work, salivary testing, or additional tests to evaluate my fertility?
- Can I change or influence my AMH levels?

- What fertility options do you offer?
- Do you provide more than prenatal nutrients?
- How would you fix a luteal phase defect without hormones?
- How do you increase the lining of the uterus?
- How do you know if I have an immune issue affecting embryo implantation?
- Is my partner's sperm quality an issue? How do I test and address this?
- How do you feel about working as a team with other providers?
- After what length of time should I consider ART options?
- How can I communicate with you if I have a question?

Before your visits, I recommend that you write down questions that you can't answer and bring them to your visit. Your doctor may need labs and other records to evaluate what recommendations they will offer to you.

Be an advocate for yourself and your healthcare. This may require taking a team approach to help you succeed. Don't be afraid to be honest with yourself and others. Sometimes the best solutions are created from asking the right questions.

YOU ARE WORTH

THE TIME

AND ENERGY

NEEDED TO

CREATE GREAT

JOY IN YOUR

LIFE.

FULFILLING YOUR BABY DREAMS:

YOUR COMPLETE FERTILITY CHECKLIST

Addressing the underlying roadblocks to fertility success is key to understanding how to realize your baby dreams. Many women spend years trying to conceive, but they fail to address the underlying issues that are blocking their success. The *Complete Fertility* recommendations in this book may or may not result in quickly getting pregnant, but they do give you the tools to create the best chance for success in less time. If you are not focusing on the things that can help you conceive, conception will take much longer, or might not succeed at all.

My hope for you is that you find the success you are looking for by understanding how your body works and how you can best support it in preparation for having a baby. Healthy pregnancy and healthy babies are paramount. It is not enough just to get pregnant. You want to prepare your body to give it the right support for growing a healthy baby, avoiding miscarriage and other complications, and creating the best environment for continued success during pregnancy and beyond. Your investment in yourself helps your own health, allows you to feel better, and improves your fertility and chances for success. You are worth the time and energy needed to help your body work optimally and create great joy in your life.

TESTING

We have discussed many tests that are useful in assessing your fertility. Some of the most helpful tests are listed below. Talk to your healthcare provider about these tests to better understand what your body needs and how to best support it.

- ✓ Basic fertility bloodwork
    - Day 3: FSH, LH, estradiol
    - Day 21: Progesterone
    - Any day: AMH levels
- ✓ Bloodwork to rule out PCOS
    - Prolactin, testosterone—free & total, DHEA sulfate, hemoglobin A1C
- ✓ Bloodwork to rule out general health conditions
    - CBC, CMP, lipid panel, vitamin D 25-Hydroxy, iron, ferritin, vitamin B 12
- ✓ Bloodwork to rule out thyroid dysfunction
    - TSH, free T3, free T4, thyroglobulin and microsomal TPO antibodies
- ✓ Bloodwork to rule out autoimmune disorders
    - ANA titer or autoimmune profile
- ✓ Rule out immune factors
    - Viral panel
- ✓ Rule out SIBO and gut dysbiosis
- ✓ Pelvic and intravaginal ultrasound and antral follicle count
- ✓ PAP and culture to rule out infections
- ✓ MTHFR genetic testing
- ✓ Salivary 24-hour cortisol testing to rule out adrenal dysfunction
- ✓ Complete sperm analysis of your partner
- ✓ Tests to complete in cases of recurrent pregnancy loss
- ✓ MTHFR and other genetic testing, clotting disorder testing

DIET AND LIFESTYLE

Creating a routine that includes regular exercise, stress management, and an anti-inflammatory diet with kidney and spleen Qi building foods, strengthens the foundation needed to conceive. Achieving ideal body weight for your height helps to normalize blood sugar and hormone regulation. Creating a network of supportive people aids in your emotional needs through this journey. Don't overlook these basic principles to contribute to optimizing your fertility. Diet and lifestyle are core to building the foundation for successful fertility.

SUPPORTING FERTILITY BASICS

Some of the basic natural and integrative supplements are listed below to increase your fertility. This is just a basic starting point. If you have PCOS, endometriosis, fibroids, or any other condition affecting your fertility, you may need additional support through supplements as well as direction from a skilled medical professional to devise the best protocol individualized for your situation. This is vital to continued success. Although many doctors who are not trained in integrative approaches may not give you the "thumbs up" for the support listed below, many of the tools are well researched and have been proven clinically to work. Having helped women conceive naturally as well as in conjunction with IVF and IUI for over nineteen years, I have seen patients get pregnant who had been unsuccessful on their own and with the help of reproductive endocrinologists (REs). That does not mean that ART is not a viable option to help you conceive; it can be a great option for some women to expand their family with success. Many REs give a success rate of about fifty to sixty percent. Some clinics report success as IVF that resulted in positive pregnancies rates. These percentages do not include miscarriage rates, which are more common than you might think. The Center for Disease Control (CDC) reports IVF success rates in terms of live births. Either way, forty to fifty percent of women are unsuccessful with IVF. These women pursed IVF because they were unsuccessful with natural conception, which means they are missing something important in their fertility success formula.

With success rates like this, it's up to you to step up your game and give your body the tools to create success. This means you have to start traveling another road. This new journey will help you improve function in your body and provide your body with the tools necessary to do what it is capable of doing—getting pregnant!

Below, you'll find a checklist for comprehensive support strategies to aid in conception.

Liver support 6 weeks prior to trying to conceive to support hormone balance
- √ Alpha lipoic acid
- √ Glutathione
- √ Liver detoxification formula for phase I and II support

Prenatal Health
- √ Prenatal vitamin with MTHF and methylcobalamin
- √ Omega-3 fatty acids (higher EPA such as EPA 850 mg, DHA 450 mg)
- √ Methyltetrahydrofolate (5-MTHF) 1–5 mg
- √ Vitamin D3 1000 iu per day

Methylation Support
- √ Methyltetrahydrofolate (5-MTHF) 1–5 mg in the morning
- √ Additional nutrients for basic methylation support
    (For example, Methylcobalamin [B 12] 1000 mg + P5P 25 mg, and B1 15 mg

- ✓ Or a physician recommended formula based on any MTHFR mutations you have

Adrenal Support
- ✓ Ginseng
- ✓ Adrenal herbal formulations to support healthy FSH and LH levels
- ✓ Adrenal glandular support
- ✓ Chinese herbal formulas to support fertility
- ✓ Acupuncture weekly

IMPROVE EGG QUALITY

Egg quality is important. If you have an egg that is poor quality, you have less of a chance to get pregnant, and an increased chance of miscarriage and other abnormalities during pregnancy. Supporting egg quality is not just about the eggs you are born with. It is about creating an environment that supports healthy cell division while the egg is maturing. The best supplements for improving egg quality are listed below.

- ✓ CoQ10
- ✓ DHEA
- ✓ 5-MTHF
- ✓ Melatonin
- ✓ Myoinositol
- ✓ Omega-3 fatty acids
- ✓ Antioxidant formula

IMPROVE SPERM PARAMETERS & DNA FRAGMENTATION

- ✓ Probiotic
- ✓ Antioxidant formula
- ✓ Methylation support
- ✓ CoQ10
- ✓ Vitamin D3
- ✓ Vitamin B12
- ✓ Carnitine

BASIC GUT HEALTH SUPPORT

✓ L-glutamine for leaky gut
✓ Gluten-free diet
✓ Address gut dysbiosis and SIBO

EATING FOR CONCEPTION

✓ Organic
✓ Kidney Yin and spleen Qi tonifying foods
✓ Avoid raw foods
✓ Avoid food allergens

UTILIZING THE BENEFITS OF ACUPUNCTURE AND CHINESE MEDICINE

Traditional Chinese Medicine (TCM) has been around for thousands of years, supporting women's and family's health before Western medicine was even established. We know that acupuncture and TCM herbal prescriptions can support normal physiology and restore optimal functioning of the body. There is a growth of scientific knowledge and research supporting the use of TCM herbal medicine and acupuncture to enhance your fertility. We know that it can help induce ovulation, increase the lining of the uterus, balance hormones, and enhance fertility. It is documented in research studies to increase the success of embryo transfer (ET) with IVF procedures using acupuncture both before and after IVF/ET and should be used as a pivotal enhancing tool to increase your IVF success.

THE IMPORTANCE OF INVOLVING YOUR PARTNER

It is important to consider your partner in the fertility equation. That means looking at his fertility health by doing a sperm analysis and optimizing his ability to produce adequate sperm that are motile, shaped well, and have reduced fragmentation. It is estimated that thirty to fifty percent of unexplained fertility is due to male factor. So it may not be all you—it could be your partner. While you are working on your body month after month and not conceiving, it could be your partner that is holding up your ability to have a baby. So it is best to work together from the beginning while you simultaneously work to improve your fertility as a couple. Or if you are using a donor, it means picking someone who has the right set of parameters that will increase your success.

It is also a good idea to discuss your fertility journey with your partner from time to time to make sure you are on the same page, aspiring toward the same goal, and supporting one another. Remember your partner's and/or your desires may change over time. He may want IVF while you don't. You may want to try naturally, but he will not take supplements to improve sperm quality. Maybe you are ready for IUI, but he is not. Maybe you want to jump into IVF and your partner does not want to do interventions other than natural ones. Whatever the situation, open communication during the journey together is important. If you are not partnered, then finding a support network and someone to bounce ideas off of will serve you well. Communicating your feelings, fears, and dreams is important for you and your partner or loved one, while maneuvering through the fertility landscape.

KNOWING YOUR OPTIONS – NEVER SAY NEVER

Remember to keep all your options open when trying to have your first baby or expand your family. Most of my patients generally prefer natural conception over other methods. Using the tools listed in these pages will increase your chances of success with natural conception. However "never say never" to other options that can make your dreams come true. That might mean that you pursue IVF or IUI cycles, or consider using a sperm donor, an egg donor, or a donor embryo; don't rule out anything that can lead to success. With modern medicine, the sky is the limit if your body is prepared.

No one knows what they will or won't do until they are in the midst of their journey and their perspective changes. It is okay to want to use IVF as an option to conceive. It is most effective if your body is functioning optimally. I have worked with patients who have had unsuccessful IVF cycles before using the integrative tools for fertility success that I've described in this book. When these patients try IVF again, when their bodies are ready, they are often successful. Some of my patients say "I will never do IVF" but later reconsider.

I am always supportive and tell my patients that ART offers viable options that should not be overlooked, especially if a woman is thirty-five or older. I am used to working with women who have tried natural conception, IUI, and IVF and not been successful until we work together to create a better outcome. Whether it is working with women who want to conceive naturally, or who want to have the best chances of success with IVF or IUI cycles, restoring optimal hormone and psychological function is paramount to their success. Be open to the possibilities that best suit you and your circumstance. Never say never, and stay the course to grow your family. There are more tools and options now than ever before that can assist you with an integration of the newest technology, combined with the age-old wisdom of Chinese medicine and acupuncture, and other natural interventions to help you be successful.

LIVING YOUR BEST LIFE

What does living your best life mean to you? For many couples, and especially women, it has to do with living a life without regret. That means exhausting all the tools possible to help you have a baby. Many times, women just don't know what tools are available until it is too late.

If you have been trying to conceive for one year or longer without success, then what you are doing is not working, and you need to do something different. Use the tools and information in this book to springboard your heart's desire into reality and live your best life without regret.

You can live your best life with or without children by empowering yourself to make your own choices, knowing you did all that you could for your best possible success. Knowledge is about empowering yourself to make the best choices for you, and not limiting yourself to one doctor's opinion. I have seen women who were told time and time again that they will never have their own children or have another child and yet, somehow, they do. So try to stay hopeful and know there are ways to get the support you need to make your baby dreams come true.

You have the tools to transform your fertility journey and live your best life. It is my deepest hope that you may be successful in your journey and create the family your heart desires.

NOTES AND REFERENCES

INTRODUCTION

(1) "American Board of Oriental Reproductive Medicine, Fertility Acupuncture, Fertility Acupuncturist." ABORM, July 31, 2019. https://aborm.org/.

CHAPTER 1

Lewis, Randine. "Fertile Soul: Part 4, Ovarian Function." Webinar, Healthy Seminars. Accessed August 4, 2013. www.healthyseminars.com.

Lyttleton, Jane. "Treatment of Infertility: Part 2." Webinar, Healthy Seminars. Accessed September 6, 2010.

Magarelli, Paul C. "Regulation of the Menstrual Cycle." Webinar, Healthy Seminars. Accessed January 3, 2016. www.healthyseminars.com.

Nedresky, Daniel, and Gurdeep Singh. "Physiology, Luteinizing Hormone." StatPearls. StatPearls Publishing, April 8, 2019. https://www.ncbi.nlm.nih.gov/pubmed/30969514.

CHAPTER 2

"Antiphospholipid Antibody Syndrome." National Heart Lung and Blood Institute. U.S. Department of Health and Human Services. Accessed October 2019. https://www.nhlbi.nih.gov/health-topics/antiphospholipid-antibody-syndrome.

Bray, David. "Essence of Infertility." AAAOM International Conference & Exposition, "Transitions in AOM," April 23–26, 2009.

Dale Pfeifer, Samantha, Marc Dale Fritz, Jeffrey Dale Goldberg, R. Dale McClure, Michael Dale Thomas, Eric Dale Widra, Glenn Dale Schatman, et al. "Evaluation and Treatment of Recurring Pregnancy Loss: a Committee Opinion." The Practice Committee of the American Society for Reproductive Medicine, Birmingham, Alabama, 2012. PDF.

Evenson, Donald P. "Sperm Chromatin Structure Assay (SCSA®)." Methods in molecular biology (Clifton, N.J.). U.S. National Library of Medicine, 2013. https://www.ncbi.nlm.nih.gov/pubmed/22992911.

Kumar, Ashim. "The Diagnostic Evaluation and Treatment of Recurrent Pregnancy Loss." UCLA School of Medicine, 2017. https://documents.pub/document/the-diagnostic-evaluation-and-treatment-of-recurrent-pregnancy-loss-ashim-kumar-md-reproductive-endocrinology-and-infertility-clinical-assistant-professor.html.

Lindsay, Tammy J, and Kirsten R Vitrikas. "Evaluation and Treatment of Infertility." American Family Physician, March 1, 2015. https://www.aafp.org/afp/2015/0301/p308.html.

Odershaw, Leslie. "Lab Testing and Hormonal Assessment for Infertility: Treatment Success Depends on Diagnosing the Real Cause." Webinar, Healthy Seminars. www.healthyseminars.com.

"Recurrent Pregnancy Loss." UCLA Obstetrics and Gynecology. Accessed October 2019. http://obgyn.ucla.edu/recurrent-pregnancy-loss.

Royal Australian College of General Practitioners. "Male Infertility—The Other Side of the Equation." RACGP. The Royal Australian College of General Practitioners. Accessed October 2019. https://www.racgp.org.au/afp/2017/september/male-infertility/.

"Women's Health Care Physicians." ACOG. Accessed October 2019. https://www.acog.org/Patients/FAQs/Evaluating-Infertility.

1. Batool Mutar Mahdi, Wafaa Hazim Salih, Annie Edmond Caitano, Bassma Maki Kadhum, and Dina Sami Ibrahim. "Frequency of Antisperm Antibodies in Infertile Women." Journal of reproduction & infertility. Avicenna Research Institute, October 2011. https://www.ncbi.nlm.nih.gov/pmc/articles/PMC3719312/.

CHAPTER 3

Elisabeth Kübler-Ross. *On Death and Dying*. Scribner, 1969.

"Depression." National Institute of Mental Health. https://www.nimh.nih.gov/health/topics/depression/index.shtml.

CHAPTER 4

1. Mehmet Firat Mutlu and Ahmet Erdem. "Evaluation of Ovarian Reserve in Infertile Patients." Journal of the Turkish German Gynecological Association. AVES, September 1, 2012. https://www.ncbi.nlm.nih.gov/pmc/articles/PMC3939241/.

2. Frank J M Broekmans, Dominique De Ziegler, Colin M. Howles, Alain Gougeon, Geoffrey Trew, and Francois Olivennes. "The Antral Follicle Count: Practical Recommendations for Better Standardization." Fertility and Sterility 94, no. 3 (2010): 1044–51. https://doi.org/10.1016/j.fertnstert.2009.04.040.

3. Akira Iwase, Tomoko Nakamura, Satoko Osuka, Sachiko Takikawa, Maki Goto, and Fumitaka Kikkawa. 2015. "Anti-Müllerian Hormone as a Marker of Ovarian Reserve: What Have We Learned, and What Should We Know?" Reproductive Medicine and Biology. John Wiley and Sons Inc. November 23, 2015. https://www.ncbi.nlm.nih.gov/pmc/articles/PMC5715856/.

4. Francisco Gaytan, Concepcion Morales, Silvia Leon, David Garcia-Galiano, Juan Roa, and Manuel Tena-Sempere. "Crowding and Follicular Fate: Spatial Determinants of Follicular Reserve and Activation of Follicular Growth in the Mammalian Ovary." PLOS ONE. Public Library of Science, December 7, 2015. https://www.ncbi.nlm.nih.gov/pmc/articles/PMC4671646/.

5. "Primordial Follicle." Primordial Follicle - An Overview, ScienceDirect Topics. Accessed October 2019. https://www.sciencedirect.com/topics/medicine-and-dentistry/primordial-follicle.

6. Jason Franasiak, Steven L Young, Christopher D Williams, and Lisa M Pastore. "Longitudinal Anti-Müllerian Hormone in Women with Polycystic Ovary Syndrome: an Acupuncture Randomized Clinical Trial." Evidence-based Complementary and Alternative Medicine: eCAM. Hindawi Publishing Corporation, 2012. https://www.ncbi.nlm.nih.gov/pubmed/22966246.

7. B Meczekalski, A Czyzyk, M Kunicki, A Podfigurna-Stopa, L Plociennik, G Jakiel, M Maciejewska-Jeske, and K Lukaszuk. 2016. "Fertility in Women of Late Reproductive Age: the Role of Serum Anti-Müllerian Hormone (AMH) Levels in Its Assessment." Journal of Endocrinological Investigation. Springer International Publishing. November 2016. https://www.ncbi.nlm.nih.gov/pmc/articles/PMC5069312/.

8. Y Himabindu, M Sriharibabu, Kk Gopinathan, Usha Satish, T Fessy Louis, and Parasuram Gopinath. 2013. "Anti-Mullerian Hormone and Antral Follicle Count as Predictors of Ovarian Response in Assisted Reproduction." Journal of Human Reproductive Sciences. Medknow Publications & Media Pvt Ltd. January 2013. https://www.ncbi.nlm.nih.gov/pmc/articles/PMC3713572/.

9. Nicola A Dennis, Lisa A Houghton, Gregory T Jones, Andre M van Rij, Kirstie Morgan, and Ian S McLennan. "The Level of Serum Anti-Müllerian Hormone Correlates with Vitamin D Status in Men and Women But Not in Boys." The Journal of Clinical Endocrinology & Metabolism 97, no. 7 (2012): 2450–55. https://doi.org/10.1210/jc.2012-1213.

10. Anne Marie Z Jukic, Anne Z Steiner, and Donna D Baird. 2015. "Association between Serum 25-Hydroxyvitamin D and Ovarian Reserve in Premenopausal Women." Menopause (New York, N.Y.). U.S. National Library of Medicine. March 2015. https://www.ncbi.nlm.nih.gov/pmc/articles/PMC4317384/.

11. Krista D Sowell, Carl L Keen, and Janet Y Uriu-Adams. "Vitamin D and Reproduction: From Gametes to Childhood." Healthcare (Basel, Switzerland). MDPI, November 9, 2015. https://www.ncbi.nlm.nih.gov/pmc/articles/PMC4934634/.

12. Sebiha Ozkan, Sangita Jindal, Keri Greenseid, Jun Shu, Gohar Zeitlian, Cheryl Hickmon, and Lubna Pal. "Replete Vitamin D Stores Predict Reproductive Success Following in Vitro Fertilization." Fertility and Sterility. U.S. National Library of Medicine, September 2010. https://www.ncbi.nlm.nih.gov/pmc/articles/PMC2888852/.

13. M Irani, D Seifer, H Minkoff, and Z Merhi. "Vitamin D Supplementation Appears to Normalize Serum AMH Levels in Vitamin D Deficient Premenopausal Women." Fertility and Sterility 100, no. 3 (2013). https://doi.org/10.1016/j.fertnstert.2013.07.892.

14. Zahra Naderi, Maryam Kashanian, Leily Chenari, and Narges Sheikhansari. "Evaluating the Effects of Administration of 25-Hydroxyvitamin D Supplement on Serum Anti-Mullerian Hormone (AMH) Levels in Infertile Women." Gynecological Endocrinology. U.S. National Library of Medicine, May 2018. https://www.ncbi.nlm.nih.gov/pubmed/29212401.

15. Nicola A Dennis, Lisa A Houghton, Michael W Pankhurst, Michelle J Harper, and Ian S McLennan. "Acute Supplementation with High Dose Vitamin D3 Increases Serum Anti-Müllerian Hormone in Young Women." Nutrients. MDPI, July 8, 2017. https://www.ncbi.nlm.nih.gov/pubmed/28698476.

16. Xiufeng Lin, Jing Du, Yan Du, Riran Wu, Xiaowu Fang, Yuechan Liao, and Song Quan. "Effects of Dehydroepiandrosterone Supplementation on Mice with Diminished Ovarian Reserve." Gynecological Endocrinology. U.S. National Library of Medicine, April 2018. https://www.ncbi.nlm.nih.gov/pubmed/29221424.

17. Yavuz Emre Sükür, Içten Balık Kıvançlı, and Batuhan Ozmen. "Ovarian Aging and Premature Ovarian Failure." Journal of the Turkish German Gynecological Association. AVES, August 8, 2014. https://www.ncbi.nlm.nih.gov/pmc/articles/PMC4195330/.

18. Charles Bankhead. "Studies: Weed Degrades Sperm, Spurs LUTS." Medical News and Free CME Online. MedpageToday, May 5, 2019. https://www.medpagetoday.com/meetingcoverage/aua/79630.

19. Henrik Leonhardt, Mikael Hellström, Berit Gull, Anna-Karin Lind, Lars Nilsson, Per Olof Janson, and Elisabet Stener-Victorin. "Serum Anti-Müllerian Hormone and Ovarian Morphology Assessed by Magnetic Resonance Imaging in Response to Acupuncture and Exercise in Women with Polycystic Ovary Syndrome: Secondary Analyses of a Randomized Controlled Trial." Acta obstetricia et gynecologica Scandinavica. U.S. National Library of Medicine, March 2015. https://www.ncbi.nlm.nih.gov/pubmed/25545309.

20. Jie Shen, Meihong Shen, Zhongren Li, Rongli Zhang, Xia Li, and Bingwei Ai. "Effects of Moxibustion at Shenshu (BL 23) on Level of Sex Hormones and AMH in Sub-Health Peri-Menopausal Women." Chinese Acupuncture & Moxibustion. U.S. National Library of Medicine, April 12, 2017. https://www.ncbi.nlm.nih.gov/pubmed/29231589.

21. Vicky Moy, Sangita Jindal, Harry Lieman, and Erkan Buyuk. "Obesity Adversely Affects Serum Anti-Müllerian Hormone (AMH) Levels in Caucasian Women." Journal of Assisted Reproduction and Genetics. Springer US, September 2015. https://www.ncbi.nlm.nih.gov/pmc/articles/PMC4595398/.

22. Seyedeh Zahra Shahrokhi, Faranak Kazerouni, and Firouzeh Ghaffari. "Anti-Müllerian Hormone: Genetic and Environmental Effects." Clinica Chimica Acta. U.S. National Library of Medicine, January 2018. https://www.ncbi.nlm.nih.gov/pubmed/29175649.

23. "BRCA1 Mutation Linked to Fewer Eggs in Ovaries." Breastcancer.org, January 24, 2019. https://www.breastcancer.org/research-news/brca1-linked-to-fewer-eggs-in-ovaries.

24. Lauren Johnson, Mary D Sammel, Susan Domchek, Allison Schanne, Maureen Prewitt, and Clarisa Gracia. "Antimüllerian Hormone Levels Are Lower in BRCA2 Mutation Carriers." Fertility and Sterility. U.S. National Library of Medicine, May 2017. https://www.ncbi.nlm.nih.gov/pmc/articles/PMC5531590/.

25. Seyedeh Z Shahrokhi, Faranak Kazerouni, Firouzeh Ghaffari, Ali Rahimipour, Mir D Omrani, Arezoo Arabipoor, Ramin Lak, and Elaheh T Ghane. "The Relationship Between the MTHFR C677T Genotypes to Serum Anti-Müllerian Hormone Concentrations and In Vitro Fertilization/Intracytoplasmic Sperm Injection Outcome." Clinical laboratory. U.S. National Library of Medicine, May 1, 2017. https://www.ncbi.nlm.nih.gov/pubmed/28627828.

CHAPTER 5

1. Osnat Bloch Damti, Orly Sarid, Eyal Sheiner, Tali Zilberstein, and Julie Cwikel. "Stress and Distress in Infertility among Women." Harefuah. U.S. National Library of Medicine, March 2008. https://www.ncbi.nlm.nih.gov/pubmed/18488870.

2. J Cwikel, Y Gidron, and E Sheiner. "Psychological Interactions with Infertility among Women." European Journal of Obstetrics, Gynecology, and Reproductive Biology. U.S. National Library of Medicine, December 1, 2004. https://www.ncbi.nlm.nih.gov/pubmed/15541845.

3. Seyedeh Z Shahrokhi, Faranak Kazerouni, Firouzeh Ghaffari, Ali Rahimipour, Mir D Omrani, Arezoo Arabipoor, Ramin Lak, and Elaheh T Ghane. "The Relationship Between the MTHFR C677T Genotypes to Serum Anti-Müllerian Hormone Concentrations and In Vitro Fertilization/Intracytoplasmic Sperm Injection Outcome." Clinical Laboratory. U.S. National Library of Medicine, May 1, 2017. https://www.ncbi.nlm.nih.gov/pubmed/28627828.

4. Sukanya Jaroenporn, Tatsuya Yamamoto, Asuka Itabashi, Katsuhiro Nakamura, Isao Azumano, Gen Watanabe, and Kazuyoshi Taya. "Effects of Pantothenic Acid Supplementation on Adrenal Steroid Secretion from Male Rats." Biological & Pharmaceutical Bulletin. U.S. National Library of Medicine, June 2008. https://www.ncbi.nlm.nih.gov/pubmed/18520055.

5. A Panossian and H Wagner. "Stimulating Effect of Adaptogens: an Overview with Particular Reference to Their Efficacy Following Single Dose Administration." Wiley Online Library. John Wiley & Sons, Ltd, October 31, 2005. https://onlinelibrary.wiley.com/doi/abs/10.1002/ptr.1751.

6. David Winston. "Adaptogens: Herbs for Strength, Stamina, and Stress Relief." Google Books. Inner Traditions / Bear & Co, March 22, 2007. https://books.google.com/books?hl=en&lr=&id=5NbXBhyQGUkC.

7. K Chandrasekhar, Jyoti Kapoor, and Sridhar Anishetty. "A Prospective, Randomized Double-Blind, Placebo-Controlled Study of Safety and Efficacy of a High-Concentration Full-Spectrum Extract of Ashwagandha Root in Reducing Stress and Anxiety in Adults." Indian Journal of Psychological Medicine. Medknow Publications & Media Pvt Ltd, July 2012. https://www.ncbi.nlm.nih.gov/pmc/articles/PMC3573577/.

8. "Eleutherococcus Senticosus." Eleutherococcus senticosus - an overview, ScienceDirect Topics. Accessed October 2019. https://www.sciencedirect.com/topics/medicine-and-dentistry/eleutherococcus-senticosus.

9. "Licorice Root." National Center for Complementary and Integrative Health. U.S. Department of Health and Human Services, December 1, 2016. https://nccih.nih.gov/health/licoriceroot.

10. Rui Yang. "The Anti-Inflammatory Activity of Licorice, a Widely Used Chinese Herb." Taylor & Francis. Accessed October 2019. https://www.tandfonline.com/doi/full/10.1080/13880209.2016.1225775.

11. Monica Damle and Bhanuben Nanavati. "Glycyrrhiza Glabra (Liquorice) - a Potent Medicinal Herb." International Journal of Herbal Medicine 2, no. 2 (May 5, 2014): 132–36. http://www.florajournal.com/archives/2014/vol2issue2/PartC/23.1.pdf.

12. Muhammad Shahzad, Arham Shabbir, Ken Wojcikowski, Hans Wohlmuth, and Glenda C. Gobe. "The Antioxidant Effects of Radix Astragali (Astragalus Membranaceus and Related Species) in Protecting Tissues from Injury and Disease." August 31, 2016. http://www.eurekaselect.com/134721/article.

13. Sung-Hoon Jo, Kyoung-Soo Ha, Kyoung-Sik Moon, Ok-Hwan Lee, Hae-Dong Jang, and Young-In Kwon. "In Vitro and in Vivo Anti-Hyperglycemic Effects of Omija (Schizandra Chinensis) Fruit." Molecular Diversity Preservation International, February 23, 2011. https://www.mdpi.com/1422-0067/12/2/1359/htm.

14. Jonathan Steven Alexander and Yuping Wang. "Therapeutic Potential of Schisandra Chinensis Extracts for Treatment of Hypertension. Introduction to: 'Antihypertensive Effect of Gomisin A from Schisandra Chinensis on Angiotensin II-Induced Hypertension via Preservation of Nitric Oxide Bioavailability' by Park Et Al." Nature News. Nature Publishing Group, July 5, 2012. https://www.nature.com/articles/hr2012101.

15. Shehua Cao, Huanping Shang, Weibing Wu, Jingrong Du, and Ramesh Putheti. "Evaluation of Anti-Athletic Fatigue Activity of Schizandra Chinensis Aqueous Extracts in Mice." African Journal of Pharmacy and Pharmacology. Academic Journals, November 30, 2009. https://academicjournals.org/journal/AJPP/article-abstract/A74B22D37372.

16. S K Gupta, Jai Prakash, and Sushma Srivastava. "Validation of Traditional Claim of Tulsi, Ocimum Sanctum Linn. as a Medicinal Plant." Indian Journal of Experimental Biology. U.S. National Library of Medicine, July 2002. https://www.ncbi.nlm.nih.gov/pubmed/12597545.

17. Beverly Yates. "Holy Basil (Ocimum sanctum): An Overview of the Research and Clinical Indications." Plant Intelligence.®, Professional Resources. Accessed October 2019. https://web.archive.org/web/20170908075309/https://www.gaiaherbs.com/uploads/1596_HPR_HolyBasil_ResearchPaper-1371567034.pdf

18. S Gholap and A Kar. "Hypoglycaemic Effects of Some Plant Extracts Are Possibly Mediated through Inhibition in Corticosteroid Concentration." Die Pharmazie. U.S. National Library of Medicine, November 2004. https://www.ncbi.nlm.nih.gov/pubmed/15587591.

19. V Rai, U Iyer, and U V Mani. "Effect of Tulasi (Ocimum Sanctum) Leaf Powder Supplementation on Blood Sugar Levels, Serum Lipids and Tissue Lipids in Diabetic Rats." Plant Foods for Human Nutrition (Dordrecht, Netherlands). U.S. National Library of Medicine, 1997. https://www.ncbi.nlm.nih.gov/pubmed/9198110.

20. Sana Ishaque, Larissa Shamseer, Cecilia Bukutu, and Sunita Vohra. "Rhodiola Rosea for Physical and Mental Fatigue: a Systematic Review." BMC Complementary and Alternative Medicine. BioMed Central, May 29, 2012. https://www.ncbi.nlm.nih.gov/pmc/articles/PMC3541197/.

21. Thomas B Walker and Robert A. Robergs. "Does Rhodiola Rosea Possess Ergogenic Properties?" International Journal of Sport Nutrition and Exercise Metabolism 16, no. 3 (2006): 305–15. https://doi.org/10.1123/ijsnem.16.3.305.

22. Kashmira J Gohil, Jagruti A Patel, and Anuradha K Gajjar. "Pharmacological Review on Centella Asiatica: A Potential Herbal Cure-All." Indian Journal of Pharmaceutical Sciences. Medknow Publications, September 2010. https://www.ncbi.nlm.nih.gov/pmc/articles/PMC3116297/.

23. Kun Marisa Farhana, Rusdy Ghazali, Wibowo, Samekto, and Abdul. "Effectiveness of Gotu Kola Extract 750 Mg and 1000 Mg Compared with Folic Acid 3 Mg in Improving Vascular Cognitive Impairment after Stroke." Evidence-Based Complementary and Alternative Medicine. Hindawi, June 1, 2016. https://www.hindawi.com/journals/ecam/2016/2795915/.

24. Rafie Hamidpour. "Medicinal Property of Gotu Kola (Centella Asiatica) from the Selection of Traditional Applications to the Novel Phytotherapy." Archives in Cancer Research 3, no. 4 (2015). https://doi.org/10.21767/2254-6081.100042.

25. K Udaya Sankarb. "Bioactive Principles from Cordyceps Sinensis: A Potent Food Supplement – A Review." Journal of Functional Foods. Elsevier, May 24, 2013. https://www.sciencedirect.com/science/article/pii/S1756464613001254.

26. H O Meissner, P Mrozikiewicz, T Bobkiewicz-Kozlowska, A Mscisz, B Kedzia, A Lowicka, H Reich-Bilinska, W Kapczynski, and I Barchia. "Hormone-Balancing Effect of Pre-Gelatinized Organic Maca (Lepidium Peruvianum Chacon): (I) Biochemical and Pharmacodynamic Study on Maca Using Clinical Laboratory Model on Ovariectomized Rats." International Journal of Biomedical Science. Master Publishing Group, September 2006. https://www.ncbi.nlm.nih.gov/pmc/articles/PMC3614604/.

CHAPTER 6

1. Yaakov Bentov, Tetyana Yavorska, Navid Esfandiari, Andrea Jurisicova, and Robert F Casper. "The Contribution of Mitochondrial Function to Reproductive Aging." Journal of assisted reproduction and genetics. Springer US, September 2011. https://www.ncbi.nlm.nih.gov/pmc/articles/PMC3169682/.

2. David R Meldrum, Robert F Casper, Antonio Diez-Juan, Carlos Simon, Alice D Domar, and Rene Frydman. "Aging and the Environment Affect Gamete and Embryo Potential: Can We Intervene?" Fertility and Sterility. U.S. National Library of Medicine, March 2016. https://www.ncbi.nlm.nih.gov/pubmed/26812244.

3. Norbert Gleicher, Mario V Vega, Sarah K Darmon, Andrea Weghofer, Yan-Guan Wu, Qi Wang, Lin Zhang, David F Albertini, David H Barad, and Vitaly A Kushnir. "Live-Birth Rates in Very Poor Prognosis Patients, Who Are Defined as Poor Responders under the Bologna Criteria, with Nonelective Single Embryo, Two-Embryo, and Three or More Embryos Transferred." Fertility and Sterility. U.S. National Library of Medicine, December 2015. https://www.ncbi.nlm.nih.gov/pubmed/26348275.

4. Yaakov Bentov, Navid Esfandiari, Eliezer Burstein, and Robert F. Casper. "The Use of Mitochondrial Nutrients to Improve the Outcome of Infertility Treatment in Older Patients." Fertility and Sterility 93, no. 1 (2010): 272–75. https://doi.org/10.1016/j.fertnstert.2009.07.988.

5. A Gvozdjakova, J Kucharska, J Lipkova, B Bartolcicova, J Dubravicky, M Vorakova, I Cernakova, and R B Singh. "Importance of the Assessment of Coenzyme Q10, Alpha-Tocopherol and Oxidative Stress for the Diagnosis and Therapy of Infertility in Men." Bratislavske lekarske listy. U.S. National Library of Medicine, 2013. https://www.ncbi.nlm.nih.gov/pubmed/24236426.

6. A Mancini, L De Marinis, G P Littarru, and G Balercia. "An Update of Coenzyme Q10 Implications in Male Infertility: Biochemical and Therapeutic Aspects." BioFactors (Oxford, England). U.S. National Library of Medicine, 2005. https://www.ncbi.nlm.nih.gov/pubmed/16873942.

7. Mohammad Reza Safarinejad. "The Effect of Coenzyme Q_{10} Supplementation on Partner Pregnancy Rate in Infertile Men with Idiopathic Oligoasthenoteratozoospermia: an Open-Label Prospective Study." International Urology and Nephrology. U.S. National Library of Medicine, June 2012. https://www.ncbi.nlm.nih.gov/pubmed/22081410.

8. Giancarlo Balercia, Eddi Buldreghini, Arianna Vignini, Luca Tiano, Francesca Paggi, Salvatore Amoroso, Giuseppe Ricciardo-Lamonica, Marco Boscaro, Andrea Lenzi, and GianPaolo Littarru. "Coenzyme Q10 Treatment in Infertile Men with Idiopathic Asthenozoospermia: a Placebo-Controlled, Double-Blind Randomized Trial." Fertility and Sterility. U.S. National Library of Medicine, May 2009. https://www.ncbi.nlm.nih.gov/pubmed/18395716.

9. Gian Paolo Littarru and Luca Tiano. "Clinical Aspects of Coenzyme Q10: an Update." Current Opinion in Clinical Nutrition and Metabolic Care. U.S. National Library of Medicine, November 2005. https://www.ncbi.nlm.nih.gov/pubmed/16205466.

10. Vittorio Unfer, G Carlomagno, P Rizzo, E Raffone, and S Roseff. "Myo-Inositol Rather than D-Chiro-Inositol Is Able to Improve Oocyte Quality in Intracytoplasmic Sperm Injection Cycles. A Prospective, Controlled, Randomized Trial." European Review for Medical and Pharmacological Sciences. U.S. National Library of Medicine, April 2011. https://www.ncbi.nlm.nih.gov/pubmed/21608442.

11. Vittorio Unfer, Emanuela Raffone, Piero Rizzo, and Silvia Buffo. "Effect of a Supplementation with Myo-Inositol plus Melatonin on Oocyte Quality in Women Who Failed to Conceive in Previous in Vitro Fertilization Cycles for Poor Oocyte Quality: a Prospective, Longitudinal, Cohort Study." Gynecological Endocrinology. U.S. National Library of Medicine, November 2011. https://www.ncbi.nlm.nih.gov/pubmed/21463230.

12. Xiangqin Zheng, Danmei Lin, Yulong Zhang, Yuan Lin, Jianrong Song, Suyu Li, and Yan Sun. "Inositol Supplement Improves Clinical Pregnancy Rate in Infertile Women Undergoing Ovulation Induction for ICSI or IVF-ET." Medicine. Wolters Kluwer Health, December 2017. https://www.ncbi.nlm.nih.gov/pubmed/29245250.

13. P Rizzo, E Raffone, and V Benedetto. "Effect of the Treatment with Myo-Inositol plus Folic Acid plus Melatonin in Comparison with a Treatment with Myo-Inositol plus Folic Acid on Oocyte Quality and Pregnancy Outcome in IVF Cycles. A Prospective, Clinical Trial." European Review for Medical and Pharmacological Sciences. U.S. National Library of Medicine, June 2010. https://www.ncbi.nlm.nih.gov/pubmed/20712264.

14. K Ravanos, G Monastra, T Pavlidou, M Goudakou, and N Prapas. "Can High Levels of D-Chiro-Inositol in Follicular Fluid Exert Detrimental Effects on Blastocyst Quality?" European Review for Medical and Pharmacological Sciences. U.S. National Library of Medicine, December 2017. https://www.ncbi.nlm.nih.gov/pubmed/29243796.

15. Rosalbino Isabella and Emanuela Raffone. "CONCERN: Does Ovary Need D-Chiro-Inositol?" Journal of Ovarian Research. BioMed Central, May 15, 2012. https://www.ncbi.nlm.nih.gov/pmc/articles/PMC3447676/.

16. Deepika Garg and Reshef Tal. "Inositol Treatment and ART Outcomes in Women with PCOS." International Journal of Endocrinology. Hindawi Publishing Corporation, 2016. https://www.ncbi.nlm.nih.gov/pmc/articles/PMC5067314/.

17. Rinchen Zangmo, Neeta Singh, Sunesh Kumar, Perumal Vanamail, and Abanish Tiwari. "Role of Dehydroepiandrosterone in Improving Oocyte and Embryo Quality in IVF Cycles." Reproductive Biomedicine Online. U.S. National Library of Medicine, June 2014. https://www.ncbi.nlm.nih.gov/pubmed/24745834.

18. Nikita Naredi, K Sandeep, V D S Jamwal, N Nagraj, and Seema Rai. "Dehydroepiandrosterone: A Panacea for the Ageing Ovary?" Medical Journal, Armed Forces India. Elsevier, July 2015. https://www.ncbi.nlm.nih.gov/pubmed/26288496.

19. Li-Te Lin, Jiin-Tsuey Cheng, Peng-Hui Wang, Chia-Jung Li, and Kuan-Hao Tsui. "Dehydroepiandrosterone as a Potential Agent to Slow down Ovarian Aging." The Journal of Obstetrics and Gynaecology Research. U.S. National Library of Medicine, December 2017. https://www.ncbi.nlm.nih.gov/pubmed/28892223.

20. Haifa A Al-Turki. "Dehydroepiandrosterone Supplementation in Women Undergoing Assisted Reproductive Technology with Poor Ovarian Response. A Prospective Case-Control Study." The Journal of International Medical Research. SAGE Publications, January 2018. https://www.ncbi.nlm.nih.gov/pubmed/28758852.

21. David Barad and Norbert Gleicher. "Effect of Dehydroepiandrosterone on Oocyte and Embryo Yields, Embryo Grade and Cell Number in IVF." Human Reproduction (Oxford, England). U.S. National Library of Medicine, November 2006. https://www.ncbi.nlm.nih.gov/pubmed/16997936.

22. Chao Song, Wei Peng, Songna Yin, Jiamin Zhao, Beibei Fu, Jingcheng Zhang, Tingchao Mao, Haibo Wu, and Yong Zhang. "Melatonin Improves Age-Induced Fertility Decline and Attenuates Ovarian Mitochondrial Oxidative Stress in Mice." Scientific Reports. Nature Publishing Group, October 12, 2016. https://www.ncbi.nlm.nih.gov/pubmed/27731402.

23. Hiroshi Tamura, Mai Kawamoto, Shun Sato, Isao Tamura, Ryo Maekawa, Toshiaki Taketani, Hiromi Aasada, et al. "Long-Term Melatonin Treatment Delays Ovarian Aging." Journal of Pineal Research. U.S. National Library of Medicine, March 2017. https://www.ncbi.nlm.nih.gov/pubmed/27889913.

24. Fatemeh Nikmard, Elham Hosseini, Mehrdad Bakhtiyari, Mahnaz Ashrafi, Fardin Amidi, and Reza Aflatoonian. "Effects of Melatonin on Oocyte Maturation in PCOS Mouse Model." Animal Science Journal. U.S. National Library of Medicine, April 2017. https://www.ncbi.nlm.nih.gov/pubmed/27530294.

25. Changjiu He, Jing Wang, Zhenzhen Zhang, Minghui Yang, Yu Li, Xiuzhi Tian, Teng Ma, et al. "Mitochondria Synthesize Melatonin to Ameliorate Its Function and Improve Mice Oocyte's Quality under in Vitro Conditions." International Journal of Molecular Sciences. MDPI, June 14, 2016. https://www.ncbi.nlm.nih.gov/pubmed/27314334.

26. Hiroshi Tamura, Akihisa Takasaki, Ichiro Miwa, Ken Taniguchi, Ryo Maekawa, Hiromi Asada, Toshiaki Taketani, et al. "Oxidative Stress Impairs Oocyte Quality and Melatonin Protects Oocytes from Free Radical Damage and Improves Fertilization Rate." Journal of Pineal Research. U.S. National Library of Medicine, April 2008. https://www.ncbi.nlm.nih.gov/pubmed/18339123.

27. Tessa Lord, Brett Nixon, Keith T Jones, and R John Aitken. "Melatonin Prevents Postovulatory Oocyte Aging in the Mouse and Extends the Window for Optimal Fertilization in Vitro." Biology of Reproduction. U.S. National Library of Medicine, March 21, 2013. https://www.ncbi.nlm.nih.gov/pubmed/23365415.

28. Deepika Nehra, Hau D Le, Erica M Fallon, Sarah J Carlson, Dori Woods, Yvonne A White, Amy H Pan, et al. "Prolonging the Female Reproductive Lifespan and Improving Egg Quality with Dietary Omega-3 Fatty Acids." Aging Cell. U.S. National Library of Medicine, December 2012. https://www.ncbi.nlm.nih.gov/pubmed/22978268.

29. Y-H Chiu, A E Karmon, A J Gaskins, M Arvizu, P L Williams, I Souter, B R Rueda, R Hauser, J E Chavarro, and EARTH Study Team. "Serum Omega-3 Fatty Acids and Treatment Outcomes among Women Undergoing Assisted Reproduction." Human Reproduction (Oxford, England). Oxford University Press, January 1, 2018. https://www.ncbi.nlm.nih.gov/pubmed/29136189.

30. Al-Safi, Zain A, Huayu Liu, Nichole E Carlson, Justin Chosich, Mary Harris, Andrew P Bradford, Celeste Robledo, Robert H Eckel, and Alex J Polotsky. "Omega-3 Fatty Acid Supplementation Lowers Serum FSH in Normal Weight But Not Obese Women." The Journal of clinical endocrinology and metabolism. Endocrine Society, January 2016. https://www.ncbi.nlm.nih.gov/pubmed/26523525.

31. K E Wonnacott, W Y Kwong, J Hughes, A M Salter, R G Lea, P C Garnsworthy, and K D Sinclair. "Dietary Omega-3 and -6 Polyunsaturated Fatty Acids Affect the Composition and Development of Sheep Granulosa Cells, Oocytes and Embryos." Reproduction (Cambridge, England). U.S. National Library of Medicine, January 2010. https://www.ncbi.nlm.nih.gov/pubmed/19789173.

32. Wiesław Szymański and Anita Kazdepka-Ziemińska. "Effect of Homocysteine Concentration in Follicular Fluid on a Degree of Oocyte Maturity." Ginekologia polska. U.S. National Library of Medicine, October 2003. https://www.ncbi.nlm.nih.gov/pubmed/14669450.

33. Bülent Berker, Cemil Kaya, Rusen Aytac, and Hakan Satiroglu. "Homocysteine Concentrations in Follicular Fluid Are Associated with Poor Oocyte and Embryo Qualities in Polycystic Ovary Syndrome Patients Undergoing Assisted Reproduction." Human Reproduction (Oxford, England). U.S. National Library of Medicine, September 2009. https://www.ncbi.nlm.nih.gov/pubmed/19443458.

34. John M Twigt, Karel Bezstarosti, Jeroen Demmers, Jan Lindemans, Joop S E Laven, and Régine P Steegers-Theunissen. "Preconception Folic Acid Use Influences the Follicle Fluid Proteome." European Journal of Clinical Investigation. U.S. National Library of Medicine, August 2015. https://www.ncbi.nlm.nih.gov/pubmed/26094490.

35. Li-Feng Liang, Shu-Tao Qi, Ye-Xing Xian, Lin Huang, Xiao-Fang Sun, and Wei-Hua Wang. "Protective Effect of Antioxidants on the Pre-Maturation Aging of Mouse Oocytes." Scientific Reports. Nature Publishing Group UK, May 3, 2017. https://www.ncbi.nlm.nih.gov/pmc/articles/PMC5431116/.

36. Ashok Agarwal and Shyam S R Allamaneni. "Role of Free Radicals in Female Reproductive Diseases and Assisted Reproduction." Reproductive Biomedicine Online. U.S. National Library of Medicine, September 2004. https://www.ncbi.nlm.nih.gov/pubmed/15353087.

37. Ashok Agarwal, Sajal Gupta, and Rakesh K Sharma. "Role of Oxidative Stress in Female Reproduction." Reproductive Biology and Endocrinology. BioMed Central, July 14, 2005. https://www.ncbi.nlm.nih.gov/pubmed/16018814.

38. Ashok Agarwal, Anamar Aponte-Mellado, Beena J Premkumar, Amani Shaman, and Sajal Gupta. "The Effects of Oxidative Stress on Female Reproduction: a Review." Reproductive Biology and Endocrinology. BioMed Central, June 29, 2012. https://www.ncbi.nlm.nih.gov/pubmed/22748101.

39. Julio Ávila, Rebeca González-Fernández, Deborah Rotoli, Jairo Hernández, and Angela Palumbo. "Oxidative Stress in Granulosa-Lutein Cells From In Vitro Fertilization Patients." Reproductive Sciences (Thousand Oaks, Calif.). U.S. National Library of Medicine, December 2016. https://www.ncbi.nlm.nih.gov/pubmed/27821562.

40. Ashok Agarwal, Damayanthi Durairajanayagam, and Stefan S du Plessis. "Utility of Antioxidants during Assisted Reproductive Techniques: an Evidence Based Review." Reproductive Biology and Endocrinology. BioMed Central, November 24, 2014. https://www.ncbi.nlm.nih.gov/pmc/articles/PMC4258799/.

41. Elizabeth H Ruder, Terryl J Hartman, Jeffrey Blumberg, and Marlene B Goldman. "Oxidative Stress and Antioxidants: Exposure and Impact on Female Fertility." Human Reproduction Update. U.S. National Library of Medicine, 2008. https://www.ncbi.nlm.nih.gov/pmc/articles/PMC2772106/.

42. Shan Wang, Guolin He, Meng Chen, Tao Zuo, Wenming Xu, and Xinghui Liu. "The Role of Antioxidant Enzymes in the Ovaries." Oxidative medicine and cellular longevity. Hindawi, 2017. https://www.ncbi.nlm.nih.gov/pmc/articles/PMC5632900/.

43. Carlo Alviggi, Federica Cariati, Alessandro Conforti, Pasquale De Rosa, Roberta Vallone, Ida Strina, Rosario Pivonello, and Giuseppe De Placido. "The Effect of FT500 Plus(®) on Ovarian Stimulation in PCOS Women." Reproductive toxicology (Elmsford, N.Y.). U.S. National Library of Medicine, January 2016. https://www.ncbi.nlm.nih.gov/pubmed/26545973.

44. Mozafar Khazaei and Faranak Aghaz. "Reactive Oxygen Species Generation and Use of Antioxidants during In Vitro Maturation of Oocytes." International Journal of Fertility & Sterility. Royan Institute, 2017. https://www.ncbi.nlm.nih.gov/pubmed/28670422.

CHAPTER 7

1. Paul B Miller, Michael R Soules. "Luteal Phase Deficiency: Pathophysiology, Diagnosis, and Treatment." Global Library of Women's Medicine [Internet], May, 2009. ISSN: 1756-2228; DOI 10.3843/GLOWM.10327.

2. Reshef Tal. "Endocrinology of Pregnancy." Endotext [Internet]. U.S. National Library of Medicine, December 7, 2015. https://www.ncbi.nlm.nih.gov/books/NBK278962/.

3. D C Daly, C A Walters, C E Soto-Albors, and D H Riddick. "Endometrial Biopsy during Treatment of Luteal Phase Defects Is Predictive of Therapeutic Outcome." Fertility and Sterility. U.S. National Library of Medicine, September 1983. https://www.ncbi.nlm.nih.gov/pubmed/6884533.

4. Fredrick Stormshak. "Biochemical and Endocrine Aspects of Oxytocin Production by the Mammalian Corpus Luteum." Reproductive Biology and Endocrinology. BioMed Central, November 10, 2003. https://www.ncbi.nlm.nih.gov/pmc/articles/PMC280731/.

5. "Histology@Yale." Ovary and Follicle Development. Accessed October 2019. http://medcell.med.yale.edu/histology/ovary_follicle.php.

6. Alexandra Ycaza Herrera, Shawn E Nielsen, and Mara Mather. "Stress-Induced Increases in Progesterone and Cortisol in Naturally Cycling Women." Neurobiology of stress. Elsevier, February 11, 2016. https://www.ncbi.nlm.nih.gov/pmc/articles/PMC5146195/.

7. D B Tully, V E Allgood, and J A Cidlowski. "Modulation of Steroid Receptor-Mediated Gene Expression by Vitamin B6." The FASEB Journal 8, no. 3 (1994): 343–49. https://doi.org/10.1096/fasebj.8.3.8143940.

8. Hirofumi Henmi, Toshiaki Endo, Yoshimitsu Kitajima, Kengo Manase, Hiroshi Hata, and Ryuich Kudo. "Effects of Ascorbic Acid Supplementation on Serum Progesterone Levels in Patients with a Luteal Phase Defect." Fertility and Sterility 80, no. 2 (2003): 459–61. https://doi.org/10.1016/s0015-0282(03)00657-5.

9. F Facchinetti, P Borella, M Valentini, L Fioroni, and A R Genazzani. "Premenstrual Increase of Intracellular Magnesium Levels in Women with Ovulatory, Asymptomatic Menstrual Cycles." Gynecological Endocrinology 2, no. 3 (1988): 249–56. https://doi.org/10.3109/09513599809029349.

10. M Zachut, I Dekel, H Lehrer, A Arieli, A Arav, L Livshitz, S Yakoby, and U Moallem. "Effects of Dietary Fats Differing in n-6:n-3 Ratio Fed to High-Yielding Dairy Cows on Fatty Acid Composition of Ovarian Compartments, Follicular Status, and Oocyte Quality." Journal of Dairy Science 93, no. 2 (2010): 529–45. https://doi.org/10.3168/jds.2009-2167.

11. S Coyral-Castel, C Ramé, A Fatet, and J Dupont. "Effects of Unsaturated Fatty Acids on Progesterone Secretion and Selected Protein Kinases in Goat Granulosa Cells." Domestic Animal Endocrinology 38, no. 4 (2010): 272–83. https://doi.org/10.1016/j.domaniend.2009.12.002.

12. Pia Saldeen and Tom Saldeen. "Women and Omega-3 Fatty Acids." Obstetrical & Gynecological Survey 59, no. 10 (2004): 722–30. https://doi.org/10.1097/01.ogx.0000140038.70473.96.

13. Ze-Peng Yu, Guo-Wei Le, and Yong-Hui Shi. "Effect Of Zinc Sulphate And Zinc Methionine On Growth, Plasma Growth Hormone Concentration, Growth Hormone Receptor And Insulin-Like Growth Factor-I Gene Expression In Mice." Clinical and Experimental Pharmacology and Physiology 32, no. 4 (2005): 273–78. https://doi.org/10.1111/j.1440-1681.2005.04183.x.

14. Rasha T Hamza, Amira I Hamed, and Mahmoud T Sallam. "Effect of Zinc Supplementation on Growth Hormone Insulin Growth Factor Axis in Short Egyptian Children with Zinc Deficiency." Italian Journal of Pediatrics 38, no. 1 (2012): 21. https://doi.org/10.1186/1824-7288-38-21.

15. S Uniyal, R P Panda, V S Chouhan, V P Yadav, I Hyder, S S Dangi, M Gupta, et al. "Expression and Localization of Insulin-like Growth Factor System in Corpus Luteum during Different Stages of Estrous Cycle in Water Buffaloes (Bubalus Bubalis) and the Effect of Insulin-like Growth Factor I on Production of Vascular Endothelial Growth Factor and Progesterone in Luteal Cells Cultured in Vitro." Theriogenology. U.S. National Library of Medicine, January 1, 2015. https://www.ncbi.nlm.nih.gov/pubmed/25304995.

16. X Tian and F J Diaz. "Zinc Depletion Causes Multiple Defects in Ovarian Function during the Periovulatory Period in Mice." Endocrinology. Endocrine Society, February 2012. https://www.ncbi.nlm.nih.gov/pmc/articles/PMC3275394/.

17. Toshiaki Taketani, Hiroshi Tamura, Akihisa Takasaki, Lifa Lee, Fumie Kizuka, Isao Tamura, Ken Taniguchi, et al. "Protective Role of Melatonin in Progesterone Production by Human Luteal Cells." Journal of Pineal Research 51, no. 2 (2011): 207–13. https://doi.org/10.1111/j.1600-079x.2011.00878.x.

18. L A Durotoye, G E Webley, and R G Rodway. "Stimulation of the Production of Progesterone by the Corpus Luteum of the Ewe by the Perfusion of Melatonin in Vivo and by Treatment of Granulosa Cells with Melatonin in Vitro." Research in Veterinary Science 62, no. 2 (1997): 87–91. https://doi.org/10.1016/s0034-5288(97)90126-0.

19. Erika Nassar, Chris Mulligan, Lem Taylor, Chad Kerksick, Melyn Galbreath, Mike Greenwood, Richard Kreider, and Darryn S Willoughby. "Effects of a Single Dose of N-Acetyl-5-Methoxytryptamine (Melatonin) and Resistance Exercise on the Growth Hormone/IGF-1 Axis in Young Males and Females." Journal of the International Society of Sports Nutrition. BioMed Central, October 23, 2007. http://www.ncbi.nlm.nih.gov/pmc/articles/PMC2174513.

20. Hong-wei Yang, Xue-yan Huang. "Effect of Acupuncture on Infertility Due to Luteal Phase Defect 刺黄体功能不足不孕的影响." SpringerLink. Shanghai Research Institute of Acupuncture and Meridian, April 4, 2012. https://link.springer.com/article/10.1007/s11726-012-0577-x.

21. H Y Zhang, X Z Yu, and G L Wang. "Preliminary Report of the Treatment of Luteal Phase Defect by Replenishing Kidney. An Analysis of 53 Cases." Chinese Journal of Integrated Traditional and Western Medicine. U.S. National Library of Medicine, August 1992. https://www.ncbi.nlm.nih.gov/pubmed/1477503/.

22. Gordon D Niswender, Jennifer L Juengel, Patrick J Silva, M Keith Rollyson, and Eric W Mcintush. "Mechanisms Controlling the Function and Life Span of the Corpus Luteum." Physiological Reviews 80, no. 1 (January 2000): 1–29. https://doi.org/10.1152/physrev.2000.80.1.1.

23. M Datta, P Roy, J Banerjee, and S Bhattacharya. "Thyroid Hormone Stimulates Progesterone Release from Human Luteal Cells by Generating a Proteinaceous Factor." Journal of Endocrinology 158, no. 3 (January 1998): 319–25. https://doi.org/10.1677/joe.0.1580319.

CHAPTER 8

1. "Metabolic Detoxification Introduction: Life Extension." LifeExtension.com. Accessed October 2019. http://www.lifeextension.com/Protocols/Metabolic-Health/Metabolic-Detoxification/Page-02.

2. Romilly E Hodges and Deanna M Minich. "Modulation of Metabolic Detoxification Pathways Using Foods and Food-Derived Components: A Scientific Review with Clinical Application." Journal of Nutrition and Metabolism. Hindawi Publishing Corporation, 2015. https://www.ncbi.nlm.nih.gov/pmc/articles/PMC4488002/.

3. Yu-Han Chiu. "Pesticide Residue Intake and Assisted Reproductive Technology Outcomes." JAMA Internal Medicine. American Medical Association, January 1, 2018. https://jamanetwork.com/journals/jamainternalmedicine/article-abstract/2659557.

4. Environmental Working Group. "EWG's 2019 Shopper's Guide to Pesticides in Produce™." EWG's 2019 Shopper's Guide to Pesticides in Produce, Summary. Accessed October 2019. https://www.ewg.org/foodnews/summary.php.

5. "Dr. Oz's Green Drink." doctoroz.com, February 15, 2010. https://www.doctoroz.com/recipe/dr-ozs-green-drink.

6. "Kale, Pineapple and Ginger Detox Drink." doctoroz.com, October 6, 2011. https://www.doctoroz.com/recipe/kale-pineapple-and-ginger-detox-drink.

CHAPTER 9

1. K Kowalczyk, G Franik, D Kowalczyk, D Pluta, Ł Blukacz, and P Madej. "Thyroid Disorders in Polycystic Ovary Syndrome." European Review for Medical and Pharmacological Sciences. U.S. National Library of Medicine, January 2017. https://www.ncbi.nlm.nih.gov/pubmed/28165551.

2. Erin K Barthelmess, and Rajesh K Naz. "Polycystic Ovary Syndrome: Current Status and Future Perspective." Frontiers in Bioscience (Elite edition). U.S. National Library of Medicine, January 1, 2014. https://www.ncbi.nlm.nih.gov/pmc/articles/PMC4341818/.

3. Richard S Legro. "Ovulation Induction in Polycystic Ovary Syndrome: Current Options." Best Practice & Research Clinical Obstetrics & Gynaecology. Baillière Tindall, September 21, 2016. https://www.sciencedirect.com/science/article/pii/S1521693416300736?via=ihub.

4. "Calculate Your BMI - Standard BMI Calculator." National Heart Lung and Blood Institute. U.S. Department of Health and Human Services. Accessed October 2019. https://www.nhlbi.nih.gov/health/educational/lose_wt/BMI/bmicalc.htm.

5. "Assessing Your Weight and Health Risk." National Heart Lung and Blood Institute. U.S. Department of Health and Human Services. Accessed October 2019. https://www.nhlbi.nih.gov/health/educational/lose_wt/risk.htm.

6. "Defining Adult Overweight and Obesity, Overweight & Obesity, CDC." Centers for Disease Control and Prevention. Centers for Disease Control and Prevention. Accessed October 2019. https://www.cdc.gov/obesity/adult/defining.html.

7. Rhonda Bentley-Lewis, Katherine Koruda, and Ellen W Seely. "The Metabolic Syndrome in Women." Nature clinical practice. Endocrinology & metabolism. U.S. National Library of Medicine, October 2007. https://www.ncbi.nlm.nih.gov/pmc/articles/PMC4428566/.

8. Zeynep Özcan Dağ and Berna Dilbaz. "Impact of Obesity on Infertility in Women." Journal of the Turkish German Gynecological Association. AVES, June 1, 2015. https://www.ncbi.nlm.nih.gov/pmc/articles/PMC4456969/.

9. Erica Silvestris, Giovanni de Pergola, Raffaele Rosania, and Giuseppe Loverro. "Obesity as Disruptor of the Female Fertility." Reproductive Biology and Endocrinology. BioMed Central, March 9, 2018. https://www.ncbi.nlm.nih.gov/pubmed/29523133.

10. Zeinab Faghfoori, Siavash Fazelian, Mahdi Shadnoush, and Reza Goodarzi. "Nutritional Management in Women with Polycystic Ovary Syndrome: A Review Study." Diabetes & metabolic syndrome. U.S. National Library of Medicine, November 2017. https://www.ncbi.nlm.nih.gov/pubmed/28416368.

11. Ajai K Pandey, Anumegha Gupta, Meenakshi Tiwari, Shilpa Prasad, Ashutosh N Pandey, Pramod K Yadav, Alka Sharma, et al. "Impact of Stress on Female Reproductive Health Disorders: Possible Beneficial Effects of Shatavari (Asparagus Racemosus)." Biomedicine & Pharmacotherapy. U.S. National Library of Medicine, July 2018. https://www.ncbi.nlm.nih.gov/pubmed/29635127.

12. M Ezhil Ratnakumari, N Manavalan, D Sathyanath, Y Rosy Ayda, and K Reka. "Study to Evaluate the Changes in Polycystic Ovarian Morphology after Naturopathic and Yogic Interventions." International Journal of Yoga. Medknow Publications & Media Pvt Ltd, 2018. https://www.ncbi.nlm.nih.gov/pubmed/29755223.

13. Valeria Tagliaferri, Daniela Romualdi, Valentina Immediata, Simona De Cicco, Christian Di Florio, Antonio Lanzone, and Maurizio Guido. "Metformin vs Myoinositol: Which Is Better in Obese Polycystic Ovary Syndrome Patients? A Randomized Controlled Crossover Study." Clinical endocrinology. U.S. National Library of Medicine, May 2017. https://www.ncbi.nlm.nih.gov/pubmed/28092404.

14. Sedigheh Esmaeilzadeh, Maryam Gholinezhad-Chari, and Reza Ghadimi. "The Effect of Metformin Treatment on the Serum Levels of Homocysteine, Folic Acid, and Vitamin B12 in Patients with Polycystic Ovary Syndrome." Journal of Human Reproductive Sciences. Medknow Publications & Media Pvt Ltd, 2017. https://www.ncbi.nlm.nih.gov/pubmed/28904497.

15. Pedro-Antonio Regidor, Adolf Eduard Schindler, Bernd Lesoine, and Rene Druckman. "Management of Women with PCOS Using Myo-Inositol and Folic Acid. New Clinical Data and Review of the Literature." Hormone Molecular Biology and Clinical Investigation. De Gruyter, June 21, 2018. https://www.degruyter.com/view/j/hmbci.2018.34.issue-2/hmbci-2017-0067/hmbci-2017-0067.xml.

16. Guluzar Arzu Turan, Fatma Eskicioglu, Oya Nermin Sivrikoz, Hakan Cengiz, Saban Adakan, Esra Bahar Gur, Sumeyra Tatar, Nur Sahin, and Osman Yilmaz. "Myo-Inositol Is a Promising Treatment for the Prevention of Ovarian Hyperstimulation Syndrome (OHSS): an Animal Study." Archives of gynecology and obstetrics. Springer Berlin Heidelberg, November 2015. https://www.ncbi.nlm.nih.gov/pubmed/25990477.

17. Francesca Caprio, Maria Diletta D'Eufemia, Carlo Trotta, Maria Rosaria Campitiello, Raffaele Ianniello, Daniela Mele, and Nicola Colacurci. "Myo-Inositol Therapy for Poor-Responders during IVF: a Prospective Controlled Observational Trial." Journal of Ovarian Research. BioMed Central, June 12, 2015. https://www.ncbi.nlm.nih.gov/pmc/articles/PMC4464995/.

18. Pedro-Antonio Regidor, Adolf Eduard Schindler, Bernd Lesoine, and Rene Druckman. "Management of Women with PCOS Using Myo-Inositol and Folic Acid. New Clinical Data and Review of the Literature." Hormone molecular biology and clinical investigation. U.S. National Library of Medicine, March 2, 2018. https://www.ncbi.nlm.nih.gov/pubmed/29498933.

19. Özlen Emekçi Özay, Ali Cenk Özay, Erkan Çağlıyan, Recep Emre Okyay, and Bülent Gülekli. "Myo-Inositol Administration Positively Effects Ovulation Induction and Intrauterine Insemination in Patients with Polycystic Ovary Syndrome: a Prospective, Controlled, Randomized Trial." Gynecological Endocrinology. U.S. National Library of Medicine, July 2017. https://www.ncbi.nlm.nih.gov/pubmed/28277112.

20. Xiangqin Zheng, Danmei Lin, Yulong Zhang, Yuan Lin, Jianrong Song, Suyu Li, and Yan Sun. "Inositol Supplement Improves Clinical Pregnancy Rate in Infertile Women Undergoing Ovulation Induction for ICSI or IVF-ET." Medicine. Wolters Kluwer Health, December 2017. https://www.ncbi.nlm.nih.gov/pmc/articles/PMC5728865/.

21. G Simi, A R Genazzani, M E R Obino, F Papini, S Pinelli, V Cela, and P G Artini. "Inositol and In Vitro Fertilization with Embryo Transfer." International Journal of Endocrinology. Hindawi Publishing Corporation, 2017. https://www.ncbi.nlm.nih.gov/pmc/articles/PMC5350329/.

22. M Stracquadanio, L Ciotta, and M A Palumbo. "Effects of Myo-Inositol, Gymnemic Acid, and L-Methylfolate in Polycystic Ovary Syndrome Patients." Gynecological Endocrinology. U.S. National Library of Medicine, June 2018. https://www.ncbi.nlm.nih.gov/pubmed/29265900.

23. Simona De Cicco, Valentina Immediata, Daniela Romualdi, Caterina Policola, Anna Tropea, Christian Di Florio, Valeria Tagliaferri, et al. "Myoinositol Combined with Alpha-Lipoic Acid May Improve the Clinical and Endocrine Features of Polycystic Ovary Syndrome through an Insulin-Independent Action." Gynecological Endocrinology. U.S. National Library of Medicine, September 2017. https://www.ncbi.nlm.nih.gov/pubmed/28434274.

24. Wei Wei, Hongmin Zhao, Aili Wang, Ming Sui, Kun Liang, Haiyun Deng, Yukun Ma, Yajuan Zhang, Hongxiu Zhang, and Yuanyuan Guan. "A Clinical Study on the Short-Term Effect of Berberine in Comparison to Metformin on the Metabolic Characteristics of Women with Polycystic Ovary Syndrome." European journal of endocrinology. U.S. National Library of Medicine, January 2012. https://www.ncbi.nlm.nih.gov/pubmed/22019891.

25. Mehri Jamilian, Maryam Maktabi, and Zatollah Asemi. "A Trial on The Effects of Magnesium-Zinc-Calcium-Vitamin D Co-Supplementation on Glycemic Control and Markers of Cardio-Metabolic Risk in Women with Polycystic Ovary Syndrome." Archives of Iranian medicine. U.S. National Library of Medicine, October 2017. https://www.ncbi.nlm.nih.gov/pubmed/29137465.

26. Heba Elhusseini, Hoda Elkafas, Mohamed Abdelaziz, Sunil Halder, Ihor Atabiekov, Noura Eziba, Nahed Ismail, Abdeljabar El Andaloussi, and Ayman Al-Hendy. "Diet-Induced Vitamin D Deficiency Triggers Inflammation and DNA Damage Profile in Murine Myometrium." International journal of women's health. Dove Medical Press, August 29, 2018. https://www.ncbi.nlm.nih.gov/pubmed/30214319.

27. C Trummer, S Pilz, V Schwetz, B Obermayer-Pietsch, and E Lerchbaum. "Vitamin D, PCOS and Androgens in Men: a Systematic Review." Endocrine connections. U.S. National Library of Medicine, March 2018. https://www.ncbi.nlm.nih.gov/pubmed/29449314.

28. M Seyyed, P Ayremlou, T Behroozi-Lak, and S Nourisaeidlou. "The Effect of Vitamin D Supplementation on Insulin Resistance, Visceral Fat and Adiponectin in Vitamin D Deficient Women with Polycystic Ovary Syndrome: a Randomized Placebo-Controlled Trial." Gynecological Endocrinology. U.S. National Library of Medicine, June 2018. https://www.ncbi.nlm.nih.gov/pubmed/29271278.

29. N Voulgaris, L Papanastasiou, G Piaditis, A Angelousi, G Kaltsas, G Mastorakos, and E Kassi. "Vitamin D and Aspects of Female Fertility." Hormones (Athens, Greece). U.S. National Library of Medicine, January 2017. https://www.ncbi.nlm.nih.gov/pubmed/28500824.

30. Mehri Jamilian, Fatemeh Foroozanfard, Elham Rahmani, Maesoomeh Talebi, Fereshteh Bahmani, and Zatollah Asemi. "Effect of Two Different Doses of Vitamin D Supplementation on Metabolic Profiles of Insulin-Resistant Patients with Polycystic Ovary Syndrome." Nutrients. MDPI, November 24, 2017. https://www.ncbi.nlm.nih.gov/pubmed/29186759.

31. G Muscogiuri, B Altieri, C de, S Palomba, R Pivonello, A Colao, and F Orio. "Shedding New Light on Female Fertility: The Role of Vitamin D." Reviews in endocrine & metabolic disorders. U.S. National Library of Medicine, September 2017. https://www.ncbi.nlm.nih.gov/pubmed/28102491.

32. Jinlu Ji, Hui Zhai, Hui Zhou, Su Song, Gil Mor, and Aihua Liao. "The Role and Mechanism of Vitamin D-Mediated Regulation of Treg/Th17 Balance in Recurrent Pregnancy Loss." American journal of reproductive immunology (New York, N.Y. : 1989). U.S. National Library of Medicine, June 2019. https://www.ncbi.nlm.nih.gov/pubmed/30903715.

33. M Azadi-Yazdi, A Nadjarzadeh, H Khosravi-Boroujeni, and A Salehi-Abargouei. "The Effect of Vitamin D Supplementation on the Androgenic Profile in Patients with Polycystic Ovary Syndrome: A Systematic Review and Meta-Analysis of Clinical Trials." Hormone and Metabolic Research. U.S. National Library of Medicine, March 2017. https://www.ncbi.nlm.nih.gov/pubmed/28351084.

34. M Jamilian, M Samimi, N Mirhosseini, F Afshar, E Aghadavod, R Talaee, S Jafarnejad, S Hashemi, and Z Asemi. "The Influences of Vitamin D and Omega-3 Co-Supplementation on Clinical, Metabolic and Genetic Parameters in Women with Polycystic Ovary Syndrome." Journal of Affective Disorders. U.S. National Library of Medicine, October 1, 2018. https://www.ncbi.nlm.nih.gov/pubmed/29859385.

35. Elisa Benetti, Raffaella Mastrocola, Fausto Chiazza, Debora Nigro, Giuseppe D'Antona, Valentina Bordano, Roberto Fantozzi, Manuela Aragno, Massimo Collino, and Marco Alessandro Minetto. "Effects of Vitamin D on Insulin Resistance and Myosteatosis in Diet-Induced Obese Mice." PLOS ONE. Public Library of Science, January 17, 2018. https://www.ncbi.nlm.nih.gov/pmc/articles/PMC5771572/.

36. A Neisy, F Zal, A Seghatoleslam, and S Alaee. "Amelioration by Quercetin of Insulin Resistance and Uterine GLUT4 and ERα Gene Expression in Rats with Polycystic Ovary Syndrome (PCOS)." Reproduction, Fertility, and Development. U.S. National Library of Medicine, January 2019. https://www.ncbi.nlm.nih.gov/pubmed/30103849.

37. Z Wang, D Zhai, D Zhang, L Bai, R Yao, J Yu, W Cheng, and C Yu. "Quercetin Decreases Insulin Resistance in a Polycystic Ovary Syndrome Rat Model by Improving Inflammatory Microenvironment." Reproductive Sciences (Thousand Oaks, Calif.). U.S. National Library of Medicine, May 2017. https://www.ncbi.nlm.nih.gov/pubmed/27634381.

38. M Khorshidi, A Moini, E Alipoor, N Rezvan, S Gorgani-Firuzjaee, M Yaseri, and M J Hosseinzadeh-Attar. "The Effects of Quercetin Supplementation on Metabolic and Hormonal Parameters as Well as Plasma Concentration and Gene Expression of Resistin in Overweight or Obese Women with Polycystic Ovary Syndrome." Phytotherapy Research. National Library of Medicine, November 2018. https://www.ncbi.nlm.nih.gov/pubmed/30062709.

39. Neda Rezvan, Ashraf Moini, Sattar Gorgani-Firuzjaee, and Mohammad Javad Hosseinzadeh-Attar. "Oral Quercetin Supplementation Enhances Adiponectin Receptor Transcript Expression in Polycystic Ovary Syndrome Patients: A Randomized Placebo-Controlled Double-Blind Clinical Trial." Cell Journal. Royan Institute, January 2018. https://www.ncbi.nlm.nih.gov/pmc/articles/PMC5672102/.

40. S Jahan, A Abid, S Khalid, T Afsar, Qurat-Ul-Ain, G Shaheen, A Almajwal, and S Razak. "Therapeutic Potentials of Quercetin in Management of Polycystic Ovarian Syndrome Using Letrozole Induced Rat Model: a Histological and a Biochemical Study." Journal of Ovarian Research. U.S. National Library of Medicine, April 3, 2018. https://www.ncbi.nlm.nih.gov/pubmed/29615083.

41. Siavash Fazelian, Mohamad H Rouhani, Sahar Saraf Bank, and Reza Amani. "Chromium Supplementation and Polycystic Ovary Syndrome: A Systematic Review and Meta-Analysis." Journal of Trace Elements in Medicine and Biology. Society for Minerals and Trace Elements. U.S. National Library of Medicine, July 2017. https://www.ncbi.nlm.nih.gov/pubmed/28595797.

42. Azam Borzoei, Maryam Rafraf, and Mohammad Asghari-Jafarabadi. "Cinnamon Improves Metabolic Factors without Detectable Effects on Adiponectin in Women with Polycystic Ovary Syndrome." Asia Pacific Journal of Clinical Nutrition. U.S. National Library of Medicine, 2018. https://www.ncbi.nlm.nih.gov/pubmed/29737802.

43. Melika Fallah, Gholamreza Askari, Alireza Soleimani, Awat Feizi, and Zatollah Asemi. "Clinical Trial of the Effects of Coenzyme Q10 Supplementation on Biomarkers of Inflammation and Oxidative Stress in Diabetic Hemodialysis Patients." International Journal of Preventive Medicine. Medknow Publications & Media Pvt Ltd, January 15, 2019. https://www.ncbi.nlm.nih.gov/pmc/articles/PMC6360842/.

44. Dan Liao, Chunhua Zhong, Cuifen Li, Lifang Mo, and Yanyan Liu. "Meta-Analysis of the Effects of Probiotic Supplementation on Glycemia, Lipidic Profiles, Weight Loss and C-Reactive Protein in Women with Polycystic Ovarian Syndrome." Minerva medica. U.S. National Library of Medicine, December 2018. https://www.ncbi.nlm.nih.gov/pubmed/30256077.

45. Maryam Karamali, Sara Eghbalpour, Sajad Rajabi, Mehri Jamilian, Fereshteh Bahmani, Maryam Tajabadi-Ebrahimi, Fariba Keneshlou, et al. "Effects of Probiotic Supplementation on Hormonal Profiles, Biomarkers of Inflammation and Oxidative Stress in Women With Polycystic Ovary Syndrome: A Randomized, Double-Blind, Placebo-Controlled Trial." Archives of Iranian Medicine. U.S. National Library of Medicine, January 1, 2018. https://www.ncbi.nlm.nih.gov/pubmed/29664663.

46. Ladan Aminlari, Seyed Shahram Shekarforoush, Saeid Hosseinzadeh, Saeed Nazifi, Javad Sajedianfard, and Mohammad Hadi Eskandari. "Effect of Probiotics Bacillus Coagulans and Lactobacillus Plantarum on Lipid Profile and Feces Bacteria of Rats Fed Cholesterol-Enriched Diet." Probiotics and Antimicrobial Proteins. U.S. National Library of Medicine, October 27, 2018. https://www.ncbi.nlm.nih.gov/pubmed/30368715.

47. Mehri Jamilian, Shirin Mansury, Fereshteh Bahmani, Zahra Heidar, Elaheh Amirani, and Zatollah Asemi. "The Effects of Probiotic and Selenium Co-Supplementation on Parameters of Mental Health, Hormonal Profiles, and Biomarkers of Inflammation and Oxidative Stress in Women with Polycystic Ovary Syndrome." Journal of Ovarian Research. BioMed Central, September 14, 2018. https://www.ncbi.nlm.nih.gov/pubmed/30217229.

48. M Jamilian, A Shojaei, M Samimi, F Afshar, E Aghadavod, M Karamali, M Taghizadeh, et al. "The Effects of Omega-3 and Vitamin E Co-Supplementation on Parameters of Mental Health and Gene Expression Related to Insulin and Inflammation in Subjects with Polycystic Ovary Syndrome." Journal of Affective Disorders. U.S. National Library of Medicine, March 15, 2018. https://www.ncbi.nlm.nih.gov/pubmed/29306057.

49. Amir Fattahi, Masoud Darabi, Layla Farzadi, Ali Salmassi, Zeinab Latifi, Amir Mehdizadeh, Maghsood Shaak, et al. "Effects of Dietary Omega-3 and -6 Supplementations on Phospholipid Fatty Acid Composition in Mice Uterus during Window of Pre-Implantation." Theriogenology. Elsevier, November 29, 2017. https://www.sciencedirect.com/science/article/pii/S0093691X17305150.

50. Fatemeh Ramezani Kapourchaliab. Bradley Feltham, and Miyoung Suh. "Food for Male Reproductive Tract Health: Omega-3 Fatty Acids." ScienceDirect. Academic Press, November 30, 2018. https://www.sciencedirect.com/science/article/pii/B9780081005965217356.

51. Mehri Jamilian, Fatemeh Foroozanfard, Fereshteh Bahmani, Rezvan Talaee, Mahshid Monavari, and Zatollah Asemi. "Effects of Zinc Supplementation on Endocrine Outcomes in Women with Polycystic Ovary Syndrome: a Randomized, Double-Blind, Placebo-Controlled Trial." Biological Trace Element Research. U.S. National Library of Medicine, April 2016. https://www.ncbi.nlm.nih.gov/pubmed/26315303.

52. Maryam Maktabi, Mehri Jamilian, and Zatollah Asemi. "Magnesium-Zinc-Calcium-Vitamin D Co-Supplementation Improves Hormonal Profiles, Biomarkers of Inflammation and Oxidative Stress in Women with Polycystic Ovary Syndrome: a Randomized, Double-Blind, Placebo-Controlled Trial." Biological Trace Element Research. U.S. National Library of Medicine, March 2018. https://www.ncbi.nlm.nih.gov/pubmed/28668998.

53. "About NCCIH." National Center for Complementary and Integrative Health. U.S. Department of Health and Human Services, September 24, 2017. https://nccih.nih.gov/about.

54. Juan-juan Song, Miao-e Yan, Xiao-ke Wu, and Li-hui Hou. "Progress of Integrative Chinese and Western Medicine in Treating Polycystic Ovarian Syndrome Caused Infertility." Chinese Journal of Integrative Medicine. U.S. National Library of Medicine, December 2006. https://www.ncbi.nlm.nih.gov/pubmed/17361532.

55. L Yu, L Cao, J Xie, and Y Shi. "[Therapeutic Effects on Ovulation and Reproduction Promotion with Acupuncture and Clomiphene in Polycystic Ovary Syndrome]." Chinese Acupuncture & Moxibustion. U.S. National Library of Medicine, March 12, 2018. https://www.ncbi.nlm.nih.gov/pubmed/29701043.

56. J Xu and Y Zuo. "[Efficacy of Acupuncture as Adjunctive Treatment on Infertility Patients with Polycystic Ovary Syndrome]." Chinese Acupuncture & Moxibustion. U.S. National Library of Medicine, April 12, 2018. https://www.ncbi.nlm.nih.gov/pubmed/29696918.

57. D Yang, M Zhao, and J Tan. "[Effect of Polycystic Ovary Syndrome Treated with the Periodic Therapy of Acupuncture]." Chinese Acupuncture & Moxibustion. U.S. National Library of Medicine, August 12, 2017. https://www.ncbi.nlm.nih.gov/pubmed/29231341.

58. J Zhou, L Yang, J Yu, Y Wang, and Z Liu. "Efficacy of Acupuncture on Menstrual Frequency in Women with Polycystic Ovary Syndrome: Protocol for a Randomized, Controlled Trial." Medicine. U.S. National Library of Medicine, November 2017. https://www.ncbi.nlm.nih.gov/pubmed/29381988.

59. Chi E D Lim and Wu S F Wong. "Current Evidence of Acupuncture on Polycystic Ovarian Syndrome." Gynecological Endocrinology 26, no. 6 (2010): 473–78. https://doi.org/10.3109/09513591003686304.

60. M H Lai, H X Ma, and X H Song. "[Electroacupuncture Combined with Clomiphene Promotes Pregnancy and Blastocyst Implantation Possibly by Up-Regulating Expression of Insulin Receptor and Insulin Receptor Substrate 1 Proteins in Endometrium in Rats with PCOS]." Acupuncture Research. U.S. National Library of Medicine, October 25, 2016. https://www.ncbi.nlm.nih.gov/pubmed/29071945.

61. F F El-Shamy, S S El-Kholy, and M M El-Rahman. "Effectiveness of Laser Acupoints on Women With Polycystic Ovarian Syndrome: A Randomized Controlled Trial." Journal of Lasers in Medical Sciences. U.S. National Library of Medicine, 2018. https://www.ncbi.nlm.nih.gov/pubmed/30026896.

62. Y Yin, Y Zhang, H Zhang, D Jiang, and G Guo. "[Clinical Therapeutic Effects of Acupuncture Combined with Chinese Herbal Medicine on Infertility of Polycystic Ovary Syndrome in the Patients with Ovulation Induction with Letrozole]." Chinese Acupuncture & Moxibustion. U.S. National Library of Medicine, January 12, 2018. https://www.ncbi.nlm.nih.gov/pubmed/29354933.

63. Richard Blitstein. "TCM for Complex Infertility Conditions: PCOS, Auto Immune and Premature Ovarian Failure." Webinar, Healthy Seminars. Accessed on September 30, 2018. www.healthyseminars.com

64. Adam H Balen, Lara C Morley, Marie Misso, Stephen Franks, Richard S Legro, Chandrika N Wijeyaratne, Elisabet Stener-Victorin, Bart C J M Fauser, Robert J Norman, and Helena Teede. "The Management of Anovulatory Infertility in Women with Polycystic Ovary Syndrome: an Analysis of the Evidence to Support the Development of Global WHO Guidance." Human Reproduction Update 22, no. 6 (October 2016): 687–708. https://doi.org/10.1093/humupd/dmw025.

CHAPTER 10

1. Natalie M Crawford and Anne Z Steiner. "Thyroid Autoimmunity and Reproductive Function." Seminars in Reproductive Medicine. U.S. National Library of Medicine, November 2016. https://www.ncbi.nlm.nih.gov/pubmed/27750361.

2. S Medenica, O Nedeljkovic, N Radojevic, M Stojkovic, B Trbojevic, and B Pajovic. "Thyroid Dysfunction and Thyroid Autoimmunity in Euthyroid Women in Achieving Fertility." European Review for Medical and Pharmacological Sciences. U.S. National Library of Medicine, 2015. https://www.ncbi.nlm.nih.gov/pubmed/25855922.

3. Gesthimani Mintziori, Dimitrios G Goulis, and Efstratios M Kolibianakis. "Thyroid Function and IVF Outcome: When to Investigate and When to Intervene?" Current Opinion in Obstetrics & Gynecology. U.S. National Library of Medicine, June 2016. https://www.ncbi.nlm.nih.gov/pubmed/26967594.

4. Andrea Weghofer, David H Barad, Sarah Darmon, Vitaly A Kushnir, and Norbert Gleicher. "What Affects Functional Ovarian Reserve, Thyroid Function or Thyroid Autoimmunity?" Reproductive Biology and Endocrinology. BioMed Central, May 10, 2016. https://www.ncbi.nlm.nih.gov/pubmed/27165095.

5. Vikas Chaudhary and Shahina Bano. "Thyroid Ultrasound." Indian Journal of Endocrinology and Metabolism. Medknow Publications & Media Pvt Ltd, March 2013. https://www.ncbi.nlm.nih.gov/pmc/articles/PMC3683194/.

6. Hillary Klonoff-Cohen. "Recommended Approach for Undiagnosed Autoimmune Diseases, Unexplained Infertility, and Fertility Treatments." Fertility and Sterility Dialog. Fertility and Sterility, October 11, 2019. https://www.fertstertdialog.com/users/16110-fertility-and-sterility/posts/19876-klonoff-cohen-consider-this.

7. Paolo Giovanni Artini, Alessia Uccelli, Francesca Papini, Giovanna Simi, Olga Maria Di Berardino, Maria Ruggiero, and Vito Cela. "Infertility and Pregnancy Loss in Euthyroid Women with Thyroid Autoimmunity." Gynecological Endocrinology. U.S. National Library of Medicine, January 2013. https://www.ncbi.nlm.nih.gov/pubmed/22835333.

8. Alban Deroux, Chantal Dumestre-Perard, Camille Dunand-Faure, Laurence Bouillet, and Pascale Hoffmann. "Female Infertility and Serum Auto-Antibodies: a Systematic Review." Clinical Reviews in Allergy & Immunology. U.S. National Library of Medicine, August 2017. https://www.ncbi.nlm.nih.gov/pubmed/27628237.

9. Andrew W Campbell. "Autoimmunity and the Gut." Autoimmune Diseases 2014 (2014): 1–12. https://doi.org/10.1155/2014/152428.

10. G E Krassas, K Poppe, and D Glinoer. "Thyroid Function and Human Reproductive Health." Endocrine Reviews. U.S. National Library of Medicine, October 2010. https://www.ncbi.nlm.nih.gov/pubmed/20573783.

11. Neal Patel and James A Kashanian. "Thyroid Dysfunction and Male Reproductive Physiology." Seminars in Reproductive Medicine. U.S. National Library of Medicine, November 2016. https://www.ncbi.nlm.nih.gov/pubmed/27741548.

CHAPTER 11

1. Melinda J Jasper, Kelton P Tremellen, and Sarah A Robertson. "Primary Unexplained Infertility Is Associated with Reduced Expression of the T-Regulatory Cell Transcription Factor Foxp3 in Endometrial Tissue." Molecular Human Reproduction. U.S. National Library of Medicine, May 2006. https://www.ncbi.nlm.nih.gov/pubmed/16574699.

2. Halyna D Koval, Valentyna V Chopyak, Oleksandr M Kamyshnyi, and Maciej K Kurpisz. "Transcription Regulatory Factor Expression in T-Helper Cell Differentiation Pathway in Eutopic Endometrial Tissue Samples of Women with Endometriosis Associated with Infertility." Central-European Journal of Immunology. Polish Society of Experimental and Clinical Immunology, 2018. https://www.ncbi.nlm.nih.gov/pmc/articles/PMC5927178/.

3. Shufang Chen, Jian Zhang, Changxiao Huang, Wen Lu, Yan Liang, and Xiaoping Wan. "Expression of the T Regulatory Cell Transcription Factor FoxP3 in Peri-Implantation Phase Endometrium in Infertile Women with Endometriosis." Reproductive Biology and Endocrinology. BioMed Central, April 27, 2012. https://www.ncbi.nlm.nih.gov/pmc/articles/PMC3443024/.

4. G Vighi, F Marcucci, L Sensi, G Di Cara, and F Frati. "Allergy and the Gastrointestinal System." Clinical and Experimental Immunology. Blackwell Science Inc, September 2008. https://www.ncbi.nlm.nih.gov/pmc/articles/PMC2515351/.

5. Taylor Thorburn, Maral Aali, and Christian Lehmann. "Immune Response to Systemic Inflammation in the Intestinal Microcirculation." Frontiers in Bioscience (Landmark edition). U.S. National Library of Medicine, January 1, 2018. https://www.ncbi.nlm.nih.gov/pubmed/28930572.

6. Andrew C Dukowicz, Brian E Lacy, and Gary M Levine. "Small Intestinal Bacterial Overgrowth: a Comprehensive Review." Gastroenterology & Hepatology. Millennium Medical Publishing, February 2007. https://www.ncbi.nlm.nih.gov/pmc/articles/PMC3099351/.

7. Whitney P Bowe and Alan C Logan. "Acne Vulgaris, Probiotics and the Gut-Brain-Skin Axis - Back to the Future?" Gut Pathogens. BioMed Central, January 31, 2011. https://www.ncbi.nlm.nih.gov/pmc/articles/PMC3038963/.

8. Andrew W Campbell. "Autoimmunity and the Gut." Autoimmune Diseases 2014 (2014): 1–12. https://doi.org/10.1155/2014/152428.

9. Outi Vaarala. "Leaking Gut in Type 1 Diabetes." Current Opinion in Gastroenterology. U.S. National Library of Medicine, November 2008. https://www.ncbi.nlm.nih.gov/pubmed/19122519.

10. Marilia Carabotti, Annunziata Scirocco, Maria Antonietta Maselli, and Carola Severi. "The Gut-Brain Axis: Interactions between Enteric Microbiota, Central and Enteric Nervous Systems." Annals of Gastroenterology. Hellenic Society of Gastroenterology, 2015. https://www.ncbi.nlm.nih.gov/pmc/articles/PMC4367209/.

11. Jennifer G Mulle, William G Sharp, and Joseph F Cubells. "The Gut Microbiome: a New Frontier in Autism Research." Current Psychiatry Reports. U.S. National Library of Medicine, February 2013. https://www.ncbi.nlm.nih.gov/pmc/articles/PMC3564498/.

12. Lora J Kasselman, Nicholas A Vernice, Joshua DeLeon, and Allison B Reiss. "The Gut Microbiome and Elevated Cardiovascular Risk in Obesity and Autoimmunity." Atherosclerosis. U.S. National Library of Medicine, April 2018. https://www.ncbi.nlm.nih.gov/pubmed/29524863.

13. S J Walsh and L M Rau. "Autoimmune Diseases: a Leading Cause of Death among Young and Middle-Aged Women in the United States." American Journal of Public Health. U.S. National Library of Medicine, September 2000. https://www.ncbi.nlm.nih.gov/pubmed/10983209.

14. "Autoimmune Disease Statistics." AARDA. Accessed October 2019. https://www.aarda.org/news-information/statistics/.

15. Xuetian Yue, Lihua Wu, and Wenwei Hu. "The Regulation of Leukemia Inhibitory Factor." Cancer Cell & Microenvironment. U.S. National Library of Medicine, 2015. https://www.ncbi.nlm.nih.gov/pmc/articles/PMC4722946/.

16. Naguib Salleh and Nelli Giribabu. "Leukemia Inhibitory Factor: Roles in Embryo Implantation and in Nonhormonal Contraception." The Scientific World Journal. Hindawi Publishing Corporation, 2014. https://www.ncbi.nlm.nih.gov/pmc/articles/PMC4131495/.

17. Edouard Hambartsoumian. "Endometrial Leukemia Inhibitory Factor (LIF) as a Possible Cause of Unexplained Infertility and Multiple Failures of Implantation." Wiley Online Library. John Wiley & Sons, Ltd (10.1111), September 6, 2011. https://onlinelibrary.wiley.com/doi/abs/10.1111/j.1600-0897.1998.tb00345.x.

18. Alban Deroux, Chantal Dumestre-Perard, Camille Dunand-Faure, Laurence Bouillet, and Pascale Hoffmann. "Female Infertility and Serum Auto-Antibodies: a Systematic Review." Clinical Reviews in Allergy & Immunology. U.S. National Library of Medicine, August 2017. https://www.ncbi.nlm.nih.gov/pubmed/27628237.

19. D A Ohl and R K Naz. "Infertility Due to Antisperm Antibodies." Urology. U.S. National Library of Medicine, October 1995. https://www.ncbi.nlm.nih.gov/pubmed/7571238.

20. A Hoek, J Schoemaker, and H A Drexhage. "Premature Ovarian Failure and Ovarian Autoimmunity." Endocrine Reviews. U.S. National Library of Medicine, February 1997. https://www.ncbi.nlm.nih.gov/pubmed/9034788.

21. Svetlana Dragojević-Dikić, Dragomir Marisavljević, Ana Mitrović, Srdjan Dikić, Tomislav Jovanović, and Svetlana Janković-Raznatović. "An Immunological Insight into Premature Ovarian Failure (POF)." Autoimmunity Reviews. U.S. National Library of Medicine, September 2010. https://www.ncbi.nlm.nih.gov/pubmed/20601203.

22. Karin De Punder and Leo Pruimboom. "The Dietary Intake of Wheat and Other Cereal Grains and Their Role in Inflammation." Nutrients 5, no. 3 (December 2013): 771–87. https://doi.org/10.3390/nu5030771.

23. Outi Vaarala, Mark A Atkinson, and Josef Neu. "The 'Perfect Storm' for Type 1 Diabetes: the Complex Interplay between Intestinal Microbiota, Gut Permeability, and Mucosal Immunity." Diabetes. American Diabetes Association, October 2008. https://www.ncbi.nlm.nih.gov/pmc/articles/PMC2551660/.

24. Taylor Thorburn, Maral Aali, and Christian Lehmann. "Immune Response to Systemic Inflammation in the Intestinal Microcirculation." Frontiers in bioscience (Landmark edition). U.S. National Library of Medicine, January 1, 2018. https://www.ncbi.nlm.nih.gov/pubmed/28930572.

25. A Venket Rao, Alison C Bested, Tracey M Beaulne, Martin A Katzman, Christina Iorio, John M Berardi, and Alan C Logan. "A Randomized, Double-Blind, Placebo-Controlled Pilot Study of a Probiotic in Emotional Symptoms of Chronic Fatigue Syndrome." Gut Pathogens. BioMed Central, March 19, 2009. https://www.ncbi.nlm.nih.gov/pmc/articles/PMC2664325/.

26. Sung Hee Lee. "Intestinal Permeability Regulation by Tight Junction: Implication on Inflammatory Bowel Diseases." Intestinal Research. Korean Association for the Study of Intestinal Diseases, January 2015. https://www.ncbi.nlm.nih.gov/pmc/articles/PMC4316216/.

27. Lisa Shaver. "Diagnosis of Celiac Disease & Ethics of Prescribing a Gluten-Free Diet." 2018 Fall Conference Gastroenterology and Dermatology, November 10–11, 2018, Scottsdale, Arizona.

28. Sveta Shah and Daniel Leffler. "Celiac Disease: an Underappreciated Issue in Womens Health." Womens Health 6, no. 5 (2010): 753–66. https://doi.org/10.2217/whe.10.57

29. A Ventura, G Magazzù, and L Greco. "Duration of Exposure to Gluten and Risk for Autoimmune Disorders in Patients with Celiac Disease. SIGEP Study Group for Autoimmune Disorders in Celiac Disease." Gastroenterology. U.S. National Library of Medicine, August 1999. https://www.ncbi.nlm.nih.gov/pubmed/10419909.

30. Anna Krigel and Benjamin Lebwohl. "Nonceliac Gluten Sensitivity." Advances in Nutrition (Bethesda, Md.). American Society for Nutrition, November 15, 2016. https://www.ncbi.nlm.nih.gov/pmc/articles/PMC5105039/.

31. Elena Moretti, Natale Figura, Maria Stella Campagna, Francesca Iacoponi, Stefano Gonnelli, and Giulia Collodel. "Infectious Burden and Semen Parameters." Urology. U.S. National Library of Medicine, February 2017. https://www.ncbi.nlm.nih.gov/pubmed/27793655.

32. G Torino, A Bizzarro, G Castello, A Daponte, A Fontana, A De Bellis, and V A Paglionico. "Cytomegalovirus and Male Infertility." Annales de biologie clinique. U.S. National Library of Medicine, 1987. https://www.ncbi.nlm.nih.gov/pubmed/2823646.

33. Roberto Marci, Valentina Gentili, Daria Bortolotti, Giuseppe Lo Monte, Elisabetta Caselli, Silvia Bolzani, Antonella Rotola, Dario Di Luca, and Roberta Rizzo "Presence of HHV-6A in Endometrial Epithelial Cells from Women with Primary Unexplained Infertility." PLOS ONE, Public Library of Science, https://journals.plos.org/plosone/article?id=10.1371/journal.pone.0158304.

34. V A Naumenko and A A Kushch. "Herpes Viruses and Male Infertility—Is There Any Relationship?" Voprosy virusologii. U.S. National Library of Medicine, 2013. https://www.ncbi.nlm.nih.gov/pubmed/24006625.

35. Tobias Marzin, Gerhard Lorkowski, Claudia Reule, Stefanie Rau, Elisabeth Pabst, Johannes C Vester, and Helmut Pabst. "Effects of a Systemic Enzyme Therapy in Healthy Active Adults after Exhaustive Eccentric Exercise: a Randomised, Two-Stage, Double-Blinded, Placebo-Controlled Trial." BMJ open sport & exercise medicine. BMJ Open Sport & Exercise Medicine, March 12, 2017. https://www.ncbi.nlm.nih.gov/pmc/articles/PMC5569274/.

36. Yang Mu, Wen-Jie Yan, Tai-Lang Yin, and Jing Yang. "Curcumin Ameliorates High Fat Diet Induced Spermatogenesis Dysfunction." Molecular medicine reports. D.A. Spandidos, October 2016. https://www.ncbi.nlm.nih.gov/pmc/articles/PMC5042768/.

37. Roya Kolahdouz Mohammadi and Tahereh Arablou. "Resveratrol and Endometriosis: In Vitro and Animal Studies and Underlying Mechanisms (Review)." Biomedicine & pharmacotherapy. U.S. National Library of Medicine, July 2017. https://www.ncbi.nlm.nih.gov/pubmed/28458160.

38. R Falchetti, M P Fuggetta, G Lanzilli, M Tricarico, and G Ravagnan. "Effects of Resveratrol on Human Immune Cell Function." Life sciences. U.S. National Library of Medicine, November 21, 2001. https://www.ncbi.nlm.nih.gov/pubmed/11764009.

39. Khushwant S Bhullar and Basil P Hubbard. "Lifespan and Healthspan Extension by Resveratrol." Biochimica et biophysica acta. U.S. National Library of Medicine, June 2015. https://www.ncbi.nlm.nih.gov/pubmed/25640851.

40. Gabriela Mazzanti and Silvia Di Giacomo. "Curcumin and Resveratrol in the Management of Cognitive Disorders: What Is the Clinical Evidence?" Molecules (Basel, Switzerland). MDPI, September 17, 2016. https://www.ncbi.nlm.nih.gov/pubmed/27649135.

41. Monika Fleshner and Camille R Crane. "Exosomes, DAMPs and MiRNA: Features of Stress Physiology and Immune Homeostasis." Trends in immunology. U.S. National Library of Medicine, October 2017. https://www.ncbi.nlm.nih.gov/pubmed/28838855.

42. Giselle Soares Passos, Dalva Poyares, Marcos Gonçalves Santana, Alexandre Abílio de Souza Teixeira, Fábio Santos Lira, Shawn D Youngstedt, Ronaldo Vagner Thomatieli dos Santos, Sergio Tufik, and Marco Túlio de Mello. "Exercise Improves Immune Function, Antidepressive Response, and Sleep Quality in Patients with Chronic Primary Insomnia." BioMed research international. Hindawi Publishing Corporation, 2014. https://www.ncbi.nlm.nih.gov/pubmed/25328886.

43. Praveen Bhandari, Praveen Rishi, and Vijay Prabha. "Positive Effect of Probiotic Lactobacillus Plantarum in Reversing LPS-Induced Infertility in a Mouse Model." Journal of Medical Microbiology. U.S. National Library of Medicine, May 2016. https://www.ncbi.nlm.nih.gov/pubmed/26872701.

44. D G Valcarce, S Genovés, M F Riesco, P Martorell, M P Herráez, D Ramón, and V Robles. "Probiotic Administration Improves Sperm Quality in Asthenozoospermic Human Donors." Beneficial microbes. U.S. National Library of Medicine, April 26, 2017. https://www.ncbi.nlm.nih.gov/pubmed/28343402.

45. Cynthia Aranow. "Vitamin D and the Immune System." Journal of Investigative Medicine. U.S. National Library of Medicine, August 2011. https://www.ncbi.nlm.nih.gov/pmc/articles/PMC3166406/.

46. Z Wieczorek, M Zimecki, M Janusz, K Staroscik, and J Lisowski. "Proline-Rich Polypeptide from Ovine Colostrum: Its Effect on Skin Permeability and on the Immune Response." Immunology. U.S. National Library of Medicine, April 1979. https://www.ncbi.nlm.nih.gov/pmc/articles/PMC1457668/.

CHAPTER 12

1. Yuanchang Zhu, Tonghua Wu, Lijun Ye, Guangui Li, Yong Zeng, and Yaou Zhang. "Prevalent Genotypes of Methylenetetrahydrofolate Reductase (MTHFR) in Recurrent Miscarriage and Recurrent Implantation Failure." Journal of Assisted Reproduction and Genetics. Springer US, August 2018. https://www.ncbi.nlm.nih.gov/pubmed/29785531.

2. Danielius Serapinas, Evelina Boreikaite, Agne Bartkeviciute, Rita Bandzeviciene, Mindaugas Silkunas, and Daiva Bartkeviciene. "The Importance of Folate, Vitamins B6 and B12 for the Lowering of Homocysteine Concentrations for Patients with Recurrent Pregnancy Loss and MTHFR Mutations." Reproductive Toxicology (Elmsford, N.Y.). U.S. National Library of Medicine, September 2017. https://www.ncbi.nlm.nih.gov/pubmed/28689805.

3. Walid Al-Achkar, Abdulsamad Wafa, Samer Ammar, Faten Moassass, and Rami A Jarjour. "Association of Methylenetetrahydrofolate Reductase C677T and A1298C Gene Polymorphisms With Recurrent Pregnancy Loss in Syrian Women." Reproductive Sciences (Thousand Oaks, Calif.). U.S. National Library of Medicine, September 2017. https://www.ncbi.nlm.nih.gov/pubmed/28814189.

4. Youngsok Choi, Jung Oh Kim, Sung Han Shim, Yubin Lee, Ji Hyang Kim, Young Joo Jeon, Jung Jae Ko, Woo Sik Lee, and Nam Keun Kim. "Genetic Variation of Methylenetetrahydrofolate Reductase (MTHFR) and Thymidylate Synthase (TS) Genes Is Associated with Idiopathic Recurrent Implantation Failure." PLOS ONE. Public Library of Science, August 25, 2016. https://www.ncbi.nlm.nih.gov/pubmed/27560137.

5. Kai-min Guo, Run-hui Tian, and Hong-liang Wang. "Relationship of MTHFR Gene Polymorphisms with Infertility." National Journal of Andrology. U.S. National Library of Medicine, February 2016. https://www.ncbi.nlm.nih.gov/pubmed/26939404.

6. Francesco Scaglione and Giscardo Panzavolta. "Folate, Folic Acid and 5-Methyltetrahydrofolate Are Not the Same Thing." Xenobiotica; the fate of foreign compounds in biological systems. U.S. National Library of Medicine, May 2014. https://www.ncbi.nlm.nih.gov/pubmed/24494987.

7. Krista S Crider, Thomas P Yang, Robert J Berry, and Lynn B Bailey. "Folate and DNA Methylation: a Review of Molecular Mechanisms and the Evidence for Folate's Role." Advances in Nutrition (Bethesda, Md.). Oxford University Press, January 2012. https://www.ncbi.nlm.nih.gov/pmc/articles/PMC3262611/.

8. P Frosst, H J Blom, R Milos, P Goyette, C A Sheppard, R G Matthews, G J Boers, M den Heijer, L A Kluijtmans, and L P van den Heuvel. "A Candidate Genetic Risk Factor for Vascular Disease: a Common Mutation in Methylenetetrahydrofolate Reductase." Nature genetics. U.S. National Library of Medicine, May 1995. https://www.ncbi.nlm.nih.gov/pubmed/7647779.

9. "MTHFR Methylenetetrahydrofolate Reductase [Homo Sapiens (Human)] - Gene - NCBI." National Center for Biotechnology Information. U.S. National Library of Medicine. Accessed October 2019. https://www.ncbi.nlm.nih.gov/gene/4524.

10. A Reyes-Engel, E Muñoz, M J Gaitan, E Fabre, M Gallo, J L Dieguez, M Ruiz, and M Morell. "Implications on Human Fertility of the 677C-->T and 1298A-->C Polymorphisms of the MTHFR Gene: Consequences of a Possible Genetic Selection." Molecular Human Reproduction. U.S. National Library of Medicine, October 2002. https://www.ncbi.nlm.nih.gov/pubmed/12356947.

11. Sahar Sibani, Daniel Leclerc, Ilan S Weisberg, Erin O'Ferrall, David Watkins, Carmen Artigas, David S Rosenblatt, and Rima Rozen. "Characterization of Mutations in Severe Methylenetetrahydrofolate Reductase Deficiency Reveals an FAD-Responsive Mutation." Human mutation. U.S. National Library of Medicine, May 2003. https://www.ncbi.nlm.nih.gov/pubmed/12673793.

12. T O Scholl and W G Johnson. "Folic Acid: Influence on the Outcome of Pregnancy." The American Journal of Clinical Nutrition. U.S. National Library of Medicine, May 2000. https://www.ncbi.nlm.nih.gov/pubmed/10799405.

13. Pelin Ocal, Bilge Ersoylu, Ismail Cepni, Onur Guralp, Nil Atakul, Tulay Irez, and Mehmet Idil. "The Association between Homocysteine in the Follicular Fluid with Embryo Quality and Pregnancy Rate in Assisted Reproductive Techniques." Journal of Assisted Reproduction and Genetics. Springer US, April 2012. https://www.ncbi.nlm.nih.gov/pmc/articles/PMC3309985/.

14. Priscilla Querioz D'Ella, Aline Amaro dos Santos, Bianca Bianco, Caio Parente Barbosa, Denise Maria Christofolini, Tsutomu Aoki. "MTHFR polymorphisms C677T and A1298C and associations with IVF outcomes in Brazilian women" Reproductive Biomedicine Online. Elsevier, June 2014. https://www.rbmojournal.com/article/S1472-6483(14)00119-9/fulltext

15. S J James, M Pogribna, I P Pogribny, S Melnyk, R J Hine, J B Gibson, P Yi, et al. "Abnormal Folate Metabolism and Mutation in the Methylenetetrahydrofolate Reductase Gene May Be Maternal Risk Factors for Down Syndrome." The American Journal of Clinical Nutrition. U.S. National Library of Medicine, October 1999. https://www.ncbi.nlm.nih.gov/pubmed/10500018.

16. Saeedeh Salimi, Mohsen Saravani, Minoo Yaghmaei, Zeinab Fazlali, Mojgan Mokhtari, Anoosh Naghavi, and Farzaneh Farajian-Mashhadi. "The Early-Onset Preeclampsia Is Associated with MTHFR and FVL Polymorphisms." Archives of gynecology and obstetrics. U.S. National Library of Medicine, June 2015. https://www.ncbi.nlm.nih.gov/pubmed/25480409.

17. Petra Bubalo, Iva Buterin, Zrinko Šalek, Vesna Đogić, and Silva Zupančić-Šalek. "Association of Plasminogen Activator Inhibitor-1 Gene Polymorphisms and Methylene Tetrahydrofolate Reductase Polymorphisms with Spontaneous Miscarriages." Acta haematologica. U.S. National Library of Medicine, 2017. https://www.ncbi.nlm.nih.gov/pubmed/28858863.

18. Han Wu, Ping Zhu, Xingyi Geng, Zhong Liu, Liangliang Cui, Zhongchun Gao, Baofa Jiang, and Liping Yang. "Genetic Polymorphism of MTHFR C677T with Preterm Birth and Low Birth Weight Susceptibility: a Meta-Analysis." Archives of gynecology and obstetrics. U.S. National Library of Medicine, May 2017. https://www.ncbi.nlm.nih.gov/pubmed/28283826.

19. R Behjati, M H Modarressi, M Jeddi-Tehrani, P Dokoohaki, J Ghasemi, A H Zarnani, M Aarabi, T Memariani, M Ghaffari, and M A Akhondi. "Thrombophilic Mutations in Iranian Patients with Infertility and Recurrent Spontaneous Abortion." Annals of hematology. U.S. National Library of Medicine, April 2006. https://www.ncbi.nlm.nih.gov/pubmed/16450127.

20. P Merviel, R Cabry, E Lourdel, S Lanta, C Amant, H Copin, and M Benkhalifa. "Comparison of Two Preventive Treatments for Patients with Recurrent Miscarriages Carrying a C677T Methylenetetrahydrofolate Reductase Mutation: 5-Year Experience." The Journal of International Medical Research. U.S. National Library of Medicine, December 2017. https://www.ncbi.nlm.nih.gov/pubmed/28703660.

21. María Enciso, Jonás Sarasa, Leoni Xanthopoulou, Sara Bristow, Megan Bowles, Elpida Fragouli, Joy Delhanty, and Dagan Wells. "Polymorphisms in the MTHFR Gene Influence Embryo Viability and the Incidence of Aneuploidy." Human Genetics. U.S. National Library of Medicine, May 2016. https://www.ncbi.nlm.nih.gov/pubmed/27068821.

22. Piet Hein Jongbloet, André Lm Verbeek, Martin den Heijer, and Nel Roeleveld. "Methylenetetrahydrofolate Reductase (MTHFR) Gene Polymorphisms Resulting in Suboptimal Oocyte Maturation: a Discussion of Folate Status, Neural Tube Defects, Schizophrenia, and Vasculopathy." Journal of Experimental & Clinical Assisted Reproduction. BioMed Central, July 10, 2008. https://www.ncbi.nlm.nih.gov/pmc/articles/PMC2500045/.

23. C J Thaler. "Folate Metabolism and Human Reproduction." Geburtshilfe und Frauenheilkunde. Georg Thieme Verlag KG, September 2014. https://www.ncbi.nlm.nih.gov/pmc/articles/PMC4175124/.

24. Edouard J Servy, Laetitia Jacquesson-Fournols, Marc Cohen, and Yves J R Menezo. "MTHFR Isoform Carriers. 5-MTHF (5-Methyl Tetrahydrofolate) vs Folic Acid: a Key to Pregnancy Outcome: a Case Series." Journal of Assisted Reproduction and Genetics. Springer US, August 2018. https://www.ncbi.nlm.nih.gov/pubmed/29882091.

25. Lesley Plumptre, Shannon P Masih, Anna Ly, Susanne Aufreiter, Kyoung-Jin Sohn, Ruth Croxford, Andrea Y Lausman, Howard Berger, Deborah L O'Connor, and Young-In Kim. "High Concentrations of Folate and Unmetabolized Folic Acid in a Cohort of Pregnant Canadian Women and Umbilical Cord Blood." The American Journal of Clinical Nutrition. U.S. National Library of Medicine, October 2015. https://www.ncbi.nlm.nih.gov/pubmed/26269367.

26. S S Li and J Li. "[MTHFR Gene Polymorphism and Male Infertility]." National Journal of Andrology. U.S. National Library of Medicine, January 2010. https://www.ncbi.nlm.nih.gov/pubmed/20180408.

27. Kiran Singh and Deepika Jaiswal. "One-Carbon Metabolism, Spermatogenesis, and Male Infertility." Reproductive Sciences (Thousand Oaks, Calif.). U.S. National Library of Medicine, June 2013. https://www.ncbi.nlm.nih.gov/pubmed/23138010.

28. Dominique Cornet, Marc Cohen, Arthur Clement, Edouard Amar, Laetitia Fournols, Patrice Clement, Paul Neveux, and Yves Ménézo. "Association between the MTHFR-C677T Isoform and Structure of Sperm DNA." Journal of Assisted Reproduction and Genetics. Springer US, October 2017. https://www.ncbi.nlm.nih.gov/pmc/articles/PMC5633564/.

29. D Cornet, M Cohen, A Clement, E Amar, L Fournols, P Clement, P Neveux, and Y Ménézo. "Association between the MTHFR-C677T Isoform and Structure of Sperm DNA." Journal of Assisted Reproduction and Genetics. U.S. National Library of Medicine, October 2017. https://www.ncbi.nlm.nih.gov/pubmed/28842818.

30. Singh Rajender, Kelsey Avery, and Ashok Agarwal. "Epigenetics, Spermatogenesis and Male Infertility." Mutation research. U.S. National Library of Medicine, 2011. https://www.ncbi.nlm.nih.gov/pubmed/21540125.

31. K Louie, A Minor, R Ng, K Poon, V Chow, and S Ma. "Evaluation of DNA Methylation at Imprinted DMRs in the Spermatozoa of Oligozoospermic Men in Association with MTHFR C677T Genotype." Andrology. U.S. National Library of Medicine, September 2016. https://www.ncbi.nlm.nih.gov/pubmed/27369467.

32. W Wu, O Shen, Y Qin, J Lu, X Niu, Z Zhou, C Lu, Y Xia, S Wang, and X Wang. "Methylenetetrahydrofolate Reductase C677T Polymorphism and the Risk of Male Infertility: a Meta-Analysis." International Journal of Andrology. U.S. National Library of Medicine, February 2012. https://www.ncbi.nlm.nih.gov/pubmed/21535009.

33. Mohammad Karimian and Abasalt Hosseinzadeh Colagar. "Association of C677T Transition of the Human Methylenetetrahydrofolate Reductase (MTHFR) Gene with Male Infertility." Reproduction, Fertility, and Development. U.S. National Library of Medicine, April 2016. https://www.ncbi.nlm.nih.gov/pubmed/25412139.

34. Hui-Hui Hong, Yan Hu, Xiao-Qing Yu, Liang Zhou, Mo-Qi Lv, Ying Sun, Wen-Juan Ren, and Dang-Xia Zhou. "Associations of C677T Polymorphism in Methylenetetrahydrofolate Reductase (MTHFR) Gene with Male Infertility Risk: A Meta-Analysis." European journal of obstetrics, gynecology, and reproductive biology. U.S. National Library of Medicine, May 2017. https://www.ncbi.nlm.nih.gov/pubmed/28363185.

35. Shin Young Kim, Jung Wook Lim, Jin Woo Kim, So Yeon Park, and Ju Tae Seo. "Association between Genetic Polymorphisms in Folate-Related Enzyme Genes and Infertile Men with Non-Obstructive Azoospermia." Systems biology in reproductive medicine. U.S. National Library of Medicine, 2015. https://www.ncbi.nlm.nih.gov/pubmed/26196053.

36. Mancheng Gong, Wenjing Dong, Tingyu He, Zhirong Shi, Guiying Huang, Rui Ren, Sichong Huang, Shaopeng Qiu, and Runqiang Yuan. "MTHFR 677C>T Polymorphism Increases the Male Infertility Risk: a Meta-Analysis Involving 26 Studies." PLOS ONE. Public Library of Science, March 20, 2015. https://www.ncbi.nlm.nih.gov/pubmed/25793386.

37. Bingbing Wei, Zhuoqun Xu, Jun Ruan, Ming Zhu, Ke Jin, Deqi Zhou, Zeqiao Xu, Qiang Hu, Qiang Wang, and Zhirong Wang. "MTHFR 677C>T and 1298A>C Polymorphisms and Male Infertility Risk: a Meta-Analysis." Molecular biology reports. U.S. National Library of Medicine, February 2012. https://www.ncbi.nlm.nih.gov/pubmed/21643754.

38. Qiang Zhang, Guo-Ying Yin, Juan Liu, Yue Liang, Yao-Yan Li, Jing-Yu Zhao, Li-Wen Zhang, Bai-Qi Wang, and Nai-Jun Tang. "Association between MTHFR A1298C Polymorphism and Male Infertility: A Meta-Analysis." Journal of Huazhong University of Science and Technology. Medical sciences. Yixue Yingdewen ban. U.S. National Library of Medicine, April 2017. https://www.ncbi.nlm.nih.gov/pubmed/28397035.

39. Zhengju Ren, Pengwei Ren, Bo Yang, Kun Fang, Shangqing Ren, Jian Liao, Shengzhuo Liu, Liangren Liu, Zhufeng Peng, and Qiang Dong. "MTHFR C677T, A1298C and MS A2756G Gene Polymorphisms and Male Infertility Risk in a Chinese Population: A Meta-Analysis." PLOS ONE. Public Library of Science, January 12, 2017. https://www.ncbi.nlm.nih.gov/pubmed/28081209.

40. K Liu, R Zhao, M Shen, J Ye, X Li, Y Huang, L Hua, Z Wang, and J Li. "Role of Genetic Mutations in Folate-Related Enzyme Genes on Male Infertility." Scientific Reports. U.S. National Library of Medicine, November 9, 2015. https://www.ncbi.nlm.nih.gov/pubmed/26549413.

41. Shin Young Kim, Jung Wook Lim, Jin Woo Kim, So Yeon Park, and Ju Tae Seo. "Association between Genetic Polymorphisms in Folate-Related Enzyme Genes and Infertile Men with Non-Obstructive Azoospermia." Systems biology in reproductive medicine. U.S. National Library of Medicine, 2015. https://www.ncbi.nlm.nih.gov/pubmed/26196053.

42. Guntram Bezold, Monika Lange, Ralf Uwe Peter. "Homozygous Methylenetetrahydrofolate Reductase C677T Mutation and Male Infertility: NEJM." New England Journal of Medicine. Accessed October 2019. https://www.nejm.org/doi/full/10.1056/NEJM200104123441517.

43. G Bentivoglio, F Melica, and P Cristoforoni. "Folinic Acid in the Treatment of Human Male Infertility." Fertility and Sterility. U.S. National Library of Medicine, October 1993. https://www.ncbi.nlm.nih.gov/pubmed/8405528.

44. R Najafipour, S Moghbelinejad, A Aleyasin, and A Jalilvand. "Effect of B9 and B12 Vitamin Intake on Semen Parameters and Fertility of Men with MTHFR Polymorphisms." Andrology. U.S. National Library of Medicine, July 2017. https://www.ncbi.nlm.nih.gov/pubmed/28440964.

45. Steven Taylor. "Association between COMT Val158Met and Psychiatric Disorders: A Comprehensive Meta-Analysis." Wiley Online Library. John Wiley & Sons, Ltd, June 13, 2017. https://onlinelibrary.wiley.com/doi/full/10.1002/ajmg.b.32556.

46. Glaucia C Akutagava-Martins, Angelica Salatino-Oliveira, Christian Kieling, Julia P Genro, Guilherme V Polanczyk, Luciana Anselmi, Ana M B Menezes, et al. "COMT and DAT1 Genes Are Associated with Hyperactivity and Inattention Traits in the 1993 Pelotas Birth Cohort: Evidence of Sex-Specific Combined Effect." Journal of psychiatry & neuroscience : JPN. Joule Inc., October 2016. https://www.ncbi.nlm.nih.gov/pmc/articles/PMC5082511/.

47. Flávia Regina Barbosa, Josie Budag Matsuda, Mendelson Mazucato, Suzelei de Castro França, Sônia Marli Zingaretti, Lucienir Maria da Silva, Nilce Maria Martinez-Rossi, Milton Faria Júnior, Mozart Marins, and Ana Lúcia Fachin. "Influence of Catechol-O-Methyltransferase (COMT) Gene Polymorphisms in Pain Sensibility of Brazilian Fibromialgia Patients." SpringerLink. Springer-Verlag, December 1, 2010. https://link.springer.com/article/10.1007/s00296-010-1659-z.

48. L Knowles, A A M Morris, and J H Walter. "Treatment with Mefolinate (5-Methyltetrahydrofolate), but Not Folic Acid or Folinic Acid, Leads to Measurable 5-Methyltetrahydrofolate in Cerebrospinal Fluid in Methylenetetrahydrofolate Reductase Deficiency." JIMD reports. Springer Berlin Heidelberg, 2016. https://www.ncbi.nlm.nih.gov/pmc/articles/PMC5059208/.

49. Lynch, Ben. *Dirty Genes: a breakthrough program to treat the root cause of illness and optimize your health.* First edition. New York, NY: HarperOne, 2018.

50. Lynch, Ben. "What is MTHFR?" MTHFR.net. Accessed October 2019. http://mthfr.net/what-is-mthfr/2011/11/04/.

CHAPTER 13

1. Toshinobu Miyamoto, Gaku Minase, Kimika Okabe, Hiroto Ueda, and Kazuo Sengoku. "Male Infertility and Its Genetic Causes." The Journal of Obstetrics and Gynaecology Research. U.S. National Library of Medicine, October 2015. https://www.ncbi.nlm.nih.gov/pubmed/26178295.

2. Victor M Brugh and Larry I Lipshultz. "Male Factor Infertility." Medical Clinics of North America 88, no. 2 (2004): 367–85. https://doi.org/10.1016/s0025-7125(03)00150-0.

3. "Male Factor - RESOLVE: The National Infertility Association." RESOLVE. Accessed October 2019. https://resolve.org/infertility-101/medical-conditions/male-factor/.

4. E Carlsen, A Giwercman, N Keiding, and N E Skakkebaek. "Evidence for Decreasing Quality of Semen during Past 50 Years." BMJ (Clinical research ed.). U.S. National Library of Medicine, September 12, 1992. https://www.ncbi.nlm.nih.gov/pubmed/1393072.

5. "What Is Male Infertility?" What is Male Infertility? - Urology Care Foundation. Accessed October 2019. https://www.urologyhealth.org/urologic-conditions/male-infertility.

6. Amr Abdel Raheem and David Ralph. "Male Infertility: Causes and Investigations." Wiley Online Library. John Wiley & Sons, Ltd, October 4, 2011. https://onlinelibrary.wiley.com/doi/pdf/10.1002/tre.216.

7. Isiah D Harris, Carolyn Fronczak, Lauren Roth, and Randall B Meacham. "Fertility and the Aging Male." Reviews in Urology. MedReviews, LLC, 2011. https://www.ncbi.nlm.nih.gov/pmc/articles/PMC3253726/.

8. Steve Paxton, Peckham, Michelle, Knibbs, and Adele. "The Leeds Histology Guide." The Histology Guide, January 1, 1970. https://www.histology.leeds.ac.uk/male/sertoli_cells.php.

9. Naina Kumar and Amit Kant Singh. "Trends of Male Factor Infertility, an Important Cause of Infertility: A Review of Literature." Journal of Human Reproductive Sciences. Medknow Publications & Media Pvt Ltd, 2015. https://www.ncbi.nlm.nih.gov/pmc/articles/PMC4691969/.

10. Damayanthi Durairajanayagam. "Lifestyle Causes of Male Infertility." Arab Journal of Urology. Elsevier, February 13, 2018. https://www.ncbi.nlm.nih.gov/pmc/articles/PMC5922227/.

11. Trevor G Cooper, Elizabeth Noonan, Sigrid Von Eckardstein, Jacques Auger, H W Gordon Baker, Hermann M. Behre, Trine B Haugen, et al. "World Health Organization Reference Values for Human Semen Characteristics." Human Reproduction Update 16, no. 3 (2009): 231–45. https://doi.org/10.1093/humupd/dmp048.

12. Christopher L R Barratt, Lars Björndahl, Christopher J De Jonge, Dolores J Lamb, Francisco Osorio Martini, Robert McLachlan, Robert D Oates, et al. "The Diagnosis of Male Infertility: an Analysis of the Evidence to Support the Development of Global WHO Guidance-Challenges and Future Research Opportunities." Human Reproduction Update. Oxford University Press, November 1, 2017. https://www.ncbi.nlm.nih.gov/pmc/articles/PMC5850791/.

13. Amir S Patela, Joon YauLeongb, and RanjithRamasamya. "Prediction of Male Infertility by the World Health Organization Laboratory Manual for Assessment of Semen Analysis: A Systematic Review." Arab Journal of Urology. Elsevier, November 20, 2017. https://www.sciencedirect.com/science/article/pii/S2090598X17301110.

14. "Optimal Evaluation of the Infertile Male." American Urological Association. Accessed October 2019. http://www.auanet.org/guidelines/male-infertility-optimal-evaluation-(reviewed-and-validity-confirmed-2011).

15. Niels E Skakkebaek. "Normal Reference Ranges for Semen Quality and Their Relations to Fecundity." Asian Journal of Andrology. Nature Publishing Group, January 2010. https://www.ncbi.nlm.nih.gov/pmc/articles/PMC3739681/.

16. Sheena E M Lewis. "Is Sperm Evaluation Useful in Predicting Human Fertility?" Reproduction 134, no. 1 (2007): 31–40. https://doi.org/10.1530/rep-07-0152.

17. L Johnson, R S Zane, C S Petty, and W B Neaves. "Quantification of the Human Sertoli Cell Population: Its Distribution, Relation to Germ Cell Numbers, and Age-Related Decline." Biology of reproduction. U.S. National Library of Medicine, November 1984. https://www.ncbi.nlm.nih.gov/pubmed/6509142.

18. Sezgin Gunes, Gulgez Neslihan Taskurt Hekim, Mehmet Alper Arslan, and Ramazan Asci. "Effects of Aging on the Male Reproductive System." Journal of Assisted Reproduction and Genetics. Springer US, April 2016. https://www.ncbi.nlm.nih.gov/pmc/articles/PMC4818633/.

19. Daniel J Mazur and Larry I Lipshultz. "Infertility in the Aging Male." Current urology reports. U.S. National Library of Medicine, May 17, 2018. https://www.ncbi.nlm.nih.gov/pubmed/29774447.

20. Rakesh Sharma, Ashok Agarwal, Vikram K Rohra, Mourad Assidi, Muhammad Abu-Elmagd, and Rola F Turki. "Effects of Increased Paternal Age on Sperm Quality, Reproductive Outcome and Associated Epigenetic Risks to Offspring." Reproductive Biology and Endocrinology. BioMed Central, April 19, 2015. https://www.ncbi.nlm.nih.gov/pmc/articles/PMC4455614/.

21. Soheila Pourmasumi, Parvin Sabeti, Tahereh Rahiminia, Esmat Mangoli, Nasim Tabibnejad, and Ali Reza Talebi. "The Etiologies of DNA Abnormalities in Male Infertility: An Assessment and Review." International journal of reproductive biomedicine (Yazd, Iran). Research and Clinical Center for Infertility, June 2017. https://www.ncbi.nlm.nih.gov/pubmed/29177237.

22. Dolores Malaspina, Caitlin Gilman, and Thorsten Manfred Kranz. "Paternal Age and Mental Health of Offspring." Fertility and Sterility. U.S. National Library of Medicine, June 2015. https://www.ncbi.nlm.nih.gov/pmc/articles/PMC4457665/.

23. Kadiliya Jueraitetibaike, Zheng Ding, Dan-Dan Wang, Long-Ping Peng, Jun Jing, Li Chen, Xie Ge, Xu-Hua Qiu, and Bing Yao. "The Effect of Vitamin D on Sperm Motility and the Underlying Mechanism." Asian Journal of Andrology. Wolters Kluwer - Medknow, 2019. https://www.ncbi.nlm.nih.gov/pubmed/30618415.

24. Sava Micic, Natasa Lalic, Dejan Djordjevic, Nebojsa Bojanic, Natasa Bogavac-Stanojevic, Gian Maria Busetto, Ashraf Virmani, and Ashok Agarwal. "Double-Blind, Randomised, Placebo-Controlled Trial on the Effect of L-Carnitine and L-Acetylcarnitine on Sperm Parameters in Men with Idiopathic Oligoasthenozoospermia." Andrologia. U.S. National Library of Medicine, July 2019. https://www.ncbi.nlm.nih.gov/pubmed/30873633.

25. Yoshitomo Kobori, Shigeyuki Ota, Ryo Sato, Hiroshi Yagi, Shigehiro Soh, Gaku Arai, and Hiroshi Okada. "Antioxidant Cosupplementation Therapy with Vitamin C, Vitamin E, and Coenzyme Q10 in Patients with Oligoasthenozoospermia." Archivio italiano di urologia, andrologia. Societa italiana di ecografia urologica e nefrologica. U.S. National Library of Medicine, March 28, 2014. https://www.ncbi.nlm.nih.gov/pubmed/24704922.

26. Sedigheh Ahmadi, Reihane Bashiri, Akram Ghadiri-Anari, and Azadeh Nadjarzadeh. "Antioxidant Supplements and Semen Parameters: An Evidence Based Review." International journal of reproductive biomedicine (Yazd, Iran). Research and Clinical Center for Infertility, December 2016. https://www.ncbi.nlm.nih.gov/pubmed/28066832.

27. Ahmad Majzoub and Ashok Agarwal. "Systematic Review of Antioxidant Types and Doses in Male Infertility: Benefits on Semen Parameters, Advanced Sperm Function, Assisted Reproduction and Live-Birth Rate." Arab Journal of Urology. Elsevier, January 2, 2018. https://www.ncbi.nlm.nih.gov/pmc/articles/PMC5922223/.

28. C Abad, M J Amengual, J Gosálvez, K Coward, N Hannaoui, J Benet, A García-Peiró, and J Prats. "Effects of Oral Antioxidant Treatment upon the Dynamics of Human Sperm DNA Fragmentation and Subpopulations of Sperm with Highly Degraded DNA." Andrologia. U.S. National Library of Medicine, June 2013. https://www.ncbi.nlm.nih.gov/pubmed/22943406.

29. A E Calogero, G Gullo, S La Vignera, R A Condorelli, and A Vaiarelli. "Myoinositol Improves Sperm Parameters and Serum Reproductive Hormones in Patients with Idiopathic Infertility: a Prospective Double-Blind Randomized Placebo-Controlled Study." Andrology. U.S. National Library of Medicine, May 2015. https://www.ncbi.nlm.nih.gov/pubmed/25854593.

30. Mario Montanino Oliva, Elisa Minutolo, Assunta Lippa, Paola Iaconianni, and Alberto Vaiarelli. "Effect of Myoinositol and Antioxidants on Sperm Quality in Men with Metabolic Syndrome." International Journal of Endocrinology. Hindawi Publishing Corporation, 2016. https://www.ncbi.nlm.nih.gov/pubmed/27752262.

31. F Mohammadi, N Varanloo, M Heydari Nasrabadi, A Vatannejad, F S Amjadi, M Javedani Masroor, L Bajelan, M Mehdizadeh, R Aflatoonian, and Z Zandieh. "Supplementation of Sperm Freezing Medium with Myoinositol Improve Human Sperm Parameters and Protects It against DNA Fragmentation and Apoptosis." Cell and tissue banking. U.S. National Library of Medicine, March 2019. https://www.ncbi.nlm.nih.gov/pubmed/30694450.

32. Rosita A Condorelli, Sandro La Vignera, Salvatore Bellanca, Enzo Vicari, and Aldo E Calogero. "Myoinositol: Does It Improve Sperm Mitochondrial Function and Sperm Motility?" Urology.. U.S. National Library of Medicine, June 2012. https://www.ncbi.nlm.nih.gov/pubmed/22656408.

33. Mohammad Reza Safarinejad. "The Effect of Coenzyme Q_{10} Supplementation on Partner Pregnancy Rate in Infertile Men with Idiopathic Oligoasthenoteratozoospermia: an Open-Label Prospective Study." International urology and nephrology. U.S. National Library of Medicine, June 2012. https://www.ncbi.nlm.nih.gov/pubmed/22081410.

34. David F Yao and Jesse N Mills. "Male Infertility: Lifestyle Factors and Holistic, Complementary, and Alternative Therapies." Asian Journal of Andrology. Medknow Publications & Media Pvt Ltd, 2016. https://www.ncbi.nlm.nih.gov/pmc/articles/PMC4854092/.

35. Kar Wah Leung and Alice St Wong. "Ginseng and Male Reproductive Function." Spermatogenesis. Landes Bioscience, July 1, 2013. https://www.ncbi.nlm.nih.gov/pmc/articles/PMC3861174/.

36. Hye Won Lee, Ki-Jung Kil, YoungJoo Lee, and Myeong Soo Lee. "Ginseng for Improving Semen Quality Parameters: A Protocol of Systematic Review." Medicine. Wolters Kluwer Health, January 2018. https://www.ncbi.nlm.nih.gov/pmc/articles/PMC5794398/.

37. Hosseini Akram, Firouz Ghaderi Pakdel, Abbas Ahmadi, and Samad Zare. "Beneficial Effects of American Ginseng on Epididymal Sperm Analyses in Cyclophosphamide Treated Rats." Cell journal. Royan Institute, 2012. https://www.ncbi.nlm.nih.gov/pmc/articles/PMC3584429/.

38. Karl Kerns, Michal Zigo, and Peter Sutovsky. "Zinc: A Necessary Ion for Mammalian Sperm Fertilization Competency." International journal of molecular sciences. MDPI, December 18, 2018. https://www.ncbi.nlm.nih.gov/pmc/articles/PMC6321397/.

39. Jiang Zhao, Xingyou Dong, Xiaoyan Hu, Zhou Long, Liang Wang, Qian Liu, Bishao Sun, Qingqing Wang, Qingjian Wu, and Longkun Li. "Zinc Levels in Seminal Plasma and Their Correlation with Male Infertility: A Systematic Review and Meta-Analysis." Scientific Reports. Nature Publishing Group, March 2, 2016. https://www.ncbi.nlm.nih.gov/pubmed/26932683.

40. Mohammad K Moslemi and Samaneh Tavanbakhsh. "Selenium-Vitamin E Supplementation in Infertile Men: Effects on Semen Parameters and Pregnancy Rate." International journal of general medicine. Dove Medical Press, January 23, 2011. https://www.ncbi.nlm.nih.gov/pmc/articles/PMC3048346/.

41. Yoshitomo Kobori, Keisuke Suzuki, Toshiyuki Iwahata, Takeshi Shin, Yuko Sadaoka, Ryo Sato, Kojiro Nishio, et al. "Improvement of Seminal Quality and Sexual Function of Men with Oligoasthenoteratozoospermia Syndrome Following Supplementation with L-Arginine and Pycnogenol®." Archivio italiano di urologia, andrologia. Societa italiana di ecografia urologica e nefrologica. U.S. National Library of Medicine, September 30, 2015. https://www.ncbi.nlm.nih.gov/pubmed/26428638.

42. R Stanislavov and P Rohdewald. "Sperm Quality in Men Is Improved by Supplementation with a Combination of L-Arginine, L-Citrullin, Roburins and Pycnogenol®." The Italian Journal of Urology and Nephrology. U.S. National Library of Medicine, December 2014. https://www.ncbi.nlm.nih.gov/pubmed/25531191/.

43. S Sinclair. "Male Infertility: Nutritional and Environmental Considerations." Alternative medicine review : a journal of clinical therapeutic. U.S. National Library of Medicine, February 2000. https://www.ncbi.nlm.nih.gov/pubmed/10696117.

44. Narmada P Gupta and Rajeev Kumar. "Lycopene Therapy in Idiopathic Male Infertility--a Preliminary Report." International urology and nephrology. U.S. National Library of Medicine, 2002. https://www.ncbi.nlm.nih.gov/pubmed/12899230.

45. Damayanthi Durairajanayagam, Ashok Agarwal, Chloe Ong, and Pallavi Prashast. "Lycopene and Male Infertility." Asian journal of andrology. Medknow Publications & Media Pvt Ltd, 2014. https://www.ncbi.nlm.nih.gov/pmc/articles/PMC4023371/.

46. Min Hu, Yuehui Zhang, Hongli Ma, Ernest H Y Ng, and Xiao-Ke Wu. "Eastern Medicine Approaches to Male Infertility." Seminars in Reproductive Medicine. U.S. National Library of Medicine, July 2013. https://www.ncbi.nlm.nih.gov/pubmed/23775386.

47. Jing Gao, Yan Zuo, Kam-Hei So, William S B Yeung, Ernest H Y Ng, and Kai-Fai Lee. "Electroacupuncture Enhances Spermatogenesis in Rats after Scrotal Heat Treatment." Spermatogenesis. Landes Bioscience, January 1, 2012. https://www.ncbi.nlm.nih.gov/pubmed/22553490.

48. Zi-Run Jin, Bo-Heng Liu, Jie Cai, Xiang-Hong Jing, Bing Zhu, and Guo-Gang Xing. "Experimental Study for the Treatment of Asthenozoospermia by Electroacupuncture in Rats." Acupuncture Research. U.S. National Library of Medicine, April 25, 2017. https://www.ncbi.nlm.nih.gov/pubmed/29071957.

49. S Siterman, F Eltes, V Wolfson, H Lederman, and B Bartoov. "Does Acupuncture Treatment Affect Sperm Density in Males with Very Low Sperm Count? A Pilot Study." Andrologia. U.S. National Library of Medicine, January 2000. https://www.ncbi.nlm.nih.gov/pubmed/10702864.

50. Lindsey E Crosnoe, Ethan Grober, Dana Ohl, and Edward D Kim. "Exogenous Testosterone: a Preventable Cause of Male Infertility." Translational Andrology and Urology. AME Publishing Company, June 2013. https://www.ncbi.nlm.nih.gov/pubmed/26813847.

51. Damayanthi Durairajanayagam. "Lifestyle Causes of Male Infertility." Arab journal of urology. Elsevier, February 13, 2018. https://www.ncbi.nlm.nih.gov/pmc/articles/PMC5922227/.

52. Mohammad Karimian and Abasalt Hosseinzadeh Colagar. "Association of C677T Transition of the Human Methylenetetrahydrofolate Reductase (MTHFR) Gene with Male Infertility." Reproduction, Fertility, and Development. U.S. National Library of Medicine, April 2016. https://www.ncbi.nlm.nih.gov/pubmed/25412139.

53. Xudong Zhu, Zhiguo Liu, Maochen Zhang, Ruihong Gong, Yajun Xu, and Baoming Wang. "Association of the Methylenetetrahydrofolate Reductase Gene C677T Polymorphism with the Risk of Male Infertility: a Meta-Analysis." Renal failure. U.S. National Library of Medicine, 2016. https://www.ncbi.nlm.nih.gov/pubmed/26584688.

54. K Singh, S K Singh, and R Raman. "MTHFR A1298C Polymorphism and Idiopathic Male Infertility." Journal of postgraduate medicine. U.S. National Library of Medicine, 2010. https://www.ncbi.nlm.nih.gov/pubmed/20935396.

55. Dominique Cornet, Marc Cohen, Arthur Clement, Edouard Amar, Laetitia Fournols, Patrice Clement, Paul Neveux, and Yves Ménézo. "Association between the MTHFR-C677T Isoform and Structure of Sperm DNA." Journal of Assisted Reproduction and Genetics. Springer US, October 2017. https://www.ncbi.nlm.nih.gov/pubmed/28842818.

56. Soheila Pourmasumi, Parvin Sabeti, Tahereh Rahiminia, Esmat Mangoli, Nasim Tabibnejad, and Ali Reza Talebi. "The Etiologies of DNA Abnormalities in Male Infertility: An Assessment and Review." International journal of reproductive biomedicine (Yazd, Iran). Research and Clinical Center for Infertility, June 2017. https://www.ncbi.nlm.nih.gov/pmc/articles/PMC5605854/.

57. K Gopalkrishnan, V Padwal, P K Meherji, J S Gokral, R Shah, and H S Juneja. "Poor Quality of Sperm as It Affects Repeated Early Pregnancy Loss." Archives of Andrology. U.S. National Library of Medicine, 2000. https://www.ncbi.nlm.nih.gov/pubmed/11028929.

58. Yang Yu, Chunshu Jia, Qingyang Shi, Yueying Zhu, and Yanhong Liu. "Hyperhomocysteinemia in Men with a Reproductive History of Fetal Neural Tube Defects: Three Case Reports and Literature Review." Medicine. Wolters Kluwer Health, January 2019. https://www.ncbi.nlm.nih.gov/pubmed/30633186.

59. "Homozygous Methylenetetrahydrofolate Reductase C677T Mutation and Male Infertility: NEJM." New England Journal of Medicine. Accessed October 2019. https://www.nejm.org/doi/full/10.1056/NEJM200104123441517.

60. R Najafipour, S Moghbelinejad, A Aleyasin, and A Jalilvand. "Effect of B9 and B12 Vitamin Intake on Semen Parameters and Fertility of Men with MTHFR Polymorphisms." Andrology. U.S. National Library of Medicine, July 2017. https://www.ncbi.nlm.nih.gov/pubmed/28440964.

61. D G Valcarce, S Genovés, M F Riesco, P Martorell, M P Herráez, D Ramón, and V Robles. "Probiotic Administration Improves Sperm Quality in Asthenozoospermic Human Donors." Beneficial Microbes. U.S. National Library of Medicine, April 26, 2017. https://www.ncbi.nlm.nih.gov/pubmed/28343402.

62. Ashok Agarwal, Gurpriya Virk, Chloe Ong, and Stefan S du Plessis. "Effect of Oxidative Stress on Male Reproduction." The World Journal of Men's Health. Korean Society for Sexual Medicine and Andrology, April 2014. https://www.ncbi.nlm.nih.gov/pmc/articles/PMC4026229/.

63. S A Suleiman, M E Ali, Z M Zaki, E M el-Malik, and M A Nasr. "Lipid Peroxidation and Human Sperm Motility: Protective Role of Vitamin E." Journal of Andrology. U.S. National Library of Medicine, 1996. https://www.ncbi.nlm.nih.gov/pubmed/8957697.

64. Mohammad K Moslemi, and Samaneh Tavanbakhsh. "Selenium-Vitamin E Supplementation in Infertile Men: Effects on Semen Parameters and Pregnancy Rate." International Journal of General Medicine. Dove Medical Press, January 23, 2011. https://www.ncbi.nlm.nih.gov/pubmed/21403799.

65. S A Ogli, O Enyikwola, and S O Odeh. "Evaluation of the Efficacy of Separate Oral Supplements Compared with the Combined Oral Supplements of Vitamins C and E on Sperm Motility in Wistar Rats." Nigerian Journal of Physiological Sciences. Physiological Society of Nigeria. U.S. National Library of Medicine, December 2009. https://www.ncbi.nlm.nih.gov/pubmed/20234752.

66. Sedigheh Ahmadi, Reihane Bashiri, Akram Ghadiri-Anari, and Azadeh Nadjarzadeh. "Antioxidant Supplements and Semen Parameters: An Evidence Based Review." International Journal of Reproductive Biomedicine (Yazd, Iran). Research and Clinical Center for Infertility, December 2016. https://www.ncbi.nlm.nih.gov/pmc/articles/PMC5203687/.

67. M G ElSheikh, M B Hosny, A Elshenoufy, H Elghamrawi, A Fayad, and S Abdelrahman. "Combination of Vitamin E and Clomiphene Citrate in Treating Patients with Idiopathic Oligoasthenozoospermia: A Prospective, Randomized Trial." Andrology. U.S. National Library of Medicine, September 2015. https://www.ncbi.nlm.nih.gov/pubmed/26235968.

68. Mohammad K Moslemi and Samaneh Tavanbakhsh. "Selenium-Vitamin E Supplementation in Infertile Men: Effects on Semen Parameters and Pregnancy Rate." International journal of general medicine. Dove Medical Press, January 23, 2011. https://www.ncbi.nlm.nih.gov/pmc/articles/PMC3048346/.

69. H Y Huang, K J Helzlsouer, and L J Appel. "The Effects of Vitamin C and Vitamin E on Oxidative DNA Damage: Results from a Randomized Controlled Trial." Cancer Epidemiology, Biomarkers & Prevention. American Association for Cancer Research, cosponsored by the American Society of Preventive Oncology. U.S. National Library of Medicine, July 2000. https://www.ncbi.nlm.nih.gov/pubmed/10919732.

70. M Dorostghoal, S R Kazeminejad, N Shahbazian, M Pourmehdi, and A Jabbari. "Oxidative Stress Status and Sperm DNA Fragmentation in Fertile and Infertile Men." Andrologia. U.S. National Library of Medicine, December 2017. https://www.ncbi.nlm.nih.gov/pubmed/28124476.

71. C Wright, S Milne, and H Leeson. "Sperm DNA Damage Caused by Oxidative Stress: Modifiable Clinical, Lifestyle and Nutritional Factors in Male Infertility." Reproductive Biomedicine Online. U.S. National Library of Medicine, June 2014. https://www.ncbi.nlm.nih.gov/pubmed/24745838.

72. Ermanno Greco, Marcello Iacobelli, Laura Rienzi, Filippo Ubaldi, Susanna Ferrero, and Jan Tesarik. "Reduction of the Incidence of Sperm DNA Fragmentation by Oral Antioxidant Treatment." Wiley Online Library. John Wiley & Sons, Ltd, January 2, 2013. https://onlinelibrary.wiley.com/doi/full/10.2164/jandrol.04146.

73. Francesco Lombardo, Andrea Sansone, Francesco Romanelli, Donatella Paoli, Loredana Gandini, and Andrea Lenzi. "The Role of Antioxidant Therapy in the Treatment of Male Infertility: an Overview." Asian Journal of Andrology. Nature Publishing Group, September 2011. https://www.ncbi.nlm.nih.gov/pmc/articles/PMC3739574/.

74. Ahmad Majzoub and Ashok Agarwal. "Antioxidant Therapy in Idiopathic Oligoasthenoteratozoospermia." Indian Journal of Urology. Urological Society of India. Medknow Publications & Media Pvt Ltd, 2017. https://www.ncbi.nlm.nih.gov/pmc/articles/PMC5508431/.

75. Ermanno Greco, Marcello Iacobelli, Laura Rienzi, Filippo Ubaldi, Susanna Ferrerro, and Jan Tesarik. "Reduction of the Incidence of Sperm DNA Fragmentation by Oral Antioxidant Treatment." Journal of Andrology 26, no. 3 (January 2, 2013). https://doi.org/10.2164/jandrol.04146.

76. Luciano Negri, Renzo Benaglia, Emanuela Monti, Emanuela Morenghi, Alessandro Pizzocaro, and Paolo E Levi Setti. "Effect of Superoxide Dismutase Supplementation on Sperm DNA Fragmentation." Archivio italiano di urologia, andrologia. Societa italiana di ecografia urologica e nefrologica. U.S. National Library of Medicine, October 3, 2017. https://www.ncbi.nlm.nih.gov/pubmed/28969406.

77. Harshit Garg and Rajeev Kumar. "An Update on the Role of Medical Treatment Including Antioxidant Therapy in Varicocele." Asian Journal of Andrology. Medknow Publications & Media Pvt Ltd, 2016. https://www.ncbi.nlm.nih.gov/pmc/articles/PMC4770490/.

78. A A Ghafarizadeh, G Vaezi, M A Shariatzadeh, and A A Malekirad. "Effect of in Vitro Selenium Supplementation on Sperm Quality in Asthenoteratozoospermic Men." Wiley Online Library. John Wiley & Sons, Ltd (10.1111), August 6, 2017. https://onlinelibrary.wiley.com/doi/abs/10.1111/and.12869.

79. Ahmad Majzoub, Ashok Agarwal, and Sandro C Esteves. "Antioxidants for Elevated Sperm DNA Fragmentation: a Mini Review." Translational Andrology and Urology. AME Publishing Company, September 2017. https://www.ncbi.nlm.nih.gov/pmc/articles/PMC5643651/.

CHAPTER 14

1. "Acupuncture: In Depth." National Center for Complementary and Integrative Health. U.S. Department of Health and Human Services, February 21, 2017. https://nccih.nih.gov/health/acupuncture/introduction.

2. Hesham Al-Inany. "Acupuncture for Infertility: A Recently Released Evidence." Middle East Fertility Society Journal 13, no. 1 (2008): 67. http://www.bioline.org.br/pdf?mf08015.

3. Mo X, Li D, Xi G, Le X, and Fu Z. "Clinical Studies on the Mechanism for Acupuncture Stimulation of Ovulation." Journal of Traditional Chinese Medicine 13, no. 2 (n.d.): 115–19. https://www.ncbi.nlm.nih.gov/pubmed/8412285.

4. Suzanne Cochrane, Caroline A Smith, Alphia Possamai-Inesedy, and Alan Bensoussan. "Prior to Conception: The Role of an Acupuncture Protocol in Improving Women's Reproductive Functioning Assessed by a Pilot Pragmatic Randomised Controlled Trial." Evidence-based Complementary and Alternative Medicine: eCAM. Hindawi Publishing Corporation, 2016. https://www.ncbi.nlm.nih.gov/pubmed/27242910.

5. Lee E Hullender Rubin, Michael S Opsahl, Klaus E Wiemer, Scott D Mist, and Aaron B Caughey. "Impact of Whole Systems Traditional Chinese Medicine on in-Vitro Fertilization Outcomes." Reproductive Biomedicine Online. U.S. National Library of Medicine, June 2015. https://www.ncbi.nlm.nih.gov/pubmed/25911598.

6. Bao-Zhi Yang, Wei Cui, and Jing Li. "Effects of Electroacupuncture Intervention on Changes of Quality of Ovum and Pregnancy out- Come in Patients with Polycystic Ovarian Syndrome." Acupuncture Research. U.S. National Library of Medicine, April 2015. https://www.ncbi.nlm.nih.gov/pubmed/26054202.

7. Wei Cui, Jing Li, Wei Sun, and Ji Wen. "Effect of Electroacupuncture on Oocyte Quality and Pregnancy for Patients with PCOS Undergoing in Vitro Fertilization and Embryo Transfervitro Fertilization and Embryo Transfer." Chinese Acupuncture & Moxibustion. U.S. National Library of Medicine, August 2011. https://www.ncbi.nlm.nih.gov/pubmed/21894688.

8. Junyoung Jo and Yoon Jae Lee. "Effectiveness of Acupuncture in Women with Polycystic Ovarian Syndrome Undergoing in Vitro Fertilisation or Intracytoplasmic Sperm Injection: a Systematic Review and Meta-Analysis." Acupuncture in Medicine. British Medical Acupuncture Society. U.S. National Library of Medicine, June 2017. https://www.ncbi.nlm.nih.gov/pubmed/28077366.

9. Eric Manheimer, Grant Zhang, Laurence Udoff, Aviad Haramati, Patricia Langenberg, Brian M Berman, and Lex M Bouter. "Effects of Acupuncture on Rates of Pregnancy and Live Birth among Women Undergoing in Vitro Fertilisation: Systematic Review and Meta-Analysis." BMJ (Clinical research ed.). BMJ Publishing Group Ltd., March 8, 2008. https://www.ncbi.nlm.nih.gov/pubmed/18258932.

10. P C Magarelli, D K Cridennda, and M Cohen. "Acupuncture and Good Prognosis IVF Patients: Synergy." Fertility and Sterility 82, no. 2 (September 2004): S80–S81. https://doi.org/https://doi.org/10.1016/j.fertnstert.2004.07.205.

11. Daniela Isoyama Manca di Villahermosa, Lara Guercio dos Santos, Mariana Balthazar Nogueira, Fabia Lima Vilarino, and Caio Parente Barbosa. "Influence of Acupuncture on the Outcomes of in Vitro Fertilisation When Embryo Implantation Has Failed: a Prospective Randomised Controlled Clinical Trial." Acupuncture in Medicine. British Medical Acupuncture Society. U.S. National Library of Medicine, June 2013. https://www.ncbi.nlm.nih.gov/pubmed/23512550.

12. Taketo Inoue, Yoshiyuki Ono, Yukiko Yonezawa, Michinobu Oi, Naomi Kobayashi, Junji Kishi, and Nobuyuki Emi. "Oocyte Quality Improvement Using a Herbal Medicine Comprising 7 Crude Drugs." Open Journal of Obstetrics and Gynecology 03, no. 01 (2013): 195–202. https://doi.org/10.4236/ojog.2013.31a036.

13. Fang Lian, Yi-li Teng, and Jian-wei Zhang. "Clinical Study on Effect of Erzhi Tiangui Granule in Improving the Quality of Oocytes and Leukemia Inhibitory Factor in Follicular Fluid of Women Undergoing in Vitro Fertilization and Embryo Transfer." Chinese Journal of Integrated Traditional and Western Medicine. U.S. National Library of Medicine, November 2007. https://www.ncbi.nlm.nih.gov/pubmed/18173139.

14. Takahisa Ushiroyama, Noriko Yokoyama, Midori Hakukawa, Kou Sakuma, Fumio Ichikawa, and Satoshi Yoshida. "Clinical Efficacy of Macrophage-Activating Chinese Mixed Herbs (MACH) in Improvement of Embryo Qualities in Women with Long-Term Infertility of Unknown Etiology." The American journal of Chinese medicine. U.S. National Library of Medicine, 2012. https://www.ncbi.nlm.nih.gov/pubmed/22298444.

15. Fang Lian, Lin Wang, and Jian-wei Zhang. "Effect of Erzhi Tiangui Recipe on Ovarian Reactivity in Elderly Sterile Women." Chinese Journal of Integrated Traditional and Western Medicine. U.S. National Library of Medicine, August 2006. https://www.ncbi.nlm.nih.gov/pubmed/16970088.

16. Li Dong, Lin Jiang, Wei Men, and Nan-sun Zhu. "Preventive and Therapeutic Effects of Bushen Huoxue Recipe on Autoimmune Premature Ovarian Failure in Mice." Journal of Chinese Integrative Medicine. U.S. National Library of Medicine, March 2008. https://www.ncbi.nlm.nih.gov/pubmed/18334152.

17. Fang Lian, Zhen-Gao Sun, and Jian-Wei Zhang. "Combined Therapy of Chinese Medicine with in Vitro Fertilization and Embryo Transplantation for Treatment of Polycystic Ovarian Syndrome." Chinese Journal of Integrated Traditional and Western Medicine. U.S. National Library of Medicine, November 2008. https://www.ncbi.nlm.nih.gov/pubmed/19213337.

18. Jing Li, Tao Teng, Qi Liang, and Wei Cui. "Effect of Chinese Herbs Combined DHEA Pretreatment on Pregnancy Outcomes of Elderly Patients with Normal Ovarian Reserve Undergoing IVF-ET." Chinese Journal of Integrated Traditional and Western Medicine. U.S. National Library of Medicine, September 2016. https://www.ncbi.nlm.nih.gov/pubmed/30645840.

19. Zheng Zhang, Xue-hong Zhang, and Tian-you He. "Smoothing Gan Reinforcing Shen Method Adjuvantly Treated Poor Response of Diminished Ovari- an Reserve Patients in in Vitro Fertilization and Embryo Transfer: a Clinical Study." Chinese Journal of Integrated Traditional and Western Medicine. U.S. National Library of Medicine, October 2015. https://www.ncbi.nlm.nih.gov/pubmed/26677665.

20. Sheng-Teng Huang and Annie Pei-Chun Chen. "Traditional Chinese Medicine and Infertility." Current Opinion in Obstetrics & Gynecology. U.S. National Library of Medicine, June 2008. https://www.ncbi.nlm.nih.gov/pubmed/18460933.

21. Trevor A Wing and Elke S Sedlmeier. "Measuring the Effectiveness of Chinese Herbal Medicine in Improving Female Fertility." Journal of Chinese Medicine 80 (February 2006): 23–28. https://pdfs.semanticscholar.org/bea4/42554d6c0bee79ed79575587f1d8ca2df1d6.pdf.

CHAPTER 15

1. Anne M Minihane, Sophie Vinoy, Wendy R Russell, Athanasia Baka, Helen M Roche, Kieran M Tuohy, Jessica L Teeling, et al. "Low-Grade Inflammation, Diet Composition and Health: Current Research Evidence and Its Translation." The British Journal of Nutrition. Cambridge University Press, October 2015. https://www.ncbi.nlm.nih.gov/pmc/articles/PMC4579563/.

2. Claudio Franceschi and Judith Campisi. "Chronic Inflammation (Inflammaging) and Its Potential Contribution to Age-Associated Diseases." The Journals of Gerontology. Series A, Biological sciences and medical sciences. U.S. National Library of Medicine, June 2014. https://www.ncbi.nlm.nih.gov/pubmed/24833586.

3. Barry Sears and Camillo Ricordi. "Anti-Inflammatory Nutrition as a Pharmacological Approach to Treat Obesity." Journal of Obesity. Hindawi Publishing Corporation, 2011. https://www.ncbi.nlm.nih.gov/pmc/articles/PMC2952901/.

4. Roma Pahwa. "Chronic Inflammation." StatPearls [Internet]. U.S. National Library of Medicine, June 4, 2019. https://www.ncbi.nlm.nih.gov/books/NBK493173/.

5. Étienne Morin, Isabelle Michaud-Létourneau, Yves Couturier, and Mathieu Roy. "A Whole-Food, Plant-Based Nutrition Program: Evaluation of Cardiovascular Outcomes and Exploration of Food Choices Determinants." Nutrition (Burbank, Los Angeles County, Calif.). U.S. National Library of Medicine, October 2019. https://www.ncbi.nlm.nih.gov/pubmed/31207440.

6. Hana Kahleova, Andrea Tura, Marta Klementova, Lenka Thieme, Martin Haluzik, Renata Pavlovicova, Martin Hill, and Terezie Pelikanova. "A Plant-Based Meal Stimulates Incretin and Insulin Secretion More Than an Energy- and Macronutrient-Matched Standard Meal in Type 2 Diabetes: A Randomized Crossover Study." Nutrients. MDPI, February 26, 2019. https://www.ncbi.nlm.nih.gov/pubmed/30813546.

7. Alice Luddi, Angela Capaldo, Riccardo Focarelli, Martina Gori, Giuseppe Morgante, Paola Piomboni, and Vincenzo De Leo. "Antioxidants Reduce Oxidative Stress in Follicular Fluid of Aged Women Undergoing IVF." Reproductive Biology and Endocrinology, BioMed Central, September 7, 2016. https://www.ncbi.nlm.nih.gov/pubmed/27604261.

8. Rahil Jannatifar, Kazem Parivar, Nasim Hayati Roodbari, and Mohammad Hossein Nasr-Esfahani. "Effects of N-Acetyl-Cysteine Supplementation on Sperm Quality, Chromatin Integrity and Level of Oxidative Stress in Infertile Men." Reproductive Biology and Endocrinology. BioMed Central, February 16, 2019. https://www.ncbi.nlm.nih.gov/pubmed/30771790.

9. Shweta Khanna, Kumar Sagar Jaiswal, and Bhawna Gupta. "Managing Rheumatoid Arthritis with Dietary Interventions." Frontiers in Nutrition. Frontiers Media S.A., November 8, 2017. https://www.ncbi.nlm.nih.gov/pmc/articles/PMC5682732/.

10. Jorge E Chavarro, Janet W Rich-Edwards, Bernard A Rosner, and Walter C Willett. "Diet and Lifestyle in the Prevention of Ovulatory Disorder Infertility." Obstetrics & Gynecology 110, no. 5 (November 2007): 1050–58. https://doi.org/10.1097/01.AOG.0000287293.25465.e1.

11. Jorge E Chavarro, Janet W Rich-Edwards, Audrey J Gaskins, Leslie V Farland, Kathryn L Terry, Cuilin Zhang, and Stacey A Missmer. "Contributions of the Nurses' Health Studies to Reproductive Health Research." American Journal of Public Health. American Public Health Association, September 2016. https://www.ncbi.nlm.nih.gov/pmc/articles/PMC4981818/.

12. Neelima Panth, Adam Gavarkovs, Martha Tamez, and Josiemer Mattei. "The Influence of Diet on Fertility and the Implications for Public Health Nutrition in the United States." Frontiers in Public Health 6, no. 211 (July 31, 2018). https://doi.org/10.3389/fpubh.2018.00211.

13. James A Greenberg, and Stacey J Bell. "Multivitamin Supplementation During Pregnancy: Emphasis on Folic Acid and l-Methylfolate." Reviews in Obstetrics & Gynecology. MedReviews, LLC, 2011. https://www.ncbi.nlm.nih.gov/pmc/articles/PMC3250974/.

14. Angelika Smidowicz and Julita Regula. "Effect of Nutritional Status and Dietary Patterns on Human Serum C-Reactive Protein and Interleukin-6 Concentrations." Advances in Nutrition (Bethesda, Md.). American Society for Nutrition, November 13, 2015. https://www.ncbi.nlm.nih.gov/pmc/articles/PMC4642421/.

15. Megu Y Baden, Ambika Satija, Frank B Hu, and Tiyani Juang. "Change in Plant-Based Diet Quality Is Associated with Changes in Plasma Adiposity-Associated Biomarker Concentrations in Women." The Journal of Nutrition 149, no. 4 (March 30, 2019): 676–86. https://doi.org/doi.org/10.1093/jn/nxy301.

16. Steven H Zeisel. "Is There a New Component of the Mediterranean Diet That Reduces Inflammation?" The American Journal of Clinical Nutrition 87, no. 2 (February 2008): 277–78. https://doi.org/10.1093/ajcn/87.2.277.

17. Philip J Tuso, Mohamed H Ismail, Benjamin P Ha, and Carole Bartolotto. "Nutritional Update for Physicians: Plant-Based Diets." The Permanente Journal. The Permanente Journal, 2013. https://www.ncbi.nlm.nih.gov/pmc/articles/PMC3662288/.

18. Sunao Shimada, Tetsuya Tanigawa, Toshio Watanabe, Akinobu Nakata, Naoki Sugimura, Shigehiro Itani, Akira Higashimori, et al. "Involvement of Gliadin, a Component of Wheat Gluten, in Increased Intestinal Permeability Leading to Non-Steroidal Anti-Inflammatory Drug-Induced Small-Intestinal Damage." PLOS ONE. Public Library of Science, February 20, 2019. https://www.ncbi.nlm.nih.gov/pubmed/30785904.

19. Karin de Punder and Leo Pruimboom. "The Dietary Intake of Wheat and Other Cereal Grains and Their Role in Inflammation." Nutrients. MDPI, March 12, 2013. https://www.ncbi.nlm.nih.gov/pmc/articles/PMC3705319/.

20. "Organic Standards." Organic Standards, Agricultural Marketing Service. Accessed October 2019. https://www.ams.usda.gov/grades-standards/organic-standards.

21. Anne Harding. "Baking Soda plus Water Best for Washing Pesticides off Apples." Reuters. Thomson Reuters, October 27, 2017. https://www.reuters.com/article/us-health-pesticides-apples/baking-soda-plus-water-best-for-washing-pesticides-off-apples-idUSKBN1CW2KV.

22. Zhi-Yong Zhangab, Xiao-YueHonga, and AbstractExperiment. "Effects of Home Preparation on Pesticide Residues in Cabbage." Food Control. Elsevier, January 16, 2007. https://www.sciencedirect.com/science/article/pii/S0956713506002696.

23. Alessandra A Z Rodrigues, Maria Eliana L R De Queiroz, André Fernando De Oliveira, Antônio Augusto Neves, Fernanda F Heleno, Laércio Zambolim, Jéssika F Freitas, and Elisa H Costa Morais. "Pesticide Residue Removal in Classic Domestic Processing of Tomato and Its Effects on Product Quality." Journal of Environmental Science and Health. Part. B, Pesticides, food contaminants, and agricultural wastes. U.S. National Library of Medicine, December 2, 2017. https://www.ncbi.nlm.nih.gov/pubmed/28956709.

24. Jorge E Chavarro, Janet W Rich-Edwards, Bernard A Rosner, and Walter C Willett. "Protein Intake and Ovulatory Infertility." American Journal of Obstetrics and Gynecology. U.S. National Library of Medicine, February 2008. https://www.ncbi.nlm.nih.gov/pmc/articles/PMC3066040/.

25. Estefania Toledo, Cristina Lopez-del Burgo, Alvaro Ruiz-Zambrana, Mikel Donazar, Iñigo Navarro-Blasco, Miguel A Martínez-González, and Jokin de Irala. "Dietary Patterns and Difficulty Conceiving: a Nested Case-Control Study." Fertility and Sterility. U.S. National Library of Medicine, November 2011. https://www.ncbi.nlm.nih.gov/pubmed/21943725.

26. Albert Salas-Huetos, Mònica Bulló, and Jordi Salas-Salvadó. "Dietary Patterns, Foods and Nutrients in Male Fertility Parameters and Fecundability: a Systematic Review of Observational Studies." Human Reproduction Update. U.S. National Library of Medicine, July 1, 2017. https://www.ncbi.nlm.nih.gov/pubmed/28333357.

27. "Anti-Inflammatory Diet & Pyramid: Nutrition: Andrew Weil, M.D." DrWeil.com, September 27, 2019. https://www.drweil.com/diet-nutrition/anti-inflammatory-diet-pyramid/dr-weils-anti-inflammatory-diet/.

28. Paul Pitchford. Healing with Whole Foods: Asian Traditions and Modern Nutrition. Berkeley, CA: North Atlantic Books, 2009.

CHAPTER 16

1. Krista S Crider, Thomas P Yang, Robert J Berry, and Lynn B Bailey. "Folate and DNA Methylation: a Review of Molecular Mechanisms and the Evidence for Folate's Role." Advances in Nutrition (Bethesda, Md.). Oxford University Press, January 2012. https://www.ncbi.nlm.nih.gov/pmc/articles/PMC3262611/.

2. P Frosst, H J Blom, R Milos, P Goyette, C A Sheppard, R G Matthews, G J Boers, M den Heijer, L A Kluijtmans, and L P van den Heuvel. "A Candidate Genetic Risk Factor for Vascular Disease: a Common Mutation in Methylenetetrahydrofolate Reductase." Nature Genetics. U.S. National Library of Medicine, May 1995. https://www.ncbi.nlm.nih.gov/pubmed/7647779.

3. Kai-min Guo, Run-hui Tian, and Hong-liang Wang. "Relationship of MTHFR Gene Polymorphisms with Infertility." National Journal of Andrology. U.S. National Library of Medicine, February 2016.

4. T O Scholl and W G Johnson. "Folic Acid: Influence on the Outcome of Pregnancy." The American Journal of Clinical Nutrition. U.S. National Library of Medicine, May 2000. https://www.ncbi.nlm.nih.gov/pubmed/10799405.

5. María Enciso, Jonás Sarasa, Leoni Xanthopoulou, Sara Bristow, Megan Bowles, Elpida Fragouli, Joy Delhanty, and Dagan Wells. "Polymorphisms in the MTHFR Gene Influence Embryo Viability and the Incidence of Aneuploidy." Human Genetics. U.S. National Library of Medicine, May 2016. https://www.ncbi.nlm.nih.gov/pubmed/27068821.

6. Piet Hein Jongbloet, André Lm Verbeek, Martin den Heijer, and Nel Roeleveld. "Methylenetetrahydrofolate Reductase (MTHFR) Gene Polymorphisms Resulting in Suboptimal Oocyte Maturation: a Discussion of Folate Status, Neural Tube Defects, Schizophrenia, and Vasculopathy." Journal of Experimental & Clinical Assisted Reproduction. BioMed Central, July 10, 2008. https://www.ncbi.nlm.nih.gov/pmc/articles/PMC2500045/.

7. S S Li and J Li. "[MTHFR Gene Polymorphism and Male Infertility]." National Journal of Andrology. U.S. National Library of Medicine, January 2010. https://www.ncbi.nlm.nih.gov/pubmed/20180408.

8. Kiran Singh and Deepika Jaiswal. "One-Carbon Metabolism, Spermatogenesis, and Male Infertility." Reproductive Sciences (Thousand Oaks, Calif.). U.S. National Library of Medicine, June 2013. https://www.ncbi.nlm.nih.gov/pubmed/23138010.

9. Dominique Cornet, Marc Cohen, Arthur Clement, Edouard Amar, Laetitia Fournols, Patrice Clement, Paul Neveux, and Yves Ménézo. "Association between the MTHFR-C677T Isoform and Structure of Sperm DNA." Journal of Assisted Reproduction and Genetics. Springer US, October 2017. https://www.ncbi.nlm.nih.gov/pmc/articles/PMC5633564/.

10. Edouard J Servy, Laetitia Jacquesson-Fournols, Marc Cohen, and Yves J R Menezo. "MTHFR Isoform Carriers. 5-MTHF (5-Methyl Tetrahydrofolate) vs Folic Acid: a Key to Pregnancy Outcome: a Case Series." Journal of Assisted Reproduction and Genetics. Springer US, August 2018. https://www.ncbi.nlm.nih.gov/pubmed/29882091.

11. D G Valcarce, S Genovés, M F Riesco, P Martorell, M P Herráez, D Ramón, and V Robles. "Probiotic Administration Improves Sperm Quality in Asthenozoospermic Human Donors." Beneficial Microbes. U.S. National Library of Medicine, April 26, 2017. https://www.ncbi.nlm.nih.gov/pubmed/28343402.

12. H Y Huang, K J Helzlsouer, and L J Appel. "The Effects of Vitamin C and Vitamin E on Oxidative DNA Damage: Results from a Randomized Controlled Trial." Cancer Epidemiology, Biomarkers & Prevention. American Association for Cancer Research, cosponsored by the American Society of Preventive Oncology. U.S. National Library of Medicine, July 2000. https://www.ncbi.nlm.nih.gov/pubmed/10919732.

13. Ashok Agarwal, Gurpriya Virk, Chloe Ong, and Stefan S du Plessis. "Effect of Oxidative Stress on Male Reproduction." The World Journal of Men's Health. Korean Society for Sexual Medicine and Andrology, April 2014. https://www.ncbi.nlm.nih.gov/pmc/articles/PMC4026229/.

14. M Dorostghoal, S R Kazeminejad, N Shahbazian, M Pourmehdi, and A Jabbari. "Oxidative Stress Status and Sperm DNA Fragmentation in Fertile and Infertile Men." Andrologia. U.S. National Library of Medicine, December 2017. https://www.ncbi.nlm.nih.gov/pubmed/28124476.

15. C Wright, S Milne, and H Leeson. "Sperm DNA Damage Caused by Oxidative Stress: Modifiable Clinical, Lifestyle and Nutritional Factors in Male Infertility." Reproductive Biomedicine Online. U.S. National Library of Medicine, June 2014. https://www.ncbi.nlm.nih.gov/pubmed/24745838.

16. Ermanno Greco, Marcello Iacobelli, Laura Rienzi, Filippo Ubaldi, Susanna Ferrerro, and Jan Tesarik. "Reduction of the Incidence of Sperm DNA Fragmentation by Oral Antioxidant Treatment." Journal of Andrology 26, no. 3 (January 2, 2013). https://doi.org/10.2164/jandrol.04146.

17. Francesco Lombardo, Andrea Sansone, Francesco Romanelli, Donatella Paoli, Loredana Gandini, and Andrea Lenzi. "The Role of Antioxidant Therapy in the Treatment of Male Infertility: an Overview." Asian Journal of Andrology. Nature Publishing Group, September 2011. https://www.ncbi.nlm.nih.gov/pmc/articles/PMC3739574/.

18. Ahmad Majzoub and Ashok Agarwal. "Antioxidant Therapy in Idiopathic Oligoasthenoteratozoospermia." Indian Journal of Urology. Urological Society of India. Medknow Publications & Media Pvt Ltd, 2017. https://www.ncbi.nlm.nih.gov/pmc/articles/PMC5508431/.

ABOUT THE AUTHOR

Dr. Kiera Lane is a Board Certified Naturopathic Medical Doctor and Acupuncturist. She received her Doctor of Naturopathic Medicine from the Southwest College of Naturopathic Medicine & Health Sciences, graduated valedictorian with her Master's degree in Acupuncture from the Phoenix Institute of Herbal Medicine and Acupuncture and received her Bachelor of Science Degree in the area of Dietetics (Clinical Nutrition) from Arizona State University. She is a Fellow of the American Board of Oriental Reproductive Medicine (ABORM), which is an international organization pioneering the best practices in acupuncture and oriental reproductive medicine. ABORM fellows are skilled Chinese medicine clinicians and educated researchers who contribute to the current body of knowledge with cutting-edge innovation and integrative evidence-based care. Dr. Lane is the founder and medical director of Arizona Natural Medicine Physicians, PLLC and has received numerous awards for her excellence in patient care. She has served as a speaker and writer, has collaborated as an expert panelist, and been featured as a regular on live radio. Dr. Lane has been actively involved in the health care field for over twenty-five years. She has been a practicing physician for more than nineteen years in primary care medicine with an emphasis in women's health and, specifically, fertility. She has been helping women and men conceive naturally as well as with assisted reproductive technology (ART) for almost two decades.

Dr. Kiera Lane has a gift for transforming technical medical concepts into understandable and usable information to non-medical readers to inspire and empower them through knowledge.

She has intimate insight into the process women go through in order to conceive. Her own road to having her child was not a straight line and required creative solutions. Successfully working with women, men, and families in the area of fertility, and having met her own personal challenges in conceiving a child, gives her a unique viewpoint to assist others in their journey to having a baby. Dr. Lane is passionate about the work she does and uses writing as a creative expression to inspire and lift others up.

You can find more information about Dr. Kiera Lane at www.drlanecompletefertility.com

PROGRAMS AND MORE INFORMATION

Trying to get pregnant just got a lot easier.

Dr. Kiera Lane offers natural and effective ways to enhance your fertility. This book is just the start. Visit www.drlanecompletefertility.com to access Dr. Lane's Complete Fertility programs for both men and women.
- Perfect for anyone trying to conceive
- Female and Male programs that include a 5-point methodology to increase your chances of pregnancy success
- Includes female and male specific diets; supplements; stress and lifestyle support; and ear (auricular) acupressure to enhance overall fertility

Don't forget the *Complete Fertility* partner book,

FERTILITY AFFIRMATIONS
for the body, mind, and spirit
365 days of the year

Use positive thinking to change your physiology and improve your chances for fertility.

"When I came to Dr. Lane I was exhausted, desperate and not trusting of doctors. I am excited to say that I'm, 37 and 7 months pregnant! I attribute this miracle to the care and love of Dr. Lane." --Vanessa

"As a woman who has invested a lot of time, emotion and money in IVF, it was deeply important to me to have my IVF cycle be successful. Not only did Dr. Lane go above and beyond but made this pregnancy a resounding success in spite of hormonal and autoimmune disease challenges I faced." --Jennifer

"After seeing Dr. Lane for a few short months, I am happy to say I am pregnant." --Michelle

www.ingramcontent.com/pod-product-compliance
Lightning Source LLC
Chambersburg PA
CBHW080332170426
43194CB00014B/2538